FORMS OF POETIC ATTENTION

Forms of
Poetic Attention

Lucy Alford

Columbia University Press
New York

Columbia University Press
Publishers Since 1893
New York   Chichester, West Sussex
cup.columbia.edu
Copyright © 2020 Columbia University Press
Paperback edition, 2021
All rights reserved

Library of Congress Cataloging-in-Publication Data
Names: Alford, Lucy, 1983– author.
Title: Forms of poetic attention / Lucy Alford.
Description: New York : Columbia University Press, 2020. | Includes bibliographical references and index.
Identifiers: LCCN 2019026948 | ISBN 9780231187541 (cloth) | ISBN 9780231187558 (pbk.) | ISBN 9780231547321 (ebook)
Subjects: LCSH: Poetry—History and criticism. | Poetry—Psychological aspects. | Attention. | Cognition in literature. | Poetics.
Classification: LCC PN1031 .A435 2020 | DDC 808.1—dc23
LC record available at https://lccn.loc.gov/2019026948

Cover image: Canary Resuscitator made by Siebe Gorman & Company Ltd. © Museum of Science & Industry/Science & Society Picture Library
Cover design: Chang Jae Lee

For Roland Greene

This pen is where the writing flows in sight
the measuring eye follows line by line,
mouth set in the mind's movement throughout attentive, tentative —

—ROBERT DUNCAN

The attentiveness a poem devotes to all encounters . . . a concentration that stays mindful of all our dates.

—PAUL CELAN

. . . When you take up your
axe, listen. Hoofbeats. Wind.
It is they who make us at home
here, not the other way around.

—ANNE CARSON

Contents

Acknowledgments xi

Introduction: What Is Poetic Attention? 1

PART I Attending to Objects

I   Modes of Transitive Attention 25

II Contemplation: Attention's Reach 53
Ponge : Heaney : Stevens : Bishop : Mullen

III Desire: Attention's Hunger 76
Dickinson : Shakespeare : Lorde : Lowell : Oppen : Hass

IV Recollection: Attending to the Departed Object 98
Al-Khansā' : Hill : Celan : Cha : Carson

V Imagination: Attention's Poiesis 125
Coleridge : Wordsworth : Rilke : Burnside

PART II   Objectless Awareness

VI   Modes of Intransitive Attention   151

VII   Vigilance: States of Suspension   167
Hölderlin : Mallarmé

VIII   Resignation: Relinquishing the Object   191
Rimbaud : Wright

IX   Idleness: Doldrums and Gardens of Time   212
O'Hara : Ammons : Retallack

X   Boredom: End-Stopped Attention   237
Bukowski : Gunn : Eliot

Coda: Toward a Practice of Poetic Attention   268

Notes   279
Bibliography   325
Permission Credits   345
Index   349

Acknowledgments

A far-reaching community of scholars, poets, friends, and family has given generously to this book and to my writing life over many years. Indeed, so many minds and hands have shared in the conception, composition, and editing of this book, it has truly become an object of sustained co-attending and copoiesis in itself.

Stanford University's Division of Literatures, Cultures, and Languages provided a dynamic and supportive environment in which to write the first version of this book. First and foremost, I am indebted to Roland Greene for his wisdom and mentorship, brilliant feedback, and clarity of mind at every stage over many years. His thinking is present in every word of this book. As adviser and friend, Hans Ulrich Gumbrecht has both encouraged and modeled true intellectual independence; his thinking, particularly on the concepts of historical latency and *Stimmung* (mood, atmosphere), has been a deep source of inspiration to me. The first draft of my reading of Charles Wright in chapter 8 emerged as a paper for Gumbrecht's graduate seminar on *Stimmung*. Joshua Landy has been a keen reader and a vital interlocutor on literature's formative capacities. Amir Eshel urged me to write the book I would like to read. This advice has stayed with me, and I've done my best to follow it. David Palumbo-Liu has been a steadfast advocate and friend in countless ways, both to me and to this book. Special thanks to Lanier Anderson, Khalil Barhoum, Karl Heinz Bohrer, John Felstiner, Kenneth Fields, Marisa Galvez, Alexander Key, Patricia

Parker, Nancy Ruttenburg, Ramzi Salti, Vered Shemtov, and, at Berkeley, Muhammad Siddiq. The Workshop in Poetics, led by Roland Greene and Nicholas Jenkins, offered an ongoing, anchoring community of poetic thinkers across periods, languages, and methodologies.

My colleagues and friends in Chicago have been heroic readers and interlocutors; our conversations brought clarity, precision, and depth to some very rough and drafty terrain. My fellow Fellows in the Society of Fellows in the Liberal Arts have offered rich interdisciplinary perspectives, both in conversation and workshop settings. Special thanks to Deborah Neibel for making everything happen. Mark Payne provided detailed feedback on the entire book, and I have returned again and again to his insightful commentary. Rosanna Warren has been a brilliant and generous mentor and friend on matters critical and creative. Epic conversations on the lyric with Christopher Davis at Northwestern have made my work and my life better. Special thanks to Marcello Barison, Alexis Becker, Aaron Benanav, Joshua Craze, Fred Donner, David Egan, Maud Ellmann, Rachel Galvin, Florian Klinger, Pablo Maurette, Françoise Meltzer, Benjamin Morgan, Sarah Nooter, Srikanth (Chicu) Reddy, Steven Rings, Na'ama Rokem, Lisa Ruddick, Michael Rutherglen, Eric Santner, Richard Strier, Christopher Taylor, Anna Elena Torres, Aaron Tugendhaft, Christopher Wild, and John Wilkinson. The Poetry and Poetics Workshop, the Comparative Literature Colloquium, and the Workshop of the Society of Fellows contributed an abundance of constructive feedback on my work in progress.

Christopher Fynsk, Adrienne Janus, and Nick Nesbitt at the University of Aberdeen's Centre for Modern Thought oversaw the research that gave rise to this project. At the University of Virginia, Jahan Ramazani, Michael Smith, Lisa Russ Spaar, and Charles Wright have been my philosophical and poetic lighthouses. At Bard College, Thomas Keenan and Joan Retallack offered early and lasting inspiration and encouragement. Heartfelt thanks to Nura Yingling, Wendy Gavin, and Virginia Masterson, my first guides into poetry.

I am sincerely grateful for the work of my editor, Philip Leventhal: for his patience and clarity, his enthusiasm for this project from our first conversation, and his willingness to invest in an unconventional first book. The anonymous readers of my manuscript helped to guide my revision process and clarify blurry patches in my own thinking. Many thanks to Columbia University Press for bringing this book into the world, especially Susan Pensak, my production editor, and Monique Briones, editorial assistant, for their attentive behind-the-scenes work on this project, and Chang Jae Lee for his beautiful cover design.

My research has been made possible by a number of institutions and awards, many of which also provided a roof over my head and an intellectual community. Many thanks to the American Comparative Literature Association for selecting this book for the Helen Tartar First Book Subvention Award. At the University of Chicago, my work has been supported by the Society of Fellows in the Liberal Arts, the Bernard Weissbourd Memorial Fund, the College, and the Departments of English and Comparative Literature. Many thanks to the Ric Weiland Graduate Fellowship for two years of interdisciplinary community and financial support and to Theodore and Frances Geballe and the Stanford Humanities Center for the unforgettable year of writing and fellowship granted by the Geballe Dissertation Prize. This book also benefited from research opportunities provided by Amir Eshel, Brian Johnsrud, and the Poetic Media Lab at Stanford's Center for Spatial and Textual Analysis; the UVA-Yarmouk University Summer Arabic Program in Jordan; the Schlegelschule and the Dahlem Center for the Humanities at the Freie Universität Berlin; and the Deutsches Literaturarchiv in Marbach.

Several portions of this book have reached early audiences. The kernel of my chapter on "Resignation" appeared as "We Know It in Our Bones: Reading a Thirty-Five-Acre Plot in Rural Virginia with Three Poems by Charles Wright" in *Philosophy and Literature*; a version of "Desire" appeared as "'Full / of Endless Distances': Forms of Desire in Poetic Attention" in *Dibur;* and a version of "Idleness" will appear as "Essaying in Idleness" in *electronic book review*. Many thanks to Garry Hagberg, Vered Karti Shemtov, and Jason Childs for publishing these essays and to the readers of these articles for their astute questions and suggestions. Additional thanks to Toril Moi, Niklas Forsberg, and the Center for Philosophy, Arts, and Literature at Duke University; to Warren Heiti, Jan Zwicky, and Tim Lilburn; and to my panel organizers and copresenters at the Association of Canadian College and University Teachers of English (ACCUTE), the Canadian Congress of the Humanities, the American Comparative Literature Association (ACLA), and the Association of Literary Scholars, Critics, and Writers (ALSCW) Annual Meetings.

This book would not have been written without the wisdom and humor of good friends. Faisal Siddiqui has been first reader of every chapter, first ear to all worries, beloved companion, and light source in all weathers.

Elizabeth Spragins, Michaela Hulstyn, and Virginia Ramos have read multiple drafts, workshopped ideas, and inspired me from this project's earliest beginnings. Their sisterhood has been vital sustenance. Dylan Montanari brought a keen editorial eye to the entire manuscript, offering a wealth of critical insight. To Joseph Boone, Frederic Clark, Alison Davis, Fabian Goppelsröder, Kathryn Hume, Kevin Larkin, Jason Lewallen, Freddie Lipmann, David Marno, Armando Mastrogiovanni, Chris Miller, Ali Naini, Priya Nelson, Thomas O'Donnell, Luke and Lauren Parker, Luke Sunderland, Bronwen Tate, Chloe Watlington, Claude Willan, and Karen Zumhagen-Yekplé: thank you for years of insight and ideas, for solidarity pints, flows of new books and music, and for sharing your work and lives with me. And to John Clegg, for kitchen dance parties, treetop writing sessions, and critical heart expansion.

I owe everything to my beautiful and branching family: especially my mother, Katherine Gerdt, for her boundless love and for her love of language; my father, Bennett Alford, for sharing his wisdom and love of teaching; and my siblings, Matthew, Katy, and Joel, for surrounding me with love and laughter from day one.

FORMS OF POETIC ATTENTION

Introduction

What Is Poetic Attention?

People are grabbing at the chance to see
the earth before the end of the world,
the world's death piece by piece each longer than we.
—ED ROBERSON

Redwood City, California

It is October. The neighborhood bar where I write is illuminated with two football games playing simultaneously. I have my phone on the bar table, my laptop open. One ear takes in (but doesn't really follow) both games, another takes in the bizarre conversation at the next table, which is somewhere between networking meeting and Tinder date. Amid all this, I've been reading and rereading a poem by James Wright, "Autumn Begins in Martins Ferry, Ohio," and a line has caught in my mind, bringing everything to stop on a word. The poem goes like this:

In the Shreve High football stadium,
I think of Polacks nursing long beers in Tiltonsville,
And gray faces of Negroes in the blast furnace at Benwood,
And the ruptured night watchman of Wheeling Steel,
Dreaming of heroes.

All the proud fathers are ashamed to go home,
Their women cluck like starved pullets,
Dying for love.

Therefore,
Their sons grow suicidally beautiful
At the beginning of October,
And gallop terribly against each other's bodies.[1]

The poem turns on the word "therefore," and the necessarily long mental space that precedes it, which it creates in its turn. Semantically, the poem enacts a series of removes, lifting off from the immediate context of the high school stadium to the mental recollections or reflections on other spaces: bars at workday's end, steel mill work lines, then the step back to the collectivity of "all the proud fathers" and "their women." "Dying for love" draws to a full stop. Rhythmically, nothing can follow the absolute downbeat of "love." At "Therefore," the poem gathers itself into a hairpin turn of pure force, a kind of blast of wind smiting from above or beyond. The language darkens toward an epicentric closure in "suicidally beautiful," and the final line and its final word, unnecessary and necessary at the same time, knock me flat. Wright could have stopped at "each other," but people don't gallop terribly: bodies do, bodies of matter and force and velocity, charged with suicidal beauty. The poem could not take a single additional line. Its brevity is power, earthbound by the working-class proper names and populational markers: Tiltonsville, Benwood, Wheeling Steel, Polacks and Negroes, grayed with labor as the watchman is ruptured by night and by long-held insomniac vigilance.

For the past ten years, partially imprinted in the pages of this book, I've been thinking about attention. More to the immediate point, I've been mulling over, in scenes like the one snapped above, what it means to read a poem like Wright's, or a psalm like 137, or a fragment of Sappho, or a line like Edward Taylor's "let this be a vent hole," in a place like this: the Silicon Valley, in the Hoover Tower's surveillant shadow, in 2016. Facebook opened up shop near my small cottage, and kombucha has made its way into the once-shabby grunge coffeeshop on the corner, and if you can say you know Drupal on a job application you're playing a whole different game than if you said you've got a reading of Dante that will change everything. And running through all these changes is an obsession with harnessing attention, attention being the one hero that might take us through the web, the webs, and leave us semi-intact at the end of the day, and the capital currency that can boost our productivity and mindfulness quotient at the same time, draining our accounts along the way. We're told to pay attention to twittering petitions and to Kickstarter campaigns, but also to the increasingly abstract flood of Syrian refugees, all while "slowing down" and baking more bread, making more things ourselves, and at the same time moving more of our lives into linked format, hypertext, bit and Bitcoin and sound bite and GIF.[2]

At a gut level, I know that the kind of operation Wright's "therefore" performs in my mind is experientially different from the kinds of attention valued at this particular cultural moment. This difference, and all the differences contained within it, are the subject of this book. Thinking about "therefore" and its reshaping of the space-time (textual and readerly) that surrounds it entails and inspires a consideration of how other poems activate and manipulate shifts in the field of spatiotemporal perception we call attention. It inspires a consideration of how attention, under the radar of all our other critical tools and terms, operates in poems as medium and mode. I house this observation and its internal investigations under the name *poetic attention:* the ways attention is formed by poetic language in readerly and writerly experience. This book is an exploration of the multitude of forms "poetic form" assumes, and an attempt to trace the dance of attention within as far-reaching an archive of poetic examples as my linguistic capabilities allow—or, if I am honest, as far as slightly beyond that horizon. Admittedly, my own capacities for both reading and attention are limited, and my exploration is the imprint of that limitation. I consider the structures I unfold to be invitations for further investigation and attention.

Form

The notion of poetic form is as old and familiar as the study of poetry itself, an easy shorthand for "how poems work." But what exactly is *formed* in a poem? Do we mean its shape on the page? Its sound in the ear? Its sequence of images? Yes and no. "Yes" because critics and students can fashion conventional interpretations of poems that have to do with shape, sound, and images. But "no" because in a sense each of these common terms stands in for something else. It is true that poetic language is densely formed. But what is formed *by* and *in* poetic language is an event of attention generated in the acts of both reading and writing. I suggest that a poem might be better understood not simply as a gathering of composed formal features, but as an instrument for tuning and composing the attention.[3] This book tests this premise, analyzing how poems compose attention and how attention is in turn poetry's most essential "raw material." Not only an interpretation of poems in terms of how they dispose attention, the book theorizes the process of attention-making itself: its objects, its coordinates, its variables. Drawing on primarily twentieth and twenty-first-century North American poets such as Emily Dickinson, T. S. Eliot, Wallace Stevens, Anne Carson, and Claudia Rankine, this book gives language to the particular forms of attention poems both produce and require.

This investigation is a kind of bidirectional lens, looking at poetic form through the lens of attention and looking at attention through the lens of poetic form. The bidirectionality of my focus is fitting, since attention itself is a bidirectional lens: the way we attend to the world changes the world we perceive, and the world we perceive changes the way we attend. Thinking about how attention operates in the context of a work of art, whether textual, sculptural, filmic, or musical, the same holds true: we bring a certain kind and quality of attention to the work by virtue of our in-the-moment cognitive and emotional capacities, our cultural context, and previous attention training, and the work, in turn, shapes and manipulates our attention through its form and thematic evocations.

Attention has been an underlying theme in poetic theory since Aristotle but has not, until recently, been explicitly acknowledged or given extended analysis. With the emergence of the rapidly growing interdisciplinary field of attention studies, this is beginning to change. Recent literary scholarship has explored the play of attention in individual poets (Donne, Lawrence, Ashbery), periods (the eighteenth century, Romanticism, the digital age), and politics (spectacle and cultural commodification, post-911 America).[4] Making explicit the centrality of attention to poetic experience *as such*, this book addresses the dynamics of poetic attention transhistorically and examines the modes of this poetic attention that take shape in specific poems. Doing so has required developing a lexicon built at the intersection of cognitive and literary studies, one that articulates the multifaceted nature of poetic attention by parsing its variables. As I show, the variety of *forms* of poetic attention yields a rich object of analysis within which we find as many nuances and subtleties as there are individual poems.

Unfolding a Language

The categories I develop in this book are intended as functional tools—they offer a flexible language for describing a variety of forms of poetic attention and how they work. They are both the products and primary offerings of this investigation. These terms derive from my direct observation of the dynamics of attention suggested in a variety of individual poems, complemented by philosophical and empirical research on attention and poetic theory. My development of these terms is thus primarily a bottom-up, phenomenological process. For ease of reference, I have included a conceptual outline at the end of this introduction. Readers may find it useful as we move into chapters that delve into the workings of specific poems.

The first half of this book focuses on the dynamics of *transitive attention*, or modes of attention that take an object. I consider how the poem, an object itself, composes the object of transitive attention formally, semantically, and figuratively. Drawing on attention studies in phenomenology, psychology, and cognitive science, I identify five dynamic coordinates, which can be thought of as the "moving parts" of transitive attention: *intentionality*, *interest*, *selectivity*, *spatiotemporal remove*, and *apprehension*. These five moving variables combine to shape a given act, event, or experience of transitive attention. I then explore this process as it plays out in four primary poetic modes: contemplation (reading Francis Ponge, Seamus Heaney, Wallace Stevens, Elizabeth Bishop, and Harryette Mullen), desire (Emily Dickinson, William Shakespeare, George Oppen, Amy Lowell, Robert Hass, and Audre Lorde), recollection (Al-Khansā', Geoffrey Hill, Paul Celan, Anne Carson, and Theresa Hak Kyung Cha), and imagination (Samuel Coleridge, William Wordsworth, Rainer Maria Rilke, and John Burnside). In each case, I constellate poems that engage with a common mode of transitive attention, showing how the coordinates come together dynamically. Exploring these common poetic modes through the lens and lexicon of attention reveals their workings as particular modes of attending, each derived through a specific combination of transitive attention's constitutive elements. For example, in the chapter on desire, I show how Emily Dickinson's poem "I had been Hungry all the Years" not only describes but composes a mode of desirous attention through the maintenance of lack, withholding the image of ample bread from the reader's eyes, syntactically keeping the reader in a state of attentional hunger.

In part 2, I turn to *intransitive attention*, exploring modes of poetic attention that are objectless. As in part 1, I begin by thinking through the variable elements that combine to generate a given act of intransitive attention. These coordinates include *intentionality*, *scope*, the presence or absence of an *indirect object*, *temporal inflection*, and the effect on the *subject-space* of poetic attention (its expansion, contraction, or kenosis). Having unpacked the moving parts of intransitive attention, I then explore how they blend and interact in four poetic modes: vigilance (in Friedrich Hölderlin and Stéphane Mallarmé), resignation (Arthur Rimbaud and Charles Wright), idleness (Frank O'Hara, A. R. Ammons, and Joan Retallack), and boredom (Charles Bukowski, Thom Gunn, and T. S. Eliot). Placing these very different poetic examples in conversation with one another serves to reveal the complexity of each mode. For example, considering three very different approaches to idled attention in the work of O'Hara, Ammons, and Retallack, I show that idleness as poetic form involves a tension between the playful, conversational, and exploratory potentials of poetry and the intensity of formal precision required to bring it about: the honing of attention toward the perfectly slack line. As I show, in O'Hara and Retallack's work idleness comes into play most actively in the compositional process, whereas in Ammons idleness is *embodied* and *produced* by the form of the poem. These three approaches highlight both the historicity and transhistoricity of idleness as a mode of poetic attention: On the one hand, all three poets are interested in a specific historical urgency surrounding the need for idleness in modern and contemporary American life. At the same time, by engaging with much older discourses on idleness, their work underscores a longer relationship between creativity and play, between idle hours and the making of song and story.

Historical Inflection

Stated simply, poetic attention is the attention produced, required, or activated by a poem. But, of course, it is not that simple: there are so many ways that poems engage our attention, so many different minds contained in this "our," and both change historically and contextually. Any event of poetic attention takes place at a complex site: the intersection of multidirectional relationships between reader, writer, and text (or other poetic material). Each of these relationships is formed and constituted by attentional dynamics, from the relationship between writer and poem-in-progress to the relationship between poem and reader. Each, moreover, is informed by and responsive to environmental factors such as sociopolitical context, poetic convention, prevailing modes of reading, and the attention cultures surrounding both the act of writing and the act of reading. Thus poetic attention is always historically inflected. Yet the phenomenon of poetic attention itself is also transhistorical, as old and as central to poetry as language itself.

Modern and contemporary America, with its intrinsic diversity of languages and national origins, the conflux of native and immigrant populations, as well as its rapid urbanization, industrialization, and technological change, offers a rich and complex site to consider attention dynamics both in poetic work and in the social and cultural environment. The attentional challenges posed by each of the modern poems considered here, from T. S. Eliot's *The Waste Land* to Anne Carson's *Nox,* must be understood as a part of a larger constellation of aesthetic movements toward increasing experimentation, nonreferentiality, and ambiguity beginning with modernity and moving through the twentieth century. At the same time, many of the attentional concerns worked out and worked over in so much modern and contemporary poetry are to be found in premodern poetry; indeed, these concerns are intrinsic to the form of poetry itself. Considering the formation and reformation of attention in modern and contemporary poetry offers a vantage point from which to look back, through the lines of influence, translation, and adaptation, at poetic attention's longer history.

In order to honor and illustrate the transhistorical yet historically inflected nature of poetic attention, this book draws from a wide-ranging archive. While focusing primarily on modern and contemporary North American poetry, I constellate my examples with earlier Western and non-Western poetries, from an ancient Egyptian love song to a Sapphic fragment to Shakespeare's Sonnet 18, that share specific attentional dynamics. In selecting my examples, I chose poems that clearly demonstrate a given mode as well as classics whose interpretation might seem conventional or rote. For example, rereading Sonnet 18 with an eye for its attentional dynamics reveals how Shakespeare accomplishes a shift in the speaker's focus, generating tension between two simultaneous objects of love—the semantic object ("thee") and the formal object ("this," the poem itself). Reading poems for how they shape, orient, and inflect a plurality of attentional pathways requires examining the formal dimensions of poetic works where they intersect with readerly attention, on the one hand, and with writerly attention, on the other, considering how both readerly and writerly attention, as well as the formal dynamics of the poem, are situated historically.

Po(i)etic Attention

In developing the term *poetic attention,* I intend the word *poetic* to function on two levels: first, the literal. The formal, material, historical, cognitive, and sensory availabilities of poetry make the attentional experiences of reading and writing poetry different from those produced by other media. Poems are made of language: aural, graphic, semantic and symbolic; on paper, on screen, in the ear, signed by the hands. Because processes of thinking, sense-making, and perception are also deeply rooted in and bound to our language-making systems, poetry takes place close to the bone of our perceptual and attentional hardware, at the least remove from the medium of thought and response. Moreover, while they are composed in such a materially minimalistic medium as language, the polyvalent nature of language *as* medium—that language lives in sound, logical pattern, rhythm, graphic sign, and bodily gesture—makes it a uniquely (and perhaps unexpectedly) multisensory aesthetic medium, engaging and requiring attention on a variety of sensory, logical, and emotional planes at the same time.

But the poetic also moves beyond the collection of loosely related entities convention has called poems. In this second sense of *poetic attention,* I intend the first term to modify the latter, suggesting modes of attention that function poetically: attentional acts and modalities that are fundamentally noninstrumental, not subjugated to the conveyance or extraction of information, and not in the service of rhetorical persuasion. Poems might *also* contain information and might *also* be argumentative, but these are not their *poetic* qualities, in the sense that I use the word here. And, usually, edification and argumentation are accomplished more effectively in other genres. Poems can do a lot of things, but they don't make the best lectures.

Given the focus of recent debates, at least in Anglophone poetics, on the history and theory of the lyric, readers may wonder why this term is not more central to this book. *The lyric* and *lyrical* are often, it's true, used as shorthand for *the poem* and *the poetic*. And, as Virginia Jackson has pointed out, the normative genre characteristics of the lyric (individual voice, temporal suspension, subjective interiority) have, since Romanticism, been imposed on a wide variety of historically specific texts (jingles, lists, and letters, but also epics and ballads) that could do with more elbow room to be what they are, not generically pigeonholed through critical "lyricization."[5] While I find this claim compelling, I also find it both important and useful to view objects of formed language comparatively and transhistorically, and the constellation of qualities that gathers around the term *lyric* offers rich veins connecting the far reaches of the porous and evolving territory of poetry. Lyric, with its ancient roots in song, voices one aspect, one modality of poetic making—of *poiesis*. And it is this act of *making*—an act I see taking place (as event) in the medium of attention, that centers my focus on the poetic rather than the lyrical. In this sense, while Jonathan Culler attributes the "ritual" dimension of the lyric poem, its standing as event, with the word *lyric,* I see the central "event" as poetic—lyric-making being one kind of poetic event.[6] I think of poems, and thus the poetic, as dynamic, porous entities. As Jahan Ramazani has shown in *Poetry and Its Others*, poems partake in, contribute to, and cross-weave the boundaries of many modalities of language use.[7] These certainly include song, but also prayer, play, propaganda, and reportage. In this book, I explore many kinds of poems. Some (including two by Dickinson) could easily be categorized as lyrics. Others (Joan Retallack's *Errata 5uite,* for example) can be seen as deliberately *anti*lyrical. Some work within and stretch the boundaries of conventional form, others draw form out of chaos. But they are all poems, and as poems they are all composed by, and compose in turn, acts and events of attention.

Reading, Reaching

As event, the poem takes place in the reading (or recitation) of it. And yet it is itself the product of an event of attention. And that event of attention, the writing and crafting of poetic language, is itself the product (to the extent that one can separate process and product) of another event of attention—the writer's attention to the world and to language. Language itself constitutes a relationship of attention to the world. Language is the site of that relationship and embodies its reach and its limitations.

This *reach* of poetic language is attentive, both phenomenologically and etymologically. In Edmund Husserl, attention is a physical act of tending- or, more aptly, *tensing*-toward.[8] My method in these investigations begins in noticing, reaching, and tensing toward poems. Based on direct phenomenological observation, the investigative work is carried out in the "twofold energy of the mind."[9] Looking at once at the poems I consider, and at the movement of my own attention in response, I use a combined process of induction and deduction to suggest possible categories for the synthetic movements of poetic attention. While I draw on literary, philosophical, and psychological research on attention and poetic experience to develop my own concepts and terminology, my reflections on the poems themselves are thus deeply subjective, rooted in firsthand acts of attention.[10]

This approach locates me in a limited position, bound by my own blind spots and conditioned lenses, which I have kept in mind throughout my theorization of poetic attention. I have chosen this precarious vantage point between subjectivity and objectivity because poetic attention is itself positioned between the subjective experiences, moods, and capacities of any given reader, and the objective formal and thematic features "really existing" in the poem. Because I am engaged in reading poems written by others, I focus for the most part on the readerly arm of this relational web. At the same time, I try to listen beyond the horizon of my individual and momentary reading experience, paying attention to how the poem works and what kind of reading it seems to ask of the hypothetical subject-space of an implied reader.[11]

Subjects and Objects

This leads to an essential question: who is the *subject* of poetic attention? The subject of poetic attention, as I conceive it here, is a postulated subject-space, the attentional space opened up (or proposed) by the form of the poem itself.[12] The subject of poetic attention should not be equated with the speaker of the poem (where there is one). The speaking voice of a lyric poem is one formal feature among others that contributes to the shaping of poetic attention—a unique feature in that it exercises an act of attention *in* the poem, and that act of attention shapes the content (thematic and formal) of the poem itself, as well as its effect on the reader's attention. The presence of a speaker is one of the effects the poem has been designed to produce. The reader's (and the writer's) relationship to the poem is a relationship of attention *to the poem itself*, however often it might be experienced as a relationship (as address or as witness) with the speaker. The object of poetic attention is yet more layered, held between the formal object that is the poem itself and the experiential object (or space of objectlessness, as the case may be) that is generated by that form and, often, its semantic content.

In its moments of composition and reception, every poem is an object of attention. The written poem stands on the page or illuminated screen, present in physical space as the object of hand and eye. In print, it might be accompanied by the smell of new paper or the warmer mustiness of a library book. The spoken poem, or the poem heard in the mind's ear, stands forth as an object of aural sense. It is an object of our listening, as we tune in, focusing, straining for rhythms, patterns. Out of this aural attention, the poem acts upon the body through rhythm, through syllables tapped out, as a poetry teacher of mine used to do, between thumb and fingertip. Its particular attentional response is a product of its form, its structure. The written poem has a shape on the page: the immediately recognizable palm-sized unit of the sonnet, the sprawling, longer-than-breath lines of Walt Whitman and Charles Wright, eating the width of the page, or the more skeletal, bladelike shapes of Federico García Lorca, Lorine Niedecker, Louis Zukofsky, and Pierre Joris, or poems by Stéphane Mallarmé, Larry Eigner, Anne-Marie Albiach, and bpNichol, which employ nonlinear layout, graphic elements, scattering, and white space. Some poems arrest the attention, some stand back a little, mute or resistant, and we might have to do some work, pushing through attention's initial brambles of boredom or confusion until we're in, caught up in the poem's engagement of us and in our own engagement with the poem's physical structure, tinkering, tapping for beams.

A consistent thread of interest in the object of the poem, and the poem *as* object, runs through modern poetry and poetics. Beginning in the first few decades of the twentieth century and again in the 1960s with the reception of Martin Heidegger in American critical theory, the *thing* became something of a keyword—from Gerard Manley Hopkins's rhythmic engagements with objects of the natural world through attunement to what he called their inscape to Gertrude Stein's ambition to conjure objects through the pure manipulation of textures of sound; from William Carlos Williams's famous line turned mantra, "no ideas but in things" to Francis Ponge's efforts to conjure the physical presence of small things (oyster, cigarette, crate); from the New Critics' formalist approach to the object of the poem at close range to Denise Levertov's writings on the revelatory potential of attending to objects in the world through the composition of "organic form"—a term adapted from Coleridge via Hopkins. One could read many—if not most—major veins of twentieth-century Anglophone poetics as engagements with the question of objective attention, each in a different way and toward different theoretical aims: a deliberate and assertively future-oriented poetics (e.g., Pound and Olson), a form of secular meditation rooted in perception of the world (Oppen, Ammons, Levertov), or a talisman of return to simpler and more earthbound relations (Robert Frost, Heaney, Mary Oliver).

Figure and Ground

At both the semantic and formal levels, the object that is the poem as well as the objects that coalesce within it are identified and constituted by attention. The ability of human perception to isolate objects (whether material or conceptual) from the general surrounding flux is attention's principal and most primal task: recognizing the shape of a face, the movement of a predator, or a source of food requires the capacity to capture, to set apart, to distinguish an object. This might be an object that captures the attention unexpectedly or the object of an active vigilant pursuit.[13] In cognitive terms, the distinction has been framed as a relationship between *figure* and *ground*.[14] The figure is an object or feature that stands out, attracting our attention. Attentional selection is thus the process of discerning figure from ground.

Cognitive and aesthetic research on attention selection, using eye-tracking and visual targets to measure attention response, have focused primarily on visual characteristics such as size, physical proximity, intactness, and color. In literary experience, by contrast, figure and ground play out in a variety of linguistic features and sensory planes—in the patterns and pattern deviations that shape and guide our attention through the written or work or oral performance.[15] Poetry offers an important addition to the conversation on the workings of aesthetic attention because, unlike single-sense artistic media such as painting or music, it requires attentional engagement across sensory experience including the visual (whether in graphic, textual, code, or performance poetry), the aural (in rhythm, rhyme, alliteration, and tone), and the tactile, as rhythm plays out on the body.[16] These elements are intensified in combination and in the interplay of moving and nonmoving elements of the poem: emotional, imaginative, and sonic experience is kinetic and changing, while the visual element does not change, except through the shifting of visual focus along the line and from page to page.

To adapt the figure-ground framework to poetry, we must identify stylistic and conceptual features that produce the patterns, shifts, and interruptions that cause certain elements of a work to capture and hold the attention even briefly. Locating these sites of linguistic deviance in a work entails, not surprisingly, sensitive reading on a number of planes within the text—phonetic, morphological, sonic, syntactic, graphological, semantic, lexical, pragmatic, and discursive.[17] The "figure," or "attractor" might change many times in the course of a single work. The relationship between figure(s) and ground is dynamic, constituted by the capture and recapture of our attention—attraction by one, distraction from another.[18] Wolfgang Iser frames a similar phenomenon in terms of a spotlight model to capture the role of selectivity in shaping the terrain of literary experience through the primary medium of attention: "While the chosen elements initially spotlight a field of reference, opening it up for perception, they also permit the perception of all those elements that the selection has excluded. These, then, form a background against which the observation is to take place. It is as if what is present in the text must be judged in the light of what is absent."[19]

The shift and gradation of these positions constitutes in large part the sense of kineticism and drama, even in a nonnarrative work, as the movement and manipulation of the attention itself enacts a play of intensification and disruptions. Moving away from a traditional cognitive model of figure and ground as binary opposites allows for a more graded and dynamic field of attention in which "figures which fade into the background by neglect can still be remembered, either unilaterally by the reader or with the active assistance of certain textual features."[20] The notion of "graded depth" captures the subtlety of linguistic modulation of attention better than a binary figure/ground distinction. As the attention moves, elements shift from figure to ground, becoming vague as they recede from focus, yet remaining in the sphere of attention as traces, resonances, and associations. For Iser, the process of selection, or the moving spotlight, reveals the "intentionality of the text, whose reality comes about through the loss of reality suffered by those empirical elements that have been torn away from their original function by being transposed into the text."[21] In this way, selection itself, the dynamic operation of focalization, constitutes the literariness of literary experience—form and fictionality—as an event combining imagination and perception within the medium of attention.

Aesthetic, Literary, and Poetic Attention

Dynamics of attention are central to reading in general, literary reading in particular, and poetic reading in even greater particularity. On a general level, attention is important in all artworks, which shape and produce it in their own ways. However, poetic attention is unique and in some ways primary to aesthetic attention more generally. In poems, the otherwise shapeless medium of language becomes an object for the senses. The specificity of language as the constitutive material of poetry is important in distinguishing the layered nature of poetic attention from the kinds of attention at play in music or visual art because of what I call, in part 1, "poetry's double transitivity"—the fact that, in poetry, attention is first given to language, and out of this primary engagement with language a multisensory, multivalent experience of dynamic attention is formed. This results in an initial high concentration of attention reading the poem itself, followed by a second-order mode of *poetic* attention. In other words, we employ a familiar focused attention in first coming to a poem, as we do in coming to any text, but then the poem, by virtue of its form, transfigures that attention into a distinct and dynamic attentional mode.

One could argue that any kind of writing does this, but I think that would be going too far. It is certainly true that attention is required by *any* act of reading—novels, the news, and even social media feeds. However, each of these broad genres of writing is characterized by a particular kind of attentional engagement. Attention to language *as* object of attention, not only as conduit of meaning, can be said to characterize the poetic—a definition resonant with Roman Jakobson's concept of the "poetic function" (in which attention is tuned, more than in other literary forms, not only to the content of the message but to the message itself).[22] Within fictional narrative, for example, I would argue that only certain kinds of novels produce something analogous to poetic attention. Most novels do not aspire primarily to stylistic innovation, focusing instead on the development of plot and character. In other words, the writing of most fictional narratives does not seek to call attention to itself *as formed language*, but aims for a transparency that foregrounds what is *conveyed*. In this case, the attention involved is typically one of immersion; one must be engaged enough to follow the forward movement of the narrative. Attention, in these cases, is a means to an end other than itself, namely understanding.

Exceptional novels that aspire, like poetry, to make of language an object for the senses, embody and produce a different kind of attention, one that is an end unto itself. Writers like Marcel Proust, Virginia Woolf, W. G. Sebald, Roberto Bolaño, Toni Morrison, Marilynne Robinson, and J. M. Coetzee demand our attention not just to understand the plot and characters of their books but also to see the kind of work being done to and by the language of their novels. These novels are sometimes called lyrical, which is telling, since it suggests their debt to the workings of poetic language and poetic attention. It is important to note, however, that it *is* possible to bring poetic attention to bear on works that are not poems, if one translates "attending poetically" to mean bringing formal attention to the ways in which attention is manipulated by the form of the language itself. The doubleness of "attention to the form of attention" is intentional here and uniquely poetic in nature.

Poetic Theory as Critical Attention

In thinking through the nature of poetic attention, its histories of theorizations under other headings, I draw from the contributions of formalist, reader-oriented, and historicist poetics to explore an alternative mode of reading. These models are united by a common concern for directing and protecting the practice of poetic attention, but are hemmed in by narrow and normative views that isolate and fix one aspect of the attentive relation between text, reader, author, or context, thereby cutting off a view of their interaction. Focusing on the attention dynamics of the text allows us to maintain close formal engagement with the work itself without neglecting the role of the historically and subjectively specific reading and writing practices and without overprivileging a universalized mode of reading that may not be elicited or supported by the text. Understanding the poem as a site of attentional relations (and poetics as a history of approaches to and prescriptions for poetic attention)[23] offers a way to engage closely with the text without severing it from its historical and contemporary reading and writing practices and without applying the same model of attention to every poetic text, privileging one mode of reading over others regardless of the specific nature of the poem.

Investigation into the workings of attention and its relationship to aesthetic objects is by no means a modern phenomenon. Questions about the object of aesthetic attention have been explored across the arts fields, beginning with Plato on real and ideal forms and Aristotle's writing on mimesis in *The Poetics*. But in the formation of aesthetics and psychology as fields of study in the eighteenth and nineteenth centuries we can see the emergence of an explicit theoretical and scientific interest in the dynamics of attention in relation to aesthetic objects.[24] Alexander Gottlieb Baumgarten isolated the aesthetic object as a unique site of attention in his redirection of the word *aesthetics* away from sensation (senses) and toward the *taste* (sense) of an objet d'art.[25] In setting such objects of taste apart, in a field outside of ordinary economies of utility and interest, the discipline of aesthetics came to study the specific dynamics of contemplative interaction with objects. Building on Baumgarten's exploration of taste, Immanuel Kant's work on phenomenal and noumenal objects addressed the mind's heavily mediated and veiled brushes with the "thing in itself," analyzing the space of disinterested contemplation experienced in relation to works of art.

Kant's description of the characteristics of aesthetic experience as a stance of contemplation without ulterior interests led to Husserl's development of phenomenology as a process of thinking through attention to perception and William James's isolation of attention as a psychological experience identified through his method of radical empiricism. This line of inquiry accompanied the growth of the psychological sciences, probing the physical processes underlying a long-acknowledged philosophical question. The rise of cognitive research fueled an increasing fascination with the nature of attention and its relationship to the art object. Turning phenomenology toward social critique, Walter Benjamin's writings on attention, boredom, and distraction in the modern urban context reflect on how different aesthetic media interact with, and generate, specific forms of attention, and how cultures of attention were reflected in the attentional dynamics of their art forms, whether storytelling, work songs, cinema, or pop lyrics. Contemporary philosophers and cultural theorists have continued to explore the mind's interaction with (and composition of) objects, leading to the emergence of, for example, "thing theory" and "object-oriented ontology."

Although it draws on a range of disciplines and methodologies, aesthetics, as Gérard Genette has articulated, has its origin in attention to the artwork and its surrounding relations.[26] Literary theory also concerns acts of attention: to formal objects, the ways they act on mind and body, and their relationship to specific environments. Yet, in the debates between various schools and methodologies, this common denominator has been largely unacknowledged or implied under different headings of scale, proximity, and contextualization.

The familiar exegetical practice of "close reading" can be seen as an act of paying attention to a text-object on its own, before considering it within a larger contextual or thematic fabric.[27] This practice, part of the modernist response to romanticism's emphasis on individual genius, underpinned the early twentieth century's formalist movements in Russia (Viktor Shklovsky, Roman Jakobson, Yuri Tynyanov) and America (John Crowe Ransom, Allen Tate, Cleanth Brooks). Yet even as formalism came under attack in the second half of the century from a variety of angles, most notably those of cultural studies, feminist theory, and new historicism, due to its neglect of literature's historical, political, and cultural embeddedness, close reading remained a dominant mode of critical and pedagogical engagement through the rise of cultural studies and new historicism in the second half of the century. The practice also remained central through deconstruction (which can itself be seen as the supreme veneration of revelatory formalism). This is perhaps because, even in order to understand its place in material or discursive histories, reading for "form" is our only way of attending to the poem itself, as a discrete object, as a form that can be touched, taken apart, questioned, and located in relationship to other texts and within larger systems.

Arguments in favor of "distant reading," in critiquing the "text-centric" model of reading that has dominated formalist and even some historicist approaches to literary criticism, essentially propose a shift in the focus of critical attention. Historicism promulgates a shift in focus from the inner workings of the text to its role as artifact in a historical setting. Distant reading reorients critical focus to patterns, movements of style, webs, and streams of exchange within and surrounding the text and constitutes a shift in the object of critical focus. Recent work on literature and the mind has approached the internal movement of close reading more specifically as an act of attention,[28] without imposing it as an unstated pseudo-theological norm.[29] As Roland Greene has observed, "The available modes of evoking such negotiations change from time to time: now they might be called history of ideas, later literary theory, still later cultural or postcolonial studies—and later again, perhaps history of ideas or formalism again."[30]

I. A. Richards once wrote, *"We are all of us learning to read all the time."*[31] Looking over the waves of schools and manifestos that have vied for supremacy through the twentieth century and into the twenty-first, I find myself, holding a poem, asking again, "how to read?"[32] "how to read a page?"[33] Looking at the (sometimes vehement, sometimes brilliant, sometimes bland) oppositions between reader-, text-, author-, psychology-, and history-centered foci that have shaped these schools, I am struck by the relative fixity of each approach and the way in which each approach levels a norm regarding what aspect of the poem merits attention, which part of the poetic relation between reader, writer, text, and their inflecting histories.

I want to propose, as a compass with which to navigate the rival schools (through their overlapping and contested territories, as well as their abandoned no-man's lands), that the method and theory of attentional analysis might fruitfully be applied not only to poetic objects (as I hope to demonstrate in this book) but also to poetic theory itself. At its core, poetics wrestles with the question of the proper attention (its scope, scale, and aims) to bring to a poem. The object of our attention (in this case, a poem) remains the same. What changes is the way we attend, the way we talk about attending, which parts of the poem we evaluate (give value to) with our attention to them, which parts merit such attention. Refinements, redirections, and relocations in the mode, manner, and scope of critical attention, in keeping with historical changes, reflect the changing attention culture of scholarship itself.[34] Understanding seemingly divergent poetic methodologies as many tools for engaging attentively with a work of literature and its surrounding cultural and historical systems offers an exciting opening for a more diverse and integrated body of critical options.

Action, thought, and belief are contained in what we attend to and what we don't, whether these choices are intentional or conditioned. The way we attend to artworks and the ways we attend in daily life are powerfully connected to structures of power, identity, and class. One could go so far as to say that the tacit manipulation and engineering of attention underpins the circulation of discourses, as language arises from specific attentional relations, stances, focal economies, and as modes of attention define relational attitudes, subject, and object. These are the ethicopolitical stakes of attention, which underpin the politics of reading, of visibility, publishing, recognition, and time spent attending (or not) to the work of people of color, women, and LGBTQ writers. The act of attending to a poem can both reveal and conceal its embeddedness in social systems of race, gender, and class. The revelation depends on turning a vigilant eye to our own attentional habits and blind spots. As Andrew Epstein puts it, "if we sleepwalk through our days, if the everyday remains naturalized and mystified, then spectacle and alienation triumph, and those forces that benefit from our distraction—usually aligned with the dominant social order, with power and capitalism—continue unchallenged."[35] Thus acts of both readerly and writerly attention (as well as the attentional dynamics we might attribute to the text independently of either) are inherently politically relevant, culturally and historically specific, and always in flux.

Attentional dynamics generate complexly interwoven webs of relation (including those of critical response) surrounding a single poem. And yet the poem itself, at least in written form, is a more or less stable object of intelligent design: its structural elements can be read for suggested purpose and effects and for their significance within larger systems, living and material.

Contingency, Form, and Attending in the World

The poem exists only in attention, held in tension, set apart. To *set apart* is the root meaning of the sacred. In this way, it is not difficult to understand the sacred as preceding and exceeding its religious uses. Attending in the secular context can be seen as a form of making-sacred that is not necessarily rooted in a metaphysics. The act of setting-apart that makes possible a poem's emergence from the backdrop of ordinary language use and ordinary perceptual experience is inevitably a confrontation with contingency through the medium of form. Seeing poems as diverse formations of attention allows us to take into account the essential event of *poiesis* as poised between the precarity of freedom and the constraints and contingencies of emergent forms.[36]

The problem of form is, at root, the problem of contingency. Contingency is the abyss out of which the form of the poem is composed. It is also the backdrop against which and out of which every act of attention takes place. The poem calls itself out of the blank noise to give itself form. Its challenge is to generate a context of necessity out of one of contingency.

This is the purpose of the invocation—to clear a space, gather attention, and *orient* attention into a clearing around itself. That clearing is both *made* by the form of the poem and *inhabited* by that form, in the same way that a conch forms its habitation around itself, building it out of itself. Every act of attention is a dance and wager with contingency. In every act of attention there is the negative of that act, that which is unattended or changed by an individual perceptive lens: at stake in this negativity is the always-present fact of the contingency of perception, not to mention the underlying ontological questions of being that attention raises. That there might be no *there* there, no object despite one's subject-feeling toward moving sense data. A blank intrudes or intervenes on the form of the poem, a reminder of what is not there and the nothing that is. Intentional practices of attention, as we find in the practices of both reading and writing poetry, engage this space of contingency.

When we practice attending to attention, we practice being in the world. Not to say that practicing attention by reading poems makes us "better people," but, insofar as this practice hones and refines our capacities for perception and response, and insofar as our capacities for perception and response underpin our powers of judgment, practicing attention—and poetic attention in particular, for reasons I discuss in the chapters that follow—holds implications for the honing and refinement of judgment.[37]

As practice, poetic attention isn't easy. Though they sometimes take hold of us by the nape, without much conscious effort on our parts, poems can be recalcitrant, withdrawn, irritating, even violent. But perhaps the difficulty is valuable in itself, and the small tears in the self that take place through this effort and exposure are necessary for building stronger cognitive and emotional muscle. Writing on the challenge posed by the poems of Wallace Stevens, Simon Critchley observed, "Yes, poetry *is* difficult and that's why it shouldn't be avoided. The difficulty is learning to love that difficulty, becoming accustomed to the experience of thinking that poetry requires and calls forth."[38] Especially now, when so many cultural and material forces drive toward productivity, profile updates, and increased public views, what is at stake in so delicate and purposeless an act as paying attention to a thing without payoff or publicity? Perhaps learning to look at poems, for how they maneuver in the medium of our own attention, for how they shape the contours of our awareness, and for how they push the horizons of our noticing, trains us in another mode of being.

Around me the bar is still humming, though the nearby meeting-date has started to sag, both parties now staring down at their phones. "Dying for love." Perhaps "learning to love that difficulty" is also learning to love. Learning, even in this twittering room of brightly lit screens, "to see the earth before the end of the world."[39]

POETIC ATTENTION: CONCEPTUAL OUTLINE

A. Transitive Attention (object-oriented attention)
    Dynamic Coordinates
        1. Interest
        2. Intentionality (endogenous / exogenous)
        3. Selectivity
            Concentration
            Resolution
            Integrity
        4. Temporal Remove
        5. Apprehension
    Modes:
        1. Contemplation
        2. Desire
        3. Recollection
        4. Imagination

B. Intransitive Attention (objectless attention)
    Dynamic Coordinates
        1. Intentionality
        2. Presence of an Indirect Object
        3. Scope
        4. Temporal Inflection
        5. Subjectivity (Constitution vs. Decreation)
    Modes
        1. Vigilance
        2. Resignation
        3. Idleness
        4. Boredom

PART ONE
Attending to Objects

CHAPTER I

Modes of Transitive Attention

My mother gave me my first book of poems when I was around six years old.[1] Its pale green cover displayed a simple sketch of a cat, nose craning downward toward a few lines that were blades of grass. Each poem, filling a small portion of one page, addressed a single object in simple language. The subject matter of each poem was plain and unassuming: pebble, watering can, cat. Nothing happened in these poems. They simply looked, for a moment. The poems themselves were pocket sized, each a pebble to be rolled between finger and thumb or tucked under the tongue. Each was accompanied by a small drawing, filling the rest of the page. The poems composed the same act they asked of the reader: hold a small object in the attention, pause with the pebble, the watering can, the cat, the poem. Pause for the duration of a few breaths and simply attend. Details came to the fore, details in stillness that I can still conjure to this day, though the book is no longer with me, tucked deep somewhere in my childhood bookcase in an upstairs room in my mother's house. I can recall the stillness they composed, the simplicity of their language, and the practice of looking they enacted and encouraged.

How does the poem, as formed object, compose a particular attentional stance? How does it compose attention toward the object or objects it presents? To what extent do environmental factors (immediate surroundings, social and historical setting, physical conditions) affect our ability to attend to the object and the shape our attention takes? How do the different sensory attentions (visual, auditory, olfactory, tactile) interact, isolate, and inform one another? These questions will inform part 1 of this book, exploring forms of what I have named transitive attention.

Transitive attention is attention *to*: it takes an object. Of course, not all objects of poetic attention are clearly identifiable as such. Poems attend not only to the face or breast of the beloved but to the edge of a sleeve, the cracked pot under the drain pipe, a certain slant of light, the crystalline comb of the pomegranate's innards, the word *blackberry*. I explore the poetic object at two levels: first, the semantic object configured by the poem, through which the poem constitutes, shapes, and colors the imagined content of its focalized object or objects (Henry Wadsworth Longfellow's daffodils, Charles Baudelaire's swan, Mahmoud Darwish's almond trees); second, the formal object that is the poem itself, of which the semantic and figurative dimension constitutes one aspect.

Poetry's Double Transitivity: Mental Representation and Direct Perception

Poetry's figurative work draws on, practices, and cultivates the ability to attend to what cognitive science identifies as objects of mental representation,[2] while the formal dynamics of the poem exercise the ability to attend to objects of direct perception. Poetry's dual nature as both formal and figurative object creates an intersection between imagined and direct perception, requiring the simultaneous practice of both modes. The present and really experienced work of attention takes place in the structural dynamics of the poem itself: the poem as an object crafts a set of attentional dynamics that take place in the real-time level of direct perception, orientation, selection, modulation, and assimilation. On the other hand, the imagination plays a central role in the descriptive and associative work of both reader and writer, in the invention of a poem's figured focal object and horizon. With the poem's composition of a semantic object, the imaginative faculty of mental representation is called upon to build in the mind a simulated experience of perception. Even the most direct observational impulse, the most faithful realism, is composed in and of the imagination. Often, within the field of mental representation, a third level opens, as objects of semantic description open to the yet more interior imaginative dimensions of metaphorization and symbolization—nested and unfolding levels of mental representation. Because of the integrated and mutually dependent nature of formal and semantic dynamics, the readings that follow move between the two levels, tracking the poems' composition of transitive attention toward both formal and represented objects.

The temporalities involved in poetic attention correspond to these two transitive modes: the location of the figured object in time (the present object of contemplation, the past object of remembrance and elegy, the potential object of future projection, anticipation, or imagination) invokes the work of mental representation, and the temporal dynamics of the poem, its attenuative, suspensive, or accelerative qualities, refer to the present action of direct perception to the formal object. Because I address the temporal dynamics of poetic language itself in detail later on, my primary reference to temporality in this chapter will refer to the temporal location of the object of mental representation, most notably in my accounts of direct contemplation and recollective attention.

In the poem's imaginative focalization, attention operates as the pure conjuring act of mind—not so very different from the Kantian subject's conjuring of the phenomenal world from the synthesis of sense data and reasoning. Imaginative focalization was itself a key aspect of Kant's philosophy—an element poised at the juncture between subjective perception and subjective cognition and between subjective cognition and the experience of objective presence.[3] The imaginative work required in both the composition and reception of poetry offers an important way not only *out of* but also *into* and *through* the ordinary experience and perception of reality. Understanding the imagination as a key element of how attention forms and responds to the poetic object foregrounds attention's location between interior and exterior, between the act of the mind on itself and the processing of objects in the world, a position that stretches between observation and meditation, at once rooted in the granularity of focalized perception and lifting off. The element of the imagination in poetry's transitive attention acknowledges the subject's active part in penetrating beyond direct perception, pushing into and opening the mystery objects hold in their modes of perceptual evasion.

We find a resonant viewpoint in Friedrich Nietzsche's philosophy of art, which saw fiction's illusion-making as a salutary alternative to truth.[4]

Wallace Stevens, on the other hand, saw poetry's imaginative work not as an alternative or escape but as our only *source* of "reality," which is constantly composed and revised by our imaginative attempts to perceive our world. In the essay "Imagination as Value," Stevens addresses the "struggle" between reason and imagination, proposing them as parts of a dialogic process of perception and synthesis: "we live in concepts of the imagination before the reason has established them. If this is true, then reason is simply the methodizer of the imagination. It may be that the imagination is a miracle of logic and that its exquisite divinations are calculations wholly within analysis."[5] Stevens is in this way a true Kantian: "We live in the mind."[6] And yet, for Stevens, imagination's revisionary power and its capacity to tune and refine the art of perception is directly linked to its fidelity to the latter's work of illuminating what is real. In this *chosen* form of belief, which enriches the real with the fullest life of the mind, rests the possibility of life without God—the supreme fiction—in the modern era.[7] Against or alongside the conjuring of imaginary objects, the poem itself, as object, produces sense data directly as well—through sonic dynamics of rhythm, rhyme, and sonic texture, through the text's visual and graphic dimensions, and through the material particulars of its transmission (its setting on page or screen, the social/environmental contexts surrounding the event of its reading or performance). The interaction between the sensory effects of the poem-object and the sensory content of its semantic object takes place between the cognitive modes of direct contemplation, desire, recollection, and imagination. The poem crafts attention to its object or objects not only through imagination but also through present sensory experience: imagined object merges with or rubs up against present object.

Dynamics of Transitive Attention

The five key coordinates of transitive attention I identify here are *interest, intentionality, selectivity, spatiotemporal remove,* and *apprehension*. These five terms will anchor us as we move into a more detailed discussion of how transitive attention *works* in the poetic context. It is important to note that these coordinates are combinatory, and combining them differently produces specific modes or inflections of transitive attention. In the sections that follow I will discuss each term, providing examples of each to show how they operate within poetic language. The chapters included in part 1 show the ways in which they combine to form and variegate poetic registers of contemplation, desire, recollection, and imagination.

Some of these coordinates concern the subject of attention, and some concern the nature of the object. Subject-oriented dynamics are those coordinates of transitive attention that concern primarily the position and attitudinal stance of the attending subject. The two subject-oriented dynamics I identify here are interest and intentionality. As mentioned earlier, it is difficult to fully extricate the subject and object in the attentive relation. However, these coordinates fall more to the side of the subject, originating in its activity, and only secondarily in the specific nature or qualities of the object. By interest, I mean the degree of investment or motivation driving the subject's relation to the object of attention. Intentionality refers, in both direct perception and mental representation, to the nature of the act of transitive attention as either active or passive: in more precise terms, the intentionality of an act of attention is classed either as endogenous (active, driven by internal goal-oriented preintention) or exogenous (passive, captured by external stimuli, and responsive to external change without preintention). In endogenous attention, the subject has the most agency, and the act of attention is a deliberate, intentional labor of focalization. In exogenous attention, primary agency lies in the object of attention, which captures or even arrests the subject's attention, whether visual or auditory, overt or covert.[8]

Object-oriented coordinates of transitive attention include selectivity (the scale, integrity, and resolution of the object of attention) and spatiotemporal remove (the location of the object in space-time, relative to the attending subject). The final category, apprehension, falls outside the subject- or object-oriented categories, or rather falls at their intersection, and refers to the degree of successful capture of the object by the act of attention. A high degree of apprehension would result in the experience of the object's full distillation and realization by the work of attention. A low degree would be those objects that resist my attentive grasp or, conversely, those forms of attention that seem always to turn up further recesses in its object, yielding an experience of resistance, evasion, and thus either perpetuation or abandonment of the work of attention. I will deal with this category last, as it relies on the other coordinates and can be seen as the crux of the attentive relationship between subject and object, accounting for the experience of revelation and crystallization of the object as well as its distance and ungraspability.

A qualification: the strength of thinking of these dynamic coordinates in terms of degrees, or scale, is also its weakness: to offer some poems as higher or lower in a given quality automatically raises questions. There are many poems that might be yet more extreme or crystallizing examples. To say that a poem, or the work of a given poet, is high or low on a given spectrum does not shut out this possibility. Rather it invites exploration into how we might account for the qualities of poems, attempting to approach their specific use of attention's many constitutive elements.

Degree of Interest and Disinterest

The notion of aesthetic experience as disinterested contemplation, while contested, has helped us to acknowledge the particular experience of a work of art as taking place in its own sphere of significance, outside of ordinary mundane interactions and relations, motivated by drives, desires, and objectives.[9] Yet, *within* the sphere of aesthetic experience, how do we recognize the dynamics of interest that complicate and pluralize the Kantian mode of contemplation? Certain modes of attention, such as desire and fascination, are primarily driven by the subject's invested interestedness toward the object, while others are geared more toward the object itself, set apart from economies of interest. These include modes of contemplation, study, meditation, and even praise predicated by an essential letting-be. While the Kantian model places the more interested modes outside of aesthetic experience, we can understand attention as necessarily bi-directional, a meeting of interested and disinterested modes. Within this meeting, it is helpful to discern the modes that fall more to one side or another of this spectrum, allowing thereby a plurality of kinds of aesthetic experience, rather than only one permitted modality. To permit dynamics of interest, and degrees of interest, into the sphere of aesthetic experience is to see the complex of motivations that take part, in textual art, in both readerly and writerly engagement. These interests might take place at the level of semantic representation, as in the fragment of Sappho I will consider, or at the level of discourse and language politics, as in the work of the Language poets.[10] Focusing on dynamics of interest at the semantic level (that is, the composed field of representation within the poem), it is nearly impossible to read Sappho's Fragment 31 without being pulled into the speaker's position of yearning, so far from disinterest:

φαίνεταί μοι κῆνος ἴσος θέοισιν	He seems to me equal to gods that man
ἔμμεν' ὤνηρ, ὄττις ἐνάντιός τοι	twhoever he is who opposite you
ἰσδάνει καὶ πλάσιον ἆδυ φωνεί-	sits and listens close
σας ὑπακούει	to your sweet speaking
καὶ γελαίσας ἰμέροεν, τό μ' ἦ μὰν	and lovely laughing—oh it
καρδίαν ἐν στήθεσιν ἐπτόαισεν	puts the heart in my chest on wings
ὡς γὰρ ἔς σ' ἴδω βρόχε', ὥς με φώναι-	for when I look at you, even a moment,
σ' οὐδ' ἓν ἔτ' εἴκει,	no speaking is left in me
ἀλλ' ἄκαν μὲν γλῶσσα †ἔαγε†, λέπτον	no: tongue breaks and thin
δ' αὔτικα χρῶι πῦρ ὐπαδεδρόμηκεν,	fire is racing under skin
ὀππάτεσσι δ' οὐδ' ἓν ὄρημμ', ἐπιρρόμ-	and in eyes no sight and drumming
βεισι δ' ἄκουαι,	fills ears
†έκαδε μ' ἴδρως ψῦχρος κακχέεται†, τρόμος δὲ	and cold sweat holds me and shaking
παῖσαν ἄγρει, χλωροτέρα δὲ ποίας	grips me all, greener than grass
ἔμμι, τεθνάκην δ' ὀλίγω 'πιδεύης	I am and dead—or almost
φαίνομ' ἔμ' αὔται·	I seem to me
ἀλλὰ πᾶν τόλματον ἐπεὶ †καὶ πένητα†	But all is to be dared, because even a person of poverty[11]

    Even as we distinguish self from speaker (I, reading, am not leaning in to the beloved leaning in to her beloved, but at yet another remove), we experience mimetically the tense triangle of desire composed by her language, looking not into the eyes of the desired but at her profile, turned in love to another. To experience this poem in a state of disinterest would be to miss the tension of attention offered by its situation, to miss the particular attentiveness of desire-in-distance it invites us to experience, vicariously. Perhaps we lean in to the turned profile of Sappho's speaker, turned in love to her beloved and not to us. The "you" is not the reader but another, so that the act of reading parallels the triangulated, asymmetrical, and unfulfilled experience of attending to an object of beauty without the return of its gaze. We read not with disinterest but with enmeshedness in the scene, participating in our own act of watching, leaning in from an outsider position.

On the other hand, some poems lend themselves more readily to the kind of disinterested, motivation-free contemplation Kant saw as primary to the aesthetic mode. Consider, for example, Derek Mahon's "A Disused Shed in Co. Wexford," with its still attention alit on small mushrooms craning up in an abandoned shed, forgotten for years and only in the moment of the poem opened to the light of attention:

> Deep in the grounds of a burnt-out hotel,
> Among the bathtubs and the washbasins
> A thousand mushrooms crowd to a keyhole.
> This is the one star in their firmament
> Or frames a star within a star.
> What should they do there but desire?[12]

Mahon's speaker wants nothing with these creatures that have been growing in darkness and only draws our attention as a way of illumination, an unexpected discovery and meditation. The mode is disinterest, and the value of attention in the second poem belongs to the object itself, the act of attention producing nothing for the speaker save the gift of discovering an unseen world and the care of stopping to give an account of it. While these poems engage with the dynamics of interest at the semantic level and involve the reader through the mimetic experience that follows the eye and interest of the "I," they also operate differently at the formal level. The latter stills the impulses of interest in its repetition of simple sentences, the syntactic breaks falling at the end of lines, not in the midst, a series of observations disrupted only by the open question "What should they do there but desire?"—an unanswered question opening a space of agency around the plants that was not there before. We are called to respond to them as subject, letting desire belong to them, letting them be, in desiring. Sappho's more complex form ignites interest, which shifts our gaze from its initial fixation on the "he," only to give way to the true object of desire, the "you," and the midline breaks of "— oh" and ", even a moment," and "dead—or almost" ratchet up the tension level, calling on our own investedness and involvement, placed within a more complex web of multidirectional attention, envy, breakages, and revisions.

In the reading experience (and, speaking personally, in the writing experience), a double movement of interest and disinterest takes place, as attention may be pulled in the direction of interest, through dynamics of desire, obsession, longing, remembrance, fascination, curiosity, and other invested subjective modes, while at the same time another grain of attention moves across the object of the poem, discovering its internal workings and rhythms, opening doors and scanning for patterns as Mahon's speaker takes in the details of bathtubs and washbasins, changing with the "slow clock of condensation," his reward the *aha!* of an encounter with life, craning toward light until he pried open the grass-bound door ("A half century, without visitors, in the dark— / Poor preparation for the cracking lock / And creak of hinges"). Staying with that encounter for the course of the poem, attending to the small objects and allowing pathways of meaning to open via figurative association, the speaker reveals a parallel between these small craning mushrooms, closed in the dark for so long, and those lives lost to human history's silent recesses: "Lost people of Treblinka and Pompeii! / 'Save us, save us,' they seem to say, / 'Let the god not abandon us / Who have come so far in darkness and in pain. / We too had our lives to live. / You with your light meter and relaxed itinerary, / Let not our naive labours have been in vain!'" The task of attention thus moves from discovery to meditation to a revelation of a deeper kind, a revelation that brings with it a burden of perdurance and a responsibility to open doors, shed light, cast the ray of attention into forgotten histories.

Degree of Intentionality: Endogenous and Exogenous Attention

Intentionality refers to the active or passive intentional mode of the attending subject toward its object. This distinction also maps onto Husserl's phenomenological classification of noetic and noemic intentionalities, while in the language of cognitive attention studies this distinction is between endogenous and exogenous modes of attention.[13] Active, or endogenous, attention is characterized by an intentional work of attention in which the subject deliberately and purposefully focuses his or her attention on the object at hand. It is top-down, goal oriented, and purposive, driven by the faculty of attention control located in the frontal cortex and basal ganglia as an executive function. The agency in this form is thus more on othe side of the subject, though the quality and complexity of the object are involved in both sparking and sustaining the subject's work. In passive, or exogenous, attention, the subject's attention is caught and held by changes or movement in the environment, or by the sheer arresting nature of the object itself. It is bottom-up, stimulus driven, powered by reflexes and receptivity networks, and sharpened by the degree of sensitivity to perceptual change. This mode of attention is not one of directed initiative, but rather one of response, and the agency is thus positioned more to the side of the object. The subject's attentive work is not goal oriented or preintended, but rather seized and engaged by the object. In poetry, this maps onto the different modes of activity and passivity that inflect the reading and writing experiences, the intentional contemplative focus or study—of an object in the world, of a difficult or opaque line of poetry— stands in contrast to the experience of arrest, surprise, and reactivity incited by change, sudden appearances, graphic and highly punctuated text, shifts in rhythm, exclamatory or interrogatory syntax, and striking imagery.

A degree of endogenous intentionality, the conscious focalization of attention, is required at the outset of any literary experience—the choice to lay pen to paper, to select a theme, the choice to open the book, to begin reading and continue long enough to *be* seized. This initial endogenous intentionality preceding the moment of inspiration or *furor poeticus* can be seen, in Plato's *Phaedrus* (244a–245a, 265a–b), as the poet's work of climbing to the muse's tripod, the work of intentionally seeking and tuning in, yet unaided by the muse's arrival to lend divine breath to her voice. In order to separate this initial requisite intentionality from the particular intentional dynamics composed by the poem, we can understand the initial prerequisite quantity of endogenous intentionality as a form of "activation energy," a threshold of intentional focalization that must be reached before a poem can do its work—as in chemistry, the amount of energy that must be present before the reaction can take place—a reaction that may require further energy (endogenous) or may produce or release an energy of its own (exogenous). Separating these two stages and accounting for this prerequisite intentionality allows us to recognize the complex interplay between modes of activity and passivity that mark the poetic experience and allows for the fact that many poems produce shifts between modes—in the activation intentionality required to step into the poem, and within the poem itself: a poem might require us to shift, mid-text, from penetrating study to passive arrest or from exogenous reactivity to a deeper and more purposive engagement. Once inspiration takes over, whether conceived as divine intervention, poetic fury, madness, or creative flow, the work takes on a momentum that cannot be reduced to the intentional labor of the poet or reader. The attention that takes place within the hold of inspiration is thus essentially *passive*, more akin to exogenous intentionality, in which the attention is guided by seemingly external influence or responsiveness, even if the influence itself lies within the poet's creative powers. The precarious balance between endogenous and exogenous attention can be found disputed throughout literary history, as thinking on the kind of attention required in poetic creation and reception has been torn between the nonagentic dynamics of inspiration, possession, and ecstasy, on the one hand, and craft, agency, and conscious making, on the other.[14] The movement of the subject, whether reading or writing, thus takes its energy and perpetuation from a locus seemingly *outside* of the subject itself. However, this does not mean that all the attentional dynamics *within* the reading and writing experience are active—to make this claim would be to overlook the real experiences of being "caught up" by a text, being "worked on" by a work.

An example of the former is found in Stevens's "A Study of Two Pears," which I discuss in the next chapter on contemplation. As an opposing example, Ezra Pound's more graphic cantos (for example 77 and 85 for their heavy use of Chinese characters, and 79 for its linguistic immediacy, image pile-up, and use of snatches of seemingly nonsensical song within the first few lines) produce an immediate exogenous reaction, with visual dynamism and linguistic playfulness, brightness of image. Yet to stay with these cantos requires a shift in modality, digging into references and translations, mining for connections in other cantos, a decidedly endogenous mode of reading. Aimé Césaire's sonically and lexically explosive poems in *Cahier d'un retour au pays natal* seem to operate primarily in the exogenous mode: they play violently upon the senses and at the same time impose a swelling tension that locks the attention in, imprisoning it through a hypnosis of repetition, tension, and momentum. Gertrude Stein's *Tender Buttons,* on the other hand, requires a radical passivity of reading, as intentional focalization and study produces far less than responsive listening and openness to the movements of the poem-objects themselves.

Degree of Selectivity

The degree of selectivity designates how and to what degree an object of attention is focalized. Unlike interest and intentionality, selectivity concerns the scale, intactness, and resolution of the attended object, qualities of the object's position within the attentional lens.

How large an area does the object or theme of attention cover? How dispersed or how narrow is attention's field? In attention studies, deconcentration denotes the widening of the focal lens, so that the object of attention, or its theme, covers a greater area, and the attention is spread thinner. In poetic attention, this translates to the capacity of poems to produce an expansive or contractive sphere of attention. Poetic language enables a heightening and concentration of the attention through the reduction and restriction of language so that within the pressurized space of the poem each word must work hard, hold a lot, and becomes a thick concentration of itself. We find this in the classic examples of Matsuo Bashō and Emily Dickinson, but also outside the microform, as in the poems of Charles Wright, whose long lines draw the breath along a single meditative strand, and whose semantic sphere is often limited to the space of a few feet of yard space, a tree, an empty snail shell. In this high concentration of the object of attention, formal and semantic, the field of attention is whittled down or compressed, and the perceptual field becomes tightly focalized. Deconcentration produces other effects, as in Walt Whitman's expansive and consuming poetics, the panoramic reach of his poems' attentive scope: "I contradict myself, I am large, I contain multitudes."[15] The quality of attention changes with the degree of concentration, as the deconcentrated mode challenges our attention with a widening horizontal expansion while necessarily remaining relatively shallow, while the concentrated mode hones in on a small area reaching inward, unfolding either greater levels of granularity or opening vertically in significance through resonance and figurative layering. As with all these dynamic coordinates, the degree of concentration in a given poem is not a fixed characteristic, and indeed part of what supports the experience of dynamism and change within a poem is its modulation between different scales: a poem may begin by composing a highly concentrated, focalized mode of attention in order to dramatize the shift to a wider scope, opening either outward to take in "the whole field" or inward to reveal layers and dimensionality within a single object.

Conversely, a poem may start in a deconcentrated mode and then home in, whittling the attention to an ever finer and more concentrated point.

While we tend to think of focalized attention as a zoom lens fixed on a single entity, attention can also be divided, alternating between multiple objects, or fragmented. In this way, the *integrity* of the object of attention, whether singularly focalized, plural (simultaneously or alternating), or fragmented, connects to the integrity of the act of attention itself, further demonstrating the degree to which subject and object are mutually constitutive in the act of attention. Poems characterized by a high degree of object integrity focus the attention on a single unified object, whether small in scope (concentrated) or expansive (deconcentrated). These are the poems of a single address, poems that compose a single transitive relation, subject to object. This mode can be expressed at both the semantic level, as in the ode or the love poem, or the formal level, as in the highly unified form. "How to Stuff a Pepper" and "Study of Two Pears" demonstrate a high degree of semantic integrity, while Shakespeare's Sonnet 18, as I show in the chapter on desire, illustrates the division of attention between two objects, the beloved addressee (semantic) and the poem itself (semantic and formal).

Whitman's poetics of largeness, multitudes, and self-contradiction in the lines offered previously illustrates the dynamics of deconcentration, but also of deintegration: the "multitude" poses not a single object of attention but many. "Song of Myself" challenges the attentive capacities to expand and deconcentrate the horizon of attention, but also to include distinct objects—multitude of objects. The multitudinous focus far exceeds the limits of human attentiveness, producing a sense of overflow, unthinkable and uncontainable (in tension with the I's act of "containment"). The multitude is "contained" only by the boundaries of the self—boundaries that are, in fact, drawn by the limits of perception and attention. And yet despite the plurality of Whitman's attention, there is a sense not of fragmentation but rather of manyness, supported by the micro-macrocosmic relationship between self and world, both mirrors and identities of one another, containing diversity beyond thought, taking place within a single horizon of consciousness. This coidentity of self and multitude in Whitman further demonstrates how the subject constitutes and is constituted by the object, how both are constituted in the particularity of a given mode of attention. In Stevens's terms, "I am what is around me."[16]

Another variety of deintegration can be found in the fragmentation of the object of attention—a mode of deintegration in which the plurality is not a collective of wholes but rather the shattering of a whole. One of the earliest pioneers (with Badr Shakir Al-Sayyab and Nazik Al-Mala'ika) of a distinctly modernist Arabic verse, Iraqi poet 'Abd al-Wahhab Al-Bayāti composed his groundbreaking 1954 collection *Abariq muhashshama* (Broken pitchers) as an exploration of the dynamic of fragmentation at both the semantic and formal levels,[17] inspired in part by translations of Eliot's *The Waste Land* into Arabic.[18] The postcolonial influence of Anglophone modernist writings in Egypt and Iraq (and of the French Surrealists in the Levant) can be seen in Al-Bayāti's fragmentary form, broken images, and attentional disruption. These respond both to colonial education and to cross-cultural resonances in the changing political and cultural terrains in both Europe and the Middle East. Political instability, emergent ideologies and revolutionary thinking, the birth of an urban and increasingly mediatic attention culture and the rise in secularism all required the development of poetic forms capable of their expression.[19] While fragmentation plays an important role at the semantic level in Al-Bayāti's collection, the most significant expression of deintegration is found at the level of rhythm, in the rejection of conventional monometer and monorhyme forms.[20] Eliot's and Al-Bayāti's explorations of fragmented objects and terrains also serve to illustrate the historical inflection of poetic attention, as changes in attention culture are reflected in changes in the forms of attention in a given poetic moment.[21]

Finally, attentional selectivity concerns the sharpness, or resolution, of the object of attention. The object can be approached with hypergranularity, or it can be perceived with a soft gaze, an inflection that greatly influences the aesthetic experience. An object constituted in high-resolution attention does not necessarily correlate with aesthetic "realism," as emotions, dreams, and subtle qualities can also have a high degree of perceptive and attentional resolution. High-resolution attention produces the experience of slowing down and zooming in, or rather focusing in. High resolution may or may not be accompanied by a shift into a high degree of concentration. Higher degrees of resolution are signaled by a greater degree of detail and granularity in perception, tuning into small details missed in the lower resolution of everyday perception. As a result of this, poetry's ability to produce (and require) greater degrees of focus can lead to an experience of discovery, as an ordinary experience, scene, or object reveals subtleties and particularities otherwise glossed over. An example of this mode of high resolution and resulting attenuation of experience can be found in Li-Young Lee's "Persimmons," in which the speaker describes the simple action of choosing and eating a fruit, transforming this mundane act through focused attention, temporal attenuation, and precisely parsed steps:

> . . .
> How to choose
>
> persimmons. This is precision.
> Ripe ones are soft and brown-spotted.
> Sniff the bottoms. The sweet one
> will be fragrant. How to eat:
> put the knife away, lay down newspaper.
> Peel the skin tenderly, not to tear the meat.
> Chew the skin, suck it,
> and swallow. Now, eat
> the meat of the fruit,
> so sweet,
> all of it, to the heart.[22]

In these lines from "Persimmons," Lee demonstrates the precision of perception and action, attending to each detail of the act of choosing, peeling, and eating, part by part. Taking each step on its own produces an experience of slowed perception and an accompanying attenuation of the passage of readerly, writerly, and represented time, as the writer slows his attention to capture the process and sensual particularity of a simple act. The attentiveness and care given to smelling the bottoms of the fruit and peeling back the thick skin is enacted physically: it occupies space and time within the poem, as do the simple preparatory actions of setting away the knife, spreading the paper. This heightened resolution is produced more by parsing and separating each particle of a single step, rather than by complex linguistic turns or descriptive thickness. As a result, Lee's high-resolution poetics offers a way into slowed perception, often as preparation and opening for memory, for revelation, or for the entrance of emotional significance, as in the last line of the above stanza, with its unexpected turn, after a stretch of precise, neutral language, "to the heart."

At the other end of the scale, the soft gaze of low-resolution attention is a mode of looking that rests upon objects and perhaps even remains with them over an extended period, without focusing in on every perceptual detail. Low-resolution attention is vital for the generation of movement, impressions, and modes of contemplation rooted less in precision of capture and more in taking in subtler moods and inflections, and for lulling the reader or writer into the desired attentive state of open and pliant receptivity, in contrast to the high energy, detail-oriented alertness associated with the high-resolution attentional object. In Stevens's "Study of Two Pears," the brittle particulars pop forth ("In the way they are modelled / There are bits of blue. / A hard dry leaf hangs / from the stem."). Yet in "Of the Surface of Things," we find an example of Stevens's use of low-resolution focalization, producing an openness of evocation:

> The gold tree is blue.
> The singer has pulled his cloak over his head.
> The moon is in the folds of the cloak.[23]

Formally, the end-stopped lines make each utterance hang as if from its own thread, occupying its own time, with minimal syntactical and semantic connective tissue. The space between the lines recruits the imaginative faculty in forming the absent connections, building imagery with sparse materials. The mind's work lies in making the gold tree blue, tucking the moon into folds. No adjectives flesh these lines out, save the gold and the blue. Even as the imaginative capacity reaches to open up the imagery, there is nonetheless a limit to proximity and granularity, and the attentive inner eye is forced to remain in soft gaze, maintaining a simplicity of evocation distilled to its minimal requirements: Shape. Color. Line. Fold. Figure. Placement. The contradiction in the first line aids in this resistance to granularity, as a little space of distance is created in the attempt to visualize the simple paradox: the tree wavers, flickers gold, then blue, then gold.

In "The Curtains in the House of the Metaphysician," Stevens conjures the mode of perception particular to the drifting movement of curtains and the grainy forms of night and sleep "as the ponderous / Deflations of distance."

> Or the changing of light, the dropping
> Of the silence, wide sleep and solitude
> Of night, in which all motion

> Is beyond us, as the firmament,
> Up-rising and down-falling, bares
> The last largeness, bold to see.[24]

The poem demonstrates the connection between resolution and concentration: as the scope of the attentional lens widens, the resolution lessens, spreading into the "beyond," to the haze of the firmament, the "last largeness." We can see the link between thematic scope and semantic resolution: nouns grow more abstract, descriptors decrease. The scale of each word opens onto a plane that cannot be granularly perceived, moving away from the more concrete and high resolution of the opening image, the curtains with their "long motions." The poem prepares us for this level of low-resolution openness with the opening pronoun, "It," deliberate in its indefinition even as it bears the only active verb, "coming about."

For Stevens, there is a powerful link between low- and high-resolution attentiveness and the relation between imagination and reality. In Stevens's poetics, both are vital, and poetry must navigate the interval between both modes of perception, neither wholly of the directly perceived "real" world nor wholly of the imagination. Drawing on Frederick Wilse Bateson, Stevens saw language as evolving "through a series of conflicts between the denotative and the connotative forces in words; between an asceticism tending to kill language by stripping words of all association and a hedonism tending to kill language by dissipating their sense in a multiplicity of associations. These conflicts are nothing more than changes in the relation between the imagination and reality."[25] In drawing on both high (denotative) and low (connotative) resolution in his poems, Stevens sought to suture what he saw as a "failed relation between imagination and reality" brought about in his historical moment by "the pressure of reality,"[26] which he defined as "the pressure of an external event or events on the consciousness to the exclusion of any power of contemplation."[27] Poetry, for Stevens, with its capacity to move between low resolution and high resolution, connotative and denotative, evocative and figurative, made possible the bidirectional reconnection of the imaginative and perceptive capacities, forming an "interdependence of the imagination and reality as equals."[28] Connotative language connects to low-resolution attention, attention that allows a certain softness and flexibility of gaze and that resists the drive toward hypergranular evocation in favor of more open reception and association.

*Spatiotemporal Remove: Relative Position of the
Object in Space-Time*

Spatiotemporal remove refers to the object's position in space and time, relative to the attending subject. It marks the interval of presence, proximity, distance, or absence that inflects the attentive relation. This dynamic is significant in distinguishing between the experience of recalling a poetic object in memory, as opposed to the experience of direct, present contemplation. As we will see, both modes may be equally marked by the experience of an object's distance or unattainability (I attend to this coffee cup, but the closer I come to it, the more complex and defamiliarized it becomes) or by the experience of proximity or closeness (though my friend is no longer with me, I can still conjure in full particularity his smell, his laughter, as though it were immediately present). Yet the variety of attention and the faculties upon which it draws (memory, direct perception, mental representation) depend greatly on the perceived spatiotemporal relationship to the object. Poems with a sense of spatiotemporal proximity include poems of direct address and direct contemplation, such as we have already seen in Stevens, Mahon, and Lee, while poems of spatiotemporal distance include the elegiac poem, as well as poems of geographical absence such as the exilic poems of Ovid, Darwish, and Agha Shahid Ali. The interval of distance between Sappho's speaker and the object of her love is what constitutes the poetics of longing, as the attending subject speaks at a remove from a relation of love that does not include her.

While in one sense the dynamic of spatiotemporal remove is the most straightforward characteristic of a poem's particular constitution of attention, this proves one of the more complex coordinates of transitive attention, as the other dynamics complicate and often contradict the simple positions of subject and object in time and space. A deconcentrated and low-resolution quality of attention to present and immediate objects at hand might suggest a displacement of the subject within the present world, while a high resolution and crystalline perception of a departed or unreal object convey the immediacy of the past, the ability of remembered or imagined objects to be rendered fully salient by the quality of attention given them. The relationship between spatiotemporal remove and the *quality* of attention brings to the fore the relationship between attention, memory, and perception: A low-resolution, deconcentrated attention to present objects brings to the fore the capacity for distance even in present perception, when there is no remove, while a high-resolution or concentrated attention to absent or past objects emphasizes the capacity for memory and imagination to work closely with attention's faculties, making what is not present *feel* immediate and conjuring an absence with the fullness and detail one would expect from direct perception. Within the context of poetic attention, spatiotemporal positioning is further complicated by the tension between the represented distance or proximity taking place at the semantic level and that experienced in the necessarily present act of reading, itself a relation of spatiotemporal remove from the act and other of the poem's authorship. For this reason, spatiotemporal positioning is also perhaps the most primary determinant of the nature of the attentive relation and the most striking location of tension between the semantic and formal realms at play within the work.

When one thinks of an object of focalized attention, *present* contemplated objects come first to mind: pebbles, problem sets, lovers, works of art. But often our attention is directed not at the present but at what is past, in the mode of attention rooted in memory. The dynamics of this elegiac attention, as we will see later in this chapter, are complex—an intersection of focalization and imagination, present composition with past perception, recollection and fictionalization. The departed object of attention can only be recalled or reconstituted to an extent, marked out (its absence and its presence), memorialized, but not regained. And yet the more time we spend with object-oriented attention, in all its forms, the more we find that even the simplest modes of attending (this coffee cup in my hands at this moment) are complex and elusive events, marked as much by objects slipping away and the limits of our perception as by the object's presence in the fullness of attention.

Degree of Apprehension: Resistance and Capture

This sixth and final coordinate of transitive attention, apprehension, stands at the border between subject-oriented and object-oriented dynamics. It refers to the degree to which the object of attention comes fully into the grasp, or into the perceptual horizon, of the attending subject. We can think of apprehension as marking out the degree of "capture." Does the object crystalize within the sphere of attention, distilled and experienced as fully present within that perceptive field, or does it seem to evade our grasp, unfolding only to reveal deeper layers of unknowability, slipping away beyond comprehension? I will consider one instance of such elusiveness in the chapter on recollection, tracing the unconjurable elegiac subject of Anne Carson's *Nox*, who never comes into focus—who will not be regathered into being. But, in other poems, objects or ideas leap into presence, fully conjured within the frame of the poem's attention, snapping in fully distilled evocation, as though present to hand or in even greater perceptual salience. In some cases, the degree of apprehension is linked strongly to the degree of resolution, yet this is not always the case. A poem may lend a high-resolution, highly concentrated attention to an object, yet this is no guarantee that the object will succumb to attention's grasp or that it will have the quality of full presence. It may yet evade or reveal only greater recesses of being with each new tuning of the attention, so that attention becomes an answer to an infinitely renewed invitation or challenge. Conversely, an image wrought by a low-resolution gesture of the attention may have the quality of total presence, though perhaps not unpacked, within the field of experience. This is because apprehension is not about thick description or analysis. Piling observation on observation or adding more and more detail to a semantic representation does not mean that the object will come to life in poetic language. The language must in fact allow elbow room for the object's recesses, more an embrace or horizoning than a probing dissection. This point has been well attested, in different terms, by poets and critics alike. For example, Philip Sidney argued, in "The Defense of Poesy," that

> many of such writings as come under the banner of unresistible love, if I were a mistress, would never persuade me they were in love; so coldly they apply fiery speeches, as men that had rather read lovers' writings, and so caught up certain swelling phrases—which hang together like a man which once told me the wind was at north-west and by south, because he would be sure to name winds enough—than that in truth they feel those passions.[29]

Seamus Heaney's early poems demonstrate a high degree of apprehension, because of the immediacy of imagery and linguistic density. Consider these lines from "Death of a Naturalist:"

> Right down the dam gross-bellied frogs were cocked
> On sods; their loose necks pulsed like sails. Some hopped:
> The slap and plop were obscene threats. Some sat
> Posed like mud grenades, their blunt heads farting.[30]

And these, from "Blackberry-Picking:"

> You ate that first one and its flesh was sweet
> Like thickened wine: summer's blood was in it
> Leaving stains upon the tongue and lust for
> Picking. Then red ones inked up and that hunger
> Sent us out with milk cans, pea tins, jam pots
> Where briars scratched and wet grass bleached our boots.
> Round hayfields, cornfields and potato drills
> We trekked and picked until the cans were full,
> Until the tinkling bottom had been covered
> With green ones, and one top big dark blobs burned
> Like a plate of eyes. Our hands were peppered
> With torn pricks, our palms sticky as Bluebeard's.[31]

Many of Heaney's poems have this quality of linguistic and representational immediacy, in which both the linguistic object and the semantic object seem thickly and palpably present and the language itself seems something fully perceived, given to the attention and to the senses. We find examples of such high degrees of apprehension and evocation throughout the early poems, as well as in the visceral bog poems of *North,* and, differently and with a lighter touch, in the prismatic sequences of *Seeing Things,* "Lightenings," "Settings," "Crossings," and "Squarings." "Death of a Naturalist" offers an example of the material density and heavy onomatopoesis of Heaney's language and its ability to render its object in full salience on the page, as though in live perception.

Heaney is certainly not the only poet of apprehension. Others might propose the object-poems of Francis Ponge—though in my opinion while Ponge's poems are explicitly interested in the project of poetic apprehension, they are not always successful at conjuring the objects on which they meditate, for reasons I discuss in my chapter on contemplation. Rather they tend to be more centered on the attending "I" and on the act of description itself. Many other poets have obtained high degrees of poetic apprehension. A more in-depth study of poetic apprehension—and this would be an important contribution indeed—might consider the apprehensional work of such diverse writers as Wordsworth, Dickinson, Baudelaire, Yves Bonnefoy, Darwish, Robert Creeley, and Frank O'Hara. But even these are merely suggestions based on one reader's intuitions: as I mentioned earlier, to catalog or hierarchize any normative scale for poetic apprehension is problematized (as are most attempts at hierarchizing normative scales in poetics) by the relatively high dependence of apprehension on the particularity of the reader and the reading moment.

It should be noted that Heaney's poems often have a strong narrative bent, so that the pull of the narrative line draws the attention along. Again, this would be an exogenous mode, with the attention drawn forward by story line. Yet the presence of a strong narrative line is not a requisite for apprehension, as demonstrated by imagists such as Ezra Pound and Amy Lowell, who sought to distill or crystallize a single object within the lens of the poem, without knitting it into a narrative fabric, or in what Jahan Ramazani called the "magnificent, subversive smallness" of E. E. Cummings.[32] What these poets achieve, in very different ways, is a sense of the fullness of "capture," whether what is captured is a childhood memory, as in the case of Heaney, or a more tactile sense of seasonal change, as in Cummings. What runs through the poems of high apprehension is the sense that the poems' objects are fully rendered in salience on the page. This does not mean that *every detail* is described, but rather that the experience of the object is caught—and perhaps held for a while—within the perceptual horizon of the poem, so that the focus is placed on what is there and not on what is absent, incomplete, or withdrawing from perception.

We find an example of low-resolution full apprehension in Gottfried Benn's poem "Astern":

Astern—schwälende Tage,	Asters—smoldering days,
alte Beschwörung, Bann,	Old incantation, spell,
die Götter halten die Waage	The gods hold the scales in balance
eine zögernde Stunde an.	A hesitant moment still.
Noch einmal die goldenen Herden	Once more the golden herds

der Himmel, das Licht, der Flor,	Of heaven, the light, the fields—
was brütet das alte Werden	Old Becoming, what do your brooding
unter den sterbenden Flügeln vor?	Slow dying wings conceal?
Noch einmal das Ersehnte,	Once more all that I longed for
den Rausch, der Rosen Du—	Rapture, the roses' "you"—
der Sommer stand und lehnte	The slanting summer stood there
und sah den Schwalben zu,	And watched the swallows too.
noch einmal ein Vermuten,	Once more a vain supposing
wo längst Gewißheit wacht:	When certainty's found its mark:
die Schwalben streifen die Fluten	The swallows are skimming the waters
und trinken Fahrt und Nacht.	And drinking flight and dark.[33]

The poem is not a systematic detailing or scientific illustration of asters, nor does it try to capture every detail of either the trees or the scene in high-resolution detail. Rather, the language itself holds open the space for a certain quality of the object to crystallize in the openness and textures of the words. It is in allowing them this space of standing without probing or detailing that this poem's fullness of apprehension lies—apprehension without full comprehension. We can see this fullness of apprehension without fullness of comprehension encoded in the poem's formal structure, and particularly its syntax: the opening word stands as a syntactic unit on its own, in apartness. The poem is bisected by an unanswered question that lies at the very center of its perfectly symmetrical form, four quatrains. The openings of the quatrains compose an object and its equally opaque echoes, dimming in the final uncapitalized iteration: "Astern," "Noch einmal," "Noch einmal," "noch einmal." The gap in the first line is mirrored after the center question mark by another, in "der Rosen Du—," so that the "Du—" is at once a reflection of "Astern—" and also its own opacity, left unexplained, unidentified and unprobed. The sentence continues but without syntactic connection across the em dash, as in line one. The two periods, at the end of the first stanza and at the end of the poem, further the pattern of echo and attenuation, as the first syntactical unit is stretched out in the second, so that the poem's final period seems also to refer to "Astern" and to bring to a close the space (the "zögernde Stunde") that opened in their wake. The poem begins with the word-object itself, Astern, followed by a long em dash. This dash, the space held open after the word, encapsulates the horizoning movement of the poem itself, which allows this space to surround and hold forth its object without any further description or articulation of the semantic representation—indeed without further mention save in the first stand-alone word and (perhaps) in the *you* of "der Rosen Du." What is described is the "schwälended Tage," the heat and heaviness in which the trees stand, and the sense of age and ritual that encircles their conjuring: "alte Beschwörung," "Bann," "alte Werden," "Noch einmal," "Noch einmal," "noch einmal." The poem's temporal suspension further enables this horizoning, creating an attenuated moment, period, hour of attention in which the only movement is that of the swallows, and in which the asters, the still center and origin of the poem, stand. The temporality of this particular attention is located in this "zögernde Stude," in the hesitancy of "anhelden," in the precarious balance of "die Waage," in the summer's stillness and witness ("stand und lehnte und sah"), and in the protracted once-again of "Fahrt und Nacht." The Astern themselves, then, are caught by the poem's wide-cast net, allowed to stand in fullness and opacity. We find a sister to this poem in Emily Dickinson's Poem 962, another instance of a poem of apprehensional fullness—moreover a poem very much *about* the quality of fullness that is simultaneous with the beginning of decline, resonant with Benn's "sterbenden Flügeln," the single moment held in the scales' equipoise:

Midsummer, was it, when They died –
A full, and perfect time –
The Summer closed upon itself
In Consummated Bloom –

The Corn, her furthest kernel filled
Before the coming Flail –
When These – leaned into Perfectness –
Through Haze of Burial –[34]

In "Of the Surface of Things," Stevens gets at the experience of a purchaseless perception of things in the world, the experience of being unable to take in such details of objects, unable to come so close to capture and containment. The lines "In my room, the world is beyond my understanding; / But when I walk I see that it consists of three or four / hills and a cloud"[35] describe different levels of apprehension—at one end of the scale, the dislocation from the world "in my room," in which attention does not reach out into things, and things do not approach to meet the speaker, remaining beyond reach. Only walking begins to align perception with world, allowing the speaker to grasp some of its forms. Somehow the rhythmic motion of walking places the speaker in their midst and medium in order to "see" them, to see what the world "consists" of. This shift can be found in the two verbs of the two lines: "is" and "consists," marking a movement, with the shift from room to walk, from a static and isolated "being" to "consisting," a verb whose root meaning, "being located in and inherent" and "standing firmly, existing," lie in the root *con* + *sistere*, standing together. Consisting suggests a more active and, importantly, relational mode of existence, only felt in walking, outside of the isolated desk environment. In it the form of the objects in the world begins to take on dimension and form, to come into apprehension. The subject only experiences the beginning of attention's ability to apprehend objects and others in the world once moving in their midst. As Stevens suggests in "The Place of the Solitaires," "There must be no cessation / Of motion, or of the noise of motion, / The renewal of noise / And manifold continuation; / And, most, of the motion of thought / And its restless iteration."[36]

The element of apprehension is in many ways the most difficult of all the dynamic coordinates to think through and to write about, standing at the intersection between subject and object, in the bidirectional reach of transitivity. The degree of apprehension depends upon the poem's crafting—it is as "objectively" present in the poem as the scales of concentration and resolution. And yet it also depends upon the attender. The experience of apprehension is a *potential* in any event of poetic attention. It is a possibility, for which the attender risks or wagers the labor of attention. Sometimes it comes, sometimes not. Both the object and the subject of attention need to align. This alignment or lack thereof may be *depicted* in poems like "Of the Surface of Things," "Astern," and *Nox*, but at the level of poetic experience, the experience of the object that is the poem, all bets are off. Contemplation opens a space, as in Benn's poem, for a thing to emerge in fullness. But the ground has to be right, the timing, the capabilities of the contemplative subject. The degree of apprehension is, more than the other dynamics I explore, the most dependent upon the capacities of the reader and the closeness and attentiveness of the acts of reading and perceiving. The perceptual invitation extended by the poem is not a guarantee, just as revelation is not a guaranteed outcome of the practice of contemplation: a revelation, like the object of the poem, *may* come together in full presence in a single moment of practice and not another and in the practice of a single individual and not another. As Thomas Merton notes, writing on this possibility without promise in contemplation, "just as the wind carries thousands of winged seeds, so each moment brings with it germs of spiritual vitality that come to rest imperceptibly in the minds and wills of men. Most of these unnumbered seeds perish and are lost, because men are not prepared to receive them: for such seeds as these cannot spring up anywhere except in the good soil of freedom, spontaneity and love."[37] Stevens sees this "genius" of poetry as the outcome of a practice of contemplation that includes the *whole* of the human being, in strength and weakness. Unlike Merton's view of contemplation as the cultivation of a certain "good" soil, Stevens sees the practice as honing the heightened expression and attunement to the complexity of human being and world through the attentive development of the senses, a "perceptual labor." "Poetry," he writes, building on Benedetto Croce's Oxford lecture of 1933 in "The Necessary Angel," "is the triumph of contemplation."[38] As the perceptual labors of contemplative practice deepen, the attentive subject builds the capacity for apprehension—not of objects and world in full, necessarily, but of the limits of perception, the apprehension of gaps and distances, spaces that withdraw or exceed the perceptual grasp, an apprehension of attention's limits and contours.

Modes of Transitive Attention: Contemplation, Desire, Recollection, and Imagination

Having explored the dynamic coordinates of transitive attention—how it functions and scales at specific axes or levels of experience—we can consider how these dynamic coordinates come together in practice. How do particular groupings and constellations of these coordinates translate into three-dimensional poems and poetic modes? The chapters that follow will consider the practice of transitive attention within the complex and graded terrain of individual poems, armed with a working vocabulary for understanding the play of attention in well-known traditional modes such as contemplative meditation, love poetry, and elegy. The particular convergence of the dynamic coordinates of transitive attention in particular degrees and relationships within the scope of a poem constitute the specific nature of the attentive mode produced and/or required by the poem.

For the purposes of clarification and orientation, I isolate four primary modes of transitive attention: contemplation, desire, recollection, and imagination. Of course, there are others: the subcategories and subtle variations in modality within the umbrella of transitive attention are many, inflected by the infinite nuances of mood, cultural and environmental moment, physical and cognitive traits, motivations. Yet these four modes serve as primary categories or cardinals, establishing a framework within which to locate particularities. I have chosen these terms precisely for their familiarity and for their ability to translate the cognitive language of subject-object relation into the language of poetic tradition; each of these terms, while invoking a key transtraditional element of poetic tradition and poetic theory, also corresponds to a specific mode of poetic attention.

Contemplation refers to the mode of attention directed to a single focal object, in which the central action and motivation is contemplation itself, not a driven interest or use for the object. Desire, on the other hand, is characterized by interest and lack. Desirous attention does not only contemplate and "let be," but leans in, reaches for, yearns. Recollection, which I consider under the rubric of elegy, is attention to a departed object that is conjured in memory. In this way, it is closely aligned with imagination in that the focalized object is not present and must be brought into a kind of presence through the reperceptive faculty of memory. Imagination, lastly, is the act of attending to objects of the mind.

Contemplation, recollection, and imagination are distinguished by the scale of spatial or temporal remove, while contemplation and desire are distinguished in terms of interest. Contemplation, desire, recollection, and imagination all have in common a transitive reach toward a central object theme. The common principle is thus focalization, or what we might call in visual terms "close looking," though the degree of concentration varies between and within poems. In focalization, while the "real" object may of course not be present, the *attentional stance* of the poem is directed toward an object or central theme.

These modes of transitive attention reflect different combinations and relationships between the dynamic coordinates I have outlined. These four modes offer, much like primary colors, a basic, skeletal, and infinitely combinatory model. There are as many potential combinations and permutations of transitive attention as there are poems, however, it is useful to begin to outline how subtle changes in the dynamic coordinates inform and in fact *compose* our most primary and elemental poetic genres and gestures, from desire to grief to flight of fancy.

The poem of transitive attention operates in a mode of close observation and description, *creating* or *evoking* a present object in the poem, whether that object is a pear, a wagon, a fall of light, a boy's face, or a single event. While this theme itself may be located in the present (contemplation), the past (remembrance), the potential (desire), or an alternative present or future (imagination, mental representation), the *act* and *event* of attention, its tensional activity, is necessarily located in an immediate present. The act of attending to a single object is a present act in which the artist, and subsequently the viewer, orients her perception toward the object. The spatiotemporal remove, or location of the object of focalized attention in space and time (present or absent, contemporaneous or past, real or unreal) determines, along with qualitative inflections of mood and cultural or historical context, the specific mode of attention and the specific poetic mode, whether contemplative, desirous, elegiac, or fantastical. Giving languages to these richly historical and readily identifiable categories as coordinates of poetic attention invites us to approach with more precision the subtler forms of noticing and attending that poems enact.

CHAPTER II

Contemplation

Attention's Reach

Ponge : Heaney : Stevens : Bishop : Mullen

> The object of contemplation is the highly complex and unified content of consciousness, which comes into being through the developing subjective attitude of the percipient.
> —GEORGE ROSTREVOR HAMILTON, *POETRY AND CONTEMPLATION*

> Look about you. Take hold of the things that are here. Let them talk to you.
> —GEORGE WASHINGTON CARVER, *INCOMPLETE LETTER*

Let us begin with a mode of poetic attention both familiar and seemingly straightforward: contemplation. In its purest sense, contemplation can be seen as a distilled form of attention, meaning simply to direct sustained focus in one direction, looking closely or reflecting deeply on one subject for a long time. For this reason, contemplation offers a starting point for thinking about the modes of transitive attention because it is immediately recognizable as attention *to*. In fact, in a certain sense contemplation is the mode of attention closest to our standard colloquial understanding of "paying attention" or "focusing"—without the inflections of interest or temporality that shape the modes I address in the chapters that follow, on desire, recollection, and imagination. In contemplation (as I treat the term here), attention is actively and consciously *paid* to its object, and all else is (more or less successfully) filtered into background. Whether pleasurable, painful, relaxed, or effortful, contemplation entails an *active* and *sustained* attention to an internal or external object.

While contemplation may seem relatively straightforward as a mode of attention, the diversity and intricate theorizations of spiritual exercises serve as a reminder that the mode of contemplation is far from simple. Even the basic distinction between focus and distraction, for example, fails to capture the inner complexity of contemplation, in which heightening attention in one area means a redistribution of attentional resources over the whole physical and mental field. To focus the attention on one object is to simultaneously divert focus away from another. Thus both focus and its opposite (diversion or distraction *from*) are attentional phenomena, and both play into the dynamic work of contemplation.

Far from simply acting on an object as though attention were something flatly applied to the world, the act of contemplation also acts on its subject. Contemplation—the act of orienting the mind and senses in a single direction—not only reveals a particular corner of world in higher resolution, but also reveals and reorients the self in relationship to world. This is why focused contemplation has played such a large role in spiritual exercises in virtually all religious and philosophical traditions, from Aristotle's notion of *theoria* to Judeo-Christian prayer and Buddhist meditation.

Contemplative attention in the context of spiritual practice can be seen as inhabiting a paradoxical relationship to intentionality, and thus to its intended object. One of the aims of devotional attention is to empty the space of the subject and its self-oriented thoughts in order to fill that space with the object of devotion or with the space of its potential entry into the soul (epiphany). On the other hand, the *aim* of practice is an intentional act. One way around this is to see the intentionality as belonging to something other than the self (for instance, God), transforming the self into a more passive vessel whose very passivity depends on the discipline and practice of extreme focus.[1] We see a similar paradox in Buddhist philosophy, though without reference to a "god" in either a monotheistic or polytheistic sense.[2] Broadly speaking, if an "aim" of meditation, in Buddhist thought, is the practice of concentration toward contemplation and ultimately toward the realization of nonself (overcoming temporal attachments and desires), this movement *toward* nonself requires deliberate focal and intentional consistency on the part of the practitioner. Thus practicing nonself depends on aligning the self (its actions, thoughts, and intent) with a path that might lead past the attached and desiring self. Releasing desire (practicing nonattachment) thus depends on mobilizing desire in right effort. In Christian thought, this would be the desire for God—the desirousness underpinning *attente* (waiting), or vigilance.

The Latin root *templum,* a consecrated space marked out and cleared for observation or worship, stems from either *tem-* (to cut, to carve out) or *temp* (to stretch, possibly referring to the act of clearing). Experientially, the act of contemplation resonates with both possible roots—carving out a site from its surroundings and clearing a space of stillness through and for the act of attending. Contemplation is thus distinguished from other modes of everyday attention by the depth of focus on the object *in and for itself*, the sanctity or separateness of the act from everyday tasks and relationships of utility, and the sense that the act contributes to an ongoing *practice* (toward grace, revelation, or deeper understanding, for example.)

In the twentieth century, Simone Weil defined prayer as "absolutely unmixed attention," drawing on Malebranche's maxim of attention as the "natural prayer" of the soul.[3] This meant that one's capacity for prayer could be cultivated through the training of attention. Secular tasks requiring sustained contemplation, including studies in geometry, science, and the arts, might train one spiritually, just as self-imposed labor and deprivation might train one to endure suffering.[4] Strikingly, but perhaps not surprisingly, rather than coming to attention through prayer, Weil came to prayer by way of poetic attention, reading George Herbert's "Love (III)." Of this experience of poetic revelation, Weil writes, "Often, at the culminating point of a violent headache, I make myself say it over, concentrating all my attention upon it and clinging with all my soul to the tenderness it enshrines. I used to think I was merely receiving it as a beautiful poem, but without my knowing it the recitation had the virtue of a prayer. It was during one of these recitations that . . . Christ himself came down and took possession of me."[5] Weil's thinking on prayer as a practice of attention offers a bridge to considering the ways in which attention has likewise offered a means of cultivating contemplative experience outside an explicitly religious framework in modern and contemporary poetry's exploration with material objects, from stones to oysters to paintings of pears.

In the readings that follow, I explore how modern and contemporary poets have turned to focused, transitive, contemplative deixis as a way of carving out an object of attention from its surroundings and clearing space and time for deepening attention. I consider the ways in which contemplation—specifically the contemplation of natural objects and life-forms—has offered, in a wide range of modern and contemporary poems, a secular form of the spiritual exercise, in the shape of an ongoing practice of being with things in close attention. I begin with two poems on oysters by Francis Ponge and Seamus Heaney, considering the ethics of metaphorization in these poets' contemplation of a single life-form. I then turn to Wallace Stevens's "Study of Two Pears" and Elizabeth Bishop's "The Fish," two poems that raise, extend, and complicate the attentional processes of observation as study, revelation, and meditation. Turning, finally, to a more contemporary example, I consider Harryette Mullen, whose tanka diary *Urban Tumbleweed* forces a reconsideration of contemplation as a historically privileged act, complicating its assumed requisites of stillness, silence, and leisure in poems that record daily walks through Los Angeles's urban jungle, weaving an awareness of racial and economic inequality and human/nonhuman disjunction and entanglement into a practice of noticing-in-motion that neither filters nor turns away. An interest in the reach and limits of attentive perception runs through all these readings, as well as an exploration of the acts of translation and ekphrasis embedded in the very nature of poetic contemplation, in the transference and transposition of an act of attending from one subject to another and from one perceptual medium to another. At the same time, I am interested in unearthing what might be seen as the ethics of contemplation underlying each of these examples in the relation between subject and object and between attending and naming.

Contemplation in Twentieth-Century Object-Oriented Poetry

The early twentieth century saw a variety of approaches to what modern poetic contemplation might look like, leading to a wealth of object-oriented poems and object-oriented theories of poetic looking, listening, and making. In the writings of Gertrude Stein, and William Carlos Williams, Wallace Stevens, Francis Ponge, George Oppen, and Louis Zukofsky, to name only a few examples, we find a shared interest in how to approach, poetically and in modern terms, objects of the phenomenal world. We also find a wide range of responses: vivid realist description, abstraction, transposition to nonsemantic sound portraits, philosophical interrogation, and symbolization. While Williams's canonized phrase "No ideas / but in things" has become something of a tag for the emergence of this early twentieth-century object-centered and plain-spoken realism in American poetry, the trend has much earlier roots—in Romanticism's relocation of grace, power, and awe in human experiences of earthly phenomena. We can see a bridge between the Romantic and modern treatments of the material world in Whitman and, from a religious angle, in Hopkins. We find efforts to slow down or even inhibit the automatic drive toward meaning-making and an ambition to find ways of living and writing poetry in a nontranscendent, mortal, material world. The exploration of animals and things independent of their human meanings or symbolic afterlives stands as a way of coming to terms with secular life, carving out a space for significant language—poetry or prayer—in a metaphysically nonsignifying terrain.

Two Ways of Looking at an Oyster

In poetic contemplation, the object of attention is composed as present before us by the formal object that is the poem. Here the formal and semantic objects are perhaps the most in sync, as the one act of attention runs parallel to the other. The mirroring of direct (formal) and imagined (representational) perception causes the gap between the two to narrow nearly to the point of immediacy. This perceptual illusion of immediacy, conjured in the poem's space-time, affords a sense of the poem's *presence* as both object and event of contemplation. As we will see, in many poems of contemplative focus, regardless of the object, the movement of the poem shows as much about the movement of the mind around and away from its focus—including in the liftoff to metaphor, in which the object serves as a starting place and a touchstone even as the attention moves to connect, to analogize, to make meaning. Language itself can only approach, not grasp, the granularity of sense-data and experiential textures, and it does so through analogy, linking one thing to a sign or symbolic framework that both illuminates and diverts from its original subject.

To get a better purchase on this tension between illumination and diversion, I will begin with two poems on the same object by Francis Ponge—one of the most canonical object poets of the modern period—and Seamus Heaney. Through these two contemplations of the oyster (a life-form both stonelike and fluid, both closed and open), we encounter one of the first challenges of object contemplation: that of metaphorization. In the drive to make meaning out of the object at hand, we find, in the case of Ponge, a *use* of the object that must in some ways leave out its otherness and complexity for the purposes of rendering it as a vessel of meaning. This approach to the oyster is complicated in Heaney by the introduction of an awareness of a more active relationship between subject and object, located historically and economically.

Ponge's *Le Parti pris des choses* (1942) takes the form of a book-length sequence of prose poems, each dedicated to a single object, natural or made.[6] These short studies, written and published during the Second World War, during which Ponge was active in the French Resistance, investigate a given object not only for the way it appears to the eye but for what one might call its inner character, its essential personality. Yet his meditations explore not only the thing itself but the objectlike qualities of language, and the relationship between external world and human meaning-making. These are studies rooted as much in the human mind and its capacity to think *with* objects as it is about the objects themselves. Metaphors and similes abound, causing the object to open and speak to human questions, human significances. The studies are self-aware as studies that reach toward their objects of contemplation but also reflect back from them. Ponge continually returns attention to the language of the poem *as* material composition. In "Mûres" ("Blackberries"), the brambled bushes are "typographiques" ("typographical"), "constitués par le poème sur une route qui ne mène hors des choses ni à l'esprit" ("Constituted by the poem on a path that leads neither out of things nor toward the mind").[7] The poet passerby draws from the brambles "la graine à raison" (the "seed" that in the section just prior was digested and excreted from a bird's anus), spins a humanist lesson about the fragility of the blackberry's blossom emerging from the tangle of thorns, and puns "Mûres" on "murs" as the material of poetic construction. We find a similar seed pun in "L'Orange"—"il faut en venir au pépin," and in "L'Huître" the oyster is echoed in the typographical bivalve of the accent circumflex.

In the poem "L'Huître," or "Oyster," Ponge begins with simple observation of the oyster—its rough exterior, its size and coloring. But with the comparison of the oyster to "un monde opiniâtrement clos," direct observation moves toward a more associative and interpretive mode of contemplation. The oyster becomes a vessel, an instrument of sign-seeking, meaning-making. The "travail grossier" of gripping the shell and working at the seam with a serrated and somewhat dull knife, cutting curious fingers and breaking nails in the process, becomes subtly laden with significance, as the marks left by the knife in the calcite shell are likened to halos. This simile forms a bridge to the second section of the poem in which references to world, firmament, heavens open the oyster (with prying blade) to widening signification. In the final line, the object is further animated in the poem's eye: it becomes a mouth, a throat in which, sometimes, a rare phrase "pearls," to be seized by the observer-consumer "à s'orner." Here, the act of looking is one of violent penetration: the closed, private world submits to repeated blows, each wound a white halo. The world that opens—heavenly iridescence above and below—is claimed for eating and drinking. The phrase that was formulating in the throat of the thing is seized.

To me, the most compelling portions of "L'Huître" are those that remain in close observation, detailing the broken nails and the blackish lace, and those efforts not only to describe but manifest the physical qualities of the oyster in language—the aqueosity of invertebrate form captured in indistinct colors: "blanchâtre," "verdâtre," "noirâtre." Yet when the oyster is opened, the life-form itself is left behind in the poet's haste to transfigure the object to a symbolic vessel for world and heavens. The last line's pearly takeaway feels too quick. In "My Creative Method," Ponge writes that poetry's purpose is "to nourish the spirit of man by giving him the cosmos to suckle. We have only to lower our standard of dominating nature and to raise our standard of participating in it in order to make the reconciliation take place."[8] This leads to what Joshua Corey describes as Ponge's "active and testing stance toward the world's things and toward language."[9] Italo Calvino likewise observed that Ponge wages "a battle to force language to become the language of *things*, starting from things and returning to us changed, with all the humanity that we have invested in things."[10] Ponge's treatment of objects in *Le Parti pris* can be seen to leave the object behind in its move toward metaphorization. In focusing on the human usefulness of things, things in themselves are used then abandoned.

Writing on the same life-form in the poem "Oysters,"[11] Seamus Heaney presents in some ways a more nuanced form of contemplation that resists simple anthropomorphization, or metaphorization, while at the same time revealing the ethical bind—the layered histories of relation that well up in objects of consumption. The oysters lie on "beds of ice," "alive and violated," each "split bulb" a "philandering sigh of ocean." The suggestion of historical casualties (human and nonhuman) echoes and intensifies: "Millions of them ripped and shucked and scattered." The speaker of Heaney's poem is confronted by a complex web of histories and associations that keep him from moving to the frictionless realm of the abstract—"poetry or freedom." His position of privileged leisure is spotlit, exposed by the objects on his plate. He is faced by his own culpability, toasting friendship after a coastal drive, "laying down a perfect memory," while at the same time tasting, in the history of shells clacking on plates, the "Glut of privilege." There is a resentment in the speaker's divided awareness that he cannot simply enjoy—his breezy repose is thwarted by historical knowledge of the "millions"—but that anger charges the speaker's relationship to the oysters with the energy of a different resolve; in place of the "clear light" of abstract nouns ("like poetry or freedom"), he finds a sharper desire: "I ate the day / Deliberately, that its tang / Might quicken me all into verb, pure verb."

While Ponge sees in the oyster a world for human extraction, Heaney finds in the shucked mollusks a history both material and collective. At the same time, Heaney's contemplation of the oyster shifts the agency of the subject from passive consumption to verb, shouldering him with a charge to action. Lingering with or opening to the oyster in this way means taking in not only its pleasures but its sharper tang, the bitterer notes of history, privilege, and violence layered in the oyster's calcite and aqueous form. It is not so much that attention turns away from the object, as it opens to the histories the object contains. This requires an act of awareness that is not simply consumptive (however much Heaney's speaker might have liked to simply kick back and enjoy) but reciprocal, open to being changed and charged by the object. The attending subject becomes the object of the oyster's gaze, or the gaze of a material history inhering therein. In this way what began as an object relation of leisurely consumption becomes a call to *verb*: to eat the oyster, seen in light of the histories that collect in it, becomes an act of eating the day and filling the body not with the static purity of an abstract noun but with the "quickening" of responsibility that emerges from fuller awareness of history and one's place in it.

Not as the Observer Wills: Reach and Resistance

We find an exploration of both the will-to-apprehension of the reader-observer and the object's refusal of this impulse in the work of Wallace Stevens. Perhaps in reaction to Romanticism's emphasis on the transcendent *meaning* of objects in the natural world, Stevens consistently investigated poetry's contemplative act, contrasting poised observation and composition, perception and imagination, receptivity and willing. From his earliest collection *Harmonium* to the late poems (particularly in *Auroras of Autumn*), Stevens turned a rigorous philosophical eye to the question of how to attend, in language, to the objects of the world, and how to square the mind's interpretive overdrive and its necessary mediation of experience with an awareness of spiritual and material finitude, as well as the realness and smallness of reality. In poetry that is, paradoxically, as abstract as it comes, we find the poet struggling in poem after poem with the problem of abstraction, with the challenge to attend to things as they are. In *The Man with the Blue Guitar,* "Not Ideas About the Thing but the Thing Itself,"[12] and in his critical prose (particularly *The Necessary Angel*), Stevens challenges poetry to see without metaphysical delusion and at the same time to find spaces of independent movement, some earthbound lateral elbow room, through his concept of imagination.

In "Study of Two Pears,"[13] Stevens critiques the misuse of objects of the world as symbolic fodder for meaning-laden flights of poetic interpretation. The poem is something of a manifesto in itself, a summary of what is wrong with the aesthetic appropriation of things for symbolic purposes and the misapplication of human meaning onto nonhuman entities. Yet does the poem do what it says? Does it attend to the pear-in-itself, or does it fail to get past the abstract level of discursive critique, an enumeration of wrong turns?

The title itself situates us in a mode of "study," which, as Charles Altieri has noted, "establishes a new space abstraction must explore, a site between art and perception, while also suggesting the basic problem that such exploration must face."[14] Meanwhile, beginning the poem in Latin underlines the cultivated and self-conscious nature of such studiousness, the artificial contemplation it connotes: "the very framework of the study may eventually prove as limiting and self-mocking as the Latin pedagogy that sets the scene. For as we become aware of how our attention becomes vital, we may feel trapped by the frames that reward its visual orientation." Though no reference to a specific artwork is given, the study suggests that the pears are painted. The poem is thus an ekphrastic poem without a visual referent. Stevens's poem suggests, then, the act of looking at pears through the impression of another's act of looking at pears. At the same time, the representational standing and medium of the two pears appears to shift in important ways during the course of the poem itself.

I.

Opusculum paedagogum.
The pears are not viols,

Nudes or bottles.
They resemble nothing else.

II.

They are yellow forms
Composed of curves
Bulging toward the base.
They are touched red.

III.

They are not flat surfaces
Having curved outlines.
They are round
Tapering toward the top.

IV.

In the way they are modeled
There are bits of blue.
A hard dry leaf hangs
From the stem.

V.

The yellow glistens.
It glistens with various yellows,
Citrons, oranges and greens
Flowering over the skin.

VI.

The shadows of the pears
Are blobs on the green cloth.
The pears are not seen
As the observer wills.

Stevens begins on the side of abstraction, the eye just coming to terms with the outlines of its object, studiously resisting figurative departures with a series of negations: "not viols, / Nudes or bottles." With the line "They resemble nothing else," we transition to something affirmative, but via a "nothing"—specificity being a "nothing else." In the statement, "They are yellow forms," the word "forms" likewise lingers between observed presence and cognitive abstraction. Function, taste, smell, as well as the pears' livingness—their past or future on tree or plate—appear notably absent. We have neither backstory nor any glimpse to the *use* or *consumption* of the object. They stand in an aesthetic moment, lifeless, static, motionless and without process.

Yet just when we grasp the pears as static forms we reach another obstacle, another wrong turn: "They are not flat surfaces / Having curved outlines. / They are round tapering toward the top." They stand out in space, three-dimensional. They are not paintings—or if they are paintings, they occupy the painting's surface with three-dimensional being, exceeding the canvas. The slipperiness of this word "forms" falls somewhere between a shape and an ideal—a vague outline or ball of formed matter, meaningless and functionless, and the ideal form of itself, the form to which the imperfect manifestation refers. Even in the first two words, we find a balancing act between abstract representation and physical conjuring: there's something pearlike in the shape of the Latin words, though their meaning has nothing to do with the object, perhaps the weight and roundness of the *opusculum*, with its deep *o*s and *u*s, and the rolling iterations of its syllables, and the more basal heaviness of *paedagogum*, which begins with two lighter tripping syllables before rounding out with the return to the heavy *o-u* pair, echoing *opusculum*. "A hard dry leaf hangs / From the stem"—these lines at once signal the age of the pears, the time that has passed since they left the tree—giving them a stale quality, as something that has stood (a form) for a long time, and also something that is in the process of changing—or something caught or frozen in one moment along a continuum of change. There is a precariousness in the leaf's dangle—dry and hard, it might fall at any moment. Here we are caught between the observation of a real pear on a table, from which the leaf might fall at any moment, and the observation, in poetry, of a painted pear that has already captured this dry leaf on the mature pear—observing a static representation of a changing thing. But the representation is not so static.

CONTEMPLATION

The use of "touched" in "They are touched red"—not "touched *with* red" but simply "touched"—raises the question of the toucher: Who touched them? Who touched them red? The painter? The poet? God? Here "red" stands forth definitively—not only as a color but as a state of being, the defining state of the pears, that with which they are touched. The reentry of the passive voice in stanza 4 raises more insistently the question of the pears' creator—"In the way they are modeled." What creator (aesthetic or otherwise) is the modeler of the pears? The passive voice signals that they are created, the only glimpse into a past life or process of composition, and yet they stand in the passive voice alone—the maker absent, they jut out of the compositional fabric seemingly without origin. Also, the present continuous tense of "are modeled" suggests a continual process of modeling, rather than a past process the result of which we witness in the poem. There are "bits of blue" *in the way* they are modeled. Not in the pears' skin, not in the paint that represents them, but in the way. The bits of blue are not inherent qualities or attributes of the pears, but rather parts of a specific *way* of modeling, a part of their ongoing composition.

With the fifth stanza, something miraculous happens: an active verb, some movement that belongs to the pears themselves: "The yellow glistens." The verb "glisten" hovers (in meaning and in evocative dynamic) between a static quality and some internal movement or a more dynamic interplay between object and light. The repetition of the verb in lines 1 and 2 ("glistens / It glistens") heightens this effect, creating an intense core of glistening that is also the belly of the chiasmus "yellow—glistens—it—glistens [. . .] yellows," which itself opens trumpet like, starting singular, passing through the doubled active verb "glistening" and becoming many, "various," "yellows"—a syntactical process of "flowering:" "Citrons, oranges and greens / Flowering over the skin." This entrance of "skin" is also the first organic and fleshly descriptor we've encountered thus far. The pears have passed from passive inert "forms," a series of disembodied negations, into an active and changing presence that "flowers" in multiple dimensions.

One can read the poem as a study of a painting which is a study of two pears, or the poem itself is the painterly study of two "real" pears. I choose to read the poem as rendering the linguistic unfurling of close attention as it struggles to "study" a simple object, and the "flowering" of thought in the translation of optical observation into language. Object and thought open through one another, even as they resist one another: "The pears are not seen / As the observer wills." B. J. Leggett has described this "final stage" in the poem's series of reductions as "a formlessness in which the object loses its familiar look and resists the mind's attempt to dictate its appearance or meaning." "Obscured" through abstraction, the pears are now "ripe for the 'early' or 'first' seeing, a result not of the will or intelligence but of what Stevens [in "Notes Toward a Supreme Fiction"] calls 'candid' seeing, an 'ever-early candor' by which 'Life's nonsense pierces us with strange relation.'"[15]

"Study of Two Pears" is in part a poem about the failure of language to capture the fullness of perception—of vision, in particular—without resorting to metaphor and analogy. Words can only gesture in the direction of things by comparing them to other things. They approximate and substitute, and some quality of the life of the thing is lost. Much is lost, too, in our original act of attending. Our senses are limited and vulnerable to mood, lighting, and fatigue. And our bodies are anchors, always pinned to one site, one vantage from which the senses reach out, as they can. The reach of the senses is thus closely linked to the reach of metaphor intrinsic to language itself and intensified in poetic attending. For this reason, Bonnie Costello has suggested that the "space of the still life," for Stevens, may not be the "'absolute foyer beyond romance,' but may stand for it, stand for a meeting place of spirit and world, and thus stand for the poem."[16] Altieri has observed that, "[a]s the pear becomes most fully itself before the eye, it must become something else: the fruit must act as a flower does if the mind is to appreciate fully its appearance as a fruit." The "flowering" takes place at both the thematic or semantic level (seed into flower into fruit), the perceptual level, as one detail opens to another, and the metaphoric level: despite our best efforts, an associative flowering enabled precisely by the distance between perception and language:

> A process of the mind's own blossoming within a world formerly perceived as only from a distance. The painting brush, the writer's recasting, and the observer's attention all here flower, suggesting that when the mind too becomes fully itself it must at the same time become other, must take on an identity that no perception qua perception can register. Perception at its most intense requires our entering the order of metaphor, requires the intensification of art. This indeed is why we need a painting to learn how to see a pear.[17]

Poetry, Painting, and Learning How to See

Over the course of the past year, I have been learning how to see fish, aided by a painting I've befriended at the Art Institute of Chicago. The painting is *North River Shad*, by William Merritt Chase. It's a medium-sized still life of the long darkly gleaming bodies of a few shad laid on a table. Beside them, in the crescent formed by the off-handed strew of the fishes' forms (one large, two small), there is a single bright crayfish, captured in free, flamelike wisps, on a plain white china plate. In the warm dark umber backdrop, filled in with wide, loose strokes, there is the suggestion of a copper pitcher—or perhaps an urn. The painting is quiet, as most still lifes are, and, in terms of subject matter, unspectacular. What caught my eye, and continues to hold it—what made me fall in love at first sight with these fish—is the quality of light on surface. The painting registers so completely the cool gleam of fish belly that looking at it feels like a lesson in seeing.

Speaking with friends, I've tried to evoke the dark gleam of Chase's fish—the way his strokes catch the light on wet scales and the dimness of the room at the same time, the way the bodies appear limp and firm to the touch, the way somehow the static image seems to convey temperature. Dead and living at the same time. Immediate and distant. But there is a quality of the untranslatable, talking about images. The same is true of talking about objects. But sometimes language comes so close that it seems to paint and then to animate and illuminate its material, as Chase does his oils and cloth. In a lyrical ekphrastic essay on seventeenth-century Dutch still life painter Jan Davidsz de Heem's *Still Life with Oysters and Lemon*, Mark Doty describes the act of returning and returning to the painting, of "looking and looking into its brimming surface for a long as [he] could," as an act of love—"a sense of tenderness toward experience, of being held within an intimacy with the things of the world."[18] A great still life reveals a fish, or an oyster, through the painter's eyes, made by physical moments of the painter's hands. It is the record of an act of sustained embodied contemplation, held open to the observer as a pathway into a translated experience akin to both sensory ekphrasis and ritual practice, where an act, object, or word serves as a medium of transfiguration.

Poems can teach us to see, too, but in the medium of imagination and the matter of words. As poet and essayist Jane Hirshfield observes, "A painter enacts perception's pleasure through brushstroke and color. For a poet, an equally material eros transforms the engagement with words."[19] Elizabeth Bishop is perhaps best known for her acute powers of visual contemplation, rendering the physical presence of objects with living immediacy on the page. Costello has described Bishop's work as an effort to "bring the difficult world into a scale of intimacy."[20] In Bishop's poems, Hirshfield observes, "closely considered objects shift continually into new life. Dignity, patient expectancy, indifference—all these human attributes are placed into fir tree and ocean with a seamless, unsentimental ease, and the objects and elements under her gaze transform, one into another, with equal ease."[21] One of Bishop's best-known poems, "The Fish,"[22] published in her 1946 collection *North and South*, both represents and enacts a moment of encounter drawn out to a suspended and arrested contemplation—faced with the strange alterity of a caught fish. Over the course of the poem, the fish flowers in perceptual and historical particularity under the speaker's arrested gaze, ultimately leading to an epiphanic climax of relation and release.

The poem begins with the speaker catching "a tremendous fish" and holding him "beside the boat / half out of water, with my hook / fast in a corner of his mouth." The power dynamic between the hunter and hunted (fisherwoman and fish) is clear—it is the fish who is held, "breathing in / the terrible oxygen," hooked fast by the lip. "He didn't fight. / He hadn't fought at all." At the beginning, the fish is "tremendous" in size ("a grunting weight"), but also plain and unspectacular: "battered and venerable / and homely." But, as the poem continues, the speaker's gaze begins to focus in on particulars, unfolding similes to grasp the specificity of this caught (stilled) life:

> . . . Here and there
> his brown skin hung in strips
> like ancient wallpaper,
> and its pattern of darker brown
> was like wallpaper:
> shapes like full-blown roses
> stained and lost through age.
> He was speckled with barnacles,
> fine rosettes of lime,
> and infested
> with tiny white sea-lice,
> and underneath two or three
> rags of green weed hung down.

In the imaginative space opened by figurative reaching ("like wallpaper," "like full-blown roses") and in the perceptual resolution opened by zooming in, visually, on the granular ("rosettes of lime," "tiny white sea lice"), the speaker's contemplation begins to move past surface and into the imagined fleshy interior.[23]

The speaker knows fish, knows fishing and gutting and scaling, and the textures of flayed interior of a fish's body. It is this familiarity with fish (their organs, their component parts) that frames the possibility of being arrested, startled out of habituation by her own act of attention, making the object strange—making it other. The vividness of the speaker's imagined gutting of the fish brings its livingness to life, while at the same time yielding a shock of beauty in the "shiny entrails'" "dramatic reds and blacks," as the "pink swim-bladder" becomes "peony": the act of attending closely, even in the mind's eye, has transformed a familiar and instrumental act (catching dinner) into an aesthetic and an ethical act at once, through proximity's estrangement: "I looked into his eyes / . . . / They shifted a little, but not / to return my stare." This is not a mutual gaze of recognition—there is no identification or communion between fisher and fish. "What she discovers," Susan McCabe has observed, "is not identity but difference, the eyes impenetrable and layered—mediated and distanced by the speaker's language."[24] The shifting textures of the fish's eyes, exposed to the light and out of its element, resemble time-weathered materials of vision and reflection—"tarnished tinfoil," "scratched isinglass." The shifting of the eye is not a response but a starkly other movement of surface and depth, beyond knowing or comprehension: "more like the tipping / of an object toward the light."[25]

As Bishop's speaker continues to gaze, holding and held by the fish for an indeterminately extended moment, she notices the fish's battle scars, or medals: the "five big hooks / grown firmly in its mouth." As in Heaney's "Oysters," contemplation reveals not only the object's present but its history. These lines and wires each tell of another near-death, another struggle. Each is a different color and size, each marked, differently, by the "strain and snap / when it broke and he got away." These remnants of past struggles hang from the fish's jaw, "Like medals with their ribbons / frayed and wavering, / a five-haired beard of wisdom." The earlier line, "He hadn't fought at all," easily passed over at the outset, resurfaces here with new significance. Why didn't the fish fight this time, after so many victories? Is his passivity as sign of hard-won wisdom, or simply exhaustion and age?

The poem's epiphanic closure does not answer these questions but dissolves them. The poem's extended meditation on the fish leads to a long culminating sentence:

> I stared and stared
> and victory filled up
> the little rented boat,
> from the pool of bilge
> where oil had spread a rainbow
> around the rusted engine
> to the bailer rusted orange,
> the sun-cracked thwarts,
> the oarlocks on their strings,
> the gunnels—until everything
> was rainbow, rainbow, rainbow!
> And I let the fish go.

Whose "victory" fills the "little rented boat?" It could be the fish's, with his five medals of life fought for and won, or the speaker's, for catching the uncatchable, for holding it in her hands. Perhaps it is shared—spreading into the world like oil on water, blurring the boundaries between things. Bishop's syntax here works a kind of miracle of convergence, in which "victory" and "rainbow" mingle and fuse in the sentence's prepositional spreading, from the bilge around the boat's engine to the bailer, the thwarts, the oarlocks, the gunnels, until victory's spreading oil transforms everything to "rainbow, rainbow, rainbow!"[26] In this spatial expansion, accompanied by a temporal suspension, what began as a moment of ordinary catching and holding gives way to closer and closer looking, deeper and deeper contemplation until it yields to an earthly and linguistic ecstasy.[27] In the act of staring and staring, something happens to the speaker, utterly altering her relationship to the object of her gaze, and to the surrounding world. She is brought to attention and held, staring and staring, until her own self-sense as agent dissolves in seeing—learning to see fish as if for the first time yields a lesson in seeing everything.

Looking, in poetry and painting, is an instruction not simply in the perceptual act of vision but in the practice of contemplation as innately relational. "To think through things, that is the still life painter's work—and the poet's," writes Doty. "Both sorts of artists require a tangible vocabulary, a worldly lexicon. A language of ideas is, in itself, a phantom language, lacking in the substance of worldly things, those containers of feeling and experience, memory and time. We are instructed by the objects that come to speak with us, those material presences."[28]

Things matter—they are our neighbors, our others, constant coinhabiters of the world, and only through them do we have a sense of both world and the "still" of still life: finitude, death's unknown, the indistinct darkness backing the objects, facing us.[29] But folded into and unfolding from artworks that contemplate things is the work of contemplation itself. At the heart of this cocontemplation is, "first, a principle of attention, simply that. A faith that if we look and look we will be surprised and we will be rewarded."[30]

When we contemplate a painting, we inhabit another's world, another's gaze and gesture. When we contemplate a poem, or contemplate an object through a poem, we inhabit these things through the prism of another's language. In the medium of another's mind, images and objects of contemplation emerge before an inner eye, in the activation of our own senses, remembered and imagined. Poems that contemplate paintings thus inhabit a double relationality in which the reader or listener receives the object through the painter's marks, transposed into language of description and association in the poet's language. These layers of reception and response create in ekphrastic writing a sense of distance (or distances) from the object itself, but also a sense of closeness in the accumulation of touches and glances and focalizations that have passed through the hands and eyes and minds of others, so that attending becomes not only attending to an object but attending to act(s) of attention. Insofar as the poetic might be thought in terms of the object of language becoming an object of attention (rather than a transparent instrument of conveyance), the ekphrastic dimension of "attending to an act of attention" cuts directly to the poetic function itself.

Any language that contemplates things as they are seen engages in an act of translation, or transposition, from one medium of perception to another. In this sense, every act of poetic contemplation, when looking gives forth language, is *ekphrastic,* if we invoke the root meaning of the word, "to call a thing by its name." The ekphrastic dimension of poetic contemplation also signals the relational leap required by attention's reach *to* and *toward.* As Anne Carson has written, thinking with Sappho's Fragment 31, "The thrill of lyric mimesis has something importantly to do with this collaboration of distance and closeness, whereby they approach, meet, and seem almost about to interchange, like a man shaking hands with himself in a mirror."[31] In poetic contemplation, the event of seeing takes place in the course of the poem itself. The poem is not a record of a past event of perception, or a representation of a past object, but an event of perception in itself—an encoding, like a musical script, that produces the perceptual event anew, each time enlivened by difference.

Poetic language is at a perceptual remove from the objects it contemplates. Unlike paint, which can convey its subject matter to the same primary sense through which we perceive the object itself, language must translate experience from the eye to an inner eye, from physical to evoked sense. This act of translation is a practice, too—ongoing, inexact, inexhaustible. We do not arrive—language does not arrive—at a total capture of the thing, any more than painting or photography gives us the thing itself. But "total capture" is not the aim of contemplation. The practice is being with, being alongside, and *staying* with. The practice is moving through time with things, either through duration or repetition, balancing temporal extension with the brevity of our moments of perception and the brevity our time on earth.

This kind of contemplative encounter might seem best suited to environments historically designated or associated with the *vita contemplativa*: hushed museum galleries, cloisters, studies, high windows, and forest clearings. And, as we have seen, contemplation is difficult even in these ideal and privileged settings. But most of us do not live in these settings, and may not even feel welcome in them. So, what happens when contemplation is removed from zones of privilege and protected spaces and integrated into urban life, with its noise and hubbub and ringtones, aggressions, and nonmetaphorical violence? How can we listen for the lily and the bird, or find the small beauty of the forest, in *this* world, at *this* time, and in *this* body, subjected to the gazes and classifications of others, marked by gender, race, and class?

Opening with the epigraph by George Washington Carver with which I (in tribute) began this chapter, Harryette Mullen's *Urban Tumbleweed* offers a contemporary example of an explicitly attention-oriented contemplative practice that takes place not in sustained stillness (or even in the smaller window offered by fresh fish),[32] but in motion, and not in conventionally "contemplative" environments, but out in the thick of urban life. The focal point—what I've described as the *indirect* object—of Mullen's attentional practice in *Urban Tumbleweed* is not a single object but an act repeated daily:

walking the streets of Los Angeles. These walks yield a sequence of 366 poems, each containing the Japanese form's thirty-one syllables, distributed over three lines, suggesting a year and a day of walks. Mullen explains in her introduction, "Walking instead of driving allows a different kind of attention to surroundings. Each outing, however brief, becomes an occasion for reflection."[33] "With the tanka diary to focus my attention, a pedestrian stroll might result in a poem."[34] The extension of contemplation, here, is produced in repetition—in place of one sustained act of "looking and looking," or "staring and staring," moments of attention and reflection are strung together to suggest both present singularity and ongoing practice. Alan Golding has observed that "attention," in *Urban Tumbleweed*, "also includes self-reflexive attention to the writing process."[35]

Mullen describes the work as "a record of meditations and migrations," and indeed both meditation's stillness and migration's transitoriness are brought together in the diary. In both its setting and in the position of the poet, the work highlights questions of belonging, nativeness, racial and sexual exclusion, and privileged environments. Inhabiting the adopted and adapted tanka form becomes, for Mullen, an extension of her meditation in nonindigenous inhabitation, assimilation, and attunement. Tanka, a genre of *waka* poetry, is a short form consisting of five lines or metrical units of 5-7-5-7-7 syllables. Mullen inhabits the formal and thematic conventions of the genre while also making it her own, balancing constraint and flexibility by distributing the thirty-one syllables over three lines instead of five to allow a more natural speech rhythm to come across in each line. This brings the tanka form closer to the more familiar haiku in English, while nodding to the older walking-meditation form, the *haibun*, in which haiku are linked by short sections of narrative, often describing journeys by foot, as in Matsuo Bashō's canonical travelogue from the seventeenth century, *Oku no Hosomichi* (*Narrow Road to the Interior*). Of the affordances of the tanka for conjuring the act of noticing in passing, Mullen writes, "The brevity and clarity of tanka make it suitable for capturing in concise form the ephemera of everyday life. With refined awareness of seasonal changes and a classical repertoire of fleeting impressions, Japanese traditional poetry contemplates, among other things, the human being's place in the natural world."[36]

The poet moves through LA's urban jungles, suburban sprawls, and rural canyons with awareness not only of the surrounding objects and others but of her own embodied position (as woman of color, as California "non-native") in the space, on the page, and in the histories of contemplative poetry, nature poetry, and the other tradition of walking poetry embodied by the *flaneur*—each of which have been disproportionately associated with whiteness and with masculinity. As Andrew Epstein has argued, the work "highlights the unacknowledged assumptions about gender and race within the long tradition that celebrates the flaneur, the *dérive*, psychogeography, and other methods of exploring the urban quotidian."[37] This critical awareness of racial, gendered, and class inequity comes through in Mullen's attention to everyday violences, which places *Urban Tumbleweed* in dialogue with Claudia Rankine's work on microaggressions in *Citizen*, as in these two tankas observing police prejudice and homelessness:

Visiting us in Los Angeles, our friend
went out for a sunny walk, returned
with wrists bound, misapprehended by cops.[38]

A homeless woman spends her days collecting
odd scraps of paper, then sits in front
of the all-night drugstore, poring over them.[39]

Yet Mullen's awareness of embodied difference and otherness in these moving meditations is not limited to identity categories of race, gender, and class. Her poems observe the convergences and chasms between "human" and "nature" thrust to the fore by urban landscapes in which humans and nonhumans are pressed into entangled, overlapping, and often contradictory cohabitation, as "Networks of tree roots, sinewy tentacles / cracking sidewalks, pushing up bulges / in asphalt streets, clogging city sewer lines."[40]

Describing California as "a place defined as much by non-native as by its native species,"[41] Mullen links her own identity as "transplant" to the state's nonindigenous fauna and flora: "Like many inhabitants of Los Angeles, I am not native to this state of elemental seasons: wind, fire, flood, mudslide, and earthquake. Like ice plant, eucalyptus, and nearly all of LA's iconic palms, I too am a transplant to this metropolis of motor vehicles with drivers who regard, and are regarded by, pedestrians and cyclists as road hazards."[42] She asks: "What is natural about being human?" What to make of a city dweller taking a 'nature walk' in a public park while listening to a podcast with ear-bud headphones?"[43]—a moment of humorous self-contradiction that emerges in one of the poems: "Walking along the green path with buds / in my ears, too engrossed in the morning news / to listen to the stillness of the garden."[44] Contemplation, for Mullen, has everything to do with the reaches and limits of attention. The way we move through and coinhabit an environment of complexly intertwined relations is determined, in large part, by what we notice and what we ignore—what we give attention to, even in moments of passing:

> Caught a quick glimpse of bright eyes,
> yellow feathers, dark wings. Never learned your name—
> and to you, bird, I also remain anonymous.[45]

Josef Pieper wrote that "the act of perception, immersed in contemplation, is the most intensive form of grasping and owning."[46] This reaching, "to touch . . . the core of all things . . . is meaningful in itself [and] can happen in countless actual forms."[47] Pieper sees the "true artist" not as one who simply observes: "So that he can create form and image (not only in bronze and stone but through word and speech as well), he must be endowed with the ability to see in an exceptionally *intensive* manner."[48] The intensification that transforms ordinary attending to contemplation likewise transforms everyday language use into the poetic. As Hirshfield, herself a lay-ordained Soto Zen practitioner, puts it,

> The writing of poems must be counted as much a contemplative practice as a communicative one, and in the contemplative byways of every tradition, a reshaped intention is the ground of change. . . . Intention welcomes the new less by force of effort than by dissolving the psyche's old habits, gestures, forms. . . . contemplative intention is translucent to what lies beyond the self. Will and choice may play a role, but creative intention's heightened speech requires an equally intensified listening.[49]

Yet, as we have seen, in poetry as in prayer and meditation, the act of contemplation turns out to be far from simple, and no small attentional feat. Weil knew this. Augustine knew this. This is why contemplation is a practice and not a default mode. Sometimes attention's reach is an intrusion, an act that changes what it tries to contemplate. Other times, the subject of contemplation is changed, acted upon, and altered by the object even in the act of consuming it. And often the object resists consumption altogether, evading the observer's drive to grasp, to metaphorize, to metabolize, to apprehend. The reach and granularity of our attention determine our ability to grasp or perceive the object, and yet the mind interferes at every turn, analyzing, moving into abstraction and away from direct perception, muddying attention's lens with distractions, ambitions, and ideas. Often the object of the poem's contemplation turns out to be other than its initial semantic object of focus, either through metaphorical liftoff or by turning attention back onto the poem itself. Perhaps because of the intrinsic limitedness of contemplation (its tendency to diversion as well as its dependence on our limited, variable, and environmentally swayed perceptual capacities), contemplative poems must grapple with thwarted apprehension as much as plentitude—the reach of attention does not always grasp. And, when it does, a further challenge lies in keeping this grasping from doing violence (through usage or fixation) to its object, thus shifting the relation out of (spiritual or aesthetic) contemplation and toward instrumentalization. In a discourse on Matthew 6:25–34, a passage from the Sermon on the Mount, Søren Kierkegaard meditates on how the lily of the field and the bird of the air, properly attended, might teach us silence, obedience, and joy. Kierkegaard finds that "the speech of the poet is very different from ordinary human speech, so solemn that in comparison with ordinary speech it is almost like silence, but it is not silence."[50] "The poet" fails to adequately contemplate the lily and the bird because of his own impulse to speech, to eloquence, and to "giving speech" to the lily and the bird. Instead of eloquence, the poet should learn, in attending to lily and bird, how to be silent,[51] how to wait unconditionally,[52] how to be present and "pay attention."[53]

What is required in poetic contemplation, then, is a balancing act: between active focus and passive reception, between drawing close and letting be. Poetic contemplation is thus caught in tension between the silent acts of looking, listening, and waiting, and the *poietic* insertion of making language, breaking the silence. In other words, contemplative poetry's open and ongoing question: how to make language resemble, produce, or shelter silence—even today, as Mullen shows us: even in the heart of the city, "distracted from distraction by distraction . . . in this twittering world."[54]

CHAPTER III

Desire

Attention's Hunger

Dickinson : Shakespeare : Lorde : Lowell : Oppen : Hass

P erhaps the oldest and most essential mode of poetic attention is that of love and its hungrier variety, desire. Tending toward a beloved object, whether earthly or divine, is a central manifestation of transitive attention in classical and contemporary poetic contexts, non-Western and Western alike. Dedication, devotion, and praise constitute central dynamics across lyric traditions. The earliest known poems of desirous attention are Egyptian love songs dated to 1305–1080 BCE; since then the genre has developed in all cultural contexts, from the erotic fragments of Sappho to Petrarch's *Canzoniere* to Donne's *Holy Sonnets* and through the present day. While much has changed in the historical and cultural settings of these poems and the particularities of the relationships they articulate, there are a great deal more constants in their formative dynamics.

Parsing the Dynamics of Love and Desire

But what *are* love and desire, and how do we identify their particular workings, dynamic shape, and stance as forms of poetic attention? What distinguishes the love poem from the ode or from the poem of descriptive observation? In the love poem, we find an essential tug between interested and disinterested attention that can be said to form the intersection between aesthetic experience and relationships in the nonaesthetic realm, the field of semantic "aboutness" that grounds the lyric's representational impulse. The relation between I and thou, or between I and the absence of a thou, is fundamental to the lyric tradition from its earliest instantiations. It is also the seat of what can be understood as the primary ethical or relational dynamic in the poem—the address of gaze and speech between one and an other.

Both contemplation and desire involve the subject's attentive reach toward its object, the subject filling with its object, perhaps even dissolving or growing porous in the act of attending to another. In *The Pleasure of the Text,* Roland Barthes convincingly explores the analogy between the attentive act of reading itself (the reader's pleasure in skimming or penetrating the text) and the play of desire.[1] Even in nondesirous contemplation something is given in the poem's attentive reach as it moves over the contours of its object with what can be seen as a kin to love. In Kantian terms, the difference is the presence of interest: in the play of desire, the object is figured in terms of the subject's interests, its drive to possession, grasp, and pleasure, while the object of contemplation is attended with disinterest: like the other of Kantian morality, it is an end in itself. Here we hear again the Kantian echoes in Stevens: "poetic value is an *intrinsic* value."[2] In Schopenhauerian terms, the object of desire is desire, its objective oscillates between satisfaction and maintenance. Unlike its interested cousin, poetic contemplation is thus more akin to Heideggerian *Gelassenheit,* a form of approach (in present focalization, memory, or imagination) predicated on letting-be.

David Schalkwyk has noted the marked absence of "love" in current critical discourse, in comparison with (or, rather, supplanted by) emphasis on power and desire. Schalkwyk suggests that this critical shift away from love stems from the perception that power and desire "promised to strip love of its murkiness and sentimentality, . . . shift[ing] our attention from a relatively naïve and common-sense obsession with what characters feel to the structural conditions that allow such feelings to be manipulated in relations of power and subjection."[3] However, as I have noted, there are important differences between desire and love, and vigilance at their boundaries is vital to an understanding of either term.

The primary distinguishing characteristic of both love and desire—as felt experience and as poetic gesture—is interest. Contemplation inflected by interest begins to move into the realm of "kinds of love," which can include parental, erotic, or fraternal loves or nonhuman attachments, such as the love felt for a particular object or place. Add to interest an interval of distance (the experience of lack that produces the dynamic of longing), and we move one step closer to the particular dynamics of desire. "Longing," wrote Robert Hass (in a poem to which I will return), occurs "because desire is full / of endless distances." This interval of distance, inflected by interest (I not only gaze at this apple and appreciate it "objectively" but also want to take it in my hand and bite), is the foundation upon which desirous attention rests, an interval of relation between subject and object formed by a particular composition of attention's dynamic characteristics. One could go further and say that, while in the poetry of *love* the interval of distance is less central and greater emphasis is placed on appreciation and enjoyment of the relation of proximity, in *desire* the relation is more dominantly characterized by distance, by not having.

The role of spatiotemporal remove is placed at the center of the attentive relationship, and the status of interest is intensified from appreciation to longing. Both love and desire require an interval of distance and difference between subject and object (otherwise there would be no relation), but in desire the interval is widened, more tensely felt, sharpened by frustration. The greater the emphasis on remove, and the more the attention is inflected with the effort (a form of interest) to reduce or eliminate the distance, the more desirous the attentional stance.

In a poem by sixth-century Sufi poet Rābi'a al-Basri, we find these lines:

أُحِبُّكَ حُبَّيْنِ: حُبَّ ٱلْهَوَى   وَحُبَّاً لِأَنَّكَ أَهْلٌ لِذَاكَا
فَأَمَّا ٱلَّذِي هُوَ حُبُّ ٱلْهَوَى   فَشُغْلِي بِذِكْرِكَ عَمَّن سِوَاكَا
وَأَمَّا ٱلَّذِي أَنْتَ أَهْلٌ لَهُ   فَكَشْفُكَ لِي ٱلحُجُبَ حَتَّى أَرَاكَا
فَمَا ٱلْحَمْدُ فِي ذَا وَلَا ذَاكَ لِي   وَلَكِنْ لَكَ ٱلْحَمْدُ فِي ذَا وَذَاكَا

I love you with a double love: I love you passionately and I love you for yourself.
Passionate love for you has put me off others.
As I love you for yourself, lower your veil and reveal yourself to me.
Praise, not for me, but praise you for yourself.[4]

The speaker grapples with love's two impulses of desire and appreciation: on the one hand the penetrative and grasping focal attention of passionate love, in which the horizon shrinks to the boundaries of the beloved and pleasure is felt in the ache of yearning, reaching, the attempt to grasp, to possess; on the other, the forgetting of the possessive drive in the act of devotion, in the attentive contemplation, rooted in love, that holds back so as to let be. Al-Basri's devotion is torn, or stretched, between these two modes of desire and devotion, grasping and *Gelassenheit*: حب الهوى and حبا لأنك أهل لذاك. In al-Basri's context, this betweenness is a condition of human love, our attention pulled between these two poles of love—that which rejoices in the beloved, *that he is*, that he is in the world, and that which yearns for closeness and for possession.

We might consider the act of readerly attention as caught between two analogous modes of "love": the consumptive act, which runs along the surfaces and plunges into the pockets of the poem, seeking to possess it, taking pleasure in it and in the act of interpretation—filling the poem's negative space with the content of our analysis and wringing it out to ensure a comprehensive reading; and the contemplative act, which can only approach the poem for itself, at an interval of distance, letting the recesses recess and the irregularities be. This second love, attention to the object on its own terms is what locates poetic attention within aesthetic experience. At the same time, it grounds what can be seen as the contribution of aesthetics to ethical relation: regardless of the passionate intensity of our enjoyment of the poem as an object. No matter how essential passionate attention's drive might be in the bringing about of an encounter to begin with, true reading necessitates (as both precondition and sustenance) this second mode, attention to the poem (the *this*) in and for itself, a mode of attention that seeks, in Weil's terms, to look rather than eat. But, in the end, a kind of eating necessarily takes place: the end of reading, the end of desire.

We find this tensed interval embodied as physical distance in one of the earliest examples of love poetry, written between the fifteenth and tenth centuries BCE. In it, the speaker stands at the bank of a river (likely the Nile), looking across the water to the lover who waits (at least in the speaker's imagination) on the distant shore:

> The little sycamore she planted
> prepares to speak—the sound of rustling leaves
> sweeter than honey.

On its lovely green limbs
is new fruit and ripe fruit red as blood jasper,
and leaves of green jasper.

Her love awaits me on the distant shore.
The river flows between us,
crocodiles at the sandbars.

Yet I plunge into the river,
my heart slicing currents, steady
as if I were walking.

O my love, it is love
that gives me strength and courage,
love that fords the river.[5]

    Spatial remove defines in large part the attentional reach of this poem. The poem inhabits the attentional stretch across the water, shore to shore. The beloved object is not present, even in imaginative or remembered description. After the initial "she" who planted the sycamore, "she" is not present even as a subjective pronoun—only as the possessor of "her love," in the plurality of "us" and in the address to "my love." Her *present* subjectivity is located in the tree itself, its anticipatory preparation to speak, the rustling of its leaves (aside from the speaker's plunge, the only movement in the poem) signaling the presence of wind, the only one capable of traversing without risk the Nile's breadth. A closer look reveals the presence of temporal remove, as well, in the dynamics of waiting: the tree's *preparation* to speak (a sound for which the speaker waits) and in the beloved's imagined vigil on the other shore, waiting, and the speaker's *preparation* to ford the currents, the barricades of crocodiles. This distance, physical and temporal, is a hallmark of desirous attention, constituted precisely by not-having, by lack. The poem's primary mode is desire, though the speaker names it love. Love itself is present primarily in the loving attention given to the little tree in the first two stanzas and in the final two stanzas' turn to action, risking death.

    The role of death in this poem is notable, positioned at the boundary between self and other. The force of desire risks two kinds of death: the peril to the subject in crossing over to the beloved (risking not only physical death but perhaps a death or change in subjectivity itself in union), on the one hand, and the death of not-having, on the other, as the subject is suspended on the shore, his life emptied into the distance separating him from her. In the shift from the first two stanzas to the last, the poem highlights a threshold at which one risk outweighs another, a tipping point at which the pleasures of memory and imagination do not suffice and the pain of distance outmeasures the pain of crossing over. The spatiotemporal reach invoked in this poem is repeated in a long history of distantial poems whose longing gaze looks not to a human beloved but to a place, a land. This longer history ranges from Psalm 137 to Goethe's *Wilhelm Meisters Lehrjahre* 3.1, to Derek Walcott's "A Far Cry from Africa" and Mahmoud Darwish's "In Her Absence I Created Her Image." Poems of homesickness and exilic longing can be seen to occupy the attentional modes of both desire and recollection—a recollection charged with the tensed interval of desire or a desire shot through with temporal pastness and the uncertainty of return.

Desire's lack holds taut the interval of attention. Even when externally imposed (by, for example, wide water and toothed beasts), the restraint or constraint of not-having maintains attention's gaze, its necessary interval of relation, the hyphen of A-B. Closing the gap risks another kind of death, that of desire itself in the closure of its prelapsarian state of hunger, curiosity, the heightened sensitivity or "plenty" of hunger. Crossing the river marks a shift toward *love* and away from desire. For this reason, some poems of desire actively maintain this hunger, resisting the closing of desire's gap. There is a sense that as soon as this gap is closed, the tautness of attention felt at the peak of longing also lapses, relaxes, dies.[6] Emily Dickinson's "I had been hungry, all the Years" is explicitly *about* the maintenance of hunger and the "hurt" of plenty:

> I had been hungry, all the Years –
> My Noon had Come – to dine –
> I trembling drew the Table near –
> And touched the Curious Wine –
>
> 'Twas this on Tables I had seen -
> When turning, hungry, Home
> I looked in Windows, for Wealth
> I could not hope – for Mine –

> I did not know the ample Bread –
> 'Twas so unlike the Crumb
> The Birds and I, had often shared
> In Nature's – Dining Room –
>
> The Plenty hurt me – 'twas so new –
> Myself felt ill – and odd –
> As Berry – of a Mountain Bush –
> Transplanted – to a Road –
>
> Nor was I hungry – so I found
> That Hunger – was a way
> Of Persons outside Windows –
> The Entering – takes away.[7]

Physical hunger becomes, for Dickinson, a metaphor for human desire, and the object of desire itself wavers in this poem between the "plenty" of the table and the plenty of desire itself. An indecisiveness emerges between these two conflicting aims—to enter and be full, or to remain outside (or on the far shore) so as to prolong and savor the pleasure of desire itself. The dashes that proliferate in this poem, and throughout Dickinson's oeuvre of hungry texts, perforate the lines with absences, breaths held. The rhythmic effect of these silences in this poem contributes to the sense of hesitation, as the speaker falters between entry and resistance, between fulfillment and abstinence. The "plenty" of "ample Bread" at life's "Noon" is made all the more sharply and acutely desired when punctuated by refusal, when held rhythmically at bay. Waiting, as the lover waits on the far shore, becomes a way of tasting without tasting, touching without entering.

We find this hesitation echoed throughout the poetry of desire, underlining its centrality to desire's attentional self-preservation in distance and delay. *Twelfth Night*'s Feste insists that "in delay there lies no plenty,"[8] while Ben Jonson's translation of Petronius Arbiter takes a comic angle on Dickinson's restraint, this time more explicitly directed at the too-brief life span of passionate "doing" in comparison to the dance of foreplay:

Foeda est in coitu, et brevis voluptas,	Doing, a filthy pleasure is, and short;
Et tœdet Veneris statim peractœ.	And done, we straight repent us of the sport:
Non ergo ut pecudes libidinosœ,	Let us not rush blindly on unto it;

Caci protinùs irruamus illuc:	Like lustful beasts, that only know to do it:
Nam languescit amor peritque flamma,	For lust will languish, and that heat decay.
Sed sic, sic, sine fine feriati,	Be thus, thus, keeping endless holiday,
Et tecum jaceamus osculantes:	Let us together closely lie and kiss.
Hic nullus labor est, ruborque nullus;	There is no labour, nor no shame in this;
Hoc juvit, juvat, et diu juvabit:	This hath pleased, doth please, and long will please; never
Hoc non deficit, incipitque semper.	Can this decay, but is beginning ever[9]

Importantly, poems that take place in or after the *crossing* of the Nile, in or after the *taking* of the ample bread, are no longer poems of desire. In these poems that attentional tension of longing, craving, and lack becomes filled and fulfilled in the act of enjoyment, description, pleasure, a fuller and less vexed mode of attention whose interested craning has been slaked and slackened. Marcus Argentarius writes of the act (or the rich memory of the act) of possession in the following poem:

Στέρνα περὶ στέρνοις, μαστῷ δ᾽ ἐπὶ μαστὸν ἐρείσας,
χείλεά τε γλυκεροῖς χείλεσι συμπιέσας
Ἀντιγόνης, καὶ χρῶτα λαβὼν πρὸς χρῶτα, τὰ λοιπὰ
σιγῶ, μάρτυς ἐφ᾽ οἷς λύχνος ἐπεγράφετο.

Her perfect naked breast
Upon my breast,
Her lips between my lips,
I lay in perfect bliss
With lovely Antigone,
Nothing caught between us.
I will not tell the rest.
Only the lamp bore witness[10]

Where Dickinson's form was riddled with suspensions and withholdings and Jonson's translation was a dance of flirtation and delay, the syntax here is notably solid, focused on the part-to-part pairing of lover to lover, in recalled physical immediacy. The only withholding is the complete picture, which rests unprecariously in memory, silenced only by discretion, a secret between the speaker and the lamp's silent witness. There is none of longing's distance here, no interval separating the object from perception. With nothing separating subject and object, breast upon breast and lips between lips, the poem produces the proximity and immediacy of love, not the tense interval of desire. The attentional stance is still inflected as strongly with interest, but this time it is the interest of possession, not of want. The poem's attentional field is full; nothing is missing or missed. The only subtle element of desire in the poem lies in the use of the past tense: that the union takes place in memory signals a lack in the present.

In the poetry of both love and desire, the attentional lens is focalized—the degrees of selectivity and concentration are high, so that the object (or figure, to use Stockwell's terminology) fills most of the attentional field,[11] and the ground recedes. Yet because of the heightened degree of interest, unlike in the ode, the subject's consciousness of its own standing in relation (either of distance or of proximity) to the object cuts into the attentional centrality of the object: I attend not only to the object on its own, in and for itself, but also to my own subjective position, my feelings for it, my longing, my distance, my proximity, my lack.

The poetics of desirous attention is in some respects unique in the way it translates across other modes of attending, inflecting the act of attention to objects of direct perception (this apple I cannot [yet] bite into), remembrance (the boy I loved and lost), and imagination (my fantasy of one who does not exist). The object of attention need not be present, human, or even real to be desired. It is useful to recognize love poetry as possessed of a specific set of dynamics that can take place in a wide variety of modes and semantic settings. This allows us to trace the working of desirous attention as it maps and reconstellates our conventional assumptions about "love poetry."

One of the easy assumptions about love poetry is that it describes a simple one-to-one relation between lover and beloved—that the poem is composed around a singular object, either of desire or of love. Yet a closer look at the dynamics of love in a given poem often troubles this assumption: looking at a well-known sonnet seemingly addressed to a single "thee," we find more than one object of attention at play, layered (and even competing with one another) in different planes of the reading experience:

Shall I compare thee to a Sommer's day?
Thou art more lovely and more temperate;
Rough winds do shake the darling buds of May,

> And Sommer's lease hath all too short a date;
> Sometime too hot the eye of heaven shines,
> And often is his gold complexion dimmed;
> And every fair from fair some-time declines,
> By chance or nature's changing course untrimm'd;
> But thy eternal Sommer shall not fade,
> Nor lose possession of that fair thou ow'st;
> Nor shall Death brag thou wandr'st in his shade,
> When in eternal lines to time thou grow'st:
> So long as men can breathe or eyes can see,
> So long lives this, and this gives life to thee.[12]

The poem opens with an address to "thee," the object of the speaker's attention. The opening line ends with a question mark, calling attention to the framing of the poem itself and involving its dedicated object in its very composition. The question's upward lilt lights the opening. Posed to the reader or listener, the opening question also serves as invocation, placing the lover/writer, the beloved/reader, into a dialogue of involvement. As the poem moves forward, this dynamic of involvement and layered address is heightened by the repeated layering of phrases separated by semicolons, so that each new rhetorical turn is contained within the one before. Interestingly, the beloved him/herself is remarkably absent from the poem, present only in the secondariness of comparison: "more lovely and more temperate." More breath by far is given to the lesser comparative objects— the rough winds, the buds of May, summer's lease, the eye of heaven. The beloved is not present in any detail, only as a greater-than behind the description of a beloved world and its seasons and present only in pronoun form: "thee," "thou," "thy." In the couplet, following the colon, we arrive at a kind of kernel of the poem's attention: the "thee" of the poem gives way to another beloved, the "this" that is the poem itself, and the poem seems to hold itself forward as the object of attention, the object that has been forming over the course of the poem through each additional layer of comparison. Indeed, the "thee" seems to morph over the course of the poem from the living beloved to the textual beloved, from the textual beloved to the life-giving text. Here, "this" (the poem) has the definitive "last word." This shift also complicates the original gesture of praise, as the beloved is, by poem's end, not only left out in the cold as attention turns to the poem itself but also, it seems, no longer living, given life only by the text. On the one hand, in its focal shift from "thee" to "this," Shakespeare's poem performs the process of aesthetic immortalization of which it speaks; on the other, we find a veneration of the poem as the "beloved" slips, unmarked, from the frame—unmarked until the final line, in which "thee" has the last word: "So long lives this, and this gives life to thee." The "thee" of the first line's open question forms a chiasmus (ABBA) with the "this-this-thee" of the final line.

Turning a fresh eye to Sonnet 18 is difficult today, when the opening line and the couplet (the lines that tend to be venerated in the sonnets, while the middle sections fall into a kind of haze) have become timeworn. Helen Vendler has noted, "To come, as a commentator, on this—the most familiar of the poems . . . is both a balm and a test: what remains to be said?"[13] To respond to this "test" requires a deliberate act of slowing down, taking each line singly, setting it apart, paying a different kind of attention. And while it is true that cultural and critical absorption of this sonnet has been high, the subtle but significant work it does on our transitive attentional lens, paired with the lack of critical account of Shakespeare's work as a trainer of the attention, merits its continued consideration from fresh vantages.

Vendler's formalist approach focuses on the "this," the formal object of attention, emphasizing not the *speaker's* attentive gaze but the reader's, exercised by Shakespeare's "compositional powers" "to confer greater and greater mental scope on any whim of the imagination, enacting that widening gradually, so that the experience of reading a poem becomes the experience of pushing back the horizons of thought." Indeed, she argues that "Shakespeare encourages alertness in his reader."[14] Yet her analysis of Sonnet 18's widening conceptual and structural horizon focuses primarily within the *semantic* field (widening representational scope, a stretch to the imaginative mind's eye, a widening of the temporal field represented in the language of the poem). Her treatment of the "object" of attention in Sonnet 18 is the object of the *speaker's* attraction, the semantic object: "It is difficult," she writes, "to settle on a word for the object of the speaker's affections. Each word prejudices the case. The 'beloved?' The 'object?' The 'friend?' The 'dark lady?'"[15] Contra arguments from the ethical criticism camp on how Shakespeare treated this shape-shifting object, she asserts, "The ethics of lyric writing lies in the accuracy of its *representation* of inner life, and in that alone"[16]—a statement that takes for granted the primacy of the poem's *representational* capacities, leaving aside the other ways in which the sonnet might "encourage alertness." The duty of the lyric is not to *produce* or *affect* inner life but to *represent* it. While her introduction identifies the compositional coup of the poem in the heightening of readerly attention, Vendler's commentary remains primarily on the representational plane. We find a similar tension between the objects of the poem's representational work and the poem's objectlike qualities, its structural dynamics, in Vendler's recognition of the contrast between the "obviousness" of the sonnets' propositional content ("love, jealousy, time's depredations") and the complexity of their effects. "Taken as a single object," she observes, the sonnet sequence as a whole displays "dispersive gaps and uncertainties between its individual units. It is on just such large uncertainties that the small certainties of single sonnets float and collide."[17] Vendler sets her attention on the "unifying forces" at play in each sonnet, aiming to bring forth each poem's "visible core." This approach suggests the unfolding of a poetic object whose constitutive semantic matter is banal but whose formal dynamics or "surface" effects are anything but. However, despite its luminous account of the "forces" and "surfaces" at play in Sonnet 18 and the vitality of its interpretive contribution, her commentary slips too easily between forms of analysis—between reading for symbolic significance, representational content, structural forces, and readerly effects—without distinction. This signals a stress point between a formalist, almost-mechanistic mode of reading and the desire to make form *mean*, to render the mechanism representational. The valued work of the poem is located not at the semantic level but in its formal dynamics, yet its significance lies not in the readerly affect (or the production of "alertness") but in what is "represented" or "displayed" in each sonnet. In contrast to this approach to the individual sonnet, Vendler's discussion of the sequence as a whole, the sum of these representations, assesses it not in terms of its representational or symbolic potential but as a "single object" in itself, an object that acts upon the reader. It does not explore the important differences at the fault lines between the representational field, the semantic content of the poem, and the related but distinct formal field of readerly attention in which representation plays a significant but nonetheless partial role. There is no mention of the *poem* as one of the several potential "objects" of the speaker's attraction, nor does she spend time on the important shift from semantic to formal object flagged *within the semantic field itself* in the poem's last line, probably because it is too obvious, a classic take on the Petrarchan convention of immortalization. And yet Sonnet 18 offers a rich example of a poem that plays actively with the convergence and divergence of semantic and formal attentional planes, in which the two engage in a bidirectional relation of translation, competition, and mutual constitution.

Some theorists have argued that modern poetry deemphasized love. Sandra. L. Bermann attributes the decline in recognizable "love lyrics" in the early twentieth century to "reigning historical assumptions" about poetry's relationship to subjective experience: for example, "the notion of poetic 'impersonality'" present in poems such as Eliot's *The Waste Land* and in critical approaches such as those of William K. Wimsatt and Monroe Curtis Beardsley and, later, Roland Barthes. Bermann suggests that this was the result of "a commendable eagerness to emphasize" (i.e., reorient attention to) "language and text," a critical focus that grated against love poetry's "seemingly 'personal' themes."[18] However, the plethora of poems inflected by and even primarily framed by love and desire in and through the modern period show the critical doubt about love in modern poetry to be a historical tremor, not the end of a form. Examples abound in Wallace Stevens, William Carlos Williams, Adrienne Rich, Pablo Neruda, Anna Akhmatova, Adunis, Mahmoud Darwish, Seamus Heaney, and Robert Hass, sufficient to rest easy in the continued exploration of poetry's transhistorical ability to compose and reflect the attentional stances of love and desire, even as the particularities of language, cultural settings, social and family structures, and poetic forms continue to change.

In the poetry of Audre Lorde—self-described as feminist, black, lesbian, mother, warrior, poet, Zami (sister)—erotic love becomes a source of personal and political power, connecting the desiring female body to the earth, to its innermost wells of feeling and truth, and to a radical sense of potentiality in the present.[19] In Lorde's poem "Sowing," originally published in *Cables to Rage* (1970), the movement of desire opens an absence in a present full of the matter of life—daily repetitive work and the lull of an afternoon offer a space in which the mind lifts off from the present occupation into fantasy. In this liftoff, desire's lack wells an absence in the everyday, which is filled by a conjuring act of imagination:

> It is the sink of the afternoon
> the children asleep or weary.
> I have finished planting the tomatoes
> in this brief sun after four days of rain
> now there is brown earth under my fingernails
> And sun full on my skin

with my head thick as honey
the tips of my fingers are stinging
from the rich earth
but more so from the lack of your body
I have been to this place before
where blood seething commanded
my fingers fresh from the earth
dream of plowing a furrow
whose name should be you.[20]

In the poem, the bodily senses, sharpened by both work and longing, create a bridge from the present to what is both recalled and longed-for—the body of the beloved. Fingers stinging, nails blackened from planting tomatoes, and sun-soaked skin making the head "thick as honey" conjure the bodily experience of desire's physical intoxication, so that an afternoon's lull after work (fingers turned now, perhaps, from one form of "sowing" to another) opens a space for the body to call out to another, feels her absence— the "furrow" the fingers long to "plow," "whose name should be you."

The poem's syntax moves with the movement of the speaker's attention. The first two lines form a run-on of information on the present: the afternoon's "sink," the children absent from the scene, their naps, their weariness from work and play allowing the mother this lull, her sink. A period falls after these first two lines, and from there to the end of the poem there is no punctuation; phrasal beginnings and endings flow into one another, marked only by only one syntax-related capitalization: "in this brief sun after four days of rain / now there is brown earth under my fingernails / And sun full on my skin."

The poem turns on the word "lack," which falls midline, almost buried in a flow of thought. The stinging fingers, raw from the "rich earth," call up desire, the blood pulsing from work, "but more so from" wanting, from "the lack of your body." In the final stretch or spill of the poem, beginning with "I have been to this place before," the syntax begins to fold and overlap. As a result, different spatiotemporal modes of attention also fold together and overlap, so that past, present, and future (acts of recollection, present sensation, and longing) bleed into one another both phrasally and attentionally. In the lines "where blood seething commanded / my fingers fresh from the earth / dream of plowing a furrow," the speaker's "fingers" are both commanded by the "blood seething" in a previous experience of "this place" and also called forward (temporally and syntactically) to a present-future act of "dreaming." Thus a single body part (the fingers' tips, responsible for so much in love) is pulled between recollection and fantasy, and the image of the furrow binds the furrows made by the fingers in the soil (in sowing), the dipping of a needle in mending, and the movement of fingers, in the speaker's recollection-fantasy, in her beloved's labial furrow.

Unfolding from present, physical experience into erotic dream, Lorde's poem shares an attentional form with an earlier lesbian love poem, Amy Lowell's "The Blue Scarf."[21] In Lowell's poem, the dream is sparked by an object—an abandoned scarf left on a chair, whose touch and lingering scent ignite an attentional liftoff from present sense into erotic fantasy. The scarf's warmth remembers the shoulders of its wearer. In the act of touching its fabric, the speaker's attention transposes to the absent body, its scent lingering in the abandoned garment: "Where is she, the woman who wore it? The scent of her lingers and drugs me." The space opened by this question, and by the scent that remains in the absence of its bearer, sparks a Proustian fan of the mind in increasing removes from the present and into imagined embrace. Yet unlike Proust's fan of forgotten time out of the present-moment taste of a madeleine or scent of steeped flowers in memory, Lowell's poem shows how attention fans from these small sensory moments into the space of imagination, fantasy, and longing. Here, as in Lorde, imagination wells up in desire's cavity, its sense of lack: "A languor, fire-shotted, runs through me, and I crush the scarf down on my face, / And gulp in the warmth and the blueness, and my eyes swim in cool-tinted heavens." The attentional "eye" of the poem drifts in this ecstatic languor, and the ambient surroundings flow by, as, in film, the camera might pan to surroundings so as to indicate lovemaking in a visual ellipsis: "columns of marble," "sun-flickered pavement," the "blow" and "patter" of rose leaves," the shadow cast by a jade jar stretching over the floor, and finally, rather abruptly and unromantically, the "plop" of a garden frog in the nearby basin.

The poem captures attention's drift, or plunge, from present sense-experience to imagined experience when, in the midst of the ambient scene, the wind's subtle movement of the scarf becomes the woman's movement, suddenly *here*, present not only in image but in action:

> . . . The west wind has lifted a scarf
> On the seat close beside me; the blue of it is a violent outrage of
>   colour.

She draws it more closely about her, and it ripples beneath her
    slight stirring.
Her kisses are sharp buds of fire; and I burn back against her, a jewel
Hard and white, a stalked, flaming flower; till I break to a handful
    of cinders,
And open my eyes to the scarf, shining blue in the afternoon
    sunshine.

All of this happens, seemingly, in the space of a moment, before the speaker opens her eyes and before her lies only the scarf, shining blue in the afternoon sun. The rupture upon "waking" from fantasy constitutes another lack—the attention has moved from a sense of absence, to an imaginative fullness, to ecstatic self-disintegration, as the self breaks "in a handful of cinders," and is thrown or flung back into the present, clear light of direct attention: the blue scarf. The utter break between ecstatic departure and shipwrecking in the light of reality is embodied in the poem's break with itself in the last line: marooned back in lack, the speaker finds only the ticking of a clock, made louder by solitude and the strange sense of bereavement from an unreal embrace: "How loud clocks can tick when a room is empty, and one is alone!"

Where Lorde and Lowell reveal the proximity between desire's lack and imagination's capacity to fill (briefly) the space of the absent beloved, an attentional space between contemplation and love forms in George Oppen's "Psalm," in which the terrain of the poem itself serves as a shelter for a mode of awe-struck silent wonder, contemplating living otherness. "Psalm" enacts a reach of attention both thematically and formally, blending an imagined contemplation of deer in the forest with a reflection back on the *this* of the poem that frames and composes them:

PSALM
VERITAS SEQUITUR. . . .

In the small beauty of the forest
The wild deer bedding down—
That they are there!

Their eyes
Effortless, the soft lips

Nuzzle and the alien small teeth
Tear at the grass

The roots of it
Dangle from their mouths
Scattering earth in the strange woods.
They who are there.

Their paths
Nibbled thru the fields, the leaves that shade them
Hang in the distances
Of sun

The small nouns
Crying faith
In this in which the wild deer
Startle, and stare out.[22]

    The poem's title announces it as both song and prayer, and positions it explicitly in the lyrical tradition of the psalms of David, in which a singular voice is addressed directly to God. But here the spiritual act of psalmic address is directed, instead, to creaturely life: to the deer in the forest. Oppen's modification of Aquinas's *Veritas sequitur esse rerum* ("Truth follows upon the existence of things") indicates this shift. Oren Izenberg has highlighted the omission of Aquinas's *esse*, "which contained in it the assumption of the divine origin of 'thing' (which, in other words, inscribes the 'truth' that follows from objects as a particular theologically sanctioned form of value) and replaces it with a paraphrase posed less as a metaphysical dogma and more as an astonished exclamatory premise."[23] The act of contemplation takes place here not in a relationship of verticality between the mortal human and the transcendent divine but horizontally, suggesting an earthly "prayer" in which, perhaps, one need not look beyond the things of the earth to experience praise, revelation, and wonder.

    The horizon of this psalm's attention is focused in the first line: "In the small beauty of the forest." "In" suggests interiority, an inwardness in which the creatures of the world (both viewer and viewed) are nested (or embedded) in a world in which they are at home. The "small beauty" of the forest presents the world of the poem as near, simple, and humble. The syntax of the poem here reflects that environment. And yet the word "forest" brings in an element of the unknown, as a terrain of shadows, darkness. The forest is a place of myth, story, wildness, pathlessness—a terrain in which the wild deer are at home in their wildness. The speaker does not bed down in the forest, but sees, or imagines, them there. The line "The wild deer bedding down" is syntactically important because its position in the present continuous suggests two things: that they are bedding down *right now*, but also that this bedding down is ongoing, habitual: that, always, in one way or another, they are there. The simple observation, whether in the eye of the speaker or in the mind's eye, is thus both a singular moment and an ongoing happening that belongs to the forest, a place that is apart from and yet existing simultaneously with the modern human world. While cars flow on freeways and digital files upload and download and headlines proliferate, there is this other realm: there is small beauty, effortless eyes, and soft lips of animals. There are their soft, simple verbs taking place: bedding down, nibbling, scattering, hanging.

The scene the poem describes is simple enough: wild deer eating grass in the forest. But in the formal layout a second, embedded poem emerges at the right-hand margin. Oppen's line breaks and indentations create a chorus effect in which, while the indented lines are syntactically connected to the others, they strike as separate utterances. "Their eyes . . . The roots of it . . . Their paths . . . The small nouns seem to form a separate, synthesizing thread that proceeds from the breath-caught formal evocation of wonder in "— / That they are there!" and feeds into the final stanza, and of which the nonindented, more descriptive lines form the attentional flesh. The use of exclamation serves to bring the attention to an emphatic present—the immediate present of looking.

The attentional crux of the poem is a single line: "In this in which," of which the final verbs "startle and stare out" are modifiers. The "this" of this line resembles Shakespeare's splitting/twinning of attentional objects in Sonnet 18, but here the "this" is a point of convergence and emergence. The poem reveals itself as the forest: an ecology formed by its own act of attending, forming a sanctuary for the earthly and creaturely lives that it safe-houses in its gaze. What is made "tangible / Because unfelt before," to borrow Charles Tomlinson's words,[24] is felt only through poetic language (figuration, lineation, spacing, timing), a reach of attention to what either is not or cannot be noticed outside the poem. But the act of attending is complicated even in the environment of the poem itself: the deer within the poem "startle and stare out," so that both writer and reader are exposed as trespassers in the poem, intruders who have interrupted the small beauty taking place in that space when no one is looking, even though the act of looking composed the poem terrain itself. Oppen believed that "true seeing is an act of love"—a phrase that echoes Richard of St. Victor's dictum *ubi amor, ibi oculus* ("where there is love, there is sight"), quoted by Pound in the *Cantos*. Izenberg sees Oppen as insisting upon an "an attention to truthfulness,"—"upon a kind of attentiveness that encourages and dramatizes the greatest possible opening of the self to the possibility that a morally salient thing could be present."[25] So, while the *this* refers at one level to the poem itself, it also forms the *this in which* of relation: this act of looking, this strange moment of a returned gaze that precedes understanding or judgment as the primary event of recognizing another being's presence, in the clearing formed by attention, widened by love: *ubi amor, ibi oculus*.[26]

And yet, and yet. While the "this" of the poem can be seen to form an almost-living clearing for attention, the deer themselves become "small nouns." The loss (or at least precarity) suggested in Shakespeare's transposition of "thee" to "this" can be seen at the semiotic level as well, in the translation of living reality into language. Just as in George Oppen's "Psalm," the relationship between the formal and the semantic object of attention also brings to the fore the essential relationship between sign and signified, word and thing (and, at the ontological level, between phenomenal representations and noumenal objects). In "Meditation at Lagunitas" Robert Hass opens with "All the new thinking is about loss." And it's true, it is. "In this it resembles all the old thinking." After Hegel, after Heidegger, after Jacques Derrida, we learned and recited the ways in which language takes away presence, the way it replaces life with markers, the living cat with its three-letter supplement, the living flower with a dry snake of symbols, the living woman with a name, a noun, nothing. We learned that living particulars are only fallen and third-order stabs at the ideal, and the ideal is a space in which no life draws breath—a canceling out that centers on language's failure in the first instance and on its capacity to harm in the second:

> The idea, for example, that each particular erases
> the luminous clarity of a general idea. That the clown-

faced woodpecker probing the dead sculpted trunk
of that black birch is, by his presence,
some tragic falling off from a first world
of undivided light. Or the other notion that,
because there is in this world no one thing
to which the bramble of *blackberry* corresponds,
a word is elegy to what it signifies.[27]

Hass's poem meditates on this thinking, new and old, inquiring about another way. The speaker, rehearsing these critical-theoretical losses in conversation with a friend, hears in the friend's voice "a thin wire of grief, a tone / almost querulous. After a while I understood that, / talking this way, everything dissolves: *justice / pine, hair, woman, you,* and *I*." What if the course of language sometimes runs, Hass's speaker seems to invite us to ask, another way? Not into the "endless distances" of desire's lacks and the small but erosive transpositions of presence into abstraction, but into presence, via the presence—far from abstract, full of mouth and tongue and the deep echo chambers of the ear—of poetic language, its body a living form among, not in the stead of, others, capable of opening rivers of memory and imagination and channeling them into the forefront of immediate perception? Speaking out of the memory of an act of love, the speaker confesses: "I felt a violent wonder at her presence / like a thirst for salt, for my childhood river / with its island willows, silly music from the pleasure boat, / muddy places where we caught little orange-silver fish / called *pumpkinseed*." "We can't do anything with an object that has no name,"[28] wrote Maurice Blanchot, one of the great theorizers of the losses inherent in language.[29] We name things in order to "do things" or even to *be* in relation to things.

There is tension between proximity and distance, between attention and neglect. Things come to the fore only to recede or refuse our grasp. The beloved is the beloved until the loving gaze alights instead on the act of love itself, the medium of the love song, the beauty of the vessel. "Thee" is wiped out, or at least neglected (she falls from the frame of my attention), in my attention to the formal beauty of "this." A blue scarf unfurls a passion of dream kisses that, back in the harsh blue of sunlight, deserts me, holding nothing, in a present desert of ticking clocks. These erasures have been articulated by Blanchot as a primary linguistic loss: "something was there and is no longer there. Something has disappeared." The question follows:

> How can I recover it, how can I turn around and look at what exists *before*, if all my power consists of making it into what exists *after*? The language of literature is a search for this moment which precedes literature. Literature usually calls it existence; it wants the cat to exist, the pebble *taking the side of things*, not man, but the pebble, and in this pebble what man rejects by saying it, what is the foundation of speech and what speech excludes in speaking. . . . My hope lies in the materiality of language, in the fact that words are things, too, are a kind of nature—this is given to me and gives me more than I can understand. Just now the reality of words was an obstacle. Now, it is my only chance.[30]

A Wallace Stevens poem comes to mind here, one of his more morbid and death-fixed poems, but one that speaks to poetry's act of bringing forth object *in the flesh*:

> Out of the tomb, we bring Badroulbadour
> Within our bellies, we her chariot.
> Here is an eye. And here are, one by one,
> The lashes of that eye and its white lid.
> Here is the cheek on which the lid declined,
> And finger after finger, here, the hand,
> The genius of that cheek. Here are the lips,
> The bundle of the body and her feet.
> . . . .
> Out of the tomb we bring Badroulbadour.[31]

This is a different lyric beloved—not the living Badroulbadour but her corpse, brought into life through language (here of course hammered home as the semantic and theoretical object of Stevens's characteristically theoretically inclined poem). The *object* of the woman is allowed to decompose a little "within our bellies," is brought forth in full material array, and is rendered present and granular, particularized, in poetic deixis: "Here is an eye. And here are, one by one, / the lashes of that eye and its white lid. / . . . / And finger after finger, here, the hand." The first and last lines bind the "bundle" of the body, head to foot. What is composed is the body of the poem, brought into terrible visceral presence not in the soft gaze of "false compare" but in the stark light of attention, its ability to meditate in hyperfocus on the materiality—and mortality—of its object.

Does Stevens's act of bringing the woman "out of the tomb" change the way we might read the transposition, or perhaps recomposition (for it does not seem a decomposition), of "thee" and "this" in Sonnet 18 or "deer" to "noun" in "Psalm?" Yes, I believe it does. Does the river of memory from woman to word in Hass's poem, each syntactical shift and each syllable a physical pathway to the next memory, remain semantically faithful to the woman herself? No, it doesn't: "It hardly had to do with her." We've moved from desire to sex to another thirst and another salt, from one river to another, backward in time, deeper into the mud, another music, sillier, more senseless, to some deeply submerged place of memory where the small fish—their name, too, a name for something even smaller— still swim. How did we get here? Syntactically, we've been led in nested degrees of reference, and the sentence never brought us back to its original object, the object of lovemaking. It comes to a full stop farthest from its original object but closest to its true love, the formal object, the triplet "lo-li-ta" name that means almost nothing: "pumpkinseed."

What faith is nested in the "this" of the poem, in the "small nouns," in "pumpkinseed" and "blackberry?" What is risked in this act of faith, what is ventured, and what's at stake in the relational reach of attention? For Blanchot, it's a matter as large and, perhaps more importantly, as small as existence: "Everything physical takes precedence: rhythm, weight, mass, shape, and then the paper on which one writes, the trail of the ink, the book. Yes, happily language is a thing: it is a written thing, a bit of bark, a sliver of rock, a fragment of clay in which the reality of the earth continues to exist."[32] Hass writes, "There are moments when the body is as numinous / as words, days that are the good flesh continuing." Lorde writes, "my body / writes into your flesh / the poem / you make of me."[33]

The good flesh, "flesh into blossom." That flesh, for being present, for bringing us back to the present, is good. That a present continues (that it is there!), at once with us and beyond us, is also good. Say it: *blackberry, blackberry, blackberry.*

CHAPTER IV

Recollection

Attending to the Departed Object

Al-Khansā' : Hill : Celan : Cha : Carson

> This is how one pictures the angel of history. His face is turned toward the past. Where we perceive a chain of events, he sees one single catastrophe which keeps piling wreckage and hurls it in front of his feet. The angel would like to stay, awaken the dead, and make whole what has been smashed. But a storm is blowing in from Paradise; it has got caught in his wings with such a violence that the angel can no longer close them. The storm irresistibly propels him into the future to which his back is turned, while the pile of debris before him grows skyward.
> —WALTER BENJAMIN, "THESES ON THE PHILOSOPHY OF HISTORY"

The practice—and problem—of recollection has held a central place among modes of poetic attention across traditions and times and has informed several conventional poetic genres, including elegy, memoir, and testimony. Yet just as the objects of both desire and direct contemplation are always at a remove, always in the process, too, of slipping farther away (not to mention slipping toward death), the object of recollective attention proves not so simple. Its contours have the dynamic and fragmentary quality of memory itself. They constitute an object of attention, but often a particularly porous and uncertain one. In what follows I will explicate some of the more challenging dynamics of recollective attention in poems of elegy, witness, and memoir by Geoffrey Hill, Paul Celan, Anne Carson, and Theresa Hak Kyung Cha.

Modes of Recollective Attention: Elegy, Testimony, Documentary, Memoir

"History and elegy are akin," writes Anne Carson in her fraternal elegy *Nox*. While we think of elegy, history, memoir, witness, and translation as isolated generic categories, a closer look shows them to share a common attentional dynamic. These forms, while apparently diverse and certainly disassociated from one another by critical approaches that treat them in isolation, can be generatively seen as permutations of a single attentive gesture or practice: the act of attending to what is no longer present. They are modes of attending *in memoriam* to departed objects, their remnants or their absence. Each is a form of looking back in poetry, gathering fragments, asking, making meaning. Each holds out the possibility of a stay against the erosive condition of contingency and finitude that moves through objects, events, and lives. Yet the work of memory seems inevitably bound up with the "work of mourning."[1] However strong and evocative our powers of memorial imagination might be, the subject is constantly reminded of its position of "tarrying with the negative."[2] In the works of recollection I consider in this chapter, the task of recollective attention seems often to undertake a "reopening" and "holding open" of the object's absence, rather than its resurrection.

The act of attending to history's abyssal archive necessitates a dance between fidelity and freedom. Writing about the task of recollective attention in the poetry of witness, Carolyn Forché argues that "memory must be kept alive; those who perish at the hands of others must not be forgotten. I'm not sure anymore if holding the memory before the eye, before consciousness, is in itself redemptive, but this work of incessant reminding seems to arise from the exigencies of conscience. In my own life, the memory of certain of those who have died remains in very few hands. I can't let go of that work if I am of that number."[3] For Forché, this work of holding-open and holding-to requires the restructuring of the material of poetry as the past carves its events and absences into our language and consciousness: "If it is true that language creates consciousness, then the self is constituted in language. To write out of . . . extremity is to incise, with language, that same wound, to open it again, and, with utterance, to inscribe the consciousness. This inscription restructures the consciousness of the poet."[4]

The restructuring of language and consciousness by events (particularly those of extremity, which might include not only traumas but also profound experiences of other kinds: love, alienation, wonder) forces the generation of new speech, marked by the past. This means, moreover, that poetic language that seeks (or is called) to attend to past objects or experiences is in some sense *bound* to break new ground, to break with conventional modes of expression. In situations of trauma, devastation, or loss, this positions the language-maker in a double bind: without adequate language to "sum up," "account for," or successfully "evoke" the object or experience of memory, and yet with the persistent drive to re-call, to collect the object or experience in language, even as the object of recollective attention evades the grasp of words, so that only the space of the seeking subject remains, itself rendered porous and contingent by its poverty of recall. Ingeborg Bachmann writes,

> Zwischen ein Wort und ein Ding
> da dringst du nur selber ein,
> wie bei einem Kranken liegst du bei beiden
> da keins je ans andre sich drängt
> du kostest einen Klang und einen Körper,
> und kostest beide uns.
>
> Es schmeckt nach Tod.[5]
>
> Between a word and a thing
> you only encounter yourself,
> lying between each as if next to someone ill,
> never able to get to either,
> tasting a sound and a body,
> and relishing both.
>
> It tastes of death.

In Bachmann's passage, the effort to attend to an object in the medium of language "tastes of death," the distance "between word and thing," regardless of subject matter, already containing so much distance, so much ungraspability and longing. The attending subject encounters only itself in the act of trying to close the gap, attention's inherent interval of distances: between thing-matter and word-matter, between noumena and phenomena, between phenomena and articulation, between focalization and vocalization.

In Mourning We Were Never Modern . . .

In Geoffrey Hill's "September Song," a poem situated uneasily between elegy and historical account, the elegizing subject runs up against this same limit Bachmann notes in "Immerzu in den Worten sein." The speaker of the poem, writing both *to* and *about* a female victim of the Holocaust, finds in this effort to recollect from bare historical records, the act of attention (and the elegy itself) turning back on itself:

> "SEPTEMBER SONG"
> *Born 19.6.32—Deported 24.9.42*
>
> Undesirable you may have been, untouchable
> you were not. Not forgotten
> or passed over at the proper time.
> As estimated, you died. Things marched,
> sufficient, to that end.
> Just so much Zyklon and leather, patented
> terror, so many routine cries.
>
> (I have made
> an elegy for myself it
> is true)
>
> September fattens on vines. Roses
> flake from the wall. The smoke
> of harmless fires drifts to my eyes.
>
> This is plenty. This is more than enough.[6]

The elegiac subject in this poem is neither transparent nor pure, as the poem underlines the terrible and unbridgeable distance between himself and the little girl, born in his birth year and "deported" ten years into his long life. The act of attending to the departed cannot get around either her absence or the easy (even complacent) fullness of the living speaker's position. Jahan Ramazani has observed Hill's "vigilance" in "preventing his rhetoric from drifting toward the redemptive" in this poem, noting the way in which, throughout, the poet "tweaks himself with constant verbal reminders of the child's inaccessibility."[7] Langdon Hammer has noted that "historical knowledge repeatedly works its way into Hill's poems . . . His work turns on itself continually, obliged to acknowledge its own lack of innocence."[8] Hammer observes the parallel between the poem's form and its self-shredding efforts at recollection: "being fourteen lines, written in free verse with traces of meter, ["September Song"] is a kind of broken sonnet (as if the paper on which a metrical poem was written had been shredded and reassembled with bits lost)."[9]

In *The English Elegy*, Peter Sacks writes that, transhistorically, the elegy is "to be regarded . . . as a work, both in the commonly accepted meaning of a product and in the more dynamic sense of the working through of an impulse or experience—the sense that underlies Freud's phrase 'the work of mourning.'"[10] Responding to Sacks, Ramazani observes a pervasive theme of resistance to consolation or resolution in modern mourning. This "anti-elegiac" movement is essential to the redefinition of mourning in a destabilized, decreated, contingent world. Modern elegy, then, is as much about resisting closure or performing its impossibility as it is about mourning as such. He goes further to suggest that elegy, and the open-ended, many-faced work of memory in the context of cultural wastelands, is essential to an understanding of modernity as it is experienced in twentieth-century poetry.[11] Exploring modern poetic articulations of cultural wasteland and their resistance to closure, consolation, or recovery after trauma, Ramazani cites research involving the personal narratives of Holocaust survivors whose testimonies resist or disrupt narrative movement "toward a consoling future," refusing pieties like 'redeeming' and 'salvation.'" He suggests that, even for poets not personally affected by political/ethnic violence, the articulation of personal losses in the twentieth century were often linguistically and experientially inscribed within the larger and more collective historical scars that systemically altered modern experience of death, violence, and loss: "even private elegies obliquely attest to the unimaginable horrors that mark the modern history of death."[12]

Ramazani argues that while the elegiac impulse might have in some periods been accomplished (or at least performed) successfully, modern poetry reveals a more vexed and unconsolable effort, in which the "working through" is never through. Far from being a "refuge for outworn nostalgias and consolations," modern poetry of recollection "offers not a guide to 'successful' mourning but a spur to rethinking the vexed experience of grief in the modern world. . . . In this view one must read modern elegy as a form deformed by its historical moment, expecting not so much solace as fractured speech, not so much answers as memorable puzzlings."[13] Poetic touchstones for claiming the uniquely vexed and nonconsolatory nature of modern efforts of recollection in the English poetic tradition include T. S. Eliot's *The Waste Land* and *Four Quartets* ("Every poem an epitaph"), William Carlos Williams's "Tract," and Dylan Thomas's "Refusal to Mourn the Death, by Fire, of a Child in London."

Certainly the twentieth century offers a substantial body of works that seem to support the modernness of the anti-elegiac impulse. But is the resistant turn in recollective writing, of which elegy is certainly the most conventionalized genre, truly a modern phenomenon? R. Clifton Spargo has noted resonant phenomena in analyzing poetries of mourning ranging from Homer to *Hamlet,* Shelley to Hardy, Dickinson to Plath, finding in each that the simple task of remembrance proves not so simple in any age, and that the labor of mourning and recollection are characterized as much by recesses and evasions as by reconstitution and recovery. Spargo sees "melancholia," as "elegy's most persistent sign of a dedication to the time and realm of the other. Even when it seems to emanate from the esoteric subjective grievances of a specific mourner, melancholia interrogates the symbolic social structures that contain and reduce the meaning of the other who is being lamented. Thus it is on the threshold of symbolic meaning that every melancholic mourner stands again as for the first time when she refuses the consolations of language."[14] Across poetic periods and traditions (at least within his Anglophone domain), Spargo finds "a strain of melancholic or anti-elegiac lyric that foresees no end to mourning—in neither the social sphere of commemoration nor in the symbolic conventions and utilitarian principles by which it is organized—I attribute ethical meaning to the elegy's resistances to elegiac convention, to social commemoration, and even to the mourner's own wishfulness."[15] In light of Spargo's earlier examples of the challenges of recollective attention in poetic language, and at the same time in light of Ramazani's rightful observation of the particular density of anti-elegies in the modern period, it might be more productive to see the twentieth century as an especially useful lens through which to gain purchase on a much more pervasive and longue-durée phenomenon.

While Hill's poem has been positioned as the sine qua non of specifically modern elegy, seventh-century Arabic female elegist Al-Khansā' (Tumadir bint 'Amr) also demonstrates an ambivalence between the departed life and its physical remains, as well as a resistance to closure. A primary contributor to the genre of elegy or *marthiya* in the early stages of Islam, Al-Khansā''s work is primarily devoted to raw dedications to her brother Sakhr and half-brother Muʿawiyah, both killed in tribal conflicts in 612. Like "September Song," the poem "يَا عَيْنِ جُودِي بِالدُّمُوعِ" reveals the double phenomena of excess and insufficiency in her works' depiction of the experience of poetic remembrance: excessive because of the imbalance between outpouring language and memory in comparison to the absence of their object and insufficient because of the ungraspability and unresponsiveness of that object, the unresolvability of the "flood" of language, which, because it reaches into an absence, runs up against no limit save the energetic and expressive capacities of the mourner:

يَا عَيْنِ جُودِي بِالدُّمُوعِ	الْمُسْتَهِلَّاتِ السَّوَافِحْ
فَيْضاً كَمَا فَاضَتْ غُرُوبُ	الْمُتْرَعاتِ مِنَ النَّواضِحْ
وَ ابْكِي لِصَخْرٍ إِذْ نَوَى	بَيْنَ الضَّرِيحَةِ وَالصَّفَائِحْ
رَمْساً لَدَى جَدَثٍ تُذِيعُ	بِتُرْبِهِ هُوجُ النَّوافِحْ
السَّيِّدُ الْجَحْجاحُ وَابْنُ	السَّادَةِ الشُّمِّ الجَحاجِحْ
الحامِلُ الثِّقَلَ المُهِمَّ	مِنَ الْمُلِمَّاتِ الفَوادِحْ[16]

O eye, well up with worthy and deserved tears,
Flooding like water flooding over arid fields;
Weep for Sakhr, who rests eternally between the grave and its
    stone cover,
The grave filled with earth, whose soil is swept away by the wind
Of this chivalrous man, son of chivalrous men,
Who bore the weight of the greatest calamities.

Much as Hill's poem walks an uneasy line between the public discourse of reportage and the private discourse of the isolate conscience, Al-Khansā''s poem compresses in a mere six بيوت (*buyut*, hemistich "houses" or lines) the intimate space between the speaker and her own grieving body (the eye, object of the opening imperative to *well up*) and the public space of memorialization suggested in words such as "worthy" or "deserved" and underlined by the fifth line's emphasis on public chivalry of both Sakhr and the tribe. Just as elegies have served a public and even political function throughout their Western history, classical Bedouin and early Islamic elegies were often sites of public statements, and their employment, as in

Al-Khansā''s poems, in response to political violence, positioned them at an uneasy intersection between the deeply personal experience of grief and the public exercise of strong rhetoric. Situating the poem as a whole within the imperative mode, the opening line's hail to the eye and call for it to weep resonates with Forché's sense of obligation and burden. At the same time, the words "يا عين" (*ya ayn,* O eye) sonically suggest the nonverbal wail, the sense that the "flood" may exceed the limits of language to express, just as the experience of loss exceeds the ability to recall.[17] The terrain of the living is, in Al-Khansā''s language, parched. There is a *need* for tears, and for their linguistic equivalents. The resolution of this need is, it seems, indefinite: the object of this attentional demand "rests eternal" as an absence made present by the wind blowing the dust of the grave into movement. The persistence of unseen movement in the space of the beloved's body long after his absence offers a metaphor for a kind of sensory remembrance, a mode of tuning in sensorially to the unseen and impalpable traces that arrest and hold the attention in the absence of the object itself.

Perhaps the "anti-elegiac" dimension in poetries of mourning—the tension between memory and forgetting, between healing and the vigilance of "never forget," is bound up in the nature of mourning itself. In thinking about the inconsolable side of elegy—the burden, the imperative left to those (victim, perpetrator, and witness alike) that remain—let us turn to Psalm 137 in its development from grief,

> By Babylon's streams,
> There we sat, oh we wept,
> When we recalled Zion

to imperative,

> Should I forget you, Jerusalem,
> May my right hand wither.
> May my tongue cleave to my palate
> If I do not recall you

from indictment,

> Recall, O Lord, the Edomites,
> On the day of Jeruaslem, saying:

> "Raze it, raze it,
> to its foundation!"

to curse:

> Daughter of Babylon the despoiler,
> Happy who pays you back in kind,
> For what you did to us.
> Happy who seizes and smashes
> Your infants against the rock.

Reading these lines, we recall Primo Levi's *Se questo è un uomo*,[18] which opens with an untitled poem, paraphrasing Deuteronomy 6:7, whose conclusion calls on the psalmic force of vengeance, imperative, and the responsibility of language in the unending task of not-forgetting:

> I commend these words to you.
> Carve them into your hearts
> At home, in the street,
> Going to bed, rising;
> Repeat them to your children,
> Or may your houses fall apart
> May illness impede you
> May your children turn their faces from you.[19]

The violence of these lines, the searing force of the imperative, sits between exigence and warning, between warning and curse. Yet even in their violence, these calls for justice are first and foremost calls to remember, to continue bearing witness, and to hold open the space of mourning. The terrain of these acts of recollection has been laid bare—by genocides and by displacements. The language that hauls its listener through such a terrain must form itself from absences, from remains. Thus language itself becomes the terrain of mourning, and of survival.

The term *elegy* suggests an act of mourning the departed, at once recalling to mind and laying to rest. And yet in the aftermath of political violence, destruction of homeland, and loss of life on a larger scale, the problem of mourning takes on a more forceful valence that goes beyond the agency of the mourner, shouldering her or him with collective responsibility. The exigency of recollection becomes tending to the past and assuming responsibility for the future—both works of "impossible witness," both exhausting and inexhaustible demands. This is, it seems, the curse of modern memory: its endlessness and inconclusiveness yield responsibility one cannot set down, a task one can never complete. Memory emerges in these poems with an agency of its own: resistant to language and to action, its shape is the absence of things, the emptiness of them and between them. Its home is the wasteland of what remains.

The works I explore here coincide with a specific culture of attention, particularly in the industrialized West. The emergence of these works amidst the rise of what has been called the "attention economy" of late twentieth- and early twenty-first-century Western cultures perhaps explains the density of works that engage so *consciously* with attentional dynamics at a formal level.[20] The exploratory, fragmentary, polyreferential, and decidedly "open" forms of Hill, Celan, Carson, and Cha suggest a lineage of analogous large-scale modern works, from Pound's *Cantos* (1917–1969) to Charles Olson's *Maximus* poems (1953–1969), Charles Reznikoff's *Testimony* (1934–1979), Peter Weiß's *Die Ermittlung* (1965), Edmond Jabès's *Le Livre des questions* (1963–1973), and Lyn Hejinian's *My Life* (1980). Taken together, they imply a particular historical affinity for explorations into poetry's capacity to engage the nonverbal, the blank, and the found and saved object, and its ability to resist "closure,"[21] as well as "unity," semantic and formal.[22] And yet in their respective modes of elegy, testimony, and memoir, the vexed dynamics of attention to departed objects are by no means a twentieth-century phenomenon, as the deep historical archive suggested by Al-Khansā', Catullus, and Hesiod evinces. Many well-rehearsed claims have been made about the impact of modernity and postmodernity on the form and, recalling Theodor Adorno, even the possibility of poetry.[23] However, while it is true that modernity brought a number of significant social, political, and aesthetic changes, so did many less routinely theorized periods.[24]

In considering artworks from any period, contemporary or classical, it is not possible to determine which dynamics are products of their contexts and which are longer-lived patterns of human expression. While acknowledging the unique historical inflection affecting any poem's particular attentional dynamics, I have chosen to focus on the phenomenology of these dynamics, rather than taking them as primarily symptomatic of a historical moment whose apparent topographical relief may be as much a product of routine overtheorization as of an actual increase in historical eventfulness relative to other epochs. It seems likely that certain historic and cultural moments have what we might consider a resonance or affinity with a particular manifestation of recollective attention's many transhistorical faces. This might explain the unique tonalities elegy assumes in specific historical moments. In this light, we may reread Benjamin's passage on the Angel of History, so often interpreted as a commentary on specifically modern historical recollection, as reflective on the historically inflected yet ultimately transhistorical challenge of attending to the past—turning the gaze backward to the debris that piles in our wake, even as time propels us away, blowing the objects of our attention ever further from our grasp.

Verbracht ins / Gelände: Wasteland and Deathworld in Paul Celan

What are the stakes, though—and what is the use—of language in the aftermath of catastrophic loss? For Romanian-born, German-language poet and Holocaust survivor Paul Celan, there was no language for "that which happened," yet language moved "through" the catastrophe—the single thread of life continuing (in human breath). Language became the only terrain in which Celan could seek shelter for the human during the too-brief years following encampment, before taking his own life in 1970. As a result, his poems grew increasingly challenging and agonized, each syllable a step made with supreme effort—a quality manifest in his long poem "Engführung."

In many ways, "Engführung" seems to share a rib with *The Waste Land*. Celan's agonizingly resistant poem situates us, like Eliot's, in unsettlement, in unhinged terrain. Written in 1958 between February and May, "Engführung" emerged partly in response to the overuse of "Todesfuge," a poem that proved too readily absorbed, interpreted, skimmed.[25] The poem begins and ends in another wasteland, but, through its de-formed language, it wrings the reader out of silence and into a different attention to the word.

Articulating the form of elegiac address possible (or nearly possible) in poetic language in his acceptance speech for the Bremen Prize, Celan described poems as "underway," "making toward something . . . toward an addressable Thou, toward an addressable reality. Such realities . . . are at stake in the poem." Embodying poetry as both way-seeking and way-making, "Engführung" suggests an exigency to forge such a way in language's bare materials of sound, trace, and breath—in Celan's words, to "go with one's very being to language." Perhaps his most difficult work, "Engführung" challenges at every stage the reader's ability to comprehend, to take hold of its language narratively or even semantically. In the failure to comprehend, there is also a failure and disconnect of memory and of the kind of recalling that both Psalm 137 and Levi's poem mandate. Instead, what emerges is something more difficult, less articulable, a space of responsibility and address that cannot be so easily summed:

Verbracht ins	Taken off into
Gelände	the terrain
mit der untrüglichen Spur:[26]	with the unmistakable trace:

In these opening lines, language and its reticence face us. Nameless, the subject(s) of the passive verb: who, or what, is *verbracht*—and by whom? In this text-"terrain" of "traces," we are thrown "here," cast upon the strangeness of these lines even as they turn away from our reading's desire for comprehension. The double definitive of "ins / Gelände" and "der untrüglichen Spur" tells us, as Peter Szondi posits in his essay on the poem, that these entities are known, but not to us. We are thus informed that the poem does not speak to us, but we enter its terrain as foreigners: faced with the simultaneous intimacy and exclusion of no-introduction.[27]

Gras, auseinandergeschrieben. Die Steine, weiß,	grass, written asunder. The stones, white
Mit den Schatten der Halme:	with the grassblades' shadows:
Lies nicht mehr—schau!	Read no more—look!
Schau nicht mehr—geh![28]	Look no more—go!

Gras, auseinandergeschrieben: literally, grass asunder-written; yet the "aus-ein-ander-geschrieben" invokes both destruction and relation in one breath, both sundering and relation, as "to-an-other-writing." Does the grass register the bodies of those driven into the terrain? Does it grow along a *Feldweg*, crushed by feet of those driven through it? It is not written *of* asunder, but written asunder, as though the act of writing both makes and unmakes.[29] There is stillness in the image of stone and blade-shadow. We do not know the identity of those driven into the "terrain," yet we sense, with the aperture of the colon, that this still(ed) scene is a part of the "terrain" into which they have been cast, with us. With the double imperative, "Lies nicht mehr—schau! / Schau nicht mehr—geh!" the poem's momentum intensifies. By whom and to whom the imperatives are directed we cannot know, but they seem to cut through the aftermath image of the grassblades to address us directly: stop reading! and stop watching! Spectatorship is insufficient in relation to the poem. A powerful critique is made in these two imperatives about the insufficiency of a certain kind of witnessing and a readership that seeks to be affected by the text or the event from a safe distance, even to be bettered by acts of guarded witness.

Der Ort, wo sie lagen, er hat einen Namen—er hat keinen. Se lagen nicht dort. Etwas lag zwischen ihnen. Sie sahn nicht hindurch. Sahn nicht, nein, redeten von Worten. Keines erwachte, der Schlaf kam über sie.[30]	The place where they lay, it has a name—it has none. They did not lie there. Something lay between them. They did not see through it. Did not see, no, spoke of words. Not one awoke, sleep came over them.

The two subjects lie close together. And yet, unnamed in a no-man's-land, they lie nowhere. They are "asked after" "nowhere." "Something lies between them" and "they did not see through it." They are unable to see or speak through whatever has come between them, and so continue being nowhere, no-one, speaking only *"of* words," *around* words. To speak around words is to refuse, to be unable, to enter into the terrain of language. It is to look away ("they did not see through it"). The "sleep" that comes over them is one of inattention, inaction, nonspeech. The line "Ich bins, ich" emerges as a voice from the text itself and haltingly recalls the earlier imperatives: "Stop reading—Look! / Stop looking—go!" To "go" into the poem-terrain begins with "I am:" "I am the one" to act, to step, to engage. The "I" here hauls itself out of nonbeing, to "go with one's very being to language."

Sprach, sprach. War, war.	Spoke, spoke. Was, was.

Wir	We
liessen nicht locker, standen	would not let go, stood firm
inmitten, ein	in the midst, a
Porenbau, und	framework of pores, and
es kam.	it came.
Kam auf uns zu, kam	Came up to us, came
hindurch, flickte	on through, it mended
unsichtbar, flickte	invisibly, mended
an der letzten Membran,	on the final membrane,
und	and
die Welt, ein Tausendkristall,	the world, thousandfaced crystal,
schoss an, schoss an.	shot out, shot out.
★	★
schoss an, schoss an.	Shot out, shot out.
Dann—[31]	Then—

At its nadir, in stifled silence and the height of obscurity, the poem turns. A kind of genesis unfolds, tentatively and slowly: "Speak, speak. / Was, was." Wrought at the final hour, "an der letzten Membran," a hard-won speech comes into being. This moment, with its echo that underlines the already-beginning process of multiplication, regeneration, and world-making, articulates the highest stakes of the poetic word. Out of the word, an event to counter the event of nullification and death: the "thousand-faced crystal" of the world surges into existence. Its hours multiply from the ground-zero of the Saying:[32] ". . . die / Welt stezt ihr / Innerstes ein / im Spiel mit den neuen / Stunden."[33]

As Celan's poem nears its close, we arrive at a prayer, spoken or sung:

. . . die	. . . the
Chöre, damals, die	choirs, back then, the
Psalmen. Ho, ho-	Psalms. Ho, ho-
sianna.	sanna.
Also	Therefore
stehen nock Tempel. Ein	temples still stand. A

Stern	star
hat wohl noch Licht.	may still give light.
Nichts,	Nothing,
nichts ist verloren.[34]	nothing is lost.

Choirs, psalms. Going in boxcars in their "final hours," the deported Jews sang and prayed together. Here the song goes up in the form of psalms, and a broken hosanna that makes an ugly laugh or a cry or both. Unlike the liturgical praise song of *Hosanna in excelsis,* the hosanna of the Hebrew psalms is a prayer for mercy meaning "Rescue us" (118:25). The relationship between the first and second stanza here is interesting. After the laugh/cry/plea of hosanna, which, given its stuttering, is *spoken* or *sung,* "audible" and in the "open," the word "Also" (therefore) comes in as an outcome or a lesson. What comes? Everything: "temples still stand," "A / star may still give light. / Nothing, / nothing is lost." The signature doubling of the "Nothing" opens a polysemic space in which both "nothing, no thing, is lost," and in which "Nothing-ness" is lost, is escaped. The prayer repeats, still broken but no longer laughing:

Ho-
sianna.
In der Eulenflucht, hier,
die Gespräche, taggrau,
der Grundwasserspuren.
★

    (— —taggrau,
               der
         Grundwasserspuren—[35]

Ho-
sanna.

At owl's flight, here,
the conversations, daygray,
of groundwater traces.

★

> (——daygray,
> of
> groundwater traces—

At "owl's flight," or dusk, the world's "daygray," we come, in "conversation" upon the "groundwater traces." What seemed parched still has the trace of moisture in it, what seemed tapped, empty, and without sustenance still bears the "trace" of "groundwater." The invocation of dwindling groundwater stands in marked relation to the desert of rock in Eliot's *The Waste Land*. In this penultimate stanza, despite the impossibility of a "return," the poem gives attention to the trace.

Twice in "Engführung" Celan locates the "final hour" reached by "us" in the moment "In der Eulenflucht."[36] The flight of the owl in the "hour that has no sisters" cannot but bring to mind the flight of the owl of Minerva,[37] when Philosophy begins to mark its own end, seeking only to "understand" the end of things. In contrast to philosophy's "speaking of words," the poetic word enters as action and as event, altering the terrain that preceded it and embodying an opening for relation.[38] Language and relation constitute the human through a "countering" (*entgegnend*) of call and response. In poetic attention, we glimpse a lost or forgotten relation between the human and its language and thus between the human and the world.[39]

Poetic language requires, for Celan, something very different from ordinary "reading" and "looking." It involves risk, labor, and participation even in suffering and lostness. Above all, it demands active and embodied attention. We must go—into the poem, perhaps, deeper into the terrain. With, or as, those who have been driven there.

Geh, deine Stunde	Go, your hour
hat keine Schwestern, du bist—	has no sisters, you are—
bist zuhause. Ein Rad, langsam,	are at home. Slowly a wheel
rollt aus sich selber, die Speichen	rolls out of itself, the spokes
klettern,	clamber,
klettern auf schwärzlichem Feld, die Nacht	clamber on the blackened field, night
braucht keine Sterne, nirgends	needs no stars, nowhere
fragt es nach dir.	are you asked after.
★	★

> Nirgends
> fragt es nach dir—[40]

> Nowhere
> are you asked after—

Picking up the imperative once again, "go"-ing into the poem-terrain, the "you" stands at the solitary hour, an hour that can only be, as Szondi points out, the last.⁴¹ And yet the hour of death is also the only possible hour of survival, the hour to which one (re)turns in remembrance of the dead. The final hour is where thought and language turn in order to bring something into the living that has passed and where the living must face nothingness with language (action) or become nothing. The "—" in "you are— / are at home" divides the homecoming with a chasm, stutter, or well of silence, while the repetition of "are" sounds differently each time, with emphasis. "To be" becomes here a fraught active verb, divided from itself. Recalling the late-world prophesies of Yeats's "Second Coming," the lines "a wheel, slowly, / rolls out of itself" and "the spokes" "clamber, / clamber" signal a slow process of coming undone that, in "clambering" cannot be reduced to a generalized condition of modernity but must be felt with the urgency of bodies vying for air. The parts of a structure, of a working and interdependent whole, unravel, the parts clattering useless on the ground. The disarrayed "spokes" resonate with the "grassblades," likewise "written asunder." The final lines of this stanza are revoiced in the fugal repetition and in the long dash that follows: "Nowhere / are you asked after."

Verbracht
ins Gelände
mit
der untrüglichen
Spur:

Gras.
Gras,
auseinandergeschrieben.)⁴²

The poem circles back to its beginning, winding back to the "setting out" into terrain. Celan says: "It is time to turn back . . . I am at the end—I am back at the beginning."⁴³ The reader, too, is back at the beginning, setting again into the terrain of the poem but with a different attention to the words and what is "underway" in them: "Once, given the attentiveness to things and creatures, we approached something open and free."⁴⁴

Talking (Why?) with Mute Ash:
Recollective Attention in *Nox*

Working between (translating, collaging) ancient elegy and contemporary docupoetics, Anne Carson's fraternal elegy *Nox* (2010) explores the labor of attention demanded by responding to her estranged brother Michael's unexpected death in Copenhagen.[45] Massive in scale, Carson's book-length elegy pulls together in collaged piecemeal the debris surrounding Michael's life and death. The book opens with an untranslated blurry image of Catullus's poem 101,[46] an elegy to his own brother. Each word of 101 is then unpacked and dilated in the course of the work. The final page contains an even blurrier, wrinkled, and water-damaged copy of Carson's translation of the poem. Threading through torn photographs and pieces of letters, brief scenes and many expanses of blank, penciled lines and paint, Carson conducts an archeological—or archaeopoetical[47]—exploration of the materiality, plainness, and irrecuperability of a life and the inevitable failure and fictionality of its telling. What surfaces in the process of sifting through Michael's remains is a negative of his life and his death. The negative becomes both object and means. Elegy emerges as a "concrete and indecipherable" negative space delineated by the poverty of memory, the paltriness of historical remnants, their inability to truly *recall*, immortalize, or evoke to any more than a trace of a life. In this way Carson's work can be seen as a *negative* elegy, a meditation on the possibility of recollection.[48]

Midway through *Nox* we find a white left-hand page, and two thickly painted (one can see the cracks in the thickly coiled pigment where the paint dried quickly) yellow ovals, one slightly larger than the other. The two yellow ovals don't function as grammarred speech or even as nonsense speech. We stare at the ovals for a while. There's a (scanned in) staple at the top, just off center to the right, pinning the thin rectangle they're painted on to the backdrop sheet. They are irregular. They say very little—are they heads? Siblings? We look at the ovals a little longer. The reader-viewer is torn between making sense and letting be. Any representation we might find is composed somewhere between the markings and what we make of them. Turning the page, we find a response to or elaboration of the ovals: "What comes to me now, as I kneel in a church in Copenhagen listening to long Danish gospels and letting the sheets of memory blow

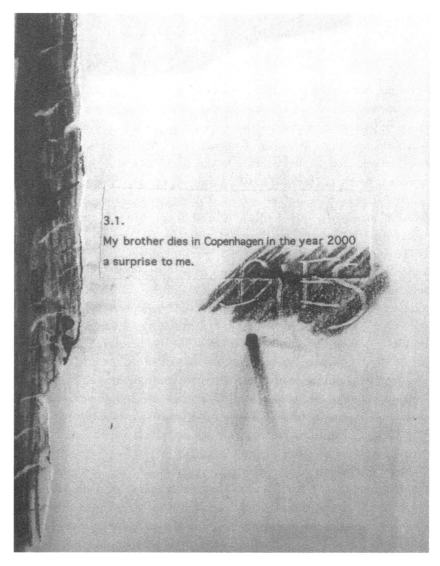

Figure 4.1 Image from *Nox*.

on the line, is that both my parents were laid out in their coffins (years apart, accidentally) in bright yellow sweaters. They looked like beautiful peaceful egg yolks. I have always admired the design of the egg – yellow circle within a white oval, as impeccable as Herodotos' explanation of the old wise saying Custom is king of all."

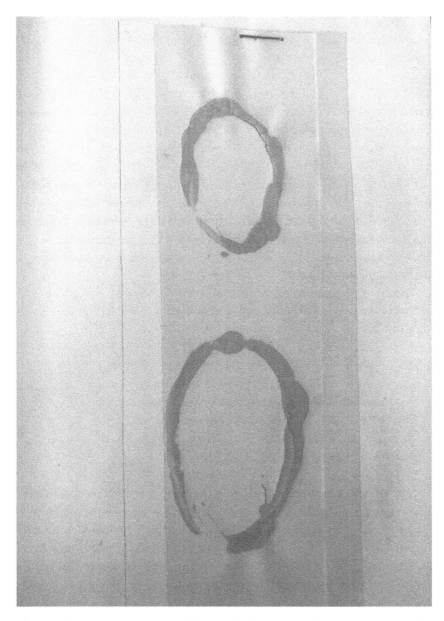

Figure 4.2 "Both my parents were laid out in their coffins (years apart, actually) in bright yellow sweaters. They looked like beautiful peaceful egg yolks." —Carson 5.5

"We want other people to have a centre," writes Carson, "a / history, an account that makes sense. We want to be / able to say This is what he did and Here's why. It / forms a lock against oblivion. Does it?" (3.3) The act of attending to the departed is driven by desire: to "fill" the space left, the "want" to "evoke," recuperating something of *life*, of *lived history* into saved matter—in this case, words and images. *"Always comforting to assume there is a secret behind what torments you"* (5.4). The struggle for immortalization is embedded throughout poetic history and its various forms of recuperative and conservationist addresses—the love lyric, conscious of its inability to save the beauty of the beloved, the elegy, conscious of its inability to bring back. In both forms, we find an uncomfortable trump when the beauty of the poem infringes on or surpasses the beloved in beauty or durability (or both). This desirous project of recollective attention is deeply rooted to the hunger of memory, reaching to hold onto things, seeking to carry them into the light.

But light doesn't always come. Sometimes both history's and elegy's recuperative projects produce only traces: hard, plain objects, the remainders of a life:

> 1.0.   I wanted to fill my elegy with light of all kinds. But death makes us stingy. There is nothing more to be expended on that, we think, he's dead. Love cannot alter it. Words cannot add to it. No matter how I try to evoke the starry lad he was, it remains a plain, odd history. So I began to think about history

The objects surrounding Michael's life remain uninterpretable, finite. Carson writes, "I am looking a long time into the muteness of my brother. It resists me." The subject of the elegy "refuses to be 'cooked' (a modern historian might say) in my transactional order." The "starry lad" is nowhere to be found in these pages of debris and insignificant scenes that collect around his passing. "Dead" is the monosyllabic and banal last word.[49] "There is something that facts lack:" "Overtakelessness," writes Carson, "*das Unumgängliche*—that which cannot be got round. Cannot be avoided or seen to the back of. About which one collects facts—it remains beyond them" (1.3.). In its insufficiency, the elegy marks out a negative space, held open for what escapes even the most meticulous translation of absence into presence, life into language.

Nox both enacts and describes recollection's double root in remembrance and collection, as one of translation:[50]

> Nothing in English can capture the passionate, slow surface of a Roman elegy. No one (even in Latin) can approximate Catullan diction, which at its most sorrowful has an air of deep festivity, like one of those trees that turns all its leaves over, silver, in the wind. I never arrived at the translation I would have liked to do of poem 101. But over the years of working at it, I came to think of translating as a room, not exactly an unknown room, where one gropes for the light switch. I guess it never ends. A brother never ends. I prowl him. He does not end.

And on the next page:

> Prowling the meanings of a word, prowling the history of a person, no use expecting a flood of light. Human words have no main switch. But all those little kidnaps in the dark. And then the luminous, big, shivering, discandied, unrepentant, barking web of them that hangs in your mind when you turn back to the page you were trying to translate.

In her labors of collection, meditation, and composition, the attending subject (elegist qua historian qua witness qua translator) "prowls," "gropes." "No use expecting a flood of light." Trolling the depths of words, the translator collects these "little kidnaps in the dark," but something essential escapes. "Looking" into the "muteness" of her brother is like looking into the "deep festivity" of the untranslatable poem, its resonance that goes beyond the fragile latticework ("luminous, big, shivering, discandied, unrepentant, barking web") of English synonyms. Late in the poem, the speaker's mother stops writing to Michael after years of vigilant, mono-directional correspondence: "Eventually she began to say he was /dead. How do you know? I said and she said When I / pray for him nothing comes back." The question is, given its apparent disillusionment with the possibility of finding her brother in elegy, why does Carson keep at it? Why does she remain, "looking a long time?" The re-collected fragments remain unmeaning and purposeless, so why continue to collect and meditate on them?

Perhaps one answer lies in the quality of purposelessness itself, the objects' resistance to interest. Disinterest and purposelessness are (returning to Kant), hallmarks of the aesthetic stance and the aesthetic object, respectively. The object of attention cannot help but become aesthetic when placed under a certain kind of sustained and active contemplation. The act of attending is the precondition for any experience of beauty and of the sublime. Removed from contexts of *interest*, recalled fragments enter into a different dynamic of attention, a different mode of "asking." Poetic elegy is repositioned as *historein,* an ongoing inquisitive attention:

> 1.1.   History and elegy are kin. The word "history" comes from an ancient Greek verb ιστωρειν meaning "to ask." One who asks about things - about their dimensions, weight, location, moods, names, holiness, smell - is a historian. But the asking is not idle. It is when you are asking about something that you realize you yourself have survived it, and so you must carry it, or fashion it into a thing that carries itself.

Carson describes this practice as a matter of surviving, of realizing one's survival in the particles gathered from the wreck. As for Forché, a responsibility follows: either to "carry" the wreckage, or to "fashion it into a thing that carries itself." To carry the whole weight of the past is impossible: it is too ungainly and fragmented, and it falls apart when we try to shoulder it. To fashion the past that it can stand on its own might be seen as the grand ambition of Carson's exhaustive practice of collection, composition, and attention. Presenting the remains of the beloved in a light of sustained and inquisitive attention, the book suggests, might be a means of transforming the parts not into the beloved himself but into something else, something that can hold its own—in other words, of *poeisis*. The fragments recalled cannot serve the function of consolation, but they can serve the poetic function of being for their own sake,[51] valued through the process of attending to them, asking about them, gathering them, and forming them into a thing that carries its own burden.

In Search of Lost Selves: Recalling the Subject of Memoir

In its use of polyvocal testimony, and in its active engagement with both the obligation and the pitfalls of a poetics of recollection, Theresa Hak Kyung Cha's *Dictee*,[52] a scrapworked memoir and portrait of Cha's mother's experiences in Busan during the Korean War, shares a vein with Carson's approach to recollection. Indeed, *Dictee* can be seen as a predecessor to *Nox*. Besides historical contemporaneity, there are important resonances between the two works' approaches to elegiac recollection: their multilingualism, their sustained reworking of classical elegies (Catullus and Hesiod), their documentarian use of gathered elements such as uncaptioned photographs and letter fragments as visual rather than linguistic remnants, their restraint in explanatory notation or commentary, their use of white space, and their minimalist and fragmentary poetic styles marked by shared elements such as the single, small-font aphorisms that thread through both works.[53]

Both *Dictee* and *Nox* engage consciously with readerly attention at a variety of levels, but "reading" is not always the required verb. With its long and frankly exhausting fan of white paper, marked as much by faint shadows of the torn edges that composed the scrapbooked original as by text, *Nox* is conscious of the place of the reader, thrown before and into the text's proliferating negative spaces. The receiver mimics the processes of composition—following entries for "ad" and "per" and "vectum," leaping between imagistic and syntactical processing, grazing over overlapping tears and large mute expanses of white, which seem to require a sustained, though contentless, meditation, and evoking an abyssal surrounding of absence surrounding the present text fragments. Anne Anlin Cheng's assessment of *Dictee's* attentional gauntlets highlights its resonance with *Nox*: "[*Dictee*] gives us a confession that does not confess, a dictation without origin, and history without names. . . . The process of memory within the text is difficult and recalcitrant—a double movement of attachment and detachment, retrieval and interment."

Throughout both texts we find the use of uncaptioned and unsituated photographs. Where these nonverbal dimensions run up against the verbal poetry, there is a degree of attentional gear-grinding as we move between very different modes of contemplation. Cheng notes that in *Dictee* the use of images without contextualizing documentation "demonstrates that historical events cannot be recaptured in all their temporal and cultural specificities, except as a record, with all the remembrance and the emptying-out of remembrance. . . . To be given a piece of historical evidence is to be given a history of its silence and revival. What we are given . . . is an afterimage of the event. . . . To see the photo is to hear its call and also witness its loss."[54] The double work of remnants in recalling presence and signaling loss is a strong theme, evident not only in the thematic content of *Dictee* but also in its use of broken but connected syntactical fragments:

> Worn. Marred, recording a past, of previous forms. The present form face to face reveals the missing, the absent. Would-be-said remnant, memory. But the remnant is the whole.
>
> The memory is the entire. The longing in the face of the lost. Maintains the missing. Fixed between the wax and wane indefinite not a sign of progress. All else age, in time. Except. Some are without.[55]

Both works produce an unstable object at the attentional levels of author, speaker, reader, and text. The many sources brought together without much connective tissue force the reader to perform a task of attention, recollection, and piecing together similar to that of the poems' speakers. Kun Jong Lee notes Cha's "revisiting" of Hesiod's *Theogony* as an organizing structure—an act of translation described by Lisa Lowe as "unfaithful to the original,"[56] and by Shelly Sunn Wong as "parodic re-uttering," signaling yet another connection to Carson's irreverence and infidelity as an adapter and translator.[57] Sue Kim argues that Cha's multiple reference points invoke and trouble, as Carson's do, "the boundaries between personal lyric and national epic" and "questions the divide between the moment of the lyric and the developmentalism of the autobiography. . . . to complicate any singular condition of speaking, to demonstrate the inextricability of multiple interrelated voices, and to interrogate the individualism and apparent self-presence of a lyric speaker."[58] Likewise, in its multisource, intertextual engagement with Catullus, Herodotus, and Bashō, *Nox* acknowledges the very long history of addressing the dead in formed language, even as its form speaks to the particular historical inflection of attention to the past at *this* particular time in cultural and intellectual history. Boundaries are called into question, rendered contingent. When genre, form, and function are thus destabilized, the attentional relation between reader, writer, and text becomes all the more tensed and focalized, its own only reference point. By problematizing the act of reading, and by requiring other modes of engagement from the reader (some of which involve being shut out from the text, rather than being drawn in), these texts demand a more valenced understanding of how attention can operate in poetry of mourning: what it can do and the kinds of materials it can involve.

Marjorie Perloff has argued that in *Dictee* "the search for identity, for personhood, is continually subverted."[59] More so than in *Nox*, *Dictee*'s act of recollection is charged with hope, with waiting, that something (albeit perhaps not the "original") will rise from the remnants, as when dead sticks are rubbed together long enough: "You remain dismembered with the belief that / magnolia blooms white even on seemingly dead / branches and you wait."[60] Early in *Dictee,* Cha asks "Why resurrect it all now. From the Past. History, the old wound."[61] Like Charles Reznikoff, for whom recollection's mission lies in an imperative "to name and to name and to name,"[62] she finds her answer in the hope that in extracting and naming the past one might avoid its repetition: "To name it now so as not to repeat history in oblivion. To extract each fragment by each fragment from the word from the image another word another image the reply that will not repeat history in oblivion." The book closes with this affirmation of vigilance as both antonym and antidote to oblivion, a way not of *resurrecting* the past but of building voice and vantage in the present: "Trees adhere / to silence in attendance of the view to come. If to / occur. In vigilance of lifting the immobile silence. Lift / me to the window to the picture image unleash the / ropes tied to weights of stones first the ropes then its / scraping on wood to break stillness as the bells fall / peal follow the sound of ropes holding weight scrap- / ing on wood to break stillness bells fall a peal to sky."[63]

The attentional task of recollection is, in *Nox*, "a room I can never leave, perhaps / dreadful for that. At the same time, a place composed / entirely of entries" (7.1.). This is how, for Carson, elegy can work in the absence of evocation, drawing up not the essence, not the intrinsic form, not the "starry lad," but a negative "latticework," a "web" of entries. An "entry" is a point in a contingent web of other points, an item in a collection. It is also a point of entrance, an aperture that leads somewhere, that leads inside something. Perhaps this notion of "entry" helps us to understand something about recollective attention in Carson, Cha, and even Celan: these texts suggest a space composed by entries, an entry held open for the attention, itself a mode of entry.

Celan wrote in the Meridian Speech, accepting the Büchner Prize: "when the talk concerns art, there's always someone who is present and . . . not really listening."[64] If there is an "enemy" in/of the poem "Engführung,"—and perhaps in elegy more broadly—that enemy has two heads: inattention (on the part of the listener) and silence (on the part of the poem). The poem of recollection emerges from and demands of its reader difficult work. It undertakes difficult terrain. But to "undertake" is to shoulder an action with responsibility, committing not to something external but to the action itself, to the poem. It is this *undertaking* and the "attentiveness" it requires that carves out, even in the absence of God, a space of reverence, a holy place. As Celan writes in "The Meridian," the poem "holds on— . . . the poem holds on at the edge of itself; so as to exist, it ceaselessly calls and hauls itself from its Now-no-more back into its Ever-yet."[65]

CHAPTER V

Imagination

Attention's Poiesis

Coleridge : Wordsworth : Rilke : Burnside

It's hard to think of a term more central to poetic experience than *imagination*. It is taken for granted that poetry involves the invention of images and resonances not available in ordinary experience. Though there has been much discussion over what imagination *is*, there has been little focus, in the expansive discourse on "poetic imagination," on how it *works*. The imaginative function marks the ability of the mind to attend to what is not present in given perception, turning inward and drawing on a combination of stored memory and creative elaboration to generate images and abstractions that take perceived realities beyond themselves, on the one hand, and bring unreal flights closer to real perception, on the other.

Recent studies in cognitive and psychological research have linked imagination to attention—considering imagination as the act of attending to objects and events of mental representation.[1] This research suggests that the processes involved in attending to directly perceived, remembered, and imagined objects are remarkably similar, with only slight variations in the timing and primary locations of brain activity.[2] This is not surprising when one considers the active role of imagination in forming and processing even direct perception, an interdependence long theorized by Aristotle, Kant, and, as we will see, Wallace Stevens.

The link between imagination and attention has not yet been explored in the poetic context and might, I think, help us to get closer to an understanding of how events of imagination take place in poems as well as how they are formed. Rethinking imagination as a mode of attention to objects of mental representation allows for an at once more detailed and more holistic conceptualization of imagination's place among other forms and faculties of experience and provides an opening for the development of a more robust, precise, and flexible lexicon for its description.

Poetry offers a unique setting for the consideration of imaginative attention for several reasons: unlike the visual arts, poetry has a linguistic basis that makes imaginative representation fundamental to poetic production and reception at the most basic level. Additionally, if one considers the crafting and manipulation of forms of attention to be among poetry's primary effects, poetry is then uniquely able to generate the states of attention prerequisite to imaginative experience, and to subsequently direct and shape these mental representations in specific ways. Finally, the density and compression of poetic language (its layering of simultaneous effective dynamics, from semantic content to evocative or symbolic figuration to rhythm, rhyme, and line breaks) yields a particularly rich and temporally concentrated frame for the imaginative experience, meaning that a great deal of imaginative impact can be considered within a tight spatiotemporal frame.

The movements of attention in imagining absent objects, or in forming objects from the raw material of experience, are subtle, ranging from the conjuring of a beloved face or room in absence before the mind's eye (a core element in recollective attention, as we've seen) to the empathic envisioning of another's suffering from a patchwork of memories of hard times, to the generation of wholly fictive objects (the ideal home, an unreal flower, a dialogue between father and son) that draw on the recombination and/or creative elaboration of objects and pieces of objects witnessed in the past. It is this power of repurposing, recycling, and rearrangement of experience that lends much poetry its double allegiance to the fictive, the new and even the revelatory, on one hand, and the recognizably "real" (visualizable, palpable, and believable) on the other. In what follows, I first explore how the reproductive, recombinatory, and inventive dimensions of imagination's attentional dynamics can be seen already at play in Samuel Taylor Coleridge's terminological parsing of imagination and fancy. I then consider the play of reproductive, elaborative, and inventive attention to imagined objects in three poems: William Wordsworth's "Tintern Abbey," Rainer Maria Rilke's "Bowl of Roses," and John Burnside's "A Fair Chase."

Attending to Imagination: Poetry *on* Imagination

Perhaps more than any other genre or mode of poetic attention, imagination holds a place not only as a significant *mode* but also as thematic subject matter and addressee. Because of the vast quantity of poetry addressed directly *to* or *about* imagination, it is important to distinguish this class of thematic explorations from the poetry *of* imagination—poems that cultivate transitive attention to an object of mental representation. In other words, those poems that enact or produce imaginative attention and those that attempt to describe its workings, for which the act of imagination itself is the object of attention.

Because I am interested in the active dynamics of attention to objects of imagination, my primary focus in this section will be on the poetry *of* imagination. However, taking an initial look at how poetic imagination has been directly conceptualized in both prose and verse treatments is helpful for understanding the historical centrality of imagination as a locus of inquiry into the workings of poetic attention under the guises of many other terms. It also highlights the conceptual and terminological instability that has plagued writings on poetic imagination—an instability that suggests the inadequate and ill-fitting nature of existing terms for acts of mental representation and the developing but unarticulated understanding of these acts as particular modes of attending. Thinking of imagination as a modality of poetic attention allows us to theorize its relationship to other elements and genres of poetic experience and develop a more workable lexicon for theorizing how poems mobilize and shape attention to imagined realms.

The role of imagination in poetic attention has long been a subject of critical thinking, from the two forms of imaginative creation in Genesis (*bara*, or *creatio ex nihilo*, from Genesis, and *yatsar*, the forming of the human from earthly dust),[3] to Aristotle's discussion of mental representation of sensory experience in *De Anima*, to John Dryden's depiction of the imagination as that power encompassing all aspects of poetic composition—the creative invention, the flight of fancy in lifting off from mere perception or description, and elocution, the imaginative crafting of evocative expression—to Stevens's discussion of the complex relationship between imagination and "reality," central to his poetics and to his philosophy of secular meaning-making. In the English poetic tradition, imagination has been described as more rooted in sensory experience and perceptual memory, while its cousin concept, fancy, suggests a free movement of creative cognition, the unfettered creative generation of the mind.[4]

Phantasia, Imaginatio, *and Their Lineage: Coleridge and the Need for a New Lexicon*

In its long history as a central concept in thinking about both poetry and attention, the generation of objects of mental representation has held many names, the definitions for which have never been clear cut—from *phantasia* to *imaginatio* to fantasy (or fancy), phantasm, imagination, imaging and even, particularly in the Renaissance, feigning, counterfeiting, and invention.[5] The roots of this terminological chaos trace to the earliest translations and responses to Aristotle and Plato, and, as illustrated by the numerous terms translatable to imagination in the writings of Al-Kindi, Avicenna, and Al-Farabi,[6] are not limited to Western discourses. By the time the Romantics were reigniting the exploration of poetic imagination as an alternative to the dominant epistemology, much had been said about all of these poetic terms, but there was little clarity or consensus on what exactly imagination and its family of terms *meant*, or which kinds of mental representation should be cultivated through poetry.

This lexical uncertainty came to a head in the Romantic period, when more pressure was placed on the significance of these terms. Marking an intersection between recollective, perceptual, creative, and elaborative attention to objects of mental representation, poetic imagination *as philosophical concept* was particularly important during the Romantic period, becoming something of a flagship emblem, a keyword signaling a philosophical departure from the dominant modes of thought, from the distressing cultural and environmental changes taking place in the public sphere: a departure at once *from* the world and *into* the world, at once *from* the mind and *into* the mind. The imaginative act of renewing perception to past and present experience as well as the fanciful world-making of creative invention offered significant pathways toward deepening attentive presence in the natural world and transcending the bare and mindless tendencies associated with ordinary perception of "reality." The marked inward turn of Romanticism has been attributed to the increased attention to imaginative processes to several factors: 1. changes in the environment of literary production and reception (notably the decline of the patron system); 2. the increased availability of and interest in mind-altering substances, particularly opiates; and 3. a shift in worldview in reaction to the mechanistic rationalism of eighteenth-century Lockean epistemology, which contributed to an experience of existential futility and spurred efforts to reimbue experience with human meaning.

The active freedom and inner world-making charge of the imagination offered a pathway out of both rationalism and mechanistic epistemology.[7] During this time we see a rise in theory and philosophy on the creative powers of the imagination as well as artistic works that emerge from or attempt to produce experiences of imaginative transport or *furor poeticus* in the reader.[8] The experience of boundless creative force linked directly to an interest in the organic over the mechanistic—to the unfolding of organic connections and interdependencies, the movement of life, growth, and change, so that the poet (as representative of the human) is positioned as part of this process of generation and unfolding, of a piece with natural ecology and living terrains.

Coleridge and Wordsworth parted ways on the subject of imagination in both theory and practice. The two poets' contributions to the *Lyrical Ballads* were originally conceived to be distinguished by their different engagements with the practice and material of imagination: Wordsworth's poems were proposed to be rooted in the imagination's responsiveness to everyday objects and experiences (placed at the intersection between direct perception, memory, and the potential of both to lift off, via the imagination, into an experience of the sublime), in order to "give the charm of novelty to things of every day, and to excite a feeling analogous to the supernatural, by awakening the mind's attention from the lethargy of custom, and directing it to the loveliness and the wonders of the world before us"; Coleridge's poems were said to be rooted in the wholly fantastical or "supernatural" realm,[9] necessitating a "willing suspension of disbelief for the moment," an act that constitutes "poetic faith." But these two approaches to imaginative attention diverged significantly—too significantly, it proved, to achieve this even split treatment in the project.[10] While Coleridge may have been the clearer of the two, neither poet's writings on imagination and fancy are exactly crystalline.[11] Yet their divergent definitions of the distinction, the motivations guiding their definitions, and their poetic application of both faculties differ significantly enough to produce in *Lyrical Ballads* an unintended demonstration of the instability of these concepts and an illustration of the plurality of forms at play within them. What began as an exploration of two ways of exercising the power of the imagination (as a renewing force in direct perception and memory or as the generation of new and unperceived objects and experiences) revealed a deeper disjuncture between these two modes.

Coleridge writes in the *Biographia Literaria* that "repeated meditations led me first to suspect . . . that fancy and imagination were two distinct and widely different faculties, instead of being, according to the general belief, either two names with one meaning, or at furthest the lower and higher degree of one and the same power."[12] Drawing on the historical synonymization of the two words, beginning with the translation of the Greek *phantasia* to the Latin *imaginatio*, he describes what he sees as a widespread "collective, unconscious good sense working progressively to desynonymize those words original of the same meaning."[13] In addition to underscoring the difference between imagination and fancy, he further subdivides imagination into primary and secondary modes, defining the primary imagination as "the living power and prime agent of all human perception, and as a repetition in the finite mind of the eternal act of creation in the infinite I AM," and the secondary as "an echo of the former, coexisting with the conscious will, yet still as identical with the primary in the *kind* of its agency, and differing only in *degree*, and in the *mode* of its operation. It dissolves, diffuses, dissipates, in order to recreate; or where this process is rendered impossible, yet still, at all events, it struggles to idealize and to unify. It is essentially *vital*, even as all objects (*as* objects) are essentially fixed and dead."[14]

Coleridge's definition of fancy is notable in its divergence from, indeed reversal of, the existing distinction. Fancy, for Coleridge, "has no other counters to play with but fixities and definites." Fancy is "no other than a mode of memory emancipated from the order of time and space; and blended with, and modified by that empirical phenomenon of the will which we express by the word CHOICE." Rooted more in recollection than in creation, fancy "receive[s] all its materials ready made from the law of association."[15] While Coleridge's attempt to distinguish and subcategorize the terms *imagination* and *fancy* may be lacking in exactitude, that very instability suggests an effort to create more specificity and nuance in the conceptualization of acts of mental representation using two ambivalently related terms that were not quite up to the job. His emphasis on the variability of *kinds, degrees,* and *modes* within both imagination and fancy reveals an attempt to parse out different essential modes of mental representation. The conventional terms themselves, whose historical definition in relationship to one another has always been blurry, get in the way of his efforts to describe and give names to the multiplicity of potential dynamics contained within the imaginative faculty itself: that forming and attending to objects of mental representation takes multiple forms, owing to variety of possible constellations of attention's dynamic coordinates. Like attention to objects of direct perception, imaginative attention can be both active, or *endogenous* (a characteristic Coleridge assigns to "imagination"), and passive, or *exogenous* (as in his use of "fancy")—in other words, rooted in an active and deliberate creative agency or rooted in a more passive play of associations and sensory recombinations.

Efforts to historicize poetic imagination have run up against a similar problem: too many terms with too little semantic clarity, too few terms to encompass or distinguish imagination's many modes and permutations. This becomes particularly clear in the scholarly writing on antiquity and even more vexed in studies of imagination in the Middle Ages and Renaissance, during which periods the terms *fantasy, fancy, imagination,* and *invention* were used sometimes in distinction from one another (and even attributed to different regions of the mind in medieval epistemological and psychological models), but more often interchangeably. In medieval and Renaissance poetics, this terminological haziness also made difficult the task of differentiating everyday psychological and pathological uses of imagination (from daydreaming to lunacy to fever dreams to erotic fantasy) from the imaginative work of reading and writing poetry.[16] The Romantic analyses of imagination by Coleridge as well as Keats, Wordsworth, and Shelley inherited this clumsy lexical and conceptual toolbox, yet their attempts to refine an understanding of the functioning of poetic imagination using these terms, by introducing plurality, subdistinctions, and an awareness of modes, forms, and degrees, begin to paint a more detailed picture of the imaginative element of poetic experience as a multiform cognitive and emotional process that can be explored systematically.[17] Moreover, we see in the Romantic analysis an effort to describe the specifically *attentional* properties of imagination's various modes and to name (using a hindering lexicon) the specific *kind* of attending—the kind of inner seeing—that the different *kinds* of imagining exercised.

Despite the quantity of writings *on* imagination in poetic experience, and the number of poems *about* the concept of imagination, what is striking about these works is how little they themselves involve the imaginative faculty. For example, poems like Keats's "Fancy," addressed directly to the semantic object of imagination, have in fact far less to do with the dynamics of the fanciful imagination than those poems that do not directly address but rather *embody* and *produce* imaginative attention, such as "This Living Hand, Now Warm and Capable," "Ode on a Grecian Urn," and "Ode to a Nightingale," to name only a few of the most canonical examples. While there have been some well-loved and well-remembered poems *on* the imagination, and arguably more in quantity than other abstract poetic concepts (in competition with "Love" and "Freedom"), their historic endurance and level of readerly attention is considerably less, perhaps because, in fixing their thematic sights on the word *imagination* (or any of its variants) abstracts what is precisely counter to abstraction. In other words, much of the poetry written *about* imagination, including substantial passages of Wordsworth's *The Prelude*, might have been expressed in prose, whereas "Tintern Abbey," "The Ruined Cottage," and the ascent of Mount Snowden would not have survived such a transposition, poetic imagination being their primary mode and medium, rather than subject matter.[18] This phenomenon holds outside the Romantic context as well (Wheatley's "On Imagination," for example, in comparison with "To a Gentleman and Lady on the Death of the Lady's Brother and Sister, and a Child of the Name *Avis*, Aged One Year") and even in contemporary poetry, not typically addressed to abstract nouns. Denise Levertov's "Everything That Acts Is Actual" moves back and forth between writing *on* and *in* imagination. Lines like "From the tawny light / from the rainy nights / from the imagination finding / itself and more than itself / alone and more than alone" and "We are faithful / only to the imagination. What the / imagination / seizes / as beauty must be truth" place us immediately outside the imaginative realm and into the rationally conceptual, while only in the lines that depart from the *subject* of imagination do we begin to feel its liftoff ("at the bottom of the well where the moon lives, / can you pull me // into December?" and "The flawed moon / acts on the truth, and makes / an autumn of tentative / silences"), yet even here interiority and abstraction prohibit the formation of a vividly somatic image.

Imagination as Mode of Attention: Poetry *of* the Imagination

Because imagination constitutes a significant element in poetry's very *poiētikos,* this turns out to necessitate not the exploration or definition of a generic category so much as the identification of specific moments and modal shifts in diverse poems' engagements with mental representation. While some poetry is more obviously engaged with enlarging the sphere of imaginative potential (Coleridge's "Kubla Kahn," for example, or Stevens's "Of Mere Being," or Yves Bonnefoy's "Du mouvement and de l'immobilité de Douve"), *all* poems, from the highly abstract to the thickly descriptive, from the liturgical to the experimental, engage a mode of imaginative attention to objects of mental representation simply by nature of their fictionality and aestheticism (not to mention the necessarily absent signified of their medium).

A poem's referentiality to objectively "real" objects, scenes, and events begins to step, and invite the reader to step with it, into this mode. This is part of what separates poems as objects of aesthetic experience as opposed to straight reportage. Because referentiality is fundamental to the essential character of poetry, it is important to examine more closely the different methods by which this takes place and the different attentional outcomes of these methods, so that we can break down the undifferentiated (and, as we have seen, often internally contradictory) Ur-category of "poetic imagination" and gain an understanding of its variants, inflections, and coordinates. As we have seen, while the terminological relationship between *imagination* and *fancy* was far from stable, the effort to distinguish between them stemmed from a move to give name to a very real experiential difference between two kinds of mental representation—that rooted in an elaboration and recombination of perception and memory (reproductive or elaborative attention, depending on the degree of recombination) and that rooted more in a purely creative impulse, generating objects of mental representation wholly outside the realm of the real or even the possible (inventive attention).[19]

It is important to note that the distinction between these two modes is not absolute but rather a matter of degrees ranging from perception itself to modes of transitive attention almost wholly severed from connection to sense data, as in transcendental, hallucinatory or ecstatic reveries.[20] Once we begin to recognize and work through the dynamics internal to imaginative attention, a number of terms in literary theory find a more precise configuration within this schema—*fictionality* itself, for example, as well as *verisimilitude* (experience approaching the real-feeling of direct perception in attending to a wholly and richly imagined object), *literary vertigo* (the puncturing of previously immersive attention to an imagined object by a reminder of its unreality), *symbolism* (stressing contemplation's potential to generate visionary moments), *imagism* (with the notion that a pure image might open what Pound called "an intellectual and emotional complex in an instant of time"), and even *metaphor* (in its mobilization of the attention from a plane of representation simulative of direct perception into other planes of representation, significance, and evocation).

In the readings that follow, I consider poems that engage particular modes of attention to imagined objects, focusing on the dynamics of reproductive, elaborative, and inventive attention and their internal variations. I then consider the temporality of imaginative attention, asking how inflections of pastness, presence, or futurity might shape a given poetic act of imagination.

Sensorum Absentium: *Reproduction, Recombination, and Elaboration of Absent Objects*

I place reproductive, recombinatory, and elaborative attention together because, while each represents a slightly different position along the continuum between imagination's recycling of recalled sense data and its capacity for pure invention or *poiesis*, they all constellate within the general category of reproductive or derivative imagination.[21] Imagination's graded continuum between perception and poiesis can be seen already articulated in Aristotle's *De Anima*, which describes the imagination as "different from either perceiving (*aisthesis*) or discursive thinking (*noesis*), though it is not found without sensation, or judgement without it."[22] While later definitions in empirical psychology distilled this intermediary position as the capacity to attend to an absent object, it was Kant who ultimately added to this definition of the faculty the distinction between absent objects of past sense experience and absent object of future or purely potential sense experience[23]—the difference between productive or poietic imagination and reproductive or empirical imagination: "Imagination (*facultas imaginandi*), as the faculty of intuition, even of an object that is not itself present, is either productive, viz., a faculty of original presentation of the latter (*exhibitio originaria*), which consequently precedes experience; or reproductive, a faculty of derivative presentation (*exhibitio derivativa*), which brings back to the mind an empirical intuition one has already had."[24] While Kant is more interested in the significance of productive imagination to the process of transcendental cognition in synthesizing perception and understanding through the essentially creative power of representation (a power "concealed within the depths of our minds which goes unnoticed even while it is being exercised" and "an art concealed within the depths of the human soul"),[25] imagination's capacity to draw on stored memory of sense perception, elaborating and recombining these perceptions to create new objects that are nonetheless rooted in experience and therefore viscerally "real" or "lifelike" is a powerful element in the fictionality of art, including poetry—the ability to generate the new within the frame of lived (and therefore believable and relatable) experience.

The roles of attention in forming and orienting toward objects of the imagination range from conjuring a beloved face in absence before the mind's eye (a core element in recollective attention, as we've seen), to envisioning another's suffering through a patchwork of our own memories of hard times, to generating wholly fictive objects (monsters, paradises, fictional dialogues) that draw on the recombination and/or creative elaboration of objects and pieces of objects witnessed in the past or adapted from received fictions. It is this power of repurposing, recycling, and rearrangement of experience that lends much poetry its double allegiance to the fictive, the new, and even the revelatory, on one hand, and the recognizably "real" (visualizable, palpable, and believable), on the other.

Kant associated reproductive imagination with attention to absent objects from the past insofar as the material of their composition lies in remembered perception. Yet when we draw on reproductive imagination, using stored sense data from past experience, this does not necessarily mean that the imagined object *itself* ever existed in the past. The faculties of elaboration and recombination allow us to draw on both productive and reproductive imagination at the same time, so that some acts of imaginative attention remain closer to the experienced "truth" of past perception, while others enact a generation of the new from material of the past, and still others seem to emerge almost without reference to any previous lived experience.[26] Kant's conceptualization of reproductive imagination can also be applied to poetic descriptions of *present* perceptions: while rooted in present sensory input (assimilated using stored memory frameworks), our perception of objects and events can be charged with imaginative associations.

We see examples of imaginative attention to the past throughout Wordsworth's contributions to *Lyrical Ballads* (notably in "Tintern Abbey") and an example of reproductive imagination at work in an act of present attention in the "Dinggedichte" of Rilke's *Neue Gedichte*. In these poems, we find a renewal of perception through the addition of imagination's "something else"—the movement of the mind's creative impulse in and around the data of direct perception sparking a different kind of attending to both past and present objects, a sensitivity to what is absent even in objects that stand before us. With both poets, we find a change in perception itself (not through conceptual analysis or argument but through language that *enacts* and *embodies* imaginative attention) toward a more active and intuitive (but nonetheless faithful) relationship to what is given to the senses.

"Tintern Abbey": Looking Newly at the Past

At the beginning of "Lines Written a Few Miles above Tintern Abbey," Wordsworth included a note on its composition, saying that he began it in his mind upon leaving Tintern, continuing to form it mentally until reaching Bristol, after a "ramble of four of five days" with his sister.[27] Wordsworth asserts that no part of the poem was written down before he reached Bristol and no changes were made to that initial transcription. However apocryphal, the note suggests that the poem resulted from a single extended act of internal composition, rather than a longer process of externalized drafting and revision. The poem is cast as revelation—not of an idea, but as an object itself. It sprang fully formed out of his being "once again" in a certain place, through the mutually constitutive acts of walking, remembering, and imagining—attending to the creative form-making of the poem itself. The poem's opening lines embody this simultaneity, enjoining recollection and imagination in the act of attending to the ecology of a specific place.

Within the first fourteen lines, the word *again* repeats four times, each time attached to a different verb: "again I hear," "again / Do I behold," "I again repose," and "again I see." Taken together, these acts of multisensory attention and repose encapsulate the mode of the poem as a whole—the act of returning to a physical place, to a site of memory, and to the act of seeing, hearing, and resting there. Harold Bloom has noted that the poem "centers upon the interplay of hearing and seeing. To 'hear' goes back to an Indo-European root (ken) which means to pay attention, watch, observe, beware, guard against, as well as to listen. To 'see' goes back to a root (sekw) that means to perceive."[28] The poem is both process and product of this act of returning in attention, and the repose of the mind forms the opening in which the attentive imagination is freed to move between past and present and future. What the speaker attends here is not only the particular deictic objects ("*these* waters," "*these* steep and lofty cliffs," "*this* dark sycamore," "*these* plots of cottage-ground, *these* orchard tufts"), but the "impression" of these things on the movement of the "picture of the mind." And, in turn, the impression of the imagination on the scene, so that the "deep seclusion" of both place and thoughts reflect one another: "Which on a wild secluded scene impress / Thoughts of a more deep seclusion; and connect / The landscape with the quiet of the sky" (6–8).

The poem emerges, according to Wordsworth's note, directly from a walk in the landscape of his childhood. The lapse of time is crucial. The place has become, in "long absence," a refuge conjured even in physical distance, "in lonely rooms, and mid the din / Of towns and cities" (26–27)—a place of imaginative repose revisited in times of "darkness and amid the many shapes / Of joyless daylight" (52–53). The speaker recalls his experience of the same landscape in the immediacy of "thoughtless youth," immersed in the pure sense experience, its "aching joys" and "dizzy raptures," with an "appetite; a feeling and a love, / That had no need of a remoter charm, / By thought supplied, nor any interest / Unborrowed from the eye;" but "That time is past" (81–84). The experience of total presence so innate to childhood is no longer available, supplanted by losses and gains weathering self and world; nor is the stretch of land recalled as a stored image, like "a landscape to a blind man's eye" (25). Rather, it becomes, in the movement of time, a living place, charged in absence with the "still, sad music of humanity" (92). It is the ability of the "picture of the mind" to "revive" again that makes it inhabitable by the imaginative attention, even in absence.

The activity of the mind in Wordsworth's poem goes beyond mere perception or recollection. Seeing "into the life of things" requires a powerful act of the imagination and a penetrating attentional faculty—not only to see but to see *into*, into the "unremembered," unperceived, and imperceptible. In the "gleams of half-extinguished thought," the seemingly magical connections between self and world, object and object, mind and ethos emerge for an inner attention.

Temporally, Wordsworth's meditations are not limited to either the present of his walk or the past of his childhood, but also reach into futurity:

The picture of the mind revives again:
While here I stand, not only with the sense
Of present pleasure, but with pleasing thoughts
That in this moment there is life and food
For future years.
(62–66)

The entrance of future experience into the speaker's act of attending suggests, darkly, a time when imagination might be the only available path of return to such wilderness—not only because of aging or death but also nature's narrowing presence in the urbanizing world. The imaginative return to the beloved site stretches between childhood and a more inward contemplation of old age, suggesting in the capacity to imagine, to conjure absent objects and places across temporal reaches, a vital resource for the renewal of human experience through a mode of attention that is half perception, half creation: "Of eye and ear, both what they half-create, / And what perceive" (107–8).

The imaginative attention at play in "Tintern Abbey" places us between recollection, direct contemplation, and a projected future act of recollection. This complex of temporalities surrounding a single walk points to the free movement of the imagination within a space held open by a walk and a poem. Distant temporal and physical experience come into "harmony" within a single attentive frame. The imagination could not strike so vividly were it not bound to the visceral and the particularity of direct perception (past and present). Perception, in turn, gains significance and depth from the movement of the attention beyond sense-data. In this way, "We see into the life of things" (49). The revelatory quality of this mode of seeing hinges precisely on its attunement to the imperceptible.

Dinggedichte: *Looking Newly at the Present*

In Rilke's collection *Neue Gedichte* (1907), we find an exploration of a related mode of attending to objects, this time rooted exclusively in present perception. The objects of meditation in "Dinggedichte" stand before the speaker and, in formed language, before the reader. They exist in the present tense of Wordsworth's walk, but without reference to a return, without reconjuring the past or projecting into the future. They seem to inhabit a kind of infinite present in which the only movement is that of attention in and through the objects themselves. Yet Rilke's object-focused poems draw out, like Wordsworth's, not only the particularities of the physical object itself but the inner reaches of both attending mind and attended form. These two interiorities coconstitute in the formal patterns of the poem. The imagination comes into play where the attention lifts away from perception, or seems to plunge beneath its surface, so that what was an inanimate object springs to life. Rilke's poem "Die Rosenschale" ("The Bowl of Roses") both enacts and produces this mode of attention charged with imagination in the context of present perception.

"Die Rosenschale" opens, unexpectedly, with a series of violent images of "caged anger" flaring: "Zornige sahst du flackern," "zwei Knaben / zu einem Etwas sich zusammenballen," "rasende Pferde, die zusammenbrachen, / den Blick wegwerfend, bläkend das Gebiß / als schälte sich der Schädel aus dem Maule" ("two boys / roll themselves up into a knot / of pure hatred, writhing on the ground / like an animal attacked by bees," and "careening horses crashing down, flinging their wild eyes away, baring their teeth / as if their skulls were peeling through their mouths"). These brutal spectacles capture the attention exogenously. Just as suddenly, the poem turns, in dramatic contrast, to quiet, endogenous contemplation: "Nun aber weißt du, wie sich das vergißt: / denn vor dir steht die volle Rosenschale" ("But now you see how such things vanish: / for before you stands the full bowl of roses.")[29]

Rilke's turn, suddenly, to an endogenous mode of contemplation brings both the thematic focus and the reader's attentiveness to the immediate here—*Dastehn*. The violence of recollection is hushed in the simple standing of the bowl, the roses, "wholly filled / with that utmost of being and bending, / of offering up, beyond power to give, of presence." What is offered in this presence, this "Dastehn?" "Das unser sein mag: Äußerstes auch uns." That it might be our utmost as well. The roses model and extend the possibility of "Lautloses Leben," ("Life lived in quietness"), of "Aufgehn ohne Ende,"—endless opening—through the simplest of directives: *Sieh. Look*—not at, but at how the roses move, and how the mind moves with them, and how the attention, resting in presence, brings to the fore a wealth of layered connections. Each rose unfolds in layers that connect at the center. The speaker asks "ist irgend etwas uns bekannt wie dies?" ("Do we know anything like this?"), and the poem, the form itself a layered unfolding, holds the question open: "Und dann wie dies." The repetition and elaboration of "Und dann wie dies . . . Und dies . . . Und dies vor allem . . . und . . . und . . . und . . ."—this and, and, and—opens nested layers of perception and association, formally enacts this unfolding process of mental representation, figured by the unfolding rose petals and the bouquet's collected variations on a single form.

We are lured deeper into particularity so that the composed roses become stable enough to support the imagination's movement in and around them, following the speaker's associative lens from this white one to the blush to the yellow, asking "Was können sie nicht sein" ("What can't they be?") as lemon-yellow petals suggest the juice of the fruit, and as one bruised bud suggests "the bitter aftertaste of lilac." And, moving further into imaginative resonance, the cambric one becomes "a dress / in which the shift still clings, soft and breath warm, both of them cast off together in the morning shadows" of a woodland pool" ("Und die batistene, its sie kein Kleid, / in dem noch zart und atemwarm das Hemd streckt, / mit dem zugleich es abgeworfen wurde / im Morgenschatten an dem alten Waldbad?"). We move from detailed description into a freer movement of imaginative association in which things become transparencies, revealing shapes behind them.

In her book on the dynamics of imagining in literature, *Dreaming by the Book*, Elaine Scarry makes the case that flowers are the ideal object for mental representation, or what she calls the "representative of the imagination," because of the "ease" of imagining them. She attributes this to the relationship between our own perceptive equipment and the physical characteristics of flowers themselves: "*their* size and the size of our heads, *their* shape and the shape of our eyes, *their* intense localization and the radius of our compositional powers."[30] It is true that the single rose seems to just fit the frame of our imaginative compositional lens: small enough for its whole to be contained at most comfortable degree of zoom, yet large enough to be visualized at a high degree of focalization. Scarry argues that these specific features of the flower "brings the work of imagining into the compass of our compositional powers." Following the writer's mental cues as we build the flower out of nothing (or out of a lifetime's stored memories of flowers) feels natural, requiring no invention of details we would not be able to perceive in direct observation. In any act of attention, but particularly in attending to objects of pure mental representation, as the reader does when imagining roses, there is a ratio between what Scarry calls *extension* (or what I describe earlier as *concentration*) and *intensity* (internal complexity at a high perceptual resolution). When one increases, another decreases. Because of their size and structural complexity, flowers allow for a high degree of both—a balance of the axes.

Given Rilke's obsession with the relationship between perception and imagination, it is not surprising that he devoted so many of his *Dinggedichte* to blossoms—roses, blue and pink hydrangeas, opium poppies, Persian heliotrope. But Rilke also noticed something vital about the formal kinship between imagination and flowers: what makes the *shape* of a bloom open so easily to the inner eye has less to do with its similarity to the "shape of our heads," which bears little significance for the act of imagining, than with the unfolding layers that constitute the form of imagination itself. Rilke not only described this form but crafted it in the unfolding stanzas of "Die Rosenschale." "A feeling arises, / because flower petals touch flower petals . . . that one opens like an eye, and beneath it lie eyelid after eyelid, / all tightly closed, as if through tenfold sleep / they might curb an inner power of sight" ("daß ein Gefühl entsteht, / weil Blütenblätter Blütenblätter rühren? / Und dies: daß eins sich aufschlägt wie ein Lid, / und drunter liegen lauter Augenlider, / geschlossene, als ob sie, zehnfach schlafend, / zu dämpfen hätten eines Innern Sehkraft"). Each circle of petals reveals an inner layer, mirroring the layered "handful of inwardness" in the process of attending, imagining, creating.

Gorgeous Nonsense and Yielding to the Unreal:
Attention in the Movement of Invention

While reproductive imagination entails an elaboration or recombination of past experience in composing the object of attention, productive or inventive imagination comes closer to the pure creative generation of its object. This mode has borne many names and assumed many generic and experiential guises: fantasy, fairy tale, hallucination, dream, myth, legend, prophesy, ecstatic vision. Because all of the senses involved in mental representation rely on some reference to sensed experience, this distinction is one of degrees: inventive experience, while drawing its perceptual legibility from stored memory, composes its thematic and structural content from the capability to create, in an intensely inward act of attention, newly imagined objects. In the readings that follow I will consider the specific dynamics of how we attend to objects generated by the inventive imagination. While the legibility and visualizability of these poems' mental representations draw from stored perceptual memory, the objects of mental representation themselves are far removed from the objects of actual experience, requiring a greater extension of the inventive faculty and greater movement (on the parts of both writer and reader) beyond the known.

In thinking of poems far to this end of the continuum between productive and reproductive imagination, some canonical examples come first to mind: Dante's *Inferno,* Coleridge's "Kubla Khan," Lewis Carroll's "Jabberwocky," Anne Carson's *Autobiography of Red*. All these works draw heavily on our capacity to compose, in a powerful attentional move, an intricate mental representation that withstands—indeed flourishes under—sustained focus, elaboration, and manipulation, all without reference to any past or present lived experience. This is the stuff of dreams, hallucinations, but also of fairy tales and childhood play, an imaginative realm capable of limitless particularity, detail. Each imagined object, each particularization of that object, enables and activates the invention of the next object, the next plane of detail, the widening of the unreal world that this actively creative attention at once constructs and contemplates.

Because this mode of attention is rooted in the unfolding process of constructing the object to which it refers, and because of the lack of (or limited) reference to recalled objects of past perception, the temporality of inventive imagination is strongly situated in the present tense, *even when narrated in the past*. The past inflection of inventive imagination is an element of the object itself, such that pastness becomes an imaginative quality. In other words, situating fantastical objects and events in the past tense, in the dynamics of legends, fairy tales, and myths, as in the case of "Kubla Khan," lends a pseudo-reality to the act of imagining. The mythic past allows as much imaginative elbow room, or as much pure potentiality, as the prophetic future. Yet, because of the lack of "real" biographical or historical referentiality, the temporal emphasis of the attentive-inventive act is still located in the present tense. The degree of imaginability—meaning to what extent a poem enables its reader to fully *attend*, with a feeling of sensory immediacy and nuance, to a purely imagined object—depends in large part on the generation of this quality of presence. In many ways, because of the lack of referential footholds in recalled experience, inventive attention requires an even greater degree of connection to the reality of the senses.

Without fleshing out the sensory dimensionality of an imagined object and its world, invented representations can have a certain poverty of presence in comparison to other modes of (even imaginative) attention more closely tied to an experience of objective reality. Without roots in the reproduction or elaboration of past experience, inventive attention must work harder to locate the reader in recognizable sense-data in order to be fully present to the inner simulative senses and to the full dimensionality of the mind—beyond the mere invention of a new object, the weight and depth of that object's resonance with the experiential weight and depth of reality. This is, in part, what distinguishes the imaginative effectiveness of "Kubla Kahn" and the *Inferno*: Coleridge's invented objects (the result of hallucinatory intoxication rather than intentional creation) never obtain weight and richness beyond the novelty and strangeness of the fantasy they evoke,[31] while even a small passage of Dante can conjure unreal scenes so fully as to strike and penetrate the inner life of the attender. While decidedly not of this world, Dante's imagined world obtains a reality of its own. Stevens highlighted a similar distinction in his critique of surrealism, which he saw to be interested in merely novelistic invention, rather than *discovery*—without, that is, a sense of the *reality* of imagined objects: "To make a clam play an accordion is to invent not to discover. The observation of the unconscious, so far as it can be observed, should reveal things of which we have previously been unconscious, not the familiar things of which we have been conscious plus imagination."[32]

"Unreal things have a reality of their own," writes Stevens, "in poetry as elsewhere. We do not hesitate, in poetry, to yield ourselves to the unreal, when it is possible to yield ourselves."[33] He is responding, here, to Plato's figure of the soul as charioteer driving his chariot across the sky and working through the paradoxical simultaneity of two opposed feelings about the figure: a feeling of its imaginative power, on the one hand—the immediacy with which one begins to place oneself in the position of the sky-traversing charioteer—and the brevity and limitedness of this power, on the other—the speed with which one is thrown out of imagining by the awareness of unreality, at which point the vividness of participation in the imaginative figuration fades. Returned to reality by the unreality of the figure, one is repositioned as "observer" and intellectual comprehender of the figure, rather than as "participant."[34] Stevens is interested in the need *as well as the limitations* of the imagination in modern experience, the historical or cognitive or metaphysical shift that made "yielding" to the unreal easier for Plato than it is for us: "The existence of the soul, of charioteers and chariots and of winged horses is immaterial. . . . Certainly a charioteer driving his chariot across the whole heaven . . . was unreal for Plato as he is for us. Plato, however, could yield himself, was free to yield himself, to this gorgeous nonsense. We cannot yield ourselves. We are not free to yield ourselves."[35] For Stevens, our inability to yield, to follow Plato's course into the sky, results from a weakened relationship between imagination and reality. Imagination and the full perception of reality are mutually dependent. In order for perception to be alive to the real, it must be rooted in the imagination, yet in order for the imagination to carry perception with it, it must be rooted in the real: "The imagination loses its vitality as it ceases to adhere to what is real. When it adheres to the unreal and intensifies what is unreal, while its first effect may be extraordinary, that effect is the maximum effect that it will ever have."[36] And yet the creative imagination was, as we see throughout his prose writings and demonstrated throughout his poetic oeuvre, vital (in the strong sense) to Stevens's vision of the task of poetry. Its work on the mind and its world-changing potential lay precisely at the meeting point of perception and imagination, to the extent that, at such a point, the two became utterly of a piece, as "silk dresses" are of a piece with "worms."[37] This interdependence and interrelation of direct perception (or "reality") and imagination was central to the identity of poetry itself, which could not survive exclusively in either mode: "Poetry is not the same thing as the imagination taken alone. Nothing is itself taken alone. Things are because of interrelations and interactions."[38] For just as "the imagination is the romantic," and "Romanticism is to poetry what the decorative is to painting," "Realism is a corruption of reality." And while "an [entirely] imaginary world is entirely without interest," poetry's "renovation" and "subtilizing" of experience can only be achieved by acknowledging and cultivating imagination's place in perception itself,[39] as a way of cultivating humanity. The "vitality" of human experience lay, for Stevens, not in sensual perception alone but in the act of "touch[ing] with the imagination in respect to reality."⁴⁰

The Blessèd Kill: Tracking the Unknown in Burnside

> What we were after there, in the horn and vellum
> shadows of the wood behind our house,
> I never knew.⁴¹

The sense of something "almost there" marks an intersection between perception and imagination—at the boundary of the known, a world of potentiality opens. In Scottish poet John Burnside's "The Fair Chase," from his 2011 collection *Black Cat Bone*, a hunt through backwoods terrain is charged with mystery by the presence of a beast—real or imagined, we never know. The setting of the poem is seemingly ordinary—a young man out hunting with others in familiar woods. Yet from the first line the poem focuses not on the known but on the unknown. The unidentified object of "what we were after" remains cloaked in shadows, and the hunt assumes mythic scope as the imagination—presented not as a fictionalizing or inventive play but as a very *real* life-force—throws to the fore reality's shadow side:

> At times, it felt like bliss, at times
> a run of musk and terror, gone to ground
> in broken wisps of ceresin and chrism,
>
> but now and then, the beast was almost there,
> glimpsed through the trees,
> or lifting its head from a stream
>
> to make us out . . .⁴²

Just enough perceptual certainty surrounds the beast to justify the hunt, and to develop movement, attitude, a dance of relation thwarted by imperceptibility. The hunter's vigilant gaze reaches a limit at the beast, whose presence is at once certain and ungraspable. The beast "lingers," and, "as if it wanted me to play," "shifted away through the trees."⁴³ When the speaker pauses for breath, the beast seems to pause, then shifts and flickers away. The reader also follows, lured as much by the almost-sensed particulars of the beast as by its shape-shifting and evasiveness:

> a phantom thing, betrayed by smoke or rain,
>
> or glimpsed through a gap in the fog, not quite discerned,
> not quite discernible: a mouth, then eyes,
> then nothing.[44]

We cannot "see it clear." And yet "by instinct" we also sense that it is "almost there," just beyond the frame of the imaginable. The attention of both speaker and poem locks in on an object that is thus both present and absent, real and unreal, perceived and imagined. Rooted in the material ground of direct perception, it is forced to push beyond perception into imaginative questioning. The hunt is haunted precisely by the boundary of the known: "what we were after"—the "something"—never reveals itself. No sooner is it present than it nothings.

In this hunt, and in this poem, a certain leap of faith is required, tracking a half-believed presence farther into wilderness, out of the woods near home and into unfamiliar terrain, where lostness compounds the defamiliarization and the horizon of the possible is pushed outside the zone of empirical reason. In this exposure to the unknown, the speaker, once an ordinary boy with his father's gun, "lost in a hand-me-down greatcoat,"[45] undergoes a mythic transformation: from "last among equals—flycatcher, dreamer, dolt, / companion to no one, / alone in a havoc of signs," to "working by scent // and instinct, finally / true to myself, / with the body and mind of a hunter."[46] Grace comes only after a relentless and exhaustive pursuit of something whose existence cannot be proved: "lucky, singled out / by death and beauty for the blesséd kill." It is stepping into the unknown, keeping the attention fixed to what can't be seen but only sensed, scented, by instinct, that transforms speaker into sacred hunter, hero—and the same step that charges an ordinary memory with archetypical power and takes the language of childhood memory into the realm of the poetic, charged by its openness to attend beyond the given, without guarantee of what, if anything, might emerge.

The crafting of attention in the poem, and the periods of intentional, focused concentration required to enter and engage, can be seen as the long trudge through pathless darkness, the hours of wait, the cold and unpromising terrain. No promises offered, only potentiality, only glimpsed movements, moments of resonance and rhythm that suggest a "something there" behind the opaque bramble of lines: something alive, something wild and moving, but whose presence is only sensed dimly or betrayed by traces, patterns that unsettle the transparency or familiarity of the language. At times, after settling into focused reading, a living image or presence unfolds suddenly, fully, exposed as in a clearing of full sunlight. Other times it might never come, and the tension of the poem is the ongoingness of the hunt, the wait, the craning senses' attention peering into darkness: only "an inkwash and blear in the grass": "no body, no warmth, no aftermath, nothing to prize."[47] This lack of guarantee in the emergence or liftoff of imaginative attention is part of what animates and rarefies experiences of vision when they come.

The movement of imagination takes place in modes of attention from distraction to daydreaming to contemplation, in contexts of joy and repose, but also in the darkest hours of human experience and under the harshest and most inhumane contexts. This is apparent when one considers the vast array of poetries that emerge under conditions of fear, exile, imprisonment, and war. Yet the "grace" of a poem's imaginative happenings is never guaranteed. They are events—flights that cannot be willed into being. Indeed, imagination stands as perhaps the most essential movement of freedom in human being—welling even in limit conditions, in the absence of other freedoms. Yet it is a freedom that exceeds even the reach of our own will to control or confine.

This is a vital component in understanding the dual nature of imaginative attention as both act and event: there is an intentional, willed action on the part of the reading or writing subject that both enables and responds to a creative event beyond of the horizon of subjective agency. The "eventfulness" of imaginative movements lies in the fact that they emerge in a field outside, though often enabled or safeguarded by, the realm of willed action. The event of imagination rises up, changes the field of thought, and becomes an object of memory in its own right. Moreover, despite the seemingly immaterial nature of imagined objects, the imaginative event is experientially corporeal, rooted in the sensing body, a physical response to unpredictably resonant points in formed language and silences.

Jean-Paul Sartre describes his attempts to deliberately exercise the imagination by imagining absent friends' faces, and fails. Yet, other times, without any effort beyond the "activation energy" provided by coming into attention, a face emerges, a scene emerges, a whole world emerges in brilliant presence and vitality. Imagination is rebellious, both in form and in arrival. There is no promise that the same poem will generate the same imaginative experience, or any imaginative experience, every time. Unlike deliberate efforts at "mental representation" in psychological experiments or in everyday life, the poem introduces a field of imaginative triggers outside of our control or invention, each formal element a carefully placed potential activation site for the imagination. The kind of imagination made possible in poetic representation differs from straight semantic representation in this way: The fact that words have meanings means that any instance of language depends on an imaginative bridge between sign and signified. But poetic imagination enables more than simple mental representation of this kind: it makes possible a coming to life that develops beyond the sphere of the words on the page. The few words present in a single line serve as potential triggers for something larger than what they represent—a leap or liftoff, an event that takes on life, layers, dimensionality, and movement. It is not surprising that the lexicon of imagination is tied to "flights."

Experientially, poetic attention can be seen as the condition of openness that makes imagination possible. It is also the act of following imagination's formations, following the movement of the mind's eye as it opens. In this way, imaginative attention relies on both endogenous and exogenous modes: an openness that is wholly self-directed sets a frame of potential imaginative experience, which, if it takes place, then captures the attention exogenously, as would an object or event unfolding in direct perception to external reality. The flowering in the activating space of the poem is at once an event that possesses an indomitable life and willfulness of its own and a phenomenon that can be, and must be, at least partially produced, crafted, and directed by the poet's formed language. Attention makes possible imagination's emergence—framed by the structured sounds and silences, the rhythms and images of the poem, and driven by the sense of "something there" worth the labor of vigilant concentration. This is the limit of its agency over imagination. In maintaining the potentiality of imagination's liftoff, it can be seen as marking the horizon of the will—half of attention (endogenous) resting within the bounds of intentionality, the other half (exogenous) beyond it. Attending is the most we can do to demarcate a space of openness within the self for poetic imagination, from visualization to revelation, to take place, when and if it does.

PART TWO

Objectless Awareness

CHAPTER VI

Modes of Intransitive Attention

veillant
    doutant
        roulant
            brillant et méditant
—STÉPHANE MALLARMÉ, *UN COUP DE DÉS*

So far we have explored forms of *transitive* attention, modes of attention to an object. As we saw in part 1, this focalization may assume a range of selectivities and concentrations, but always oriented toward an object, whether present or absent, real or imagined, narrow or expansive, bounded or fragmented. Yet not all modes of attending work in this way. Some kinds of attention are not directed toward a focalized object and are instead constituted by a particular state of attention, without a central figure or "content." I house these modes within the category of *intransitive* attention.

Intransitive forms of attention are in many ways more challenging to conceptualize, yet they produce important (and importantly different) cognitive, emotional, and even spiritual effects. Intransitive attention may take the form of a widening of the lens to include background as well as figure (in other words, they are produced by an extreme *deconcentration* of the attention) or may be the result of an emptying out of the attentional field, sometimes with the aid of what I will define as an *indirect object*. We can see this dynamic in operation in various meditative practices, including a repeated word or mantra or a focus on breath in which the inhalation and exhalation act not as objects of direct attention but rather as indirect objects whose repetition offers a negative framework for the emptying of awareness of sense-data.

In the sections that follow, I offer a phenomenology of the dynamics of intransitive attention, exploring how poetic attention functions when, aside from the formal object that is the poem itself, there is not a central object of contemplation. Having explored these dynamics in detail, I then identify several applied modes, including vigilance, resignation, idleness, and boredom. These are, in turn, the subjects of the chapters in part 2. Because these macrocategories contain nuance and variation, in each case I constellate several close readings together as a way of unfolding the complexity of each mode.

Because transitive attention dominates everyday usage of the word "attention," particularly (and increasingly) in the post-digital industrialized context, this mode has become almost synonymous with attention itself in current discourse. We exercise transitive attention in a variety of situations, most often with a very narrow and productivity-driven intentional focus—the kind of focus required by driving, texting, web surfing, focused conversation, and most forms of intellectual work and problem solving. Yet this kind of attention, while a powerful engine for certain kinds of thinking, is only one of the forms of attention available to us. There are a variety of attentional modes that do not center on a subject-object relationship of desire, problem-solving, remembrance, or direct perception, but are instead rooted in more open and objectless awareness. We glimpse these kinds of objectless attention in experiences as diverse as meditation and prayer, daydreaming, relaxation, or "just being," in which we are simply present without locking our attention in on a given object, idea, or problem. At the extreme of disengaged intransitivity, we find boredom, a state in which the attention finds no foothold for engagement, yielding an experiential void.

Dynamics of Intransitive Attention

As with transitive attention, intransitive attention can be understood through a constellation of dynamic coordinates, the variable elements that shape a particular mode. I have identified and named five of these coordinates. These include *intentionality*, or whether the state is active or passive (whether the meditative state is achieved through deliberate effort, as in meditation, or entered unintentionally or without agency, as in arrest or distraction); the presence or absence of an *indirect object* (a tool or mantra that is used for the purposes of achieving meditation or an object attended idly and without centrality, as in distraction, the attentive equivalent of doodling); *scope* (inclusivity or exclusivity) of the attentive state in relationship to the field of sensory and mental data; *temporal inflection* (whether the state is inflected with pastness or futurity or is rather an experience of suspended present, a moment cut off from its temporal fabric); and, finally, *subjectivity*, which refers in this case to whether in the act of attention the subject-consciousness is magnified or reduced (decreation or kenosis).

Intransitive Intentionality—Passive Activity, Active Passivity

Like transitive attention, intransitive modes of attention are inflected by the intentionality of the attending subject. Forms of objectless attention can be endogenous, intentionally cultivated and practiced, as in practices of meditation, prayer, or deliberate vigilance, or they can come upon the subject exogenously, as in such unintentional, unwilled states such as daydreaming, boredom, objectless anxiety, or ecstasy. Yet, more so than transitive attention, intransitive attention is difficult to intentionally produce. It is an easy and familiar thing to turn our attention *to* something. Focus on your hand. Think of a pear. Recall your first kiss. It is not so easy to attend, deliberately, to *nothing*. This is because the subject itself, with its comfort zone in sensory perception and ongoing content-filled thought, gets in the way. The active, endogenous effort to achieve intransitive states of awareness can be self-defeating as the ambition, the objective, becomes the object or becomes an object of imagination and desire. The centrality and attentional salience of both subject and object are bolstered in this striving. Yet some of the modes of intransitive attention are, from various spiritual, psychological, and physiological standpoints, desirable—thought to be conducive to experiences beyond the typical experience of self and world (relaxation and stress relief, spiritual and emotional receptivity, and even deepening the capacity for focus, including transitive focus) by making the attentional mechanisms less reactive, tight, and rigid. Because it is difficult to intentionally shift into intransitive states at will, this capability must be practiced, though cognitive exercises, rituals, and, in poetry, the use of repetition, semantic ambiguity, and constraints. Because of the interfering nature of *striving* for intransitive attention, these practices are often aimed at letting go—of effort, of self, of objective, of ambition—primarily so as to allow the subject to slip toward immersion in objectlessness awareness. Active or endogenous modes of intransitive attention are thus unique in that they are formed around this seeming antithetical move—intentional unintentionality or active passivity. To attend to nothing (or, conversely, to attend to the whole field of perception without focalizing on a single figure) requires an act of letting go, a deliberate and intentional passivity that does not latch on to either content or objective, as doing so would result in fixation.

This practical tension inherent to intentional intransitivity produces several poetic modes—poems that *embody* a state of intransitive attention, poems with the potential to *produce* such a state in the reader, poems that in themselves *enact* a kind of practice toward the cultivation of such a state (more on this in the discussion of indirect objects), and poems that are in fact *about* intransitive attention rather than *of* it. We see this final class in poems that describe or discursively propose a specific kind of awareness as well as in poems that invoke something outside themselves to bring this about. In the first case, attention itself is a semantic object (not practiced but described); in the second, it is a semantic object of desire. This latter case falls more to the side of the intransitive simply by virtue of the formal position of the poem in the passive voice, addressed to an unknown or unknowable force, so that while the ultimate state may be longed for (as a transitive object), the *mode* of passivity and waiting creates in itself a dynamic of intransitive suspension and letting go. In other words, a poetics of *entreaty* can sometimes produce a double dynamic in which transitive, desirous attention turns into intransitive vigilance. The acts of desiring and of asking are transitive, yet their respective objects in these cases are ultimately unknowable, ungraspable, and unguaranteed. We see this intentional passivity of entreaty in devotional poetry such as that of fifteenth-century Rajasthani mystic Mirabai, whose devotional (*bhakti*) poems are often positioned in the form of a plea for the overtaking of the self by the divine ("Dark One, take this girl as your servant. / Then cut the cords and set her free")[1] or in secular calls for unselfing, a darker example of which would be Lady Macbeth's famous plea: "Come, you spirits / That tend on mortal thoughts, unsex me here, / And fill me from the crown to the toe top-full / Of direst cruelty."[2]

In poems that exhibit a practice toward intransitive attention, we find another combination of endogenous and exogenous, transitive and intransitive attentions. The practice of attention is deliberate, an intentional act set in the active voice. Yet the effect of the practice is the giving over of intentionality and choice to the practice itself, to its carrying out. While a given outcome (the stilling of the mind, the cultivation of spiritual receptivity, etc.) may guide the originating intentionality, process overtakes outcome as a point of focus, and, with repetition, process itself recedes into the attentional background, leaving only empty or open focus, depending on the nature of the practice and its cognitive, psychological, or spiritual aims. The focus of practice is, then, not the content of the practice itself but rather the space of potentiality it opens up—the unguaranteed outcome of a given practice, paired with the negative space held open by its formal structure, enacts a wager of sorts in which the objective content of attention is replaced by potentiality and the suspension of content. The intentionality involved in this process begins in an endogenous mode, then grows increasingly exogenous as agency is given over to the external formal constraints of the practice itself. What began as an intentional act of focalization evolves into a passive mode of *being acted upon*. The "practice" might be a deliberate way of looking or being, a poetic or linguistic constraint imposed for the purposes of acting on the attention or limiting thought, or a more intricate procedural method that interferes with the role of intentionality (readerly and writerly) at a more fundamental level, as with in the work of Oulipo (Ouvroir de littérature potentielle) and other practitioners of procedural, constraint-based poetics,[3] as we will see in the following section on indirect objects and the attentionality of praxis.[4] This particular mode of intentional practice is closely tied to the function of indirect objects of attention, which I address in the following section.

Intransitive modes of attention are not only the object of desire or the result of willed practice and labor; some forms of intransitive attention come upon the subject unintentionally. These unintentional modes might be experienced as positive or negative, desired or undesired, might develop gradually in the mind or overtake the subject suddenly and unforeseen. What characterizes them is the experience of unwilled emptying or opening of the attentional field, without deliberate intent or effort. Examples of these modes of unintentional intransitivity range from boredom and "zoning out" to objectless anxiety, ecstatic reverie, and simply being, without an object of focus or aim.

Indirect Objects—Meditation, Constraint, and Means of Praxis

To speak of "objectless attention" in the context of poetic experience may seem like an impossible contradiction. Poems, being composed of language, a medium of representation, are full of semantic objects. Moreover, they are, as we saw in part 1, objects themselves. Both reading and listening to poetry entail, at a basic level, an inherently transitive mode of attention. Yet some poems produce a very different experience *out of* this transitivity. Sometimes the object of attention serves as a frame and foothold that allows the attention to open into a wider awareness or that allows the mind to still, to grow experientially empty. I define this as the *indirect object*: an object or theme of focus that serves to empty the attention of content without ascending to the level of focal object ultimately receding from attentive consciousness through repetition or duration. When an object of attention is focalized not with an active interest toward the object, but rather as a frame for awareness itself, brought into the foreground lightly and marginally—just enough to release awareness from other content, to bring the attending mind to stillness around its structure, to minimize or desensationalize surrounding perceptive input, or to provide a space for attentional letting be, the object forms a house for the awareness, without becoming the direct object of attention (that is, *without becoming the subject of a narrative* and *without drawing interest or emotionally inflected focus to itself*). Unlike the direct object, the formal and semantic properties of the indirect object are not actively grasped or probed from an interested or emotionally driven angle—perceived indirectly and without being singled out by a particular interest or investment, the object's presence and form can act as a catalyst for the experience of contentless awareness, intentionally or otherwise. In some cases, it does so by offering a skeleton for a negative space of otherwise contentless awareness; in others it fills the attention to such an extent that awareness itself is immersed *within* it. When the figure fills the entire attentional field, there is no longer a focalization of figure against ground: what was figure becomes ground, and, when it is not replaced by another figure (for example, a detail), an experience of nonfocalized intransitivity emerges within the newly defined field.

When the achievement of objectless awareness is purposeful, as in meditative practices, we can best understand the function of the indirect object of attention as a *tool*, whose sole purpose is the freeing of attention from other objects *and ultimately, perhaps, from itself.* While some poetries of active-intentional praxis are rooted in specific spiritual, religious, and psychological objectives, others stem merely from a cultivation of awareness and attentional stillness, an experiential end in itself. When the perception of objects as indirect objects of otherwise contentless attention is *un*intentional, purposeless and unwilled, we find states such as boredom, depression, and "absent-mindedness" in which things are perceived as *there,* but never attain centrality, and what is centrally experienced is an attentive absence: not a lack of attention, but an attention in which all objects are nonfocalized or marginal, lacking in attentional adhesiveness, and somehow lacking *presence for the subject.*

Objectless Scope: Inclusivity and Exclusivity

Like transitive attention, intransitive attention also contains a variable of selectivity or scope. Given the absence of a direct object of attention, the perceived scope of intransitive attention is a result of the particular mode of awareness and the process that brings the objectless state about—whether it is a product of radically full (deconcentrated) attention or radically empty attention stemming either from awareness of negativity, or absence, or from the elimination of attentional content. In the former, inclusive variety, the degree of selectivity is very low; the attention takes in so much content that its lens fills completely, to the extent that there is no distinction between figure and ground. The figure or figures spread to the horizons of awareness, so that, rather than zeroing in on any part, awareness is spread evenly over the entire field, generalized to the point of nonfocalization. Paradoxically, the total fullness of object-consciousness results, then, in a state of objectlessness (where the "object" is defined as a focalized theme attended to in contact to a nonfocalized ground). In the exclusive mode of intransitivity, object-consciousness is reduced—either by attention to absence, negative space, or nothingness, or by whittling attention down to a thin foothold of content, as in the use of an indirect object. In contrast to the defocalized fullness of inclusive awareness, exclusivity is thus often the result of a hyperfocalization down to a single point (then nothing); exclusive intransitivity is attention that is *emptied* of content. While both the inclusive and exclusive modes might begin in a state of transitive "awareness *of*" or "attention *to*," by either widening or narrowing focus past the point of possible focalization, the *of* or *to* is ultimately canceled out, leaving only awareness, pure attending.

In part 1, we considered Whitman's long lines and multitudinous foci as examples of selectivity's low end—his poetic form an embodiment of attention's deconcentration. Yet some of Whitman's poems test the very limits of focalization itself and ultimately exceed it. In other words, they cross a threshold at which attention moves beyond the scope of the transitive and into the intransitive—beyond the contemplation of a deconcentrated object or beyond the contemplation of multiple objects to embody an experience of open, inclusive, panoramic receptivity, a mode of attention so full that there remains no figure/ground distinction, only an open-ended and nonfocalized field of perception. Whitman's poems play the boundary between transitive and intransitive attentions in this way, often moving between them, employing (and producing) both modes in a single section. What begins with an attentive contemplation—of the self, of the Hudson, of the butcher boys or the wild gander—gathers in scope and number of foci, in lists and in layered hypotactic clauses, until what is produced is not a mode of looking *at,* but rather a synthesis of open, all-consuming, and departicularized receptivity and, at the same time, in all this taking in, a kind of gradually emerging sense of indifference, or at least a lack of choosiness with regard to the particular objects themselves, which grow increasingly lost in the oceanic flux of content.

At the other end of the scope spectrum, Dickinson's poetry exhibits a whittling away or emptying out of attentional content—a movement toward intransitive attention that hinges on holding open spaces of emptiness and potentiality. We find a formal and semantic articulation of this movement in Dickinson's poem 466,[5] in which to "dwell in Possibility" depends on the holding open of structural apertures—windows, doors, and hands open and empty. The poem begins with a single "I," whose dwelling is a practice of *this*, the poem, opposed to "Prose" by its formal beauty ("a fairer House"), a beauty defined in terms of its negative spaces, its formal openness, as well as its resistance to capture by any object that might fill it. The poem both describes and embodies an act of opening and *remaining open*, a resistance to fullness and the closure brought by gasping, taking in, akin to the maintenance of hunger we saw in her poem 76 in part 1's discussion of desire's necessary lack. The subject of the poem's single sentence, "I," has no direct object, only a series of metaphorical openings on the subject's prepositional dwelling place, "Possibility," each modifying clause itself prepositional. The function, or "occupation" of Possibility itself is a verb, an ongoing intentional action (or what I described as a *practice*): "the spreading of my narrow Hands / To gather Paradise." But with hands eternally spreading open, and an "everlasting Roof" as open as the sky, and with an eye that, to maintain its vigil in potentiality, must also remain "impregnable," "Paradise" must itself be a negative or a pure potentiality that is "gathered" precisely by not gathering, held by holding nothing. Whether the present continuous "spreading" of the hands *precedes* a potential future "to gather Paradise" or whether gathering Paradise is included in the present continuous action of spreading hands remains syntactically indeterminable. Yet, in either reading, gathering paradise requires an act of refusal: maintaining receptivity to the possibility of grace depends on remaining open—composing the self as a dwelling in potentiality whose structural form is defined both by its openings and by its resistance to being filled. And grace—here glimpsed (perhaps) as beauty—is already present *in the act of spreading hands to gather*, whether gathering is present or future. The subject is lonely in this poem without objects; it holds itself (or dwells) in a condition of both openness (exposure and shelterlessness) and exclusion or impregnability. Its occupation is "this," the act of the poem, the poem's act of attention, open because empty of objects.

Temporal Inflection

Considering the effects of temporal inflection in the context of transitive attention is relatively straightforward: the temporal location of the object in relation to the subject creates a temporal remove that shaped the particular kind of attention as one of direct contemplation, future imagining, or recollection. But when there is no object of focalization, does time cease to play a role? It turns out that intransitive attention can also be inflected by temporality, but this experience of time relates not to the standing of a particular object but directly to the kind of attentional mode.

Attention registers temporality primarily through the relationship between the attending subject and the object or objects of attention. Modes of intransitive attention are by nature more firmly rooted in the act of attending itself, which is a present act. When intransitive attention has duration, what is produced is an experience of extended presentness, a suspension in present attending without the temporal demarcation and contrast that comes with the remove between attender and attendee. Yet the quality of intransitive attention may itself be inflected with a quality of temporality—a quality modifying not subject or object but the particular mode of attending itself. Inflections of presence, pastness, or futurity then become qualities of a present and (to varying degrees) ongoing attention, rather than indicators of an interval of transtemporal or transspatial relation between subject and object. In other words, intransitive attention in all its modes is primarily an experience of heightened *presence*, but that present may be colored and shaded by different effects, one of which is temporal inflection.

The mode, the state of attention, takes place in the present. The experience of temporality within that state modifies the mode itself. Without an object to externally determine attention's temporal quality, the experience of time or the leaning in a particular temporal direction can be seen as a quality of the attention itself—akin to mood, a quality that affects the experience of the subject from within, rather than an emotional response to external cause, or intentional content. Nostalgia, for example, can be seen as an inflection of the past without direct contemplation of a past object. It is rooted in a feeling of pastness that pervades the attentional tone of the present, but is not itself an act of remembrance. Likewise, vigilance and anxiety both inflect present attention with futurity, but are not directed at the imagination of a specific future event or potential event. They are rather states that charge the present with futurity, through generalized and nonfocalized anticipation, positive or negative. All three are closely connected to emotional states, and all three (nostalgia and anxiety in particular) have been justly endowed with a significant body of research and theorization in psychology, philosophy, and literary studies; however, what concerns me here is their suggestion of temporal experience without the presence of a temporally located object of attention.

Formally, poetic language crafts temporality in a variety of ways: not only through verb tenses but through the intricacies of syntax. Parataxis locks the reader in the present, as one clause follows another, each reasserting a new and self-contained "here," while hypotaxis, with placement of resolution in a clause not yet disclosed, positions reading in an anticipatory state, waiting for a yet undisclosed clause while the meaning or semantic direction of what is read remains unknown. Breaks in lines, stanzas, or strophes, as well as the use of in-line gaps, em dashes, and parenthetical clauses, have the ability to suspend a poetic utterance over a silence or interruption, generating, depending on the specific usage, a sense of present suspension, an intrusion of pastness or absence into present articulation, or a sense of futurity in suspense. In my discussion of vigilance in the next chapter, I trace how these forms of formal suspense play out in the poetry of Friedrich Hölderlin and Stéphane Mallarmé. Like a musical notation, a single formal trait has the capacity to create a variety of temporal inflections, depending on its place within the dynamics of the composition.

Consciousness and Decreation: Subjectivity in Intransitive Attention

Without fixation on an object, what happens to the subject of attention? Whether the product of emptying out or total inclusivity, whether it moves directly to objectlessness, or employs the mediating presence of an indirect object in its praxis, whether it occupies a suspended and timeless present or is inflected with pastness or futurity, the experience of intransitive attention is rooted in the attentional act of the subject, without a focalized object or other to give shape and contour and semantic content to that experience. The act of attention is, in other words, not an act of relation *to* or being *toward,* but rather a mode of being, full stop. The particular characteristics of a given act or enduring state of intransitive attention coconstitute the subject—building and expanding, introducing suspensions and porosities, or emptying, hollowing, decreating the very subjectivity as it undergoes a terrain composed by its own attending. These movements of constitution and kenosis within the attending subject are directly linked to the particular practice of attention itself—the dynamics of emptying or filling, immersion in sense perception or withdrawal from it, openness to world or closure from it. What takes place in attention takes place in the subject. Like the poem itself, subjectivity is fundamentally composed by, in, and of attention. The opposing forces of subjective constitution and kenosis can be understood as the experiential outcome of the noetic and noemic elements shaping attention's intentionality—noetic or endogenous modes constitute and bolster the presence of the subject in the act of attending, while noemic or exogenous modes quiet, soften, and surrender the intentional subject through attentional passivity, willed or unwilled.

"*Pan tolmaton:* all is to be dared." Reading decreation in Sappho's Fragment 31, Anne Carson describes the simultaneous breakdown of poetic subject and poem as an act of emptying into ecstasy. Positioned in jealousy, outside of the relationship of love between the beloved and her beloved, the speaker's senses begin to fray and decline: "Sappho describes her own perceptual abilities (visual, aural, tactile) reduced to dysfunction one after another; she shows us the objects of outer sense emptying themselves; and there on the brightly lit stage at the center of her perception appears her own Being: I am . . ."[6] In Carson's reading, however, this emptying and self-dissolution is not a breakdown but a revelation of the subject's being in the experience of ecstasy: "*ekstasis*, literally 'standing outside oneself.'" Translating line 17 as "But all is to be dared because even a person of poverty," Carson draws out the nature of this "daring" as an opening at the limit of affliction and lack: the subject is thrown outside herself by impoverishment, and in that abyssal lack (the total absence of an object to grasp) all that is present is her being in its pure potentiality. Carson's reading is hemmed in by the breaking off of the poem itself, where the papyrus's incompleteness necessitates a reading of the poem's own potential development: "Unfortunately we don't reach the end, the poem breaks off. But we do see Sappho begin to turn toward it, toward this unreachable end. We see her senses empty themselves, we see her Being thrown outside its own center where it stands observing her as if she were grass or dead." What remains is "*absolute* potential." Thrown from its comfortable house of the self, the subject is in the open, a mode of total wager whose precondition is poverty and whose outcome is unknown. Yet the wager, the dare, to leave behind the self, is accepted. Reading the potential turn of the poem's lost conclusion, Carson asks, "Why does she consent?" only to reframe the question according to the condition of the Sapphic subject: "*What is it that love dares the self to do? . . . Love dares the self to leave itself behind, to enter into poverty.*"[7]

Carson focuses her reading on the second half of the extant fragment, only briefly summing up the opening as an experience of jealousy, the precursor to the more interesting shift into recreation and thrown subjectivity. Yet the opening offers a vital contrast and allows us to witness a shift not only into ecstasy but from one mode of attention to another: transitive to intransitive. As I showed in my discussion of Fragment 31 in part 1, the opening offers a complexly layered example of transitive attention, operating both semantically (at the level of the speaker's described experience) and formally (in the focalization of third-person pronouns and transitive sense verbs (seeming, listening, looking, speaking). This changes at "no,"—after which sensations begin to break down, references to the external scene vanish, and senses are presented one after the other *from the inside*, as feelings and changes in the subject rather than perceptions *of external objects*. What Carson rightly describes as an event of subjective decreation—ecstasy's unselfing—can be understood as a shift from ordinary perception in transitive attention into intransitive attention, in which the subject's attention to external objects and others begins to fray, empty, and dissolve, leaving only "I am," irreducible and exposed. Raw subjectivity remains after external fixations and their narrative accompaniments have fallen away. All of this happens in "a moment." But the moment stretches and by the fragment's end seems potentially endless, drawing down to a solitary point of presence.

In the example of Whitman's open-focus poetics—the extended moments in some of his poems when the scope of attention widens to such a degree that there is no longer an act of focalization—we found a very different kind of intransitivity: one constituted by an extreme fullness, rather than emptying out or breaking down, of perception. The subject in this mode would seem to expand and gain presence in attention, an example of constitution rather than decreation. At the same time, the radical openness of Whitman's attentional scope brings with it—or is perhaps brought about by—a kind of radical passivity, even though the act of widening scope is intentional and deliberately all-consuming. In opening to perceptual and intellectual input from all sides, the subject of Whitman's open focus dissolves and disperses, its structure of selfhood diminishing as receptivity increases. By contrast, in the Dickinson poem, with its exclusionary reduction of object content in favor of pure "possibility" (resonant with Sappho's *pan tolmaton*), the poetic subject is, in its withdrawal from objects (and thus from relation), reduced to the irreducible—the self is made more agonizingly present against a backdrop of void. In "daring all," or "dwelling in possibility," objective presence is lost in a wager for x, leaving the subject starkly present. This is one of the more unsettling qualities of Dickinson's work—the fact that, in poems hollowed out by gaps and dashes and faltering over capitalizations and arrhythmic rhythm, in which often what is said is an opaque abstraction of what is not, and what is not is as unsayable as a void, the persistent and unwavering "voice" of the subject—not that of the speaker but of the poem itself as speaking subject—juts from the poem's negatived space like Berenice's teeth.

Modes of Intransitive Attention: Vigilance, Resignation, Idleness, and Boredom

Having considered the formative elements of intransitive attention, it is helpful to consider how they combine to form specific modes. In the chapters that follow, I show how particular gatherings of intentionality, scope, temporality, subjectivity, and the presence or absence of indirect objects bring about recognizable states of intransitive attention. This helps us understand how these modes both shape and are shaped by poetic language in context. Exploring how the diverse formal and semantic elements of specific poems converge to bring about shifts into and out of intransitive attentionalities gives us traction on how some of the more subtle, nuanced, and difficult to grasp qualities of poetic attention function in practice. With a foothold in the workings of intransitive attention, the following chapters will consider several distinct attentional states and the poems that produce them. The relatively unexplored nature of intransitive attention correlates with the underexamined nature of its associated poetries. While, as we saw in part 1, there is a host of generic categories that map onto modes of transitive, object-oriented attention, we find a scarcity of generic categories that name, historicize, or offer a hermeneutical consideration of the poetics of intransitive attention, even though these modes are practiced and embodied in poetries from diverse historical moments. For this reason, instead of exploring the attentional dynamics of explicitly poetic modes, I will consider the poetic dynamics of several modes of intransitive attention, namely vigilance, resignation, idleness, and boredom. This approach offers an opportunity to consider in detail the coming-together of intransitive attention's dynamic coordinates in specific sites of poetic language and, at the same time, yields an opening to uncover the workings of poetic modes that have heretofore not been recognized or addressed.

My purpose here is not to label new genres of poetry, but rather to show how an examination of the subtler forms of attention—particularly those that are not addressed to a focal object—illuminates poetic qualities that play a vital and substantial role in poetic history and practice, but have fallen beneath and between the generic spotlights. Giving language and attention to these modes enables a deeper understanding of poetry's harder-to-pinpoint effects. It also enables a recognition of poetic dynamics that cut across existing generic boundaries, causing them to either be overlooked or lumped into an ill-fitting mold. Finally, exploring existing *attentional* categories through the highly particularized and irreproducible lens of an individual poem (or more, an individual reading of an individual poem) pluralizes our understanding of attention's forms from within, showing the infinite plurality, complexity, and variety that are possible under a single category of attention. Vigilance is never simply vigilance, boredom never boredom, resignation never resignation. Within the complex formal structure of a single poem, there is enough dynamic particularity to problematize and complicate all the names we give to attentional states, states of mind, and states of being. Seeing this nuance in action underscores the utter singularity and complexity of any poetic object or event; turning this awareness back to attention itself serves as a reminder of the singularity and complexity of attention's composition, moment to moment.

Intransitive Attention in the Modern Age

In his book on gardens, Robert Harrison begins a chapter "On the Lost Art of Seeing" with the following meditation: "Almost a century ago Rainer Maria Rilke hypothesized in his Duino Elegies that it was the earth's destiny to become invisible, that a process of transmutation of the visible into the invisible had begun to take place." The "transmutation of the visible into the invisible" stood, in this case, as a symptomatic loss, disappearance, or drawing back into itself, of the world in modernity:

> It's not that the world is any less visible than it was in the past; rather its plenitude registers with us less and less. It is in us that the transmutation takes place. Thus it is not a question of generational deficiency but of epochal transformations in the framework in and through which the world reveals itself. . . . The basic inability to see a garden in its full-bodied presence is the consequence of a historical metamorphosis of our mode of vision, which is bound up with our mode of being. For as our mode of being changes, so too does our way of seeing. . . . What our vision sees (and just as important, what

it doesn't see) is determined by historically unfolding frameworks that preorganize or predispose the empirical reach of our perception.[8]

It's not the world that changes in modernity, or the human brain, but the prevailing mode of looking, increasingly characterized by selectivity, narrowing, and elimination of the environment in favor of an increasingly closely defined set of technological, aesthetic, and political concerns. This constitutes a shift in human attention—a heightening of attention in the sense of narrowing our focus and ratcheting our discipline and a slackening of attention in the form of more circumferential awareness, sensitivity, readiness, vigilance, and reflection: modern subjects have become conditioned, by industrial, economic, and even architectural and aesthetic forces, to a disciplinary "attention"—the narrowing of one's perceptive horizon to the object of a given task or interest.[9]

Whether metonymized as vision or perception, attention is a layered and contextually inflected action, never an isolated event of agency or autonomous will, but embedded within larger attentional dispositions in human thought. Rather than the increasing invisibility of the world implying something about the world itself, what is significant is the shift in attention: the eye that sees or does not see, the human beings that attend or do not attend. It is the human ability to attend to the world, not the world itself, that is growing weak. Paradoxically, this comes about through an increasing reliance on—or even addiction to—narrow-focus, object-oriented attention. Opening the attentional scope beyond a narrowly focalized site, or emptying it of objects to allow for negativity and spaciousness, opens new possibility for being in the world and in the self as well as possibilities for releasing the vise grip on world and self—both paths to a different kind of presence in space-time, sociality, and subjectivity.

CHAPTER VII

Vigilance

States of Suspension

Hölderlin : Mallarmé

Whether invoked in spiritual, military, or occupational contexts, vigilance constitutes a state of attention in which there is no present object of focus, but rather an openness to *potential* objects, a vigilant scanning of the attentional field. This practice of sustained awareness or alertness is marked by a readiness to detect the appearance of a potential but unpredictable object, signal, or change. While this might seem like a passive or purely receptive mode, vigilance is incredibly challenging to maintain, requiring focalization not on a concentrated theme but on the potential emergence of such a target.[12] And yet the practice of vigilance or sustained objectless attention—itself a form of meditation—has been found to improve both sustained focal attention *and* sustained vigilance, significantly delaying and attenuating their decrement. A variety of forms of attention, including vigilance, can be trained through repeated engagement, through practice. As a craft of attention, poetic language might itself offer such a practice or training, one capable of tuning, refining, deepening and extending the attention, and perhaps one that is transferable from the poetic context outward into other contexts requiring sustained and granular attention. In this chapter's readings of Friedrich Hölderlin and Stéphane Mallarmé, I show how formal elements of syntax and spatial layout both embody and produce two kinds of vigilance: revelatory (characterized by the sudden emergence of an object or event after a prolonged period of waiting) and nonrevelatory (in which vigilance is maintained and cultivated even in the absence of epiphany).

The notion that attention—and specifically vigilant attention—might be trained through practice was of vital importance to one the twentieth century's most enigmatic and poetic thinkers of attention, Simone Weil. Echoing Malebranche, Kafka, and Benjamin, Weil famously saw attention as "the natural prayer of the soul." Yet her definition of attention in its most acute form reveals itself as a mode of vigilance:

> Attention consists of suspending our thought, leaving it detached [*disponible*], empty [*vide*], and ready to be penetrated by the object; it means holding in our minds, within the reach of this thought, but on the lower level and not in contact with it, the diverse knowledge we have acquired which we are forced to make use of. . . . Above all our thought should be empty [*vide*], waiting [*en attente*], not seeking anything [*ne rien chercher*], but ready to receive in its naked truth the object that is to penetrate it.[3]

In many ways, one might think vigilance as the mode of attention that comes the closest to the root meaning of the word, as "reach." Indeed, attention's reach is better captured in French than in English: *attendre,* both attending and waiting. In English, these also come together in *vigilance*—keeping wakeful vigil.

Reading Weil, Maurice Blanchot writes, "Attention is the reception of what escapes attention, an opening, upon the unexpected, a waiting that is the unawaited of all waiting."[4] In this notion of *the unawaited of all waiting,* we find the state of vigilance: a waiting that is not waiting *for,* an attention that has, in a sense, neither subject nor object, held empty except for the sum of potential relations, a waiting that is not *waiting for a turn to speak, or waiting for a chance to strike,* but simply waiting. It is this waiting, this hush of attention that marks out a space as sacred. This "space" of suspension can be thought temporally as well, in the sense of keeping vigil. Blanchot emphasizes the temporal inflection of vigilance, its location in a present attention to *potential* futurity:

> Attention is waiting: not the effort, the tension, or the mobilization of knowledge around something with which one might concern oneself. . . . Attention waits. It waits without precipitation, leaving

empty what is empty and keeping our haste, our impatient desire, and, even more, our horror of emptiness of thought oriented by a gentle force and maintained in an accord with the empty intimacy of time.[5]

Vigilance also actively *keeps*, holds present (for an eternal instant) the subject's forward thrust (in self-narration, action and reaction, causal thinking), suspended in waiting.

Françoise Meltzer has pointed out that, for Weil, "attention is not to be confused with will; it is rather bound up in desire (here Weil is strongly influenced by her reading of the Stoics). Attention specifically requires the passivity of the I and the disappearance of the subject."[6] This distinction between attention and the will hinges on Weil's notion of decreation: the kenotic emptying of the self in devotion and sacrifice, the dissolution of what Weil called "all that I call 'I.'" Weil writes that in the work of prayer, "all that I call 'I' has to be passive. Attention alone—that attention which is so full that the 'I' disappears—is required of me. I have to deprive all that I call 'I' of the light of my attention and turn it on that which cannot be conceived."[7] In this sense, paradoxically, attention at once requires and produces the muting and dissolution of the will in opening to the other (or to the big Other, God). On this self-emptying movement of vigilant attention, Maurice Blanchot writes, "Attention is impersonal. It is not the self that is attentive in attention; rather, with an extreme delicacy and through insensible, constant contacts, attention has always already detached me from myself, freeing me for the attention that I for an instant become."

For Weil, attention's decreative potential depends on the soul's ability to overcome attachments and desires, which she saw as antithetical to devotion. It requires a relinquishment of the self, and specifically the desiring self. She writes, "The extinction of desire (Buddhism)—or detachment—or *amor fati*—or desire for the absolute good—these all amount to the same: to empty desire, finality of all content, to desire in the void, to desire without any wishes. To detach our desire from all good things and to wait."[8] In her notebooks we find the passage:

> *Amor fati.* To extend it to one's own past and future acts. I have never disturbed, I will never disturb the order of the world. In that case, what does my fate matter?. . . Order of the world. Macrocosm and microcosm (amor fati, bridge between the two). An ordered universe

is a condition of existence for an ordered body, and an ordered body for a spirit united to flesh. . . . To renounce everything which is not grace, and not to desire grace.[9]

Weil's vigilance thus poses an impossible paradox, torn between waiting *for* grace (the moment of revelation) and waiting without desire for grace. The immense waiting-for seems to rely on immense desire for what is awaited. Yet precisely this desire gets in the way of true waiting. In this sense, Weilian vigilance asks us to inhabit a space of impossibility. This impossibility itself may be seen as essential to vigilance: waiting without expectation or desire, holding open of the space of the "I," in the act of *attente*, for the possible moment of grace. The unattainability of this mode of waiting without desire is precisely what makes it divine.[10] Only in the moment of grace can the human soul achieve what is required by grace: the complete surrendering of desire. This impossibility (embodied, formally, as paradox) is the gateway to paradise, the instant between mortality and eternity.

Weil's attention depends on the *possibility* of revelation and also on the renunciation of desire for revelation. In this sense, her notion of attention can be seen as poised between the two kinds of *formal* poetic vigilance that I will trace in this chapter through the work of Hölderlin and Mallarmé. Hölderlin's use of syntactical delays followed by sudden shifts into emphatic present tense suggests a mode of *revelatory vigilance*: a preparation *for* the epiphanic moment of arrival. In Mallarmé's *Un Coup de dés*, reading across white space and scanning for syntactical connections over multiple typographically interspersed threads of text requires a nonrevelatory vigilance, navigating contingencies and afflictions here on earth, toward a more gradual, horizontal transformation.

Der Kommende Gott: Vigilance and Immediacy in Hölderlin

Friedrich Hölderlin's long poem "Wie wenn am Feiertage . . ." ("As on a Holiday . . .") begins with a scenic embodiment of stillness and silence: early morning coming slowly to country fields after a summer night's rain.[11] At the level of "plot," very little happens in the course of the long poem. Yet, at the formal and figurative levels, the poem composes a dynamic terrain of suspense, expectation, and waiting, punctuated and brought to climax by dramatic turns, composed primarily through a highly crafted syntax of extended hypotaxis punctuated by sudden reversals and emphatic declarations. The opening sentence extends for thirteen lines, halfway into the second stanza. The opening and titular clause, "Wie wenn am Feiertage . . . ," already positions the line in dependence on what follows, yet the relationships between each part of the sentence seem vague, somehow suspenseful yet opaquely so. The "Wie wenn" of the first line links to the countryman's mode of walking out to the field, but also seems to link conditionally to something to come, of which the countryman's amble is a part of the initial comparative clause, rather than its resolution.

Semantically, the poem begins in a representational mode and takes off, increasingly, into a zone of greater and greater abstraction and mythicism. The field, thunder, rain, trees, and grapevines give way to more abstract and spiritual evocations:

> So stehn sie unter günstiger Witterung
> Sie die kein Meister allein, die wunderbar
> Allgegenwärtig erzieht in leichtem Umfangen
> Die mächtige, die göttlichschöne Natur.

> So now in favourable weather they stand
> Whom no mere master teaches, but in
> A light embrace, miraculously omnipresent,
> God-like in power and beauty, Nature brings up.

Each clause seems to hang on the next, not in urgent suspense but in suspension, eternity, a place of indeterminate unmarked time—time as on holiday. The verbs are predominantly intransitive (*standing, growing, sleeping, shining,* and *divining*), verbs of stillness and of very slow and ongoing development. In a process of increasing deconcentration, the phrase arrives at *Natur*, an embodiment of panorama taken to the point of contentlessness. In "nature" taken in its abstract fullness and generality, there is not enough focalization to produce action or movement, only open all-containing and temporally indeterminate presence. The only temporal inflection in the opening two stanzas emerges from the repeated delay and deferral of syntactical resolution, a trend exemplified by the colon separating stanzas 1 and 2.

This changes at stanza 3, with the sudden shift into an active and emphatic now: "Jezt aber Tags!" ("But now day breaks!") The verbs, previously positioned in an ongoing present tense, are suddenly shifted to past, a move that, paradoxically, produces a greater effect of action, or *action taken*. The third stanza ushers in a sudden and unexpected shift into a different kind of present, an active *now* ("jezt") echoed several lines later, and again in stanzas 4 and 7. The speaking subject enters in for the first time, and day becomes both active agent and object of active and transitive verbs: "Ich harrt und sah es kommen" ("I waited and saw it come"). Yet the emphatic present ushered in by this line is interrupted, immediately, by the subject's urge to speak the event: "Und was ich sah, das Heilige sei mein Wort" ("And what I saw, the hallowed, my word shall convey.")

Writing on these lines in *L'Etretien infini*, Blanchot notes their common interpretation in French translations (retranslated to English) as "And what I saw, the holy, may it be my word," in which what is seen, or "the viewed of the vision," is *das Heilige*, read as direct object in a syntactically unusual phrase. This interpretive option is upheld in Michael Hamburger's English translation: "And what I saw, the hallowed, my word shall convey." Yet Blanchot reads in the original text another, more faithful syntax, in which the comma signals a pause, a caesura in the phrase, interrupting and cutting off the undefined object of Hölderlin's vision:

> At the moment of breaking the seal and finally revealing what we were destined to see, once, thought the poet's intervention, the line interrupts itself, becoming silent for an instant before gathering impetus to give form with an urgent force to a new present; but which one? The present of desire (in which, therefore, absence presents itself), or poetic desire in its highest form: *the holy be my word*. May my word be the holy. Here, in this sort of exclamatory prayer and desiring appeal, is all that is given to us of the relation that holds between the poet, speech, and the Sacred. Hölderlin does not say that he saw the holy—this he could not say—he can only, having seen, give himself in a movement that evokes to the future of the fundamental wish: *the holy be my word*.[12]

The "new present" Blanchot sees in the shift from *sah* to *sei* is not the same present of the poem's beginning, but the vigilant present of poetic potential itself—the potentiality, or *hoped for* potential of poetic saying—that it must do more than describe the sacred event but must *be* it, its embodied and experiential form transposed to a different flesh, the material of language. Or to draw from Hölderlin's own language in the short poem "Der Winkel von Hahrdt," "Ein groß Schiksaal / Bereit, an übrigem Orte."[13] The potentiality of the poetic utterance is a kind of presence—one, in Blanchot's words, "in whose nuance . . . our entire poetic destiny is at stake." This ambition for poetic language is one of both reach and restraint: reach, because it entails language moving beyond the level of meaning and into a highly singular *being* ("The Sacred must be speech, and, even more, my very speech"); restraint, because of its constrained standing as wish, a standing that is perhaps the sole constituent of its singular being: "all is limited to the exigency of a fervent wish so that, finally, 'what I saw' is perhaps nothing more than the present of this wish, this provoking resolution that gathers in an intimacy of belonging and through an already sacrilegious contact with the Sacred and speech in the space of the extremity of desire."[14]

What is important in Blanchot's emphasis on the potentiality of Hölderlin's desire that *the holy be my word* is its reinflection of the poetic present with futurity. The declarative suddenness of "Jezt aber Tags!" marked a momentary breakthrough of present experience made possible only by the vigilant stillness and suspension that preceded it. The revelatory vision—unspeakable except by the tonal cry of exclamation and by the space left silent by the comma following *sah*, depends upon the prior stanza's production and deepening of a meditative vigil, the mind turning inward from the opening comparative scene, the second half of the comparison left open, unresolved. In Hölderlin's poetic syntax, it is also the shift into presence, the sudden turn of direction, that throws the preceding vigil into contrast, making it sensible. While the breakthrough of exclamatory daybreak signals a breaking into immediate present, this breakthrough is only possible from the position of vigilant "waiting," that came before, a vigil that is at once impoverished and charged with potentiality. Blanchot puts it this way:

> The *now* that Bonnefoy proposed to us as what is at stake in poetry, and that irrupts from the beginning of the line with the impatience of a first light: *But now day breaks!* Then, immediately after the burst of this present in which the day dawns, we fall back, having lost it, to the past, and we must again live the infinite of waiting, the time

of distress and destitution without companionship: *I waited*. A waiting without a term, existence reduced to a fruitless waiting without a present that is nevertheless also a waiting rich and full of the presentiment in which the coming and the vision of what always comes is prepared: *I waited and saw it come*.[15]

Through the repetition of this cycle of attenuated vigilant contemplation followed by abrupt turns into the present of deixis and declaration, Hölderlin crafts a flow of intransitive attention whose semantic content pales in importance beside the continual modulation of temporal and contemplative intensities. Writing on Hölderlin, Blanchot, and Heidegger together, William Allen has noted the importance of the caesura, or suspensive *entretemps*, for both writers as a form of suspending time in a present that lies between active registers, suspending the attention in this liminal present.[16] This is a mode that is not described in language, only played out or made present in language's material form: what takes place is not a description or expression of attentive experience and attentional shifts, but rather the attentive experience itself, embodied and produced in the protosemantic matter of poetic language.[17] It is only experienceable in contrast to what it is not—not action, not object, not past or future. It is a kind of chasm between terrains of positive content. As such, and having nothing, as it were, to talk about, it can be suspended, characterized, and sustained only by patience.

We find a sustained example of this cycle of modulatory turns in the long poem "Brod und Wein," in which the shift between the vigilant present and the emphatic present takes place not through an explicit repositioning of temporal cues, and not through the contrast between syntactical futurity (hypotaxis, colon, and conditional) and immediacy (declaration and exclamation), but rather through a series of hairpin turns that take as their hinge the uniquely Hölderlinian *aber* ("but") found in "Jezt aber Tags!" Looking over the poem with writer and translator John Felstiner, I pointed out Hölderlin's persistent use of the word *aber* to bring about an attentional shift into the present. Scanning again down the length of the poem, Felstiner nodded: "Yes, one could write an entire book only on Hölderlin's *aber*." And it's true, one could, and hopefully someday that book will exist. No doubt the significances of Hölderlin's repeated use of the word reach much farther than its role in maintaining and modulating a certain kind of vigilant attention, but for now that will be my focus.

Like "Wie wenn am Feiertage . . . ," "Brod und Wein" begins in stillness and suspension, this time cast in the imagistic frame of a town settling into evening and in the form of lulling sonic and lexical repetition:

Rings um ruhet die Stadt; still wird die erleuchtete Gasse,
    Und, mit Fakeln geschmükt, rauschen die Wagen hinweg.
Satt gehn heim von Freuden des Tags zu ruhen die Menschen,
    Und Gewinn und Verlust wäget ein sinniges Haupt
Wohlzufrieden zu Haus; leer steht von Trauben und Blumen,
    Und von Werken der Hand ruht der geschäfftige Markt.[18]

Round us the town is at rest; the street, in pale lamplight, falls quiet
    And, their torchlights ablaze, coaches rush through and away.
People go home to rest, replete with the day and its pleasures,
    There to weigh up in their heads, pensive, the gain and the loss,
Finding the balance good; stripped bare now of grapes and of
    flowers,
    As of their handmade goods, quiet the market stalls lie.

As the pensive heads make their way home to weigh the day's gains and losses, town, people, and emptied markets now find rest. In the somnolent roll of repeated *r*s, *s*s, and the open vowel phonemes of *u* and *au*, the language of these opening lines does more than describe and mirror its semantic landscape: it creates, in lulling incantation, the same slow restfulness in the reader's attention. The repetition of "still," and the various conjugations of *ruhen*, toll in the mind, conjuring a state of soft-focus contemplation and pensive reflection: "Rings um ruhet die Stadt," "Satt gehn heim . . . zu ruhen die Menschen," "Ruht der geschäfftige Markt." The position of the collective, generic terms of "die Stadt," "die Menschen," and "der Markt" in the present tense emphasizes the opening's soft-focus, dreamlike quality: this could be anywhere, anyone. The only semiparticular term is *um*, placing "us" in the evening's midst.

As with the "Jezt aber Tags!" of "Wie wenn am Feiertage . . . ," the poem shifts course with a reversal, softer but still signaled by "aber": "Aber das Saitenspiel tönt fern aus Gärten." The line depicts the breaking of silence semantically with the sound of distant strings, but the form has already had the equivalent attentional effect with the leading *aber*, whose role in this case is not to dispute or change what has come before, but to interrupt it, for the purpose of bringing the reader to attention. The calls to presence echo through the rest of the stanza, with proliferating sounds (from a possible love song, or lonesome song, to a fountain's splash, church bells, a watchman's call, and a rustling breeze in branches) and an increasingly insistent shift from rest into a more active and alert *now*:

> Aber das Saitenspiel tönt fern aus Gärten; vieleicht, daß
>   Dort ein Liebendes spielt oder ein einsamer Mann
> Ferner Freunde gedenkt und der Jugendzeit; und die Brunnen
>   Immerquillend und frisch rauschen an duftendem Beet.
> Still in dämmriger Luft ertönen geläutete Gloken,
>   Und der Stunden gedenk rufet ein Wächter die Zahl.
> Jetzt auch kommet ein Wehn und regt die Gipfel des Hains auf,

> But faint music of strings comes drifting from gardens; it could be
>   Someone in love who plays there, could be a man all alone
> Thinking of distant friends, the days of his youth; and the
>   fountains,
>   Ever welling and new, plash amid balm-breathing beds.
> Church bells ring; every stroke calls out, mindful, no less, of the
>   hour.
>   Now a breeze rises too and ruffles the crests of the coppice,

The tension of the lines increases with the increase of noticed sounds—as more is taken in from all sides, more sounds puncturing the silence of rest, the syntax takes on velocity: *und* clauses proliferate, each bringing a new layer of volume and unseen movement to the terrain. "Jezt auch kommet" further focalizes the active present—not only by its literal meaning but by its syntactical intensification of the interruptive present, in line with "aber" (and, for that matter, "jezt aber"). Moreover, its situation of the incoming sensory details in a *now*, and *now this*, signals a mode of attention that does not know what is coming, or where sounds and movements come from, but can only crane outward with increasing alertness. The vigilant tension culminates with a syntactical shift into exclamatory imperative with "Sieh!" And from this hypersensitized, open attention comes what can only be described as sublime defamiliarization—to crane one's senses out into the darkness is to discover a night that is neither ordinary nor the picturesque idyll with which the poem began, but Night, utterly strange-making, utterly other-than-human, astonishing and *there*:

> Sieh! Und das Schattenbild unserer Erde, der Mond
> Kommet geheim nun auch; die Schwärmerische, die Nacht kommt,
>   Voll mit Sternen und wohl wenig bekümmert um uns,
> Glänzt die Erstaunende dort, die Fremdlingin unter den Menschen
>   Über Gebirgeshöhn traurig und prächtig herauf.[19]

> Look! and in secret our globe's shadowy image, the moon,
> Slowly is rising too; and Night, the fantastical, comes now
>   Full of stars and, I think, little concerned about us,
> Night, the astonishing, there, the stranger to all that is human,
>   Over the mountain-tops mournful and gleaming draws on.

The speechless wonder of this transfiguration is allowed to resonate and extend through the pause of the stanza break, yet, while stanza 2 opens with an iteration of this wonder in "Wunderbar ist die Gunst der Hocherhabnen," we have already shifted back into contemplation, as the speaker ponders discursively man's relationship to night's strangeness in contrast to "der besonnene Tag." The syntax slows, grows steady, point by point, until the next reversal, again with "Aber," to call into question man's preference for clarity and reason: "Aber zuweilen liebt auch klares Auge den Schatten." The reasoning folds back on itself, casting itself in shadow with rethinking and redoubling: "Oder es blikt auch gern ein treuer Mann in die Nacht hin." These turns in contemplation, subtler than the emphatic daybreak of *now*, hold the reader in tension, each turn disallowing philosophical or narrative onward march, modulating the present with the dialecticism of autocritical hesitancy. Temporally and attentionally, what is produced in these modulations is a *zaudernden Weile*, a wavering moment—a present continually representing in question and rerouting:

> Aber sie muß uns auch, daß in der zaudernden Weile,
>   Daß im Finstern für uns einiges Haltbare sei,
> Uns die Vergessenheit und das Heiligtrunkene gönnen,
>   Gönnen das strömende Wort, das, wie die Liebenden, sei,
> Schlummerlos und vollern Pokal und kühneres Leben,
>   Heilig Gedächtniß auch, wachend zu bleiben bei Nacht.[20]

> But to us in her turn, so that in the wavering moment,
>   Deep in the dark there shall be something at least that endures,
> Holy drunkenness she must grant and frenzied oblivion,
>   Grant the on-rushing word, sleepless as lovers are too,
> And a wine-cup more full, a life more intense and more daring,
>   Holy remembrance too, keeping us wakeful by night.

In this wavering moment of night, in which objects of the senses are veiled in darkness and ordinary perception is strained, in which gazing is not *at* but *into* the night's depths, a different experience of the present emerges, one of immersion and awareness, wakefulness. Hölderlin crafts this wakefulness in the syntax of modulatory turns, holding the mind in suspension so as, perhaps, to sense that which endures, "daß im Finstern für ins einiges Haltbares sei." This suspension is drawn between two poles: lulling toward night's Dionysian potentialities of oblivion and ecstasy—"die Vergessenheit," "das Heiligtrunkene," "wie die Liebenden, sei, / Schlummerlos und vollern Pokal und kühneres Leben"—yet continually ushered back into the present, called into "Heilig Gedächtniß" by the language itself, "das strömende Wort." Grant us now the "on-rushing word."

The word, sacred to Hölderlin's poetics, flows only in the moment, deep in the stillness of suspension held by a taut line of attention. Its position is at once forceful and precarious—at once *strömende* (brilliantly translated by Hamburg as "on-rushing") and that which, unguaranteed, must be *granted* ("gönnen, / Gönnen"). The granting of the word requires vigil, keeping wakeful by night, keeping tension on the line, keeping present and alert through a series of autocritical checks. The charge of this vigilant mode gains in tension until Hölderlin's syntax again breaks in, breaks through with declaration and exclamation, bursting the contemplative mode with a new iteration of emphatic *jetzt*:

> Göttliches Feuer auch treibet, bei Tag und bei Nacht
> Aufzubrechen. So komm! daß wir das Offene schauen,
>   Daß ein Eigenes wir suchen, so weit es auch ist.
>
> Day-long, night-long, we're urged on by a fire that's divine.
> Urged to be gone. Let us go, then! Off to see open spaces,
>   Where we may seek what is ours, distant, remote though it be!

The exclamatory setting-forth into active present takes place, here semantically as well, yet the lack of narrative content positions the drama of the words in a purely linguistic relief of tone, inflection, punctuation, and lineation.

This cyclic modulation through different tensions and intensities of attentional present, from the vigilant to the emphatic to the revelatory to the explosive and back again, takes place repeatedly, almost exhaustingly, over the course of the poem's nine long stanzas. In nine stanzas we find no less than sixteen *aber*s, each signaling a hairpin turn into a different present. We also find scatterings of emphasis and intensity in Hölderlin's interrogatory clusters, pilings of question after question, each starting with the same word, as in the series of "wo?" questions in stanza 4 or the "warum?" cluster at stanza 6. A similar effect of attentional suddenness (*Plötzlichkeit*) without objective content can be found in the exclamatory imperatives of stanza 3,[21] whose breaking effect flows into an extended series of clauses piling modifiers onto a multidirectional and mythic *there*:

Drum! und spotten des Spotts mag gern frohlokkender Wahnsinn,
    Wenn er in heiliger Nacht plözlich die Sänger ergreift.
Drum an den Isthmos komm! dorthin, wo das offene Meer rauscht
    Am Parnaß und der Schnee delphische Felsen umglänzt,
Dort ins Land des Olymps, dort auf die Höhe Cithärons,
    Unter die Fichten dort, unter die Trauben, von wo
Thebe drunten und Ismenos rauscht im Lande des Kadmos,
    Dorther kommt und zurük deutet der kommende Gott.[22]

Well! Then may jubilant madness laugh at those who deride it,
    When in hallowed Night poets are seized by its power;
Off to Isthmus, then! To land where wide open the sea roars
    Near Parnassus and snow glistens on Delphian rocks;
Off to Olympian regions, up to the heights of Cithaeron,
    Up to the pine trees there, up to the grapes, from which rush
Thebe down there and Ismenos, loud in the country of Cadmus:
    Thence has come and back there points the God who's to come.

While the literal sites of the *dort* ("to," or "off to") here are important for the figurative and symbolic dimensions of the poem, it is secondary to its function in generating movement, the attentional quality of suddenness and kinetic emphasis. The attentional dynamics of this passage, particularly from a temporal standpoint, are complexly nuanced and polyvalenced: the repeated emphatic imperative-invitation "Drum!" and its echoing follow-through in "Dort . . . dort . . . unter . . . drunten . . . Dorther" bring an element of activity and propulsion, a building tension of readiness and departure. The stillness, the "heiliger Nacht," that has been cultivated in the poem's language up to this point is thrown into contrast by the suddenness of song ("plözlich die Sänger ergreift"). Yet this suddenness is cast in futurity, a potentiality and contingency underscored by the propositional nature of the flight, and by the conclusion of the stanza with the double iteration of "kommen" in "Dorther kommt und zurük deutet der kommende Gott." The use of the verb *ergreifen* signals not only lyrical flight but also a more active and assertive action of *grasping*, physically and apprehensionally. The suddenness of the potential poetic event, possible only in the stillness of vigil and sacred, contemplative, wakeful night, is one of grasping, active seizing, and making-present: a sudden shift from highly endogenous intransitive attention to radically exogenous transitive apprehension: revelation. In stark contrast to both the meditative stillness and the contemplative inquiry of the preceding stanzas, this passage breaks in with an almost violent, ecstatic urgency of near liftoff—but the urgency is nonetheless vigilant insofar as it is winding back and gearing up for a coming that is emphatically *to come*. At the same time, the intensifying near-present futurity of approach coincides with a mode of looking back: the approaching departure is aimed at sites of greco-mythic past, and the approach of the "kommende Gott" is at once a coming (*kommen*) and a pointing back (*zurük deuten*). This image of propulsive and onrushing arrival of a god that looks back resonates more than a century later in Klee's forward-driven, backward-glancing *Angelus Novus,* interpreted by Walter Benjamin as the Angel of History.[23] In both works, the position of the poetic or artistic event can be seen in a similar temporal position—torn between meditation on the past (mythic or historical) and exposure to the potentiality of the future, a present event rooted in the stillness of meditation but charged by anticipation of what is to come. What emerges is a poetic vigilance that casts back, in meditation, autocritical rerouting and doubt even as it cranes into futurity, making ready for the potential event of revelatory apprehension.

Nonrevelatory Vigilance: Contingency and the Practice of Alertness in *Un Coup de dés*

While the suspensive temporality of Hölderlinian vigilance is felt in the slow, quietly building passages and in the accumulation of futurity through the repeated use of hypotaxis and delayed syntactical conclusion, this effect is sharpened by the moments of revelatory breakthrough, which enhance the preceding vigilant state by the suddenness of contrast. Hölderlin thus accentuates the effect of poetic vigilance by repeatedly interrupting it with a poetics of epiphanic immediacy. Yet this is not always the case. In other poetries we find modes of vigilance that continue without, as it were, revelatory relief—without the hairpin turns into immediate presence offered by Hölderlin's uses of *aber* and *jezt*. We find one such example in Stéphane Mallarmé's long and visually dynamic *Un Coup de dés jamais n'abolira le hasard* (A throw of the dice will never abolish chance). In this masterpiece of multisensory attentional suspense, Mallarmé produces an effect of nonrevelatory vigilance, a state of alertness and multisensory tuning rooted in a background condition of contingency that lends precarity to attention's probe.

Unlike in Hölderlin, the effortful state of alertness required even to find footing through a single page is immense; moreover, this demand not only remains but accumulates over the course of eleven double-page panes of text and white space. Rather than rewarding vigilance with flashes of breakthrough performed and (in Hölderlin) even *announced* by the poem, Mallarmé's text offers only microvictories, such as the feat of determining which line follows which, and these decisions, made throughout the highly opaque and layered text, seem contingent to the end, dependent on other decisions made and on some cues from Mallarmé's prose writings. The precision and intricacy of composition disallows any easy conclusion of "ambiguity" or "indeterminacy" in the text, yet sleuthing for unambiguous and determinate readings requires almost superhuman attentional acuity and endurance. The text not only supports but *demands* repeated, potentially endless, rereading. Yet reading, in this poem, is hazarded, and each step is a process of deliberation and multidirectional scanning for possible alignments enabling the next and the next. As with Anne Carson's *Nox*, *reading* seems too narrow and linear a verb to account for the multisensory, multidirectional, nonlinear activity required by this text.

Attending to *Un Coup de dés* feels not so much like quiet contemplation leading to sudden visionary openings, but more like trying to cross an abyssal ravine by building a bridge, plank by plank, beneath one's feet as one goes. Each plank is a small stay of necessity against contingency. The progress is gradual, and the suspensive state exhaustive of all one's resources. This agonizing and hypervigilant exercise of the attention is linked, for Mallarmé, to a historically inflected condition affecting the very foundations of language-making at the turn of the twentieth century. What is practiced, in the text, is a slow and precarious exercise of rigorous attention to the sites of noncontingency (or necessity) language (and in particular the structure of syntax) affords amidst, and in the face of, the groundlessness (freedom's shadow side) that accompanied the shift away from received forms.

UN COUP DE DÉS

The poem begins not with words but with the blank that precedes them. The first page, to the left, is left blank, and the first and titular line is positioned on the second page. Then comes language: UN COUP DE DÉS, thrown to the far right margin, so that the line both announces its form semantically and performs its meaning formally. The "coup de dés" (throw of the dice) hangs there after page 2, falling through the wholly white expanse of page 3. The alternation created between these opening four pages: unmarked, marked; unmarked, marked. We can see numerous patterns of alternating oppositions throughout the poem: ABAB—thesis and antithesis in recurrence, a relation of alternation without synthesis or conciliation.[24] If a C emerges in this poetics of opposition, it is the ongoing sequence itself, a whole composed of opposing elements—containing opposition rather than resolving it.

This beginning places white space in visual opposition to the marked space of language. The intricate composition of blanks runs throughout the poem, indicating silence at the aural level and, at the conceptual level, Mallarmé's notion of *l'abîme* (blank, abyss). These blanks suggest both contingency and potentiality out of which language must emerge. In the blank, anything is possible—an at once empowering and terrible condition. The expanse of silence surrounding the words of the text is thus double in nature: it signals *l'abîme*'s pure potentiality, but also highlights the contingency, and thus the existential groundlessness, that plagues language and action that exit the realm of potentiality, as when language, with its capacity for both overconstraint and ambiguity, leaves the realm of unuttered mind. The white space is the absence out of which *something*—language, action, existence—might emerge. The pure potentiality of the blank dramatizes both the contingency (the risk of randomness or ambiguity) and the ambition of (at least) formal necessity (the pursuit of the *mot juste*) in the linguistic acts that take place in and out of it. Against some interpretations that see *le hasard* (chance) as a kind of enemy, or the opposite of the order made possible in verse, I would like to suggest that *le hasard* concerns the precarity and risk that characterize poetic language in a condition of contingency: imperfect, impure, and limited as soon as it exits the domain of mind. As Mallarmé writes in *Crise de vers,*

> Les langues imparfaites en cela que plusieurs, manque la suprême: penser étant écrire sans accessoires ni chuchotement mais tacite encore l'immortelle parole, la diversité, sur terre, des idiomes empêche personne de proférer les mots qui, sinon se trouveraient, par une frappe unique, elle-même matériellement la vérité.[25]

> Languages imperfect insofar as they are many; the absolute one is lacking; thought considered as writing without accessories, not even whispers, still *stills* immortal speech; the diversity, on earth, of idioms prevents anyone from proffering words that would otherwise be, when made uniquely, the material truth.

If language is inherently imperfect and imprecise (each sign pointing in too many directions), poetry alone might be able to master contingency, achieving the seemingly impossible: absolute necessity, which would be immortal truth. This condition of existential contingency was central to Mallarmé's view of the human condition in modernity. The sources of this contingency, for Mallarmé, were both existential and historical: the death of Victor Hugo, who so thoroughly determined the reading and writing of French poetry that his absence left a "desert of silence" in which too much possibility yawned;[26] the death of a clear (if "habitual") understanding of what makes poetry poetry and who can write it; the terror of foundationlessness or arbitrarity; the death of the author:

> Une ordonnance du livre de vers point innée ou partout, élimine le hasard; encore la faut-il, pour omettre l'auteur: or, un sujet, fatal, implique, parmi les morceaux ensemble, tel accord quant à la place, dans le volume, qui correspond.[27]

> An order innate to the book of verse exists inherently or everywhere, eliminating chance; it's also necessary, to eliminate the author: now, any subject is fated to imply, among the fragments brought together, a strange certainty about its appropriate place in the volume.

In the wake of the death(s) of the "Master(s)" of the previous "phase" (Hugo, God, tradition, metaphysical certainty), poetry responds not by reasserting the qualities of these masters in their orderly necessity, but by hazarding new courses in direct engagement with abyssal potentiality, contingency, and freedom:

> Le vers, je crois, avec respect attendit que le géant qui l'identifiait à sa main tenace et plus ferme toujours de forgeron, vînt à manquer; pour, lui, se rompre. Toute la langue, ajustée à la métrique, y recouvrant ses coupes vitales, s'évade, selon une libre disjonction aux mille éléments simples . . .[28]

> Verse, I think, respectfully waited until the giant who identified it with his tenacious and firm blacksmith's hand came to be missing, in order to, itself, break. All of language, measured by meter, recovering therin its vitality, escapes, broken down into thousands of simple elements . . .

The composition of the words and the white space has the air of scattering, randomness, and chance—yet it is precisely composed, using the whole space of the page as a blank canvas and the range of typeface sizes to highlight the complex weave of different syntactical strands. Blanchot notes in a letter Mallarmé's assertion that " 'the intellectual armature of the poem' . . . is less in the organization of the words (the rhymes or the rhythms) than in the space which isolates them. '*Significant silence no less beautiful to compose, than verses.'* "[29] Mallarmé speaks of *composing* the blanks, as one would compose a piece of music. Mallarmé is up to something highly nuanced in which the abyss of the blank, the horizon of nonbeing, is always at hand, and its pure potentiality remains a part of what comes contingently into being.

The handful of words that form the smaller capitalized strand on page 3, "quand bien même lancé dans des circonstances / éternelles // du fond d'un naufrage" ("even when launched in eternal / circumstances / from the depths of a shipwreck"), begins in a modifying clause that only gradually becomes intelligible as grammared speech. We see a similar semantic opacity or delay in the opening line of the short poem "Éventail de Madame Mallarmé": "Avec comme pour langage / rien . . ."[30] Both lines heighten an awareness of language as composed by discrete particles (*des éléments simples*) strung together and only afterward acquiring a kind of precarious relation to one another. At the bottom of the page, "du fond d'un naufrage" offers us a hint of location, even as it leaves us (still in need of a verb) wondering whether and how the "un coup de dés jamais" of the large strand ties in with the "quan bien même . . ." of the small strand. The shipwreck's ambiguity renders it at once a clear image and an orphaned image without apparent connection to the poem except sensorially: it lies at the floor of the page, surrounded by line fragments of varying sizes and a lot of white space. Semantically, the line of tension in these lines forms between the particularity, randomness, and materiality of *circonstances* and the word *éternelles*, a suspension and duration of time at odds with the momentariness and unpredictability of circumstances as they take place.[31]

"SOIT / que // l'Abîme . . .": at last a verb, but not a main verb, and situated in an uneasy tense.[32] Already the preceding page has prepared us to be uncertain as to whether this next step down, into typographic granularity in the smaller lowercase font, should be read as a continuation of the preceding strand or as a new and syntactically independent voice. Should the "soit" be connected syntactically to "l'Abîme?" They are in different typographic strands, which elsewhere seem to want to be read horizontally through the poem. And yet the syntax connects ("il faut une garantie— // La Syntaxe—").[33] Can it be that the "soit" connects to multiple strands— syntactically and typographically? Already the reading stalls and encounters friction with its own processes of deliberation. The reader brushes against a kind of metalevel of semantic judgment that usually goes on unnoticed behind every act of reading. Now this process is brought forward by a multifront ratcheting-up of uncertainty, producing an attentional grinding of gears.

One of the formal features that contributes to the precarious, hovering quality of attention required and performed by this text is the emergence of perfect and quasi-Alexandrine lines. We find Alexandrines that are broken and scattered, only brought together by the act of pinning lines together: "d'un bâtiment / penché de l'un ou l'autre bord," and "que / / l'Abîme / blanchi / étale / furieux," and "sous une inclinaison / plane désespérément" which asks us to locate and scan the line as prose, without the sounded *e*. These lines' manner of hovering around the twelve-syllable line recalls Mallarmé's comparison, in *Crise de vers,* of an "intermediate" approach to prosody, between faithful loyalty to "our hexameter" and unmetered "free verse:"

> Le poëte d'un tact aigu qui considère cet alexandrin toujours comme le joyau définitif, mais à ne sortir, épée, fleur, que peu et selon quelque motif prémédité, y touche comme pudiquement ou se joue à l'entour, il en octroie de voisins accords, avant de le donner superbe et nu : laissant son doigté défaillir contre la onzième syllabe ou se propager jusqu'à une treizième maintes fois.[34]

> The poet with acute tact who consideres the alexandrine the definitive jewel, but not to bring out, sword, flower, very often and according to some premeditated end, touches it shyly or plays around it—he gives us neighboring chords before releasing it, superb and naked: letting his fingers drag against the eleventh syllable or go on to a thirteenth, many times.

These pinned-together "lines" or twelve-syllable groups, such as "très à l'intérieur résume," "jusqu'adapter," and "à l'envergure," which cut vertically through a long line spanning the width of the page ("l'ombre enfouie . . ."), require a process of multidirectional scanning. In these constellations we are asked to detect the line, even when it is interrupted by another line, or to sense the convergence of a syllabic unit that is formed of dispersed elements.

Midway through the poem, with the entrance of the sole character, "le Maître," contingency comes to the fore in its more violent aspect, chaos. It is chaos against which the willing subject is pitted and chaos that overtakes it. Chaos is linked to an extremity of contingency, the terrifying condition of existence and judgment without foundation. The crisis contingency poses for subjectivity (the problem of judgment in a context governed by chaos) is dramatized by the Master. The subject's struggle against chaos, his struggle to assert reason, or ordering intellect, comes to its final stand against *l'Abîme*, in a last gasp at obtaining a basis for judgment, at obtaining a ground for probability—the throw of the dice.

The entrance of a human subject into the poem is accompanied by several changes in the form. First, the visual chaos of the poem's layout is heightened, and following Mallarmé's instruction to take syntax as our guide, we must follow the lines back and forth across the page. The subject, presented as *le Maître*, cannot help but bring to mind Kant's sovereign subject as well as the Master of Hegel, particularly apt in its effort to sustain its mastery, having built itself up and set out, buoyed by the vast entity over which he tries to hold dominion and that now rises up like an immense slave population—to overtake him. The capitalized and isolated *Esprit*, the divided line "l'unique Nombre qui ne peut pas /// être un autre," as well as the line "en reployer la division et passer fier" underline Mallarmé's Hegelian influences in the suggestion of an oppositional struggle of coming-into-being, the emergence of something out of nothing. Meanwhile, the diction surrounding the sovereign—"surgi," "cadavre," "jouer," "en maniaque chenu"—emphasizes the proximity of reason to madness, the horizon of chaos always at hand even within the subject itself.

The poem's repeated leaping of the page's fold brings forth the fold's own physical qualities as an element of the text: the depth of the book, where it becomes its own vanishing point. The text moves on the surface, and the eye each time skims over the deep ravine—*le gouffre*—between the pages, simulating vertigo, a Borgesian idea of reading of which there is an abundance in this text. Reading slows even more here. The reader is placed in a position of the Master—clinging to a frail handrail of syntax for judging the next step, looking for possible grammatical connections to signal a way through the text. We hold onto a subject and a verb; we match tenses; we line things up.

The ninth double-page pane reaches an apex in which all the strands, or voices, converge, their various syntaxes and tonalities combining and competing. The text takes up by far the most room here than in any of the other panes, stretching to the corners of the page. This pane is most explicitly about existence and gives name to the central problem of the poem's particular attentional grappling: *le hasard*. From "C'ÉTAIT" to "CE SERAIT" to "EXISTÂT-IL," there is a movement from the past to the conditional to the future. *LE HASARD* lies at the center, referring, it would seem, to all the verbs at once. This suggests a temporal condition unique to *le hasard*, which concerns the contingency of the present and the potentiality of the future. Again, this transtemporal suspense is at odds with that of the suddenness and temporally bounded events of wreck, dice throw, and poem. The poem thus dramatizes a tension between contingency and potentiality, playing out a head-to-head of present and future temporalities that results in a suspension of the present.

"RIEN . . . N'AURA EU LIEU . . . QUE LE LIEU": *Nothing will have taken place but the place*. This ties back to Mallarmé's insistence on the physicality of poetic language when it is allowed to obtain vitality as a topography. And yet nothing is contained in the location of the poem except the poem. There is nothing *outside* of its sounds, visual play, and rhythms. It refers to nothing beyond and is precisely what is created out of nothing. It is, in this sense, an empty act, without meaning, but with *effects*, just as the dice throw is in itself meaningless, but renders an effect, an outcome. What is important here is that the language acts: this requires a precision of timing and location that, accomplished, allows the author to recede and the poem to step out as a vital entity.

If anything "takes place" in the course of the COUP besides "le lieu," it is (perhaps) a *fusionne* of the place with *au delà*—the fusion of the *hereness* or *presence* of the poetic event in its particularity with the Infinite, understood not as an "out there," or a transcendent realm or divinity, but the distillation of the particular to its pure resonance—the Mallarméan *Idée*, or that which slips through the gap between our flawed language and the things it tries to contain:

> Je dis: une fleur! et, hors de l'oubli où ma voix relègue aucun contour, en tant que quelque chose d'autre que les calices sus, musicalement se lève, idée même et suave, l'absente de tous bouquets.[35]
>
> I say: a flower! And, out of the oblivion where my voice casts every contour, insofar as it is something other than the known bloom, there arises, musically, the very idea in its mellowness; in other words, what is absent from every bouquet.

"RIEN . . . N'AURA EU LIEU . . . QUE LE LIEU" "EXCEPTÉ . . . PEUT-ÊTRE . . . UNE CONSTELLATION." Particles of singular exception such as *excepté, sauf,* and *rien/que* appear repeatedly throughout the the poem, forming reversals and conditional contradictions whose effects are similar to that of the Hölderlinian *aber*. Both techniques lend a quality of the precarious and the conditional to the poem's utterances and affirmations. Inspired by Hegelian opposition, this movement of contradiction or doubling back (ABA) does not resolve synthetically (the dialectic C), but continues in a seemingly irresolvable process of thesis and antithesis, creation (poiesis) and decreation (antipoiesis.) It is in this way that the poem stays in motion, stays alert, and resists the (lifeless) fixity of synthetic resolution. The poem closes, appropriately, in the unresolved anticipation of eleven sections. The last page is full of line constellations that either strike the Alexandrine squarely ("veillant / doutant / roulant / brillant et méditant"; "EXCEPTÉ . . . PEUT-ÊTRE . . . UNE CONSTELLATION") or hover around it ("sur quelque surface vacante et supérieure"; "vers ce doit être / le Septentrion aussi Nord"). These approaches, paired with the precision of the poem's composure of approach, combine to produce a text that cultivates multidirectional and multisensory vigilance without rewarding this attention, as Hölderlin does, with emphatic breakthrough or revelation. The poem remains in the mode of vigilant potential, without that vigilance leading to a culminating or interruptive event. The deliberateness with which the poem's form resists synthetic resolution exhibits a greater restraint than would a more traditionally resolving closure.

What mode of reading, an action so predicated on judgment, is possible in a state of contingency? "Lire— // Cette pratique": the text is above all an exercise in attention. Even as the subject is overtaken by l'Abîme, the poem gains traction, as does the reader. The poem exercises a multisensory, multidirectional, vigilant attention to language, one that attends not only to rhythm, rhyme, and semantic content, but to color, lighting, percussion, and the fugal weaving of voices. Mallarmé writes: "Let an average group of words, under the comprehension of the gaze, line up in definitive traits, surrounded by silence."

  veillant
 doutant
  roulant
    brillant et méditant[36]

These verbs provide a description of the movement of Mallarmé's language and instructions on how to read: come close, remain bent to the page for a long time, to test the syntax and look for points of connection, and keep paying attention without epiphanic relief, *hors l'intérêt*, within a condition of contingency in which the sole guarantee is a syntax that is stretched *almost* to the breaking point: *doutant, méditant*. If there is a payoff in this poetic process, it is not one of revelation or transcendence, but rather of the slower transfigurative effects of vigilant praxis, which, even as it meditates the poem into being, dissolves the subject into the negative space held open by ongoing vigilant attention and the ever proximal potentiality and contingency of the nothing. The work of poetic attention in Mallarmé becomes an ongoing labor of guarding both the something (being) and the nothing (potentiality) against the anything (arbitrarity).

CHAPTER VIII

Resignation

Relinquishing the Object

Rimbaud : Wright

You could not be born at a better period than the present,
when we have lost everything.
—SIMONE WEIL, GRAVITY AND GRACE

In an essay on Wallace Stevens, J. Hillis Miller writes, "First something happens which 'decreates,' which destroys an earlier imagination of the world. Then man is left face to face with the bare rock of reality."[1] A number of poets—Eliot, Baudelaire, Rimbaud, Williams, Stevens, Celan—have addressed this "bare rock of reality" as the terrain of twentieth-century poetry. Eliot saw it as a wasteland of "stony rubbish"[2]— and a site for "The Burial of the Dead"; Stevens, a "barrenness," a "mind of winter," "a grappling with rocks."[3] Many modern poems seem to have been written in the face of giving up certain beliefs, forging new paths within the condition of resignation—making a home in the wasteland in and through poetic practice. The "something" was felt as the ripples of numerous historical events that shook the collective psyche and moral bedrock: the two world wars, the catastrophe that Paul Celan called "that which happened,"[4] the escalating pace of cultural and technological change, and the alienation that accompanied the "death of god."[5]

While poems of resignation can be found in other periods (poems of existential doubt and spiritual crisis, for example, are by no means unique to the modern period), a particular quality of poetic resignation can be traced as an unmistakable characteristic of modern poetry—as explicit or implicit theme, as formal denouement, as tone. If we take the late nineteenth century as a starting point, with Baudelaire's ushering in of a specifically modernist discourse of ennui, urbanity, and the profane, and add in the distinct voices of Eliot, Yeats, and Stevens in the early twentieth century, we find a period of pervasive struggle with the limits of meaning and the pursuit of possible responses to the perceived impossibility or untenability of genuine belief: that is, a period dominated by a mode of resignation that assumes different names, forms, and styles and led to different existential and poetic outcomes, from silence to conversion to madness to dry, blank humor. Taking in a little more of the twentieth century, we can see that the direct and explicit grappling with resignation in modernism's first and second generations gradually seeped out of the semantic and into a formal and tonal attitude increasingly pervasive in a great deal of Western and non-Western poetries alike from the mid-twentieth century through the 1990s, after which point we find, at least in the increasingly program-driven American scene, a surprising renewal of a poetics of sincerity. This specifically mid- and late-twentieth-century *tone* of resignation runs through the poetry of A. R. Ammons, Charles Bukowski, John Ashbery, Robert Creeley, and Charles Wright, to name only a few canonical American examples.

To think of resignation as a mode of attention might seem incongruent—even a contradiction in terms. On closer consideration, we find that the act of letting go, of disengaging from a given pursuit, constitutes a shift into a different mode of attention—a release from an interested, transitive attending into a nonattached, disinterested attention.[6] In resignation, attention has given up one form and either forged or given in to another form. This act of letting go, in shifting its relationship to intentionality and interest, also shifts its relationship to time. Like vigilance, resignation occupies a particular—necessarily *present*—temporality. But unlike vigilance, resignation is inflected by a relationship to the past more than the future. It is an experience of attentional present in which the futurity of interested striving has been resigned, and the new present is inflected by the former state, and by the now past-tense act of resigning. Because resignation, as an attentional state, is shaped by something having been let go, its intransitivity derives partly from the contrast to what has been let go: intransitivity is thus an experience of negativity or empty-handedness after the relinquishment or giving up of something previously held as an object of ambition, desire, or potentiality. The present of this particular mode of intransitivity is one that is inflected by the shadow of the past, the shadow that remembers what has been let go. In other words, unlike vigilance's inflection by a future or potential event of attention, resignation is inflected by a past or prior event of attention. While the first is an intransitivity whose absence is a not-yet, the second is an intransitivity whose absence of an object is a no-longer. Both represent a state fundamentally rooted in an experience of the present that is inflected by a presently unavailable temporality.

Resignation also shares with vigilance a wake of religious and spiritual connotations and usages, but it, too, is fundamentally descriptive of an attentional condition. Given that attention is an ordering and shaping of consciousness, the resonances between attentional modes and the terminology of spiritual experience is neither surprising nor coincidental, nor does it suggest a hidden allegiance between attention studies and a given religious or spiritual philosophy. It is rather the opposite: the more we come to understand attention, the more we understand religious and spiritual theories for what (I think) they are: languages and narratives that seek to describe shifts in consciousness through various practices and events of attention. Simone Weil famously defined attention as "the natural prayer of the soul," but also inverted this to define prayer as "absolute unmixed attention."

Historical inflections of poetic attention can be traced as latent, often unrecognized themes in the criticism of a given period. In critical theorizations of modernism and postmodernism, for example, the inflection of a particular mode of poetic attention can be discerned as a shared latency, an underlying tonal quality, running through a forest of seemingly starkly diverging theories. In the next few pages, I offer a sketch of how diverse theorizations of the twentieth century describe, by different names and from different scholarly and ideological angles, a mode of resignation that runs through modern and postmodern poetry.

One of the challenges with writing about the qualities of twentieth-century poetry is that many of the attentional states crucial to the kinds of aesthetic and poetic experience explored during this period are, to borrow Robert Musil's oft-borrowed phrase, experiences without qualities. The poetry of resignation feeds, is fed by, and often bleeds into poetries of boredom, depression, distraction, lethargy, mindlessness, detachment, despair, and silence. Yet each of these constitutes a response to a limit, a shift in which something has been let go, in which a paradigm of positive, future-oriented belief (religious or secular) gives way to a resignation to its absence, nonexistence, or untenability. For this reason, while life and even poetry might go on through a resignative shift, whatever comes after this shift will be shaped at least in part by the *absence* of what was held in faith before. To be clear, this need not be religious faith: cultural norms, moral foundations, social values, political convictions, personal ambitions—all of these are forms of secular faith-based, future-oriented thinking; examples of their abandonments can be found throughout poetic imprints of the twentieth century.

Critics from diverse theoretical approaches have given different names to the particular quality of emptiness welling in and between the lines of so much twentieth-century poetry. This has yielded a plethora of terms for and variously trending evaluations of what I argue is a historically inflected shift of attention. It is a testament to both the ubiquity and the subtlety of this attentional shift that, despite so many theorizations, it has remained unrecognized. Upon closer inspection, the sense of postness that runs through so much early- to mid-twentieth-century poetry, and implicitly in so many critical characterizations of the period, reveals itself as a mode of resignation. This paradigm is reflected throughout theories of the modern and postmodern as well, though it has been given so many different names that the underlying modal shift has been obscured, as has its essential character as a shift—or, indeed, series of shifts—in the prevailing inflection of poetic attention.

This is particularly vital in a consideration of modern and postmodern poetics of resignation because it serves as a reminder that it is not only the production of poetic works that changed in (and after) modernity but the culture of readerly attention as well. Given the high degree of salience of the mode of resignation in the shift to modernism and, even more, to postmodernism, the reception of any work will reflect the features available or unavailable to perception and thinking: in other words, any text read in postmodernity is susceptible to reconfiguration in terms of the resignations of the period.[7]

This notion of resignation in fact runs beneath all of the various terms this shift has been pegged with, from *alienation* and *estrangement* to *absurdity, cynicism, disenchantment, camp,* and *Verwindung*.[8] Gianni Vattimo has positioned the Heideggerian conception of *Verwindung* at the center of the resignative shift to postmodernity, defining the word as "something similar to yet distinct from Überwindung ('going beyond') in that Verwindung contains no notion of dialectical sublimation (Aufhebung) nor of a 'leaving behind' which characterizes the connection we have with a past that no longer has anything to say to us." This is particularly true when one considers the roots of *resignation* itself: re+signare—un-seal, cancel, un-sign. Each of the above terms represents an effort to name a subtle quality of "un-sealing," or "dis-connecting," as well as "un-signing," the ungluing of name from thing, subject from object, noumena from phenomena. In this light, we can understand the twentieth century's litany of endings as so many letters of resignation.[9]

The sociohistorical conditions of reading and writing in the postmodern era are characterized by a provisionality, a contingency, and a lowering of expectations that can be reread as a phenomenon of attentional resignation, a choiceless shift from one attentional mode, or from one perception of salience, to another. Fredric Jameson reads the shift between modern and postmodern modalities as not merely a shift in stylistic choices or literary fashions, but a necessary environmental response to social conditions overwhelmed by spectacle, repetition, and arbitrarily, externally determined valuations and devaluations.[10] This response is reflected in the role of the poet, whose alienation, in the words of Stathis Gourgouris, "is chronicled by registering . . . the place of their displacement": "The recognition that, in this world, lies are the order of the day comes with an understanding that under such conditions, truth cannot overcome them. In this order of things, when purity is impossible, one must fight to find a place that ensures survival and readiness for a time of truth to come."[11] If, through disillusion or fatigue, this fight fails, and one resigns to the absence of a "truth to come," the survival mode yields to endurance without the hopeful vigil implied in "making ready." Brian Crews has described this in other terms: a resignation to the "sure knowledge that the past is irrecoverable."[12] Philippe Lacoue-Labarthe has argued that this condition affects not only the thematic content of writing but its form and very possibility, producing a halting, futile, self-swallowing language: "stuttering is the only 'language' of the age. The end of meaning—hiccuping, halting."[13]

The question is this: when the possibility (or point) of meaning is in question, when there seems to be little ground for meaningful or "sincere" speech, why not fall silent? Under such a condition, what was thought to be the space of poetic utterance is no longer available; the poet is "always being thrown back from the dialogue one had thought possible and then, in withdrawal, 'huddling,' as Heidegger says of Hölderlin, no longer able to speak; stuttering, swallowed up in idiom. Or falling silent."[14] In other words, there is a choice, at this limit, between a poetry of resignation and the resignation of poetry. This limit, and this choice, are the central problematic I explore in the readings that compose the remainder of this chapter.

I draw a similar distinction between poems *about* resignation and poems *of* resignation, as I did in the earlier chapter on imagination. There are a number of poems *about* resignation—with a sweep of poems of the same title by Henry Wadsworth Longfellow, Matthew Arnold, J. D. McClatchy, and Nikki Giovanni, as well as Coleridge's "The Pains of Sleep," Robert Burns's "Winter: A Dirge" and Hopkins's "I wake and feel the fell of dark, not day" and "No worst, there is none. Pitched past pitch of grief"—poems that grapple with the experience of distance from God or that wrestle with the subject matter of faith and doubt. While these are interesting from a thematic standpoint, I will focus in this section on the poetry *of* resignation—a poetry that is shaped by, seems to emerge from, and formally reflects the state of resignation as an attentional state, or that more indirectly evokes the shift into resignation by other means. Poems in this category include Eliot's *The Waste Land* and *Ash Wednesday,* Stevens's "The Plain Sense of Things" and "Sunday Morning," Les Murray's "A Retrospect of Humidity," and Audre Lorde's "Afterimages."

In what follows I turn to two very different forms of poetic resignation in the work of Arthur Rimbaud and Charles Wright. Each exhibits a particular response to the reaching or realization of a spiritual, epistemological, or existential limit. These limits are felt culturally, personally, emotionally, but each represents an essentially metaphysical limit and a metaphysical resignation thereto. While Baudelaire's writing on ennui can be seen as a starting point for modern resignation, I have chosen to focus here on Rimbaud, whose poetry and writing career embody an extremity of the poetics of resignation—an extreme that can end only in silence. Rimbaud responds to the limit of possible meaning-making by a convulsive oscillation between boredom and ecstatic madness ending in despair and his resignation *from* poetry and Western modernity wholesale; Wright responds with an ongoing practice of meditating on resignation while holding open the "idea of God," which Stevens forecloses, as impetus for the necessary continuation of poetic practice.

From the Poetry of Resignation to the Resignation of Poetry: Arthur Rimbaud

Rimbaud's final works, *Une Saison en enfer* and *Les Illuminations*,[15] take us through the fitful stages of arrival at a limit of experience, thought, and belief, ultimately demonstrating a limit of the poetics of resignation in the poet's decision to resign from poetry wholesale. While it is impossible to know the full spectrum of reasons for this final "adieu" to the written word, in the poems themselves we find a speaker wrestling with disillusionment with the Western industrialized world (a world embodied in London, the city where Rimbaud spent the final years of his poetic career before quitting both writing and Europe at the age of twenty, ultimately to settle in Yemen). The poems shift between modes of cynical reflection on the cityscape and its inhabitants, responding sometimes with boredom, sometimes with attempted (often failed, always temporary) escapes to delirium. Their oscillation between fragmented, short-line *vers libre* and the unconfined velocities of the prose form suggest this torn position between indulgence and renunciation.[16]

Throughout *Une Saison en enfer* we find exclamations of distress, disgust, and removal from the modern world. Despite the emotional intensity of the poems, a quality of detachment and disconnection pervades, as though the speaker were constantly, willfully, and forcibly repelled or repulsed from any proximity or involvement with the human life and terrains around him. The speaker of *Une Saison* is seemingly crowded by the world and at the same time isolated from it. The speaker is, in many ways, the sole subject of the poems as a whole, for despite the cramming of descriptive fragments of the world, the "I" is the obsessive center of every poem's every line. The "I" is one who is "no longer in the world": "Ah ça! l'horloge de la vie s'est arrêtée tout à l'heure. Je ne suis plus au monde."[17] Rimbaud's poetics of resignation is one of a speaker expelled from connection with the world. There is no object of attention in these poems outside of the speaker's own voice, an echo chamber of estrangements and exclamations, unable to attend to or connect to—to be at home in—the world as it has become: "Décidément, nous sommes hors du monde. Plus aucun son. Mon tact a disparu. Ah! mon château, ma Saxe, mon bois de saules. Les soirs, les matins, les nuits, les jours . . . Suis-je las!"[18] While *Les Illuminations* was probably completed after *Une Saison en enfer*, the latter forms the most direct address to Rimbaud's final resignation from the modern world and his poetic *adieu*. He writes in the prose poem "L'impossible," "J'ai eu raison de mépriser ces bonshommes qui ne perdraient pas l'occasion d'une caresse, parasites de la propreté et de la santé de nos femmes, aujourd'hui qu'elles sont si peu d'accord avec nous. / J'ai eu raison dans tous mes dédains: puisque je m'évade! / Je m'évade!"[19]

Central to both *Une Saison en enfer* and *Les Illuminations* is a quality of fatigue that runs through even the most convulsive passages. As Rimbaud puts it, "Ma vie est usée."[20] As in the lines quoted previously, senses are dulled, connection to the living world is lost despite the most concerted efforts to regain it through sex, intoxication, and satiric laughter: "Je meurs de lassitude. C'est le tombeau, je m'en vais aux vers, horreur de l'horreur! Satan, farceur, tu veux me dissoudre, avec tes charmes. Je réclame. Je réclame! un coup de fourche, une goutte de feu."[21] We find this sensory and attentional void in the poem "Faim," in which appetite is reduced to the taste of dust, broken stones, and air. The speaker pleads with himself (again the folding back on the self that underscores Rimbaud's subjective echo chamber) to be hungry, to find hunger even for what paltry remnants remain in the voided terrain:

Si j'ai du goût, ce n'est guère
Que pour la terre et les pierres.
Je déjeune toujours d'air,
De roc, de charbons, de fer.

Mes faims, tournez. Passez, faims,
    Le pré des sons.
Attirez le gai venin
    Des liserons.

Mangez les cailloux qu'on brise,
Les vieilles pierres d'églises;
Les galets des vieux déluges,
Pains semés dans les vallées grises.[22]

The repugnance of the modern world is tied, in *Une Saison en enfer*, to Rimbaud's disillusionment with both Christian "delusion" and the rise of rational-scientific thinking, which placates modern man with "proofs," obscuring any deeper and arational search for truth in the world: "n'y a-t-il pas un supplice réel en ce que, depuis cette déclaration de la science, le christianisme, l'homme *se joue,* se prouve les évidences, se gonfle du plaisir de répéter des preuves, et ne vit que comme cela!"[23] And yet the speaker of *Une Saison* scorns his own "spiritual meanderings" and the "madness" of his early writings no less: "Torture subtile, niaise; source de mes divagations spirituelles."²⁴ He sees his own efforts to break through the "fog" of a mechanized and mind-numbing world (through poetry, through intoxication, through spontaneity) as further examples of a nature gone awry, just so many forms of ignorance, lumped in with scientific and religious self-delusions: "N'est-ce pas parce que nous cultivons la brume! Nous mangeons la fièvre avec nos légumes aqueux. Et l'ivrognerie! et le tabac! et l'ignorance! et les dévouements!"²⁵ All these seemingly inescapable errors and inevitable failings typify for Rimbaud the sleep of the modern spirit, dulled to experience, numbing itself through reflexive belief, moral dogmatism ("La morale est la faiblesse de la cervelle"),²⁶ scientific oversimplifications, and the repetitive bored flailings of an indulgent lifestyle whose paltry stimulations are short-lived at best: "—Mais je m'aperçois que mon esprit dort. / S'il était bien éveillé toujours à partir de ce moment, nous serions bientôt à la vérité, qui peut-être nous entoure avec ses anges pleurant! . . . —S'il avait été éveillé jusqu'à ce moment-ci, c'est que je n'aurais pas cédé aux instincts délétères, à une époque immémoriale! . . . —S'il avait toujours été bien éveillé, je voguerais en pleine sagesse!"²⁷

In these lines Rimbaud opposes the sleep of spirit to a possible alternative in wakefulness. Staying "wide awake" offers in this passage the only glimpse of a "way out" in *Une Saison* that is neither despair nor silence. At the same time, staying awake in the spiritual and perceptual sense suggests a possible pathway toward truth. But staying awake, or keeping the "veille" or "vigil," as he refers to it in both *Une Saison* and *Les Illuminations,* is not simple, particularly in a world that seems overwhelmed by a cultural, spiritual, intellectual, and environmental torpor whose characteristic impulses are speed, repetition, and unfulfilling shortcuts. It seems that Rimbaud at once identifies a possible way out, even as he rejects this option, foreclosing the vigil as a presupposed impossibility.

"Adieu," the last poem in *Une Saison en enfer,* both describes and embodies this battle between a glimpsed possibility of wakeful vigilance, and the ultimate resignation to despair: "L'automne. Notre barque élevée dans les brumes immobiles tourne vers le port de la misère, la cité énorme au ciel taché de feu et de boue. . . . Il faut être absolument moderne. / Point de cantiques: tenir le pas gagné. Dure nuit! le sang séché fume sur ma face, et je n'ai rien derrière moi, que cet horrible arbrisseau!"²⁸ Aside from its titular self-description and the finality of its position in Rimbaud's career, "Adieu" enacts the fitful movement of the poet's battle with the limits of meaning-making and, more crucially, communicability—a "spiritual battle" that, in this case, ends in despair. We see the poem wrestle with its own possibility in the syntactical enjambment of its prose through repeated unanswered, self-reflexive questions, statements that begin and break with em dashes or trail off in ellipses and exclamations that seem to lead nowhere.

The speaker of *Une Saison* and *Les Illuminations* is a disaffected observer, disengaged from and separate from the fabric of modern urban life. The position is obsessively self-descriptive, commenting on both self and world with the same dispossessed apartness, as exemplified in "Ville": Je suis un éphémère et point trop mécontent citoyen d'une métropole crue moderne parce que tout goût connu a été éludé dans les ameublements et l'extérieur des maisons aussi bien que dans le plan de la ville. Ici vous ne signaleriez les traces d'aucun monument de superstition. La morale et la langue sont réduites à leur plus simple expression, enfin!"[29] In the world perceived in these lines, all values are replaced by and all actions predetermined by the rule of efficiency and reproducibility. The prose form positions the act of the poem somewhere between commentary and craft—a poetic event that seems to take place outside of the poem, a movement of thought separated from both itself and the living world by the window's pane of glass. Appropriately, and in perfect complement to the dramatic farewell of *Une Saison*, *Les Illuminations* concludes in a postpoetic shrug, in a poem in which everything—from sport, fantasy, and comforts to voice, body, anarchy and salvation—is "à vendre."[30]

Writing on Rimbaud's resignation from poetry in *L'Expérience intérieure*, Georges Bataille reads the final poetry as an encounter with the "extreme limit" of the possible, and an account of a battle to either reach or communicate this limit that ultimately, for Rimbaud, ends in despair. He argues that "the last known poem of Rimbaud is not the extreme limit. If Rimbaud reached the extreme limit, he only attained the communication of it by means of his despair: he suppressed possible communication, he no longer wrote poems."[31] Despair, in Bataille's reading, embodied in Rimbaud's "giving up" and "turning his back on" poetic communication, is itself a final and most desperate form of communication, as a vow of silence is itself an ultimate speech act. Elaborating on this understanding of final resignation to silence *as itself a communicative poetic act,* Bataille writes,

> The refusal to communicate is a more hostile means of communication, but the most powerful. . . . No one will know if horror (weakness) or modesty was responsible for Rimbaud's giving up. It is

possible that the limits of horror have been extended (no more God). In any case, to speak of weakness makes little sense: Rimbaud maintained his will for the extreme limits on other levels (that above all of giving up). It is possible that he gave up, failing having attained it (the extreme limit is not disorder or luxuriance) being too demanding to bear it, too lucid not to see. It is even possible that after having attained it, but doubting that this should have a meaning or event that this should take place—as the state of one who attains it does not last—he couldn't bear doubt. A longer search would be useless, although the will for the extreme limit stops at nothing (we can't really attain it).[32]

In Bataille's thinking, despair represents a powerful form of meditation—a supreme act of attention or "inner mastery" akin to yoga but without yoga's potential to become either physical exercise or spiritual dogma: "This mastery of our innermost movements, which in the long run we can acquire, is well known: it is *yoga*. But *yoga* . . . practiced for its own sake, advances no further than an aesthetics or a hygiene, whereas I have recourse to the same means (laid bare), *in despair*."[33] He holds up Jesus's moment of doubt on the cross ("my God, my God, why hast thou forsaken me?") as a moment of nonknowledge, a moment at the extremity of both reason and faith.[34]

Whether Rimbaud's resignation from the world of letters was, as Bataille suggests here, a choice in favor of a more powerful albeit "more hostile" mode of communication, or whether it was a final result of a less noble, more all-too-human combination of boredom, fear, and giving up, we cannot know. But given the deliberateness of the move—not simply a matter of prolonged writer's block, loss of a habit, or a more pragmatic giving up of poetry's foolery in favor of a career in trade—it seems more likely that Rimbaud's resignation had something of the vastness of intention that Bataille's note suggests. His boredom is existential, his despair and ultimate renunciation of poetic language an extreme poetic act in itself. The writing itself is self-mocking: "Quel ennui, l'heure du 'cher corps' et 'cher coeur.'"[35] So is the speaking subject, having "seen enough . . . had enough . . . known enough," as "Départ" ("Departure") puts it bluntly: "Assez vu. La vision s'est rencontrée à tous les airs. / Assez eu. Rumeurs des villes, le soir, et au soleil, et toujours. / Assez connu. Les arrêts de la vie.—Ô Rumeurs et Visions! / Départ dans l'affection et le bruit neufs!"[36] And, as the resigned attention forms a resigned world, so the world too has had enough: "Les sentiers sont âpres. Les monticules se couvrent de genêts. L'air est immobile. Que les oiseaux et les sources sont loin! Ce ne peut être que la fin du monde, en avançant."[37]

"This must be the end of the world, lying ahead"—the voice throughout *Les Illuminations* is uniquely positioned between three temporalities: one of postness (postfailure, postresignation, with and without regret), one of futurity, by turns apocalyptic and messianic, and one of presence torn between these modes, yielding a present-tense cocktail of boredom, frustration, mourning, premonition, and tragic hero songs: "Cela commença par quelques dégoûts et cela finit,—ne pouvant nous saisir sur-le-champ de cette éternité,—cela finit par une débandade de parfums."[38] Rimbaud's writing occupies a temporality shaped by this convergence of leanings toward a nostalgic past, repulsion from the present moment, and grasping for a possible future that might offer an escape from things as they are. This particular temporal convergence is central to a poetics in which the poet's primary role is that of displaced and self-destructive witness—a witness whose ultimate act is a kind of suicidal detonation at the limit of the unknown. As Rimbaud puts it in a letter to Paul Demeny, "I say one must be a *seer, make oneself a seer*. The Poet makes himself a seer by a long, gigantic and rational derangement of all the senses. All forms of love, suffering, and madness. He searches himself. . . . He reaches the unknown, and when, bewildered, he ends by losing the intelligence of his visions, he has seen them. Let him die as he leaps through unheard of and unnamable things."[39] This passage offers a glimpse of a larger project or practice with which Rimbaud's resignation—both stylistic and professional—is involved. It is a practice that has an endpoint in extremity of thought and perception, in which the poetic subject itself is renounced in an act of divestment from the poetic itself. Yet Rimbaud's discussion of this aim is positioned in terms of responsibility. In the same letter to Demeny, Rimbaud describes the poet as "responsible for humanity, even for the *animals*; he will have to have his inventions smelt, felt, and heard; if what he brings back *from down there* has form, he gives form; if it is formless, he gives formlessness. A language must be found."[40] Aside from the self-destructive sacrificial end of ultimate resignation itself, the ongoing task of poetry lies, here, in a responsibility to "find the language" for both form and formlessness. That this practice takes Rimbaud to a limit of resignation becomes an integral part, and perhaps even a necessary outcome, of modern poetic practice in itself, rather than an abandonment.

The problem with Rimbaud's silence as a poetic act is that it is the last one. Even if we take Bataille's view that poetic despair is itself a powerfully communicative noncommunication, as poetic practice, this act is incredibly short-lived. In total silence, there is no way for the poet to practice what Rimbaud sees as poetic responsibility—that is, the finding of a language for what he "brings back" from the depths of experience, for form and formlessness. What emerges is a problem familiar to semiotics: without language, there is no approach to the ineffable. Yet language will of course never reach the ineffable—only silence can do that. On the other hand, silence is only notable as such within a context of nonsilence. Bataille puts the paradox this way: "Words, their labyrinths, the exhausting immensity of their 'possibles,' in short their treachery, have something of quicksand about them." "This difficulty is expressed in this way: *the word silence is still a sound*, to speak is in itself to imagine knowing; and to no longer know, it would be necessary to no longer speak."[41] In other words, the communication of nonknowledge or an epistemological limit is possible only in the cessation of speech. Bataille attributes this to the "quicksand" quality of words,[42] constantly pulling us back into the realm of positive knowledge or its semblance, the assertions of the subject over its perceived "objects" and the lure of categories, concepts, and subjective ambition (a mode Bataille calls "Project"). There is not an easy "way out" of this subjective default mode, since "trying to get out," he points out, is a project in itself, possessed of all the same problematic claims to knowledge and subjective assertions.

While silence is one fail-safe response to the problem of language's alliance with knowledge, Bataille and Rimbaud both suggest an alternative path latent in words' other, more hidden alliance with the world of sense—perception taking place in interior moments of attention, not in reason's conceptualizing process. Bataille's writing on this other side of language bears strong resemblance to Blanchot's writing on the "unlit slope" of language, with Celan's writing on attention and the "breath turn" of language, and, interestingly, with Buddhist writings on forms of language that elicit objectless awareness and nonknowledge and move us into attentive presence and away from the mediating impulse of concepts:[43]

> We would not get out of this sand, without some sort of cord which is extended to us. Although words drain almost all life from within

us—there is almost not a single sprig of life which the bustling host of these ants (words) hasn't seized, dragged, accumulated without respite—there subsists in us a silent, elusive, ungraspable part. In the region of words, of discourse, this part is neglected. Thus it usually escapes us. We can only attain it or have it at our disposal on certain terms. They are the vague inner movements, which depend on no object and have no intent—states which, similar to others linked to the purity of the sky, the room, to which it can refer, and which directs attention towards what it grasps—is dispossessed, can say nothing, is limited to stealing these states from attention (profiting from their lack of precision, it right away draws attention elsewhere).[44]

Here Bataille seems to suggest an alternative to the ordinary bustling swarm of language use, through the channeling of attention inward, away from a fixation on objects (even including word-objects) toward an inner realm, felt in "des mouvements intérieurs vagues," that is, objectless, suspended, and expansive. This redirection of attention away from the transitive and toward the intransitive constitutes an ongoing practice of meditation. If this can take place *in the material of language* without being overtaken by language's tendency toward focalization, conceptualization, and endless referentiality, there might be a space for a poetics of resignation without despair. This meditative alternative offers itself, in Battaille's thinking, as a life raft, a rope out of the quicksand, a last sprig of life that might pull one, through language, out of despair in language. In other words, there is hope: "The limit is crossed with a weary horror: hope seems a respect which fatigue grants to the necessity of the world."[45] In the work of Charles Wright, resignative attention can be seen as a practice of poetic perseverance and the maintenance of possibility in the absence of faith.

Architectures of Absence: Resignation as Meditation in Charles Wright

Writing under the influence of Rimbaud, Eliot, and Stevens (as well as Dante, Dickinson, Pound, Yeats, Montale, and Justice), Wright offers an example of a late-twentieth-century American poetics of resignation. Yet the attentional state of resignation felt throughout Wright's poems—indeed throughout his entire oeuvre—does not translate to a poetics of despair (if resignation were an ending, or automatically ended in despair, there might be only one poem of resignation, after which nothing to say—as was the case with Rimbaud). Rather, resignation in Wright is an opening to an ongoing meditative practice that represents what is possible given the limited, constrained reality of experience in the world.[46] The practice of resigned meditation in Wright's work is rooted in an ongoing inquiry into the limits of experience, the limits of the soul, the limits of the body in its terrain of physical matter and memory, and the keeping of a practice, even in the absence of faith: "Attention's a gift, Simone Weil thought— / The world becomes more abundant in severest light."[47] The practice of attention, in Wright, is paradoxical: first, it centers on paying attention and asking questions of the world, even having resigned oneself to the absence (or at least the unavailability) of answers. At the same time, it requires holding open the question (or, in Wright's words, the "idea") of God, even while knowing that he does not exist, or will not reveal himself except (perhaps) through material objects and landscapes. This is, to borrow Mark Jarman's apt term, Wright's "metaphysics of absence."[48] In practice, and indeed *as* practice, resigned meditation in Wright translates to a ceaseless exercise of attention to "little and mortal things," yard, tree, word, line: "Through Language, strict attention—".[49]

> We *are* our final vocabulary,
>   and how we use it.
> There is no secret contingency.
> There's only the rearrangement, the redescription
> Of little and mortal things.
> There's only this single body, this tiny garment
> Gathering the past against itself,
>   making it otherwise.[50]

Laboring away in rearrangement and redescription, Wright's poems begin in and return to disillusionment and the relinquishing of belief ("a paltry thing / and will betray us, soul's load scotched / Against the invisible"). This relinquishment becomes reconfirmation that "we are what we've always thought we were— / . . . Butting the nothingness—/ in the wrong place, in the wrong body."[51] We go about endlessly redescribing and repositioning ourselves in terms of some higher meaning, "The definer of all things," which "cannot be spoken of." Wright's poetry seems to practice letting go, letting the great definer be if not nonexistent at least inaccessible to our spiritual and linguistic reachings:

> It is not knowledge or truth.
> We get no closer than next-to-it.
> Beyond wisdom, beyond denial,
>   it asks us for nothing,
> According to Pseudo-Dionysus, which sounds good to me.[52]

"Sounds good to me"—a signature Wrightian turn, clipping the sweeping metaphysical declaration's wings with a wry drop into the plainspoken. Similarly, in "Sitting Outside at the End of Autumn," "Everything comes from something, / only something comes from nothing, / Lao Tzu says, more or less. / Eminently sensible, I say."[53] The drift into contemplative abstraction is pulled back to earth again and again. The speaking voice offers a check on the mind's impulse toward the infinite, as the body's limits pin the voice to the grounded *here*.

Fault lines of worry seem to be carved into the voice of these poems, embodied arrhythmically in their slow, measured pulse. Despite the vividness of imagery in his poems, semantic content often seems an embellishment of the rhythm, which, devoid of semantic content, could carry on alone. Wright describes his metrics as a stretching and contracting of an "iambic base," a flexing of the core meter inspired by Eliot's "freed verse:" "I count every syllable and every stress. . . . I'm always conscious of this. All my lines are extensions of seven-syllable lines, or contractions."[54] These elastic, odd-syllabled lines, usually of seven, nine, thirteen, or fifteen syllables, "have the iambic ghost tapping behind them all the way through," combining "the felicities of the metric line, and the possibilities of the free line."[55] Wright's use of repetition and syncopation echo the old country and blues music he grew up listening to: plain speech and not too much of it. Meanwhile, repetition allows the echo of things to emerge, made strange in recurrence, heavier with weight and patience: "We know hell in our bones— / outside time, outside comprehension, / We know it in our bones." Skip James sings: "Hard times here and every where you go. . . . These hard times will drive you from door to door."[56]

Wright's characteristic long lines (often spanning the width of the page) are often spaced by dropped lines. These dropped lines create rhythmic cadence and shifts in volume, a small decline in tone, like an echo or afterthought or the sonic equivalent of shadow. Visually, the dropped line appears to have grown tired under its own weight and stepped down. Spatially, it allows the poem to occupy more of the page, while at the same time aerating it with white space, a significant element in his poetics.[57] Light and white space, formally present in the white space of the page, held open by ellipses, interstanzaic blanks, and dropped lines, prove as crucial in Wright's poetic practice as the objects it illuminates. Wright explains in an interview, "Space has everything to do with the line, it's what the line lives in and breathes in, if it is to breathe at all."[58] Throughout Wright's poems, one encounters this persistent awareness of negativity and blanks, as we saw in Mallarmé.[59] But unlike Mallarmé's *l'Abîme*, a locus of potentiality and anteriority, Wright's interest in negativity carries a temporal inflection of postness. Perhaps not surprisingly, many of Wright's poems are temporally located in late times—the "end of autumn," the "snub end" of the year. Even those set in spring and summer have an autumnal postness about them.[60]

In and against the white space, images, often of late-season remains, litter the lines. A shadow accompanies each thing—"The shadow that everything casts." These images operate with a potency and charge indicative of the significant influence of Pound, whose work Wright encountered through a borrowed copy of the *Cantos* during his first stay in Italy. The image is the flashpoint and "center of attention" surrounded by empty space, bound by and binding together the whole formal structure of the poem, so that parts are no longer parts but inseparable elements in an indivisible systemic whole. In Wright's revision of imagism, the image "takes on, gives off, and reflects light. . . . It both holds the poem together and extends it. And it does its work in just about the length of time it takes to read the image. . . . All the connections happen simultaneously, if you have been paying attention."[61] In lines like "Like a late pear in the autumn sun, / Hard, green, indigestible, / It hangs in front of our eyes," the words, too, hang from the line, then break off. Indigestible. There's a sense of barrenness in these nonripening, indigestible fruits, late and stunted: what wasn't chosen, didn't ripen, held too long, and now can only wait or fade out: A small snail shell becomes a pregnant absence: "it carries its emptiness like a child / It would be rid of."[62]

In some ways this image encapsulates Wright's poetics of resignation: what is held is an emptiness, the hollow spiral shell left by that which shaped it, now dead or departed. A kinship forms between what remains after the life of a thing and what never makes it, aborted or unchosen—what "hangs there and grows dark." In this way November brushes elbows with March. Both understand fruitlessness and the cross-gap between birth and death. Even language is presented as the dried husk of a once growing thing: A "dead script of vines scrawls unintelligibly / Over the arbor vitae." Emptiness serves as refrain throughout these poems, a bare summing of things in which "one and one make nothing."

In Wright's opposition between what is present and the absences welling up within and around them, there is a sense of time's passage and the erosion of vigilance to resignation. No epiphany comes. Things shrug into themselves and turn away, "Toward the night's shrugged shoulder / with its epaulet of stars."[63] Wright's poems both emerge from and produce a state of resigned being in the world, after trying at revelation for a long time. Yet what emerges is not lethargy but meditation—an ongoing resignation, without hope or promise of salvation, to contemplative practice. In Wright's words, "All my poems seem to be an ongoing argument with myself about the unlikelihood of salvation . . ."[64] Unlike the more confirmedly secular Stevens, for whom the "idea of God" was more of a closed book, if nonetheless an essential poetic driver, Wright is either unable or disinclined to shut down the conversation with the infinite.[65] This "ongoing argument" takes place as a practice of attention to objects and forms in the world—to the moments of connection and presence possible in the poetic line: "It's the closest I got to 'salvation,' since salvation doesn't exist except through the natural world."[66] In this nontranscendent form of salvation, all is staked on relentless effort toward the perfect form—an unattainable vanishing point.

If Wright's poetics proposes that "the true purpose and result of poetry is a contemplation of the divine and its attendant mysteries," this contemplation takes place within a resignation to the limits of the knowable and a commitment to staying close to the finite world that is all we have—to what is *here* rather than what might be *out there*: "Words, like all things, are caught in their finitude. / They start here, they finish here."[67] Language is pinned to the horizon of the knowable. Contemplation of the infinite must resign itself to our imperfect tools of perception and making: finite words for finite things. Poetry can only gesture, signal the presence of the infinite—it cannot reach it. "Words are wrong. / Structures are wrong. / Even the questions are compromise."[68] And yet, even in their finitude and failure, words provide a formal shelter for things of the world and for the infinite that worlds around and through them (silence, space, light). Poems shelter and signal the presence of what can't summed up. Thinking of language in this way requires an act of letting be, of relinquishment. The work of giving form to language—creating a space for being in language—requires a practice of ongoing, if resigned, attention.

In Hölderlin, the attentional pivot was the word *aber*, marking a shift, a turn, into a different present and giving relief and contour to the suspended state of vigilance. In Wright, the equivalent pivot is *still*, indicating the point at which resignation becomes meditation and marking the difference between Wright's resigned metaphysics and despair. *Still* is the life raft of the present, the narrow foothold in the realm of the living. As Wright said in an interview, "All poems are about not dying."[69] As with Hölderlin's *aber*, once one notices the frequency and consistency of Wright's *still* (importantly signaling both a semantic turn of perseverance in the sense of "nevertheless" and a call to *still*ness), attention alights on it everywhere:

>   The silence is cold, like an instrument in the hand
> Which cannot be set aside,
> Unlike our suffering, so easy, so difficult.
>
> Still, the warmth on our skin is nice,
>   and the neighbor's pears,
> Late pears, dangle like golden hourglasses above our heads.[70]

Wright's *still* is a turn to *keep going* in the face of and indeed within the presence of resignation. *Still* operates in Wright as an autocritical urging to attend, to keep paying "serious and lasting and constant attention," a refusal of ending in despair or denial, a refusal of the lethargy that might accompany resignation, and a call back to the world despite the failings of the soul, despite the bleakness of mortality and the blank tedium of days: "Still must we praise you, nothing, / still must we call to you."[71] At the same time, as with Wright's tonal checks of plain speech, the still is a check on the reach toward transcendence: "Death's still the secret of life, / the garden reminds us. / Or vice versa. It's complicated."[72] Often the "still" comes as a reversal or a rethinking of everything that has come before, creating a shift in direction, rerouting thought and calling it back from whichever closure it has been trending toward.

Disallowing either the refuge of belief (a. unavailable, and b. too easy) or that of closing down the question of belief, the "idea of God,"[73] Wright's "still" serves to keep walking the line, keep open the synapse, resisting either refuge: both offer a kind of closure and a respite from holding open the big questions—the "supreme act of the spirit,"[74] as he calls it. This self-contradictory "still" is Wright's way of "working in the synapse,"[75] "Between Buddha-stare and potting shed."[76] Helen Vendler has observed that "Wright's poetry reproduces the circling and deepening concentration that aims at either obliteration or transcendence, blankness or mysticism. But Wright stops short of either polarity because he remains bound to the materiality and the temporal rhythm of language, whereas both Eastern nothingness and Western transcendence, at their utmost point, renounce as meaningless both materiality and time."[77] In his "Commonplace Notebook," a gathering of saved lines and quotations, Wright includes two lines from Simone Weil: the first, the definition of prayer, quoted earlier, as "absolute unmixed attention"; the second, "Contradiction is a lever of transcendence," sheds insight on Wright's use of the autocritical *still*. Yet, in Wright, even transcendence is everywhere contradicted and contradictory, every word provisional. In a similar comparison between Wright's and Roethke's contemplative processes, James McCorkle notes that, while both poets "search out communions with a natural landscape," Roethke "assumes the attainment of transcendence" and "sees the possibility of embracing the world," while Wright "cannot assume such a stance spiritually because each link forged—transcendent as each link may be—remains provisional and at best only a suggestion of a larger harmony."[78] But despite the unavailability of transcendence in Wright's poetry, the constancy of its meditative attention is unwavering and, if anything, more urgent: a meditation on a condition of endless and everywhere contradiction, a kind of faithful faithless practice, grace without grace.

Keeping open the synapse as a workspace for attention requires a constant guard against the "last word." The poems practice, in Wright's words, "a search for the small, still center of everything . . . where all things come together and intersect . . . what can one say but Good Luck. So that's what I say to myself. Good Luck."[79] "Good Luck"—cold comfort in a world in which a nonexistent (or at least unavailable) God says, "watch your back," but these lines signal the stress point in Wright's meditation, the "search" that keeps him coming back, "like a tongue to a broken tooth."[80] To write toward the still, the small, the "brightly lit center of attention at the heart of the universe": "concentrate, listen hard."[81]

CHAPTER IX

Idleness

Doldrums and Gardens of Time

O'Hara : Ammons : Retallack

Japanese plum. Summer
and sunset, the peace
of the writing desk

and the habitual peace
of writing, these things
form an order I only

belong to in the idleness
of attention.

—ROBERT HASS, "MEASURE"

Today, when attention has become colloquially synonymous with only one of its many aspects, that of focalized concentration, to think of states like boredom and idleness as modes of attention might seem oxymoronic. After all, isn't boredom, as the inability to engage "attentively" with the task at hand or with the world in general, attention's opposite? And isn't idleness, the mental version of "hanging out," just another mode of *in*attention?

I would argue, no. This chapter and the one that follows will show that both these modes of unstructured or unengaged awareness in fact constitute specific modes of attention in which there is a low degree of both intentionality and interest. In both cases, the attention is passively present without focalized engagement. In the case of boredom, there may be some degree of intentional effort toward engagement itself—not out of interest in a given object or task, but out of interest in escaping the state of boredom itself. In other cases, boredom is experienced as a more generalized and existential condition of boredom *with the world*.

Boredom and idleness share many characteristics in terms of structure, orientation (or, more aptly, lack thereof), and the absence of willed executive control on the attention. However, they differ in the degrees of intent and acceptance: in idling, there is an acceptance, even an embrace, of the unstructured attentional state, while in boredom there is an unhappy consciousness of the lack of engagement paired with an inability or unwillingness to engage.[1] Put another way, both boredom and idleness are attentional modalities in which there is no intentional object, but they differ with regard to the degree of intentionality toward their own intransitivity.

To think of idleness in terms of attention is not entirely new in the discourses of literary aesthetics, spiritual practice, and, most recently, in psychological research. However, despite explicit links between cognitive idling and specific attention dynamics, little has been done to flesh out the specific nature of idleness as a mode of attention or what this might mean in poetry. This is in large part because of the negative cultural evaluation of idleness and the privileging of task-driven executive attention in the present age of productivity apps and Getting Things Done. When "paying attention" becomes synonymous with a narrow branch of focused, intentional, transitive attention, the states that lie on the other side of the attention spectrum—nonfocalized, nonintentional, intransitive attention—get categorized as "failures," "lapses" in attention, or examples of *in*attention.

With recent cognitive research, this limited view of attention is beginning to change. A number of studies have linked passive, "task-negative" modes of attention to the cognitive system known as the "default mode network," which activates when the mind is not engaged in intentional executive tasks.[2] Daydreaming, wandering mind, and zoning out fall into this type of nondirected, nonfocalized attention, as do all the subtle movements of the mind when it is awake and at rest, not engaged in any particular task: when it is, in other words, idling.

Another way to understand attentional idling is through a similar concept of ambience, which in art, film, and music theory has only very recently been explicitly linked to a form of attention, most notably in the work of Lutz Koepnick on installation and video artworks that exceed the perceptual boundaries of aesthetic contemplation in its conventionally focused, directed sense, encouraging instead a more wandering, idle, ambient engagement on the part of viewer, listener, or user.[3] But the notion of "ambient attention" has not been sufficiently explored in relation to written works. The necessarily focused and, at least to some degree, linear act of reading offers a new set of challenges for understanding the dynamics of idled, aimless, and ambient forms of attention.

In these last two chapters, I show how idleness and boredom, respectively, operate formally as modes of poetic attention. In this chapter, I first consider the attentional structure of idleness, using the Roman notion of *otium* as a starting point and connecting this notion to the development of a poetry of idleness—a poetry of courtyards, wine, friendship, and leisure time distinct from the task-positive, productive, and externally directed attention in the hours of work and public life. I then consider how the dynamics of idled attention play out in the context of modern and contemporary poetry, drawing on poems by Joan Retallack, Frank O'Hara, and A. R. Ammons. The chapter on boredom that follows will take a similar structure: I first elucidate the phenomenal structure of boredom itself, with reference to philosophical accounts by Schopenhauer and Heidegger, then turn to several poems by Charles Bukowski, Thom Gunn, and T. S. Eliot to show how a poetics of boredom forms in the attentional dynamics—slack, ambient, suspended, agonized, even tedious—of each poem.

In both chapters, I focus primarily on twentieth-century American poets, framing my considerations of boredom and idleness in light of their meanings in modern thought. However—and this is most important in the case of boredom—I do not limit my definitions of these phenomenon to modern life, nor do I hold that boredom did not exist before the modern period. While the language surrounding these attentional modes has, of course, developed in meaning and association over the course of the nineteenth and twentieth centuries, to definitionally sever modern boredom from its longer phenomenological history would be shortsighted in the context of this investigation. I therefore situate boredom within a constellation of experientially closely related, older terms for states of unwilled and undesired attentional nonengagement, including *acedia,* the demon of noontide, *taedium vitae,* and ennui.[4] To consider boredom as one linguistic and historical inflection of a wider-ranging attentional phenomenon is not to erase or disavow the important distinctions (psychological, theological, sociological, and material) that mark each of these terms; it is rather to look beneath these distinctions for the structural commonalities revealing each as a particular inflection of a common constellation of attentional characteristics. Doing so also allows us to situate boredom within the fabric of contemporary terms for similar but different mental and emotional states: doing so allows a more nuanced understanding of the basic frameworks that run through unintentional intransitive states and the subtle but important divergences that make boredom different from "going blank," "zoning out," "checking out," and other evocations of attentional wandering or stallings.

Attentional Idling: *Otium,* Aimlessness, Ambience

> Idleness is enough for me and, provided I do nothing, I prefer to dream waking than sleeping . . . to live without constraints and eternally at leisure. . . . The idleness I love is not that of an indolent fellow who stands with folded arms in perfect inactivity and thinks as little as he acts. It is the idleness of a child who is incessantly on the move without ever doing anything, and at the same time the idleness of the rambling old man whose mind wanders while his arms are still.
>
> —ROUSSEAU, THE CONFESSIONS

In his first public volume of poems, *Hours of Idleness,* written during periods of distraction at university, Lord Byron brought together a slim collection of conventional poems written in the style of several Latin poetic genres. The volume was sharply criticized in the *Edinburgh Review* and has since been evaluated by critics primarily for the way its critical bashing spurred Byron to write his first "great" work of satirical vengeance. Yet the volume is important in its own right, for its demonstration of an attempt (untimely though it was) to revise and exercise two venerable poetic traditions—that of *otium* and that of *imitatio.* While I will not delve into an extended reading of the volume here, the collection offers a starting point for a consideration of the poetics of idling because of its implicit linking of the traditions of otium and the practice of imitatio via a poetic idling whose primary nonliterary analogue is friendship. In its adaptation of earlier forms and in its exploration of the themes of play, friendship, and noninstrumentalized writing, *Hours of Idleness* offers a kind of ungainly bridge between modern experimental poetics and the classical conception of otium. In Roman antiquity, *otium,* the unstructured private hours of leisure, was defined in contrast to the hours of work and public engagement, *negotium*. In otium, an individual was free to let the mind rest by spending time in the gardens and courtyards of the home, having philosophical discussions with friends, writing poetry (often, notably for an understanding of Byron's first work, in the mode of imitatio, or rewriting the work of other poets, ancient or contemporary), drinking wine, and generally cultivating the arts of idle pleasure, hobby, and taste. Byron's depiction in *Hours of Idleness* of friendship as "amour sans ailes" suggests a parallel distinction between the attentionality of nonfocalized being-with implied by companionship and the focalized transitive attentionality of desire.

In idleness, the attention is allowed to wander. With no externally or intentionally determined object of focus, attention becomes literally *aimless*. Perceptions and thoughts enter and exit the field of attention, as though passing through a background, leaving the foreground expansive and soft. This is the mode of undirected, unstructured awareness that accompanies various kinds of just being: hanging out with friends, drinking wine, sitting on porches or park benches, and generally whiling away time.

In Catullus 51, we find a poetic mulling of *otium,* as the speaker turns the word over and over in mind, an "over and over" of mind only possible in hours of idleness. As a rewriting of Sappho (Fragment 31), the poem offers a rich locus for considering how the poetic convention of imitatio can be seen as itself a formal and practical expression of the mode of attentional idleness, as the poem is not attended to as a unique and original object in its own right, but rather for the ways it enters into conversation with other poems, in homage or competition—often a complex layering of the two. Yet when Catullus breaks off his inhabitation of Sappho's lovelorn daydreaming, the poem becomes a warning against idleness's mental quicksands:

> otium, Catulle, tibi molestum est:
> otio exsultas nimiumque gestis:
> otium et reges prius et beatas
>   Perdidit urbes.

> Idleness, Catullus, is trouble for you:
> In idleness you revel and delight too much:
> Idleness has destroyed both kings and
>   blessèd cities before.[5]

Whether and how idleness is valued and employed changes historically; The rhetoric surrounding nonproductive time and the use of leisure time (its allocation to a particular class, its particular load of normative values, etc.) tells us a great deal about a society's attention culture.[6] The cultural standing of idleness shifted considerably over the course of the nineteenth and twentieth centuries. No longer held as a value to be cultivated and savored, as it was for Epicurus and even for later writers such as Andrew Marvell, whose poem "The Garden" delves deeply into the temporal suspension of idle hours, idleness's other cultural identity as "devil's plaything" came to the fore, repositioning it as a source of malaise, emotional instability, and, most sinfully for an increasingly secular and postindustrial West, nonproductivity. Idleness was opposed to the triadic forces shaping modern attention culture: Protestant work ethic, capitalist productivity, and a rising belief in individual entrepreneurship that would eclipse the boundary between work and personal life.[7]

Idleness has been denigrated not only in modern productivity culture but in earlier writings on the dangers of laziness and lethargy, from Catullus's cautionary portrayal of idleness, or otium, in 51 ("otium, Catulle, tibi molest'est") to the Christian Desert Father Evagrius Ponticus's ascetic exercises for coping with acedia, or the noonday demon, in fourth-century Egypt.[8] Yet there are a number of significant ways in which idleness has been valued and intentionally cultivated across historical periods: as a source of pleasure, as a way of stopping or passing time, as a way of achieving *ataraxia,* as a way of being with friends and forming a friendship with the world.[9] At stake in these practices and temporal whilings is the cultivation of what I think of as a garden of unstructured time—composed of noninstrumentalized attention and nonproductive being.

In an essay on Robert Louis Stevenson's *An Inland Voyage* (1898) and William Morris's *News from Nowhere* (1890),[10] Stephen Arata proposes, "I would like to begin by drifting idly down one river and then rowing vigorously—but not at all strenuously—up another. The ultimate destination of both journeys is a certain abstraction of mind." In both "drift" and easy "row," Arata tracks in the two writers' work a movement—both formal and thematic—away from the burgeoning modern *coup de définition* taking place in the meaning of attention, in which the word came to be associated with only one of its modalities, and toward an exploration, veneration, and indeed formal *cultivation* of a very different attentional practice—what Arata calls inattention and what I define as in fact a mode of intransitive attention. Arata's essay touches on the formal and phenomenological structure of idling that I explore here in the poetic tense: "abstraction of the mind" constitutes a practice of idling the attention toward passive reception and nonselective awareness. The experience of drifting downstream, or of rowing, at leisure and without particular object, upstream for the sake of the rowing itself and the river, evokes some of the practices considered in what follows.

To understand the *poetics* of these forms of idled attention, I explore how formal aspects of these modes have been translated into formed language. Reading, in other words, not only for the ways in which idleness has been *described* in poetry, but for the ways it has been *brought to form*—given spatiotemporal form in language.[11]

"How does poetry idle itself?" asks Charles Bernstein, "It is the product of the most intensive labor, concentration, attention. Attention to measure, to the ordering of occurrences, that such occurrences are instances of how the world itself comes to mean." Perhaps the only poetics theorist to focus on the political value of idleness (and idleness as the political value of poetry in particular), Bernstein sees idleness as a core impulse "of a writing that is just for itself, not to be used for some other thing . . . call it noninstrumental . . . where language is not in gear, is idling."[12] Bernstein envisions this noninstrumental, idled poetics in this way: "Writing as stupor, writing as out-to-lunch. Writing as vacation. Writing degree zero. Idleness as antistatic (functionless, it becomes estranged). Writing as idled thinking (not just the means to a displaced end), becomes world revelation."[13]

How do specific poems produce and require *idled* attention? In the poetry of Frank O'Hara, A. R. Ammons, and Joan Retallack, we find a common formal and thematic exploration of poetry's otiose center. While approaching from very different angles within American poetics, each of these poets seeks to loosen literature from the externally dictated agendas of usefulness and functionality. As I'll show in the readings that follow, in O'Hara and Retallack's work idleness comes into play most actively in the compositional process, whereas in Ammons idleness is *embodied* and *produced* by the form of the poem. In other words, while O'Hara's and Retallack's idlenesses are *procedural,* Ammons's is *formal* and *perceptual*. In each case, idleness as poetic form involves a tension between the playful, conversational, and exploratory potentials of poetry and the intensity of formal precision required to bring it about: the honing of attention toward the perfectly slack line.

Small Sentiments / Lunging Robustly: O'Hara and the Attentionality of Banter

Describing the abrasiveness of Frank O'Hara's early poems, Harvard friend and fellow New Yorker John Ashbery wrote,

> One frequently feels that the poet is trying on various pairs of brass knuckles until he finds the one which fits comfortably. It is not just that it is often aggressive in tone—it simply doesn't care. A poet who in the academic atmosphere of the late 1940s could begin a poem
>
> > At night Chinamen jump
> > On Asia with a thump
>
> was amusing himself, another highly suspect activity.[14]

While O'Hara's poetry did not retain the "brass knuckles" of his earlier works, it did maintain the quality of not-caring, noninvestment, and, most importantly (and most heretically in post–New Critical America), amusement. Describing O'Hara's writing process, Ashbery once recalled that Frank would "dash the poems off at odd moments—in his office at the Museum of Modern Art, in the street at lunchtime or even in a room full of people—then he would put them away in drawers and cartons and half forget about them" (vii). He relates one instance when a publisher requested a manuscript and O'Hara "spent weeks and months combing through the apartment, enthusiastic and bored at the same time, trying to assemble the poems. Finally he let the project drop, not because he didn't wish his work to appear, but because his thoughts were elsewhere." These anecdotes gesture toward a quality of noncaring and *amusement* that run through O'Hara's unrevised, unfinished, and often only belatedly collected body of work.

Getting at this quality of radical nonselectivity that characterizes much of O'Hara's poetry, Ashbery notes in the poem "Easter," an example of "Frank's 'French Zen' period," "faults don't impair but rather make the poem—whose form is that of a bag into which anything is put and ends up belonging there."[15] Ashbery makes an explicit link between O'Hara's approach to poetic making and a particular mode of attention—a shift and expansion of the mind's perceptive horizon, a widening of scope that does

IDLENESS [219]

not, despite its inclusivity, lose the bone structure and particularity of composition. Ashbery describes O'Hara's practice in this way: "words and colors could be borrowed freely from everywhere to build up big, airy structures unlike anything previous in American poetry and indeed unlike poetry, more like the inspired ramblings of *a mind open to the point of distraction.*"

I opened with Ashbery's reading of O'Hara because both poets, individually and in conversation, introduced the formal characteristics of friendship (as a particular form of idleness) into twentieth-century American poetry. One of the most striking qualities of O'Hara and Ashbery is their ability to capture in poetic form friendship's rhythms, tonal qualities, and the sense of shared but open proximity. This mode is neither the circumscribed one-to-one of Dickinson, the reverberating singularity of Yeats, the fragmented chorus of Eliot, nor Stevens's sound-of-one-man-thinking. O'Hara's version of friendship poetics is decidedly airier and chattier than that of Ashbery, but the resonance and, yes, friendship between their poetic explorations is clear. In O'Hara, the quality of friendship's idle banter comes through in a lightness of tone, a quickness of perceptual switches, and an assemblage of quips and parries. Friendly banter inhabits a mode of idled attention because it takes place in the unstructured space between "us"—close but unwedded—in the easy rhythms of our interactions. These easy rhythms make the world feel different.[16] It is the difference between sitting across from a lover at a candlelit table, locked in gaze, and sitting beside a friend on a park bench, facing out, shooting the breeze.

The poem "Very rainy light, an eclogue," posed as a dialogue between Daphnis and Chloe, the shepherd and shepherdess of the second-century novel by Longus, captures this kind of idleness in its attentional structure—a dialogue between two voices shot through with both love and friendship but not focalized desire. They poke fun of each other, and their rhythms create a kind of momentum in interplay, each line falling in medias res:

"VERY RAINY LIGHT, AN ECLOGUE"
(*DAPHNIS AND CHLOE*)

D: Remembering at best bitterly
that peacocks are not a hit with

you. Chinchilla, you are beautiful.
All that you've given me's at one.
I'm not chilly thinking or bones.

C: Someone has glued my castanets
together. And this morning early I
became aimlessly apparent 'cause
I woke up first and the dew jetted
from your armpits of ambergris.
I smelled burning rubber, I did
not receive a cable from your Europe
every being at war at the time.

D: All praise to Juno, she as disaster
cuts a fine figure. Your diamonds
are dripping like spit. Am enamored.

C: The whistle of your gaze cuts across
my hair like spurs. You're the big
breeze in halflight, don't think I
don't know it. At dawn when I'm milking
the aphids I hear your stomach
coming up like thunder. Oh baby.

D: Onto what Nizhni sifts, ja ja,
the appealing moo? Under which
nasty mummer skips the coral rope?
I like you, but perhaps you, fiery,
are no fit companion on field trips?

C: You must come when my throaty heart
traces the wiry meteors to breathe
in your ear its invitation at the beach.
I will scare up the money to chase
you into my arms where, like winter
flowers, you'll find small sentiments
lunging robustly. Warm. Is as if

I am your sheeted will for windward.
I shall leave a jar of powdered coffee
on your tongue. Be wakefully mine.

D: O joy! O joy! today's the day, eh?
I've quit pictures for the grassy knolls
of knees and the apple of your nut.
No more greys for me! You. Artichoke.

C: O infinite languor of railroads!
truly you master a heady scent.[17]

Flights of pure sonic joy suggest lines spun for pleasure, evoking a quality of *being* more than semantic content. Insofar as this is a kind of love poem, it's a love poem between two idle wits. Directed at nothing, the quality of "talk" in the poem is there in and for itself—a kind of dance of talk, which is the essence of banter. At the same time, lines like "I smelled burning rubber . . ." cast postwar shadows on the pastoral and bacchic references to Longus's *Daphnis and Chloe*, a juxtaposition that recalls Ravel's ballet adaptation, written during the buildup to the First World War. Later in the poem, O'Hara makes reference to Vaslav Nijinsky of the Ballet Russe, who performed the role of Daphnis in the Paris premier. The poem's linguistic pirouettes take place in the wake of the Second World War, evoked in the entrance of Juno, "as disaster," anticipated by the peacocks in stanza 1. Juno's presence carries both elements of the poem's tonal invocations: that of playful youthfulness, and that of fiery force, both warlike and sexual. These qualities leap, crash, and court one another in the poem, and the dialogue has the air of both careless abandon and energetic eruption. Yet, despite the intensity of some of O'Hara's imagery, what is most striking in the delivery of this intensity is its levity and the mode of friendship and play that banters and wits through the stanzas' interplay.

The jaunty staccato call and response anticipates the abbreviated linguistic jousts of contemporary texting, where intimacy lies not in the depth of emotional content but in quickness of response, inside jokes and epithets, keeping the flow going during a particular errant thread of attention: "Am enamored." Writing on O'Hara's eclogues in the context of an extended study of digression in modern American poetry, Srikanth Reddy has noted that O'Hara's poetics of banter—his "ongoing attempts to replicate the mercurial designs of casual talk within poetic form"—"reprises, in miniature, a history of the conversation-poem in the Western literary tradition."[18] Reddy suggests that "such sequences of digressive locutions may shed light on the origins of poetry itself" in playful, ambient, and idled attention.[19]

This playful quality in O'Hara's work—its liveliness and ease—suggests quick sketches in motion. This quality is both tonal and procedural—rooted not in the semantic content of the snippets of urban life he describes, but rather in the act of snipping itself. The snippets are not even so much valued in themselves, but are rather parings from the play of glances that generates them. The poems themselves are important, but more important is the lightfooted play of time and conversation that runs through their unrevised, in-progress accumulation.

The light touch of O'Hara's poems tells us something about how poetry itself changed in the twentieth century. The criteria of what constituted poetic attention shifted from a long-valorized crafted perfection toward a more irreverent, curious, off-handed modality. Ashbery's characterization of O'Hara's work as "anything but literary" indicates the narrow mode that counted as literary at the time, which O'Hara's artistic guides—John Cage, Guillaume Apollinaire, Vladimir Mayakovsky, and Jackson Pollock—were pushing against. O'Hara's degree of influence on the literary itself shows us something about how aesthetic and poetic attention shifted and expanded in the twentieth century to include a greater variety of modalities, including the irreverent, the unintentional, the nonfocalized and nonselective, and, as Marjorie Perloff has noted, the unoriginal.[20] O'Hara's self-described "I do this I do that" poems did not single-handedly inaugurate this shift and expansion of poetic attention so much as ran with it, riffed on it, inhabited it, and stretched its limits.

He was the product of specific changes in American attention culture—the increasing association of focus and intentionality with the workplace, and the increasing artistic, spiritual, political, and psychological exploration of nonproductive, noninstrumentalized modes of being. This accompanied the emergence of an aesthetics of "cool" in twentieth-century literature and art, with its body language of informality and easy unconcern.[21] It also accompanied an increasing interest in poetic *practices*, rather than the perfection and honing of the final work. O'Hara's poetry shares with

Language poetry and Oulipo an interest in processes that resist the fixity of overly crafted composition. O'Hara's interest in poetic practice also put him in conversation with Beat poets such as Ginsberg and Bukowski, and the idiosyncratic rural walker A. R. Ammons, whose work fuses a relaxed conversational tone with a syntactically meandering contemplative practice of walking.

Whatever Coming and Going Is: Nonselective Receptivity in A. R. Ammons

> I don't know somehow it seems sufficient
> to see and hear whatever coming and going is . . .

While O'Hara's conversational poems *perform* a mode of relaxed play, A.R. Ammons's use of form *embodies* idled awareness and brings the reader into this mode through minimalist paradox and extended syntax. As I will demonstrate, these serve to both *formally figure* the shape of idled awareness and *produce* that state in the reader.

Throughout his work, Ammons formally summons a perceptual experience of open-focus awareness or nonselective receptivity. He describes this quality as "—a stir: not a gale," in "Fasting," the first poem in his last, posthumously collected volume, *Bosh and Flapdoodle*.[22] The name of the collection itself summons up nonsense, play, and linguistic irreverence, the contentless and nonpurposive motion of doodling. Like O'Hara, Ammons is a master of conversational banter, though more often in Ammons the banter is between mind and world and between the mind and itself. His meditations are couched in slang, slants of humor, and slouched turns of Southern idiom. The reader is brought close alongside the speaker by that tone, even when the poems drift into abstraction.

"Fasting" follows the movement of air currents, motions that are discernible only in their rustling of other things, "gusts that show up / out of nowhere, presences that are not there, little twirls of leaves that scoot across the // street and then just wilt out, forms, / air-whorls that are made out of nothing."[23] Attending to the movement of air—always all around us but perceptible only when it brushes against something else—becomes a practice of craning outward and around, taking in the circulation of matter in space. Ammons thus inverts the focus to attend not to the "figure" but the "ground" of perception, its movements, circulations, diffusions.[24]

This idled attention to the ground of perception is the practice that brings together an oeuvre characterized by the book-length sentences of *Tape for the Turn of the Year* and the more fragmented *Glare* as well as the very short poems of *Briefings*.[25] Both Ammons's macro- and micropoems are practices of meditation toward this end. The first practice is one of intentional nonselective receptivity: perceptions move through the poem, neither sought nor held. The poem takes the open-ended form of this modality of perception: long lines open on all sides, phrases held open at both ends with wide-eyed colons, the scope of one trail or movement eddying into the next. The short poems that marked his 1970s foray into minimalism offer not a countering but a complementary, negative practice. Rather than letting in the flood of moving particulars without filter (as some of O'Hara's seem to do), these short poems touch one single point without fixation, letting the reverberation of that single point call attention to its surrounding expanses. Often the briefest poems, such as "Timing," "Mirrorment" ("Birds are flowers flying / and flowers perched birds"), and "Small Song" ("The reeds give / way to the // wind and give / the wind away")[26] take the form of a single Dogenesque paradox or x-is/not-x structure that, in its resistance to both sameness and separateness, holds the mind open for an extended moment. Both of Ammons's seemingly opposed approaches to formal scale can thus be read as methods of holding open a meditative space of objectless yet dynamically world-full attention.

Describing the attempt to take in a field of bay rushes in one of the *Briefings* poems, aptly called "Attention," Ammons explicitly refers to this balance between taking-in and letting-go:

Down by the bay I
kept in mind
at once
the tips of all the rushleaves
and so
came to know
balance's cost and true:
somewhere though in the whole field

> is the one
> tip
> I will someday
> lose out of mind
> and fall through.[27]

The practice of taking-in and letting-go, so often formally ambulatory in Ammons, is a process of moving through space and time, with the mind's movement another current among currents: "motion gives its form away by / picking up miscellany and throwing it off, motion / the closest cousin to spirit and spirit the / closest neighbor to the other world."[28] Ammons's walking meditations are at once scientific notation and spiritual communion. His vocabulary ranges from biochemistry and quantum physics to theology. The scales of both notation and contemplation are the microscopic and the infinite. At the limit point of both, we find the poem's ekstasis:[29] a self-emptying movement from keeping "in mind" to falling "out of mind."[30] As Ammons writes in *Tape for the Turn of the Year*,

> the biochemist, first
>   seeing how
>   two molecules select each
> other & interlink
>   must think he
>   beholds
>   a face of god:[31]

Unlike other poets who write of beholding "a face of a god" in small things (from Hölderlin to Mary Oliver), Ammons's poems don't follow the epiphanic structure of sudden revelation. As he writes, "where but in the asshole of comedown is / redemption." Redemption comes not in a flash of vision but rather in an ongoing maintenance of openness, a relaxed and wandering attention that moves through things, idly taking in what's around. This is the way one walks through a field—picking out threading paths and taking in the terrain without agenda or project. The mind is held open and things pass through. In fact, holding open the mind constitutes the only act of intentional effort, formally manifest in the signature element that binds together Ammons's entire body of work, the extended sentence.

Published in 1993, Ammons's book-length poem *Garbage* offers perhaps the richest exploration of this open-focus attending, both formally and semantically.[32] The book is composed of a single, self-reflexive and self-decomposing meditation on and around a garbage dump. Passing through its wide and wandering ambulations of mind meeting mound, "crippled aluminum lawn chairs, lemon crates / with busted slats or hinges, strollers with // whacking or shiningly idle wheels: stub ends / of hot dogs" are broken down (with the help of gulls and worms, the "deities of unpleasant / necessities") in "terrifying transformations, the disappearances of anything of interest // morsel, gobbet, trace of maple syrop, fat / worm: addling intensity at the center // where only special clothes and designated / offices allay the risk, the pure center."[33] Accumulation and circulation build through the gathering of particles around a sustained syntactical current that runs through the book.[34]

The act of syntactically maintaining a single phrase, over a few lines or an entire book, requires a sustained act of attention, both readerly and writerly. Syntactical gymnastics involving em dashes and semicolons, parentheses, and the all-pervasive Ammonsian colon, its two eyes looking out on "the ongoing," produce a line of sustained attention—what Ammons called the "dispositional axis" (20) or "spindle of energy" (24) coursing through the poem.

The intense formal craft that composes the long phrase and its wide-ranging semantic tendrils is leavened by tone. "Gravelly Run," the ultimate poem in *Corsons Inlet*, and to my mind one of his best, begins mid-thought, already downplaying its speaker's authority, or decentering the speaker as both subject and object of knowing:

> I don't know somehow it seems sufficient
> to see and hear whatever coming and going is,
> losing the self to the victory of
>   of stones and trees,[35]

The conversational shrug of "I don't know somehow" evokes the easy familiarity of friends talking on a porch or on a walk, mulling things over without needing to solve anything. The reader is brought up along the speaker by that tone. The friends within the poem are called by their names: "dwarf pine," "cedar cone," "algal hair," "snowbroken weeds." Familiarity with the terrain of particulars situates the eye of the poem in the world, surrounded on all sides: one of many, master of nothing—"for it is not so much to know the self / as to know it as it is known / by galaxy and cedar cone." At the same time, to lose the self is defamiliarizing and to maintain nonknowing is to maintain a strangely relation to the world. Describing the "move toward self-extinction" in Ammons's early poems, Frederick Buell has observed a quality of "incomplete suffocation"[36]—a lack of catharsis or peace in self-emptying in the poet's "fall out of being." Here self-extinction is perhaps more complete than in his early work, but not necessarily comforting: it is a refusal to replace blank being with fictions of meaning, religious or philosophical, or to construct a metaphysical "home" in the world through the addition of significance, either of self or of cedar cone: "no use to make any philosophies here: / I see no / god in the holly, hear no song from / the snowbroken weeds."

By the time he wrote *Garbage* three decades later, Ammons talked less about god (even as absentia) and was less bleak about both things in the world and the self.[37] He was also, perhaps, at least in lyric self-presentation, a bit more at ease: the "I don't know somehow"s are more frequent, the language less conventionally beautiful, less curated in its selection of images. The soulful, psalmlike quality that runs through *Corsons Inlet* is replaced by a very earthly, quirky, irreverent voice that manages to remain all of the above even when quite profound in statement. He writes early on in the long poem, "if this is not the best poem of the // century, can it be about the worst poem of the / century: it comes, at least, toward the end, // so a long tracing of bad stuff can swell / under its measure." Letting all the "bad stuff" swell, letting it fill and expand the field of his attention, the reader's, and the definitional horizon of poetic attention at the same time, can be seen as the "free offering" of the poem.

For Ammons, the decomposition, mixing, and compression of the garbage dump also cuts close to something vital about poetic language as a workable medium of attention. He writes in *Garbage*,

. . . there is a mound,

too, in the poet's mind dead language is hauled
off to and burned down on, the energy held and

shaped into new turns and clusters, the mind
strengthened by what it strengthens . . .

Ammons writes, "Garbage has to be the poem of our time, because / garbage is spiritual, believable enough // to get our attention, getting in the way, piling / up, stinking, turning brooks brownish and // creamy white." But rather than deep meaning or grand epiphanies, the aim of Ammons's spiritual exercises is understated. His walks, his wide reach and rambling lines, and the phrasal sinew that courses through the poem are tools toward a kind of secular, scientific practice of mindfulness meditation. They are "the mixed // means by which we stay attentive and keep to / the round of our ongoing." Just shy of midway through *Garbage*, we find a passage that, read on its own, could as easily hail from an instruction manual on mindfulness meditation:

. . . on writing a poem—you sit vacant and
relaxed (if possible), your mind wandering

freely, unengaged and in search of focus: you
may sit this way for several minutes till the

void unsettles you a bit and you become impatient
with the intrusion of an awareness of yourself

sitting with a touch of unwelcome exasperation
over a great blank: but you keep your mind

open and on the move and eventually there is a
trace of feeling like a bit of mist on a backroad

but then it reappears stronger and more central,
still coming and going, so the mind can't

grab it and hold on to it: but the mind begins
to make an effort, to shed from itself all

awareness except that of going with the feeling,
to relax and hold the feeling—the feeling

is a brutal burning, a rich, raw urgency:
the mind knows that it is nothing without the

> feeling, so concentrating on the feeling, it
> dreams of imminent shapes, emergences, of
>
> clust'ral abundances, of free flow, forms discernible,
> material, concrete, shapes on the move, and
>
> then the mind gives way from its triggering, and
> the mechanisms of necessity fall into, grasping the
>
> upheaval, the action of making;[38]

I am not the first to note the resonances between Ammons's poetics and various practices of meditation. He has been positioned as a reviver of transcendentalism and Romantic contemplation (Harold Bloom),[39] an Emersonian natural theologian (J. T. Barbarese),[40] a practitioner of Whitmanesque ecstatic immersion (Patricia Parker),[41] a mystic (Marius Bewley),[42] and a religious visionary (Hyatt H. Waggoner, Helen Vendler, and Frank Leprowski).[43] Bridging the latter two, Abrams saw Ammons as a poet of "displaced and reconstituted theology, or . . . a secularized form of devotional experience."[44] More recently, the contemplative nature of Ammons's work has been brought under the heading of ecopoetics, highlighting its resonance with the meditative practices of Gary Snyder, W. S. Merwin, and Wendell Berry.[45] Recognizing the variousness of Ammons's affective styles, from "Whitmanian urgency" to "breezily chatty," Buell has highlighted the less-acknowledged modal strain that cuts through his various lengths and attitudes; even deeper than the oft-cited and self-evident theme of "motion and the mind," Buell observes "an underlying receptivity in both the cosmos and man." He emphasizes, as I have, the practice that produces this receptivity: "In a walk, one loiters and absorbs as much as one attempts to get anywhere; in a repeated, daily walk, this passive absorbtiveness is emphasized."[46]

While diverse in their attributions of theological/metaphysical influence, these critical insights come together on the particular attentional qualities that characterize Ammons's poetic practice: nonselective receptivity, all-inclusive vision, nongrasping awareness, and the dissolution of the attending subject in the widening scope of perception.[47] Ammons's poetry finds, in "swerves of action" and "the overall wandering of mirroring mind," a way of being "released from forms" in attention's "field of action / with moving, incalculable center." Without recategorizing Ammons as a Buddhist poet, I would argue that the poems I've considered demonstrate a spectrum of attentional idlings: widening the scope of awareness and emptying the space of the subject "to see and hear whatever coming and going is."

Idleness of the Running Mechanism: Joan Retallack's Procedural Passivity

While Ammons *perceptually* manifests idle and errant attention through formal and syntactical meanders and swerves, Language poet Joan Retallack uses *procedural* errancy to disrupt focalized attention and inhibit the drive toward intentional meaning-making. To distinguish between O'Hara's and Retallack's procedural idlings, one could say that O'Hara's is *affective* and *gestural,* Retallack's is *causative* and *interventionist.*

In both her poetry and her essays (which she sees as intimately connected modes of thinking),[48] Retallack makes of idleness an interventionist procedural methodology, mixing a variety of formal constraints with intuitive play to perform and produce "swerves" in poetic experience. These swerves effectively deemphasize intentional predetermination and linear logic. The methodology is writerly, but the effect on the reader is one of forced disarming: linear reading and comprehension are replaced by a poetics of play, semantic and syntactic puzzles and jumbles, found in bits and pieces. Retallack's 1994 volume *Errata 5uite* is a procedural play on, in, and as the errata sheet or errata slip,[49] an editorial catalog of errors that, in itself, offers a potent space for exploring nonintentional, accidental sites of language.[50]

As one can see in the following passages, the "suite" is musical, and each five-line fragment was actually composed on five-bar musical composition sheets. Meanwhile, the language, which draws from a range of texts from Augustine to Kierkegaard to Wittgenstein, is also generated by numerical constraints (every fifth book on a library shelf, every fifth word from every fifth page, and so on). Each page contains only one of these five-bar stanzas, surrounded on all sides by white space:

erratums for the tummy La La tin *erratum* neuter past *errare* all history lies behind before Poetique Terrible delete as/like Duchamp as Fred Astaire to read epit ess pref b iv b neut p pple sundry errats' distended verse to wander err erratic nudging **ers** root erratum rrroneous erroar The World's a Book 'Tis falsely writ.... et ... cet ... era

(15)

errat to curiositas clubbed Medieval sin should read (between 1 word next) zero *sum* (led by her) I found the silent water's error genus now reading *les* for *le* in holocauste (homme-dieu) or Khmer read noire in *ANGR* old as Old Norse grief were still it here a trouble to my dreams this earth im parts (slowly through the mind) its silence

(18)

to read read real denied being there at all that is to cause to follow these the choices that make us defacto human bacchae melanesia cafeteria ergot cert to be inclued a error for mirror interroregnum regulaterrrata p.8 forementioned bag-O-bugs the gardeners friends late evenings inadverdant soar remarks to others to mak ammendes

(48)

The near-total lack of semantic figuration in lines like these prohibits meaning-making, continually denying liftoff from the formal object of language to the plane of mental representation. This produces a baffling reading experience in which one wanders through a text terrain where linear, focused reading seems all but impossible, and in which tinkering, toying, skipping around, or skimming over the surface of words is the only mode of attention available. The pleasure of the text becomes, here, at once intellectual and sensual. Retallack's poetry moves in and out of making sense via procedurally generated randomness, aiming-not-aiming for "a poetics that keeps mind in motion amidst chaos." The result is a poetic modality predicated on errant experiences of nonintentional, nonfocalized attention. As she writes in "Essay as Wager," "To wager on a poetics of the conceptual swerve is to believe in the constancy of the unexpected—source of terror, humor, hope."[51]

Describing what she proposes as a "poetics of the swerve," Retallack begins with a discussion of Epicurus's concept of the clinamen or atomic swerve—the necessary randomness and free movement of particles that enables natural change. Retallack theorizes the swerve as poetic principle, suggesting that vital change takes place in language that "produces disorientation, even estrangement, by radically altering geometries of attention."[52]

Moreover, Epicurus's concept of the swerve (a crucial touchstone for the French Oulipo group as well) links to the cultural and creative swerve embodied in his vision for an alternative community called The Garden, a commune devoted to "friendship, philosophical conversation, and delight in simple pleasures of the senses." The Garden was conceived as a civil, intellectual, and creative utopia premised on the cultivation of otium through a defined structure for unstructured time. In otium, an individual was free to let the mind rest.

That Retallack begins her career-defining book on poetic experimentation with the concept of otium is significant for an understanding of how attentional idling manifests in contemporary poetics. Even as Retallack roots the swerve in classical reference, her methodology is driven by the urgent need for practices of idleness and errancy in modern and contemporary life—a need evoked in Walter Benjamin's discussion of his chosen methodology in *Origin of the German Trauerspiel*: "Method is indirection. Presentation as indirection, as the roundabout way. . . . Renunciation of the unbroken course of intention—this, then, is the methodological character of the tractatus. Renunciation of the unbroken course of intention is its immediately distinguishing feature. In its persevering, thinking constantly begins anew; with its sense of the circumstantial, it goes back to the thing itself."[53]

Situating postmodern experimentation within a cross-cultural historical engagement with the relation between idleness and poetic practice is vital for an understanding of the forces at play in the procedural poetics shaping the work of Retallack as well as other practitioners of poetic passivity, ambience, and spontaneity from Raymond Queneau and the Oulipo movement to Olson, Ashbery, and the contemporary procedural poetics of Fady Joudah's *textu* and Solmaz Sharif's erasure-inspired surveillance poems. In each of these artists' works we find strong ties between active passivity, noninterference, and *intentional attention practice* (or meditation), enacting a twentieth-century hybrid adaptation of the classical practice of otium with Buddhist philosophies of meditative nonattachment.

While the significant influence of Western fascination with Eastern spirituality on mid- and late-twentieth-century American art, music, and writing is common knowledge and has been widely documented, less has been said about the relationship of this fascination to a rebirth of otium as a rethinking of the aesthetic, psychological, and political value of leisure in an increasingly productivity-driven cultural economy. In Retallack's thinking, the nature of the poetic "wager" (itself a swerve concept) hinges on the embrace of nonintentional, nonfocalized attention that underlies otium and frames the values of the Epicurean Garden. At the same time, this thought is intimately connected to the American adoption and adaptation of Zen philosophy, practiced by Retallack's principle creative and intellectual interlocutor, John Cage.[54]

Retallack's work across genres can be seen as an ongoing exploration and practice of focused nonfocalization, intentional nonintentionality, through a poetic adaptation of what Cage called chance operations. Chance operations aimed to disrupt the habitual structure of music, using formal procedures to generate patterns and structures dependent on nontonal factors such as duration rather than pitch. Their ultimate effect was to challenge the listener to cultivate a fine-grained but nonselective attention predicated on nongrasping and purely passive (but ambiently sensitive) reception.

The diversion of attention away from pitch results in a diversion away from the sense-making side of music, in the same way that Retallack uses formal procedure to disrupt the semantic coherence of a written work.[55] Both processes are characterized by what Christopher Shultis has described as "interchangeability of content in a fixed structure";[56] they aim to produce an act of listening or reading in which the tendency to generate anticipatory meanings and retroactively fit the experience of the work into a unified sense-object is rendered impossible, so that the only available mode of attending is one of present, passive experience.

While both Retallack and Cage engage with attentional idling in their poetic practices, Retallack's idleness remains primarily on the side of the writer—a procedural tool for linguistic-attentional disruption on the part of the writer and a kind of gauntlet thrown to the reader. Retallack's work is far from easy on the reader, and certainly does not always conjure the leisure of otium, but it does produce swerves, forcing a consideration of the relationship between spontaneity and passivity, between letting be and letting happen. *Errata 5uite* manages not only to execute idleness as procedural relinquishment of artistic control (or, in Benjamin's terms, intention's "unbroken course") but also lets some of the spirit of idled attention translate to the receptive experience. There is a quality of motion in the words, though they are jumbled and often quite literally sense-less. Here *all* of the meanings of "play"—as music-making, wordplay, and childhood's imaginative improvisation—come *into play*. Meanwhile, her use of white space creates large expanses of visual silence, so that reading becomes adept at learning to listen to silence, an act that is not object oriented but nonetheless wholly present, temporally and attentively. Reading Retallack's poetry thus requires an attentional act of letting go of typical footholds in intentionality and meaning-making and a release into a more idle, though certainly not *in*attentive, mode of receiving the work, discovering and simply perceiving the sense-data unfolding therein.

O'Hara, Ammons, and Retallack approach the poetics of idled attention in distinct ways—from the performative to the perceptual to the procedural. Yet their approaches highlight both the historicity and transhistoricity of idleness as a mode of poetic attention. On the one hand, all three poets are interested in a specific historical urgency surrounding the need for idleness in modern and contemporary American life. At the same time, their work serves to remind us of a longer relationship between creativity and play, between idle hours and the making of song and story.

Poetries that explore mental states conventionally understood to be "inattentive"—whether distracted, unintentional, or roundabout—can and should be reread as explorations and experimentations in attention's margins, its unrecognized and unsung regions. They can be seen as the "others" contained within the category of poetic attention itself. Any given mode of poetic attention, from contemplation to desire to vigilance, constitutes an inflection of the attentive faculty—its orientation, selectivity, and degrees of interest and absorption. Rather than upping the intensity of these variables, poets working in idled attention downshift, exploring familiar but uncelebrated mental states, perhaps especially in modern and contemporary life. The result is a rethinking of the boundaries of attention and a retuning of what has been thought to be poetry's designated modality. In other words, they break down the unstated normative assumptions surrounding poetic attention.

At the same time, these poets turn the lens of attention onto attention itself, practicing a keen perceptual attunement that breaks open the categorical assumptions limiting attention to a narrow range of experience and attitude. That is, they show the internal structures and experiential forms underlying seemingly vacant and formless attentional doldrums. These doldrums are conventionally categorized out of the permissible registers of "attention" and "the poetic" because of their distance from the normative ideals imposed on both categories. But they have a vital role to play in understanding a variety of poetic and attentional modes that work differently—modes that became increasingly fundamental to life and art over the course of the twentieth century.

The work of attentional idling creates a structure within which an experience of unstructured attention is possible. In the same way that a garden or park offers a spatial frame for passing unstructured time, the poem of idleness is a garden of unstructured attention.

CHAPTER X

Boredom

End-Stopped Attention

Bukowski : Gunn : Eliot

> Society is now one polish'd horde,
> Form'd of two mighty tribes, the *Bores* and *Bored*.
> —LORD BYRON, *DON JUAN*

We all—at least, those willing to admit it—know what boredom feels like. Time crawls. Things stand around and before us, but apart, as though behind a glass partition we can't reach through. In the chamber of experience, thoughts are loud and staccato, falling with a thud. The longer we stay in this airless space the more the tempo of thoughts increases, and the more fixed the thoughts themselves become—not on any particular object, idea, or task, but on the unease of boredom itself and the question of how to escape it. The hand on the clock does not progress, and an afternoon seems interminable. We can't engage with the conversation we're supposedly "in," or move beyond the paragraph we keep re-"reading," or even just let go into idleness and enjoy a stretch of undirected time. We can't get out of the loop of repeating thoughts or get around the glass separating us from the world. We look around for a distraction, but nothing catches. We can't get traction. We can mime attention with our posture but we can't *pay* attention. Can't. Pay. Attention.

Because attention has come to be taken for a narrowly defined slice (focused, engaged, interested, selective, endogenous, transitive) of its fuller definitional and experiential field, and because this slice has been loaded with positive cultural, economic, and theological norms, boredom is often described, with distraction, as attention's opposite. It has been defined as an inability or refusal to engage with the world, a failure or insufficiency of attention, or a misalignment between subjective attention and the task at hand. And yet, when one considers the experiential contours and textures of boredom, and when one considers the forms boredom has assumed in literary and artistic expressions of the mood or condition, boredom emerges not as the *opposite* of attention, but as a condition of attention itself in which active focalization, or engaged concentration, is challenged.

This intuition has been given scholarly voice in cognitive research on the phenomenon of boredom, which has in recent years started to define boredom *in terms of attention*, rather than as its opposite or antithesis.[1] Most research still positions boredom in negative terms—in terms of insufficiency and failure[2]—but some have argued for thinking this experience of insufficient engagement as an experience *within* the horizon of attention itself, as a mode of attention shaped by unfulfilled desire. As John Eastwood and his colleagues have argued, "Boredom has at its core the desiring of satisfying engagement but not being able to achieve that. . . . Putting attention at the center of the experience . . . allow[s] us to explain the subjective experience of boredom: time passing slowly, difficulty focusing, disordered arousal, disrupted agency, negative affect."[3]

At the top of the list provided by Eastwood and his coauthors is perhaps the most consistent—and (ironically perhaps) interesting—thread in the various transhistorical definitions of boredom: time's slow passage. The centrality of slowness, or an experience of temporal suspension, is also one of the structural elements that positions boredom most convincingly as a form of attention. For, as I have discussed, attention takes place in time, inflecting and inflected by the particular experiential shape of the present moment on the perceiving body and mind. In fact, beginning a piece of writing on boredom with a play-by-play description of waiting seems to have become a standard practice. Seneca's early analysis of boredom's experiential form plays out this quality of suspension in repetition:

> How long the same things? Surely I will yawn, I will sleep, I will eat, I will be thirsty, I will be cold, I will be hot. Is there no end? But do all things go in a circle? Night overcomes day, day night, summer gives way to autumn, winter presses on autumn, which is checked by spring. All things pass that they may return. I do nothing new, I see nothing new. Sometimes this makes me seasick [*fit aliquando et huius- reinausia*]. There are many who judge living not painful but empty.[4]

Likewise, Heidegger opens his consideration of *tiefe Langeweile* with a tedium-inducing account of killing time while waiting for a train:

> We are sitting, for example, at the tasteless station of some lonely minor railway. It is four hours until the next train arrives. The district is unattractive. We do have a book in our rucksack, though—shall we read? No. Or think through a problem, some question? We are unable to. We read the timetables or study the table giving the various distances from this station to other places we are not otherwise acquainted with at all. We look at the clock—only a quarter of an hour has gone by. Then we go out onto the main road. We walk up and down, just to have something to do. But it is no use. Then we count the trees along the main road, look at our watch again—exactly five minutes since we last looked at it. Fed up with walking back and forth, we sit down on a stone, draw all kinds of figures in the sand, and in doing so catch ourselves looking at our watch yet again—half an hour—and so on.[5]

Giorgio Agamben later reproduces the scene, in full (as I have just done), in his own account of profound boredom.[6] Eastwood and his team likewise begin their paper on boredom in the waiting room of a doctor's office, with its uninteresting magazines, its dull wall ornaments, and, above all, the clock on the wall whose second hand seems to be frozen in place.[7] Rasmus Johnsen puts it this way: "To the bored the present seems to be dragging itself along unbearably, it is as if nothing leads up to it and nothing will come of it. Along with the feeling that the present will not pass, comes the feeling that all eternity is going to be like this, that forever is reduced to the self-sameness and obviousness of a single moment."[8] Importantly for a consideration of boredom in and as poetic form, Johnsen connects, via Husserl's concept of the synthesis of *retention* (holding in the mind what has just passed) and *protension* (the anticipation of what is to come), the *rhythmic* experience of subjectivity-in-time and how the single note struck by the world experienced in boredom accounts for the feeling of temporal suspension.[9]

Largely due to the rise of boredom as an all-purpose sign of dissatisfaction in modern Anglophone speech, and to the particular urgency of boredom's temporal gear-grinding amid the contemporary technologically enhanced speed culture, boredom has predominantly been considered as a modern phenomenon. Scholars such as Patricia Meyers Spacks, Elizabeth Goodstein, and Saikat Majumdar have made important observations about the specific modernity of literary boredom. Spacks has rightly observed that "designating books as boring acquires cultural usefulness and energy from its capacity to obviate difficulty; it justifies inertia. Interest is always constructed: literary critics, in the business of creating and sustaining it, know that. Boredom is constructed too."[10] Goodstein sees boredom as a symptomatic invention of transnational modernization and its accompanying experiential transformations tied to the "changing temporal rhythms of everyday life"—changes such as technological and economic developments, urbanization and factory labor, an increasingly secular interpretation of human life, and decreased faith in narratives of redemption, meaning-making, life purpose, and divine consequences. She argues that "the nineteenth-century discourse on boredom registers this epochal transformation in the rhetoric of reflection on human existence. In it, the impact of modernization on subjective experience was articulated, existential questions linked to a peculiarly modern experience of empty, meaningless time."[11] Reading boredom as a modern by-product of Weberian disenchantment, she further argues that the experience of boredom is ontologically rooted in a specifically post-Enlightenment subjectivity.

Majumdar also emphasizes boredom's dependence on secularization, arguing that "the double meaning in the related word 'mundane,' implying both the ordinary and the secular, indicates these cultural symptoms of modernity as embedded in a secular vision."[12] He goes on to tie boredom to the banality of colonial and postcolonial life, reading boredom as sign of both the colonizer's nonchalant dominance and the colonized's experience of time without agency. "The dread of banality," he argues, is "rooted in an inability to transcend the immediate condition of life surrounding the experiencing subject," an inability he links to the colonial and postcolonial cultural and literary contexts.[13]

While it is crucial to situate boredom and its accompanying cultural connotations and evaluations historically, the discourse surrounding boredom has suffered, in the modern literary field, from *over*historicization. Each of the examples I have given offers an important perspective into the specific valence of boredom's thwarted attentional condition in modernity. Yet their analyses, in limiting boredom to the modern postindustrial context, often fail to recognize its longer-durée history, archived in a ranging lexical wake that includes malaise, lethargy, sloth, melancholy, acedia, horror loci, the noonday demon, and *taedium vitae*. Isolating boredom to a single vacuum-sealed set of historical conditions short-circuits our ability to consider this longer range of philosophical and poetic approaches to what is, in fact, an essential condition in human world perception and the experience of time, as suggested by the writing of Seneca and Catullus as well as the Desert Fathers, up through the work of Schopenhauer, Nietzsche, and Heidegger. Goodstein's own definition of boredom suggests a condition that can hardly be reduced to boredom's contemporary manifestations, cutting to a deeper and more foundational experiential terrain: "An experience without qualities, with the deficits of the self masquerading as the poverty of the world. In boredom there is no distinguishing in here from out there, for the world in its failure to engage collapses into an extension of the bored subject who empties out in the vain search for an interest, a pleasure, a meaning."[14] In its contemplative demand, its material understatement, and historical association with pockets of idled, inward time, poetic language cuts to boredom's longer history, drawing out under various guises an ongoing issue of language in and out of slackened time, non-productive moods, and stalled activity.

A Slackened Line: The Poetics of Boredom

In nearly every mode of poetic attention I've considered thus far, there has been an important distinction to be made between "poems on" and "poems of." Boredom seems at first like it should be the exception to this rule—and it usually is. Poems that are symptomatically boring are often just bad poems, or so ill-fitted to the capabilities of the reader that full reception is impossible, making any attempt at sustained interest or attention painful. This is precisely because of poetry's rootedness in and dependence on the dynamics of sustained attention, and due to the fraught place of boredom among the other forms of attention—positioned as such a fallen angel as to be pitted as attention's nemesis, antithesis, and antonym. Yet boredom, used intentionally as a mode of attention, makes a comeback—and often a very striking one, particularly in the modern period—as an aesthetic tool, challenge, and ultimately a potentially generative, albeit not exactly pleasurable, mode. When poems engage with boredom intentionally, they undertake a dance with the seeming enemy of art within the frame of the work itself. Moreover, *what* bores us also tells us something important about *how* readers attend, individually and historically. And how writers manipulate the boredoms and attentional limits of their postulated readers is equally informative about the contingencies and constraints shaping literature at a given moment.

I love poems about boredom. And I love how many there are, and by what a diverse gathering of poets (not even to mention the novelists, all of whom are, in a sense, always in a conversation with boredom, though I think more antagonistically than writers of poetry). Andrew Epstein sees the "wave of interest in boredom as a phenomenon" in contemporary writing as a way of "mourning the loss" of real quotidian life, amid "all the microblogging, self-documentation and life-blogging, and the photographic food diaries."[15] To be sure, there is a hunger, in the obsession with the everyday, for the "the lost art of simply doing nothing," even though boredom itself might have more to do with the condition of human life itself—its desires and discontents. "Life, friends, is boring," writes John Berryman in "Dreamsong 14," a poem that, despite its subject matter, never ceases to fascinate me. Perhaps it is Berryman's dance of self-correction: "We must not say so. / After all, the sky flashes, the great sea yearns, / we ourselves flash and yearn." These lines underline what others have observed about contemporary productivity culture, with its emphasis on individual responsibility and its equally Christian-inherited ethic of work, when it condemns boredom (a condemnation inherited from the Desert Fathers grappling with the sin of acedia) as self-indulgent, a stagnation of the soul. Or, in Berryman's telling of the lesson, "and moreover my mother told me as a boy / (repeatedly) 'Ever to confess you're bored / means you have no // Inner Resources.' I conclude now I have no / inner resources, because I am heavy bored." In Charles Simic's poem "To Boredom," the speaking voice is shared ambivalently by both the sufferer of boredom and boredom itself, so that the two are indistinguishable, from the first lines ("I'm the child of your rainy Sundays. / I watched time crawl / Over the ceiling / Like a wounded fly") to the last ("In eternity's classrooms, / The angels sit like bored children / With their heads bowed").[16] Margaret Atwood's boredom poem is longer, both nostalgic and self-corrective, recalling her boredom with the chores and monotonies of her childhood in the shadow of her father, always pointing things out: "I could hardly wait to get / the hell out of there to / anywhere else.... Now I wouldn't be bored. / Now I would know too much. / Now I would know."[17] And in Charles Bukowski, as I will show, boredom hangs in his entire body of work, as tone, posture, and persona.[18]

The Forms Boredom Makes

Up to this point I have considered boredom as a transhistorical phenomenon, an inflection of the attentive faculty, a particularly dominant theme in modern experience, and a thematic vein in modern and contemporary poetry. In the readings that follow, I will focus on the work of three poets whose work engages with the attentional shape of boredom *formally*, not only semantically or descriptively. I will be particularly interested in the ways in which, in these poems, the form of boredom as a form of attention is given form in language. In what follows, I explore the forms boredom makes in Charles Bukowski, Thom Gunn, and T. S. Eliot. In Bukowski, I consider the poet's bored process and performative affect in light of his self-claimed philosophy or poetic motto, "Don't try." In Gunn, I locate the articulation of a kind of boredom (whether intentional or unintentional) in the pursuit of the perfect form. In their highly crafted lines, airless rhymes, and closed-circuit forms, Gunn's early poems enact boredom as a formal rigidity that I call the incredible boredom of the perfect form. Turning finally to Eliot, I trace a move from the description of boredom as a social symptom in *The Waste Land* to the formal enactment or production of boredom as spiritual practice in the *Four Quartets*.

Deadbeat: Bukowski and the Poetics of Dropping Out

Charles Bukowski's tombstone in the Green Hills Memorial Park in Los Angeles County's Rancho Palos Verdes reads, simply, "Don't Try." It's the kernel of a dropped anecdote about giving advice to budding artists, from a 1963 letter to fellow poet and friend-by-correspondence John William Corrington: "Somebody . . . asked me: 'What do you do? How do you write, create?' You don't, I told them. You don't try. . . . You wait, and if nothing happens, you wait some more." It also turns out to be one of the guiding kernels of his poetic praxis—a praxis in which boredom figures simultaneously as attitudinal response, performative persona, critical stance, and creative methodology.

Bukowski's work is often rejected in toto as "bad poetry" because it is difficult to know how to engage with his poems as poetry, when the "poetic" has become so strongly associated with a certain intensity of formalist contemplation on the parts of both reader and writer. Bukowski's writing flies consistently-delinquently in the face of these attentional norms that to this day shape conversations about what "good poetry" can, or rather should, do. What separates Bukowski from other bards of boredom is the quality of acceptance. Boredom's lack of engagement is a source of suffering. The boredom of Bukowski's poems edges toward intentional idleness in that it is, at least in some minimal way, chosen, even embraced, as a way of being in the world outside of a cultural economy of ambition and productivity predicated upon the dominance of highly focused, object-oriented attention. Boredom mixes with idleness to form both a politics and a poetics of "dropping out." In short, his oeuvre suggests a sustained exploration, through poetic form, of the resignation of effort and ambition—or, in attentional terms, of intentional foci and executive orientation—in favor of a passive, stripped down observational commentary on passing moments.

The line "Don't try" first appears in an uncollected poem from 1982 in which "the old big time" sends off for the 1982–83 copy of *Who's Who in America,* which arrives in two big volumes. The speaker opens the box with his wife, who flips to his entry. He tells her that the editors had asked for "some / comment upon / life, some / philosophy." She reads out: "it says: 'don't / try.'" // "right," I answered / "what's good on / TV tonight?"[19] Both formally and semantically, the poem is stripped down to the bare bones of an interaction characterized by a generalized attitudinal shrug. Against a conventional characterization of poetry as necessarily—even definitionally—crafted, honed, concentrated, or distilled, this piece is a lazy snapshot of a few lines of dialogue, seemingly dashed off before switching on the tube. At no point does the poem lift off into metaphor or symbolism or go out of its way to add complexity, layered significances, hidden references, or any of the other formal elements one might expect from a literary work. In other words, the poem seems to enact the motto it describes by refusing to try, having given up or rejected the notion of "working" at poetry.

To any writer for whom writing is effortful, Bukowski had one suggestion: "don't do it." He describes the creative process as one of intentional passivity, with as little concern over the "finished" work or its reception as possible. As a mode of intransitive attention, his poetics suggests an extremity of passivity or exogeneity—the opposite of active intentional (endogenous) focus. Bukowski's poetics present a kind of working-class white man's blues—a musical influence made explicit in poems like "bluebird," whose title and refrain call up Sonny Boy Williamson's "Bluebird Blues," recorded with the cheap label Bluebird Records in 1937; "copulation blues," about trying to "fuck" in the age of distraction;[20] and "somebody," a poem that shows a darker ethical delinquency in Bukowski's bored blues: "I've got the sad sads / all I want to do is / fuck you."[21]

In "somebody," a demoralizing and demoralized scene of sexual violence tumbles out in a series of spoken lines that switch without punctuation or distinction between the poet's voice and that of the woman he's chatting with, until the voices disappear as he forces himself on her in order to feel like "Charles Somebody." The linguistic juxtaposition of dirty colloquial and the lyricism of "O I just looked up her long slim legs of heaven," with the "O" a jarring importation from the conventional poetic beauty otherwise rejected in the poem, produces the effect of a series of wrong turns and violations. The conventional aesthetic beauty of "long slim legs" gives way to the unexpected bodily organs of "liver" and "quivering intestines" as the poem's pace picks up, lines shorten, dialogue disappears and violence ratchets up, driven by hammering monosyllabic verbs ("walked over," "grabbed her," "ripped her shirt over her head"). The ethical stance is bluntly explicit: "I didn't care." With pathetic machismo, the speaker shrugs off his own rape admission, suggesting a total resignation to boredom's drive to diversion through sexual predation.

Equally repugnant scenes litter Bukowski's writing. At the same time, a subtler element of the human that keeps the poems from being predictable misogynistic caricatures, or mere spectacles of American lowlife, is the unexpected currents of tenderness that run underground through many of them, understated nearly to the point of evaporation. That element is, surprisingly, love—and a strikingly realist love, because stripped of romance and sentimentality. In Bukowski's poems, love is not a pathway to anything, not a message from anywhere, not a sign of anything. It's a creaturely necessity, simply one of the few things to celebrate in life or writing.

Bukowskian love is more companionship than focused desire. We see it in poems like "the shower,"[22] describing a postcoital bath with Linda King and the rhythms of cohabitation and physical ease that make up an afternoon, and the poem "like a flower in the rain,"[23] in which the speaker makes love to his girlfriend after her bath while she puts lotion on her legs and smokes a cigarette, the scene unfolding with easy candor and idle banter. What is remarkable about both poems is that their direct and detailed sexuality is neither erotic nor particularly vulgar, lacking the requisite performativity of either mode. Despite the blow-by-blow explicitness of its physical description, the locus of "like a flower" is not the sex itself but everything else, all the material marginalia of not-being-alone—laughter, fast food, feeling good in the imperfect sufficiency of companionship. The theme of taking comfort in basic sufficiency also appears in "grass,"[24] where the speaker watches the incessant patterns of a power mower in the neighboring yard, taking in "what's left of my life" like a feast of mediocre comforts: "the grass is green enough / and the sun is sun enough / . . . / it is / interesting enough."

If Bukowski's "Don't try" forms a poetic or political practice, it is a refusal of the intentionality and agency of poetic craft, as with Bataille's refusal of "project." At the same time, both poet and poems do seem intentional about "acting out" boredom as poetic strategy, public persona, and political nonstance. In the poems themselves, boredom is primarily present in the tone of the speaker, in the representation of the scenes and the overall drab and deadbeat depiction of the world. In their lack of formal complexity or polish, they also present themselves as the products of boredom's almost nonexistent attention span and so do not always capture the focused attention of the reader, except as snatches of voice and attitude. This raises the question: how might boredom operate poetically as form? That is, what would it look like for the very form of a poem to inhabit and produce the structural characteristics of boredom as a mode of poetic attention?

The Boredom of the Perfect Form: The Early Poetry of Thom Gunn

In a collection of images called The Terrible Boredom of Paradise, photographer Derek Henderson captures a series of landscapes from the window of a car driving through his native New Zealand. In a note on the collection, Henderson writes: "I was trying to recapture what I saw as a child in the backseat of my parents' car when we went on holidays. Even though the car was moving fast the car window seemed to frame, isolate and freeze these moments which have stayed with me more as emotions rather than as images."[25] The images themselves are imbued with a diffuse light, with a flat, pale tonality of color. Most are of roadsides, others of the ocean, with a couple of still-life-like interiors in the mix. The location of these photographs, often talked about as a kind of paradise on earth, and a top ecotourism destination, makes of the stretch of time these images evoke and recall a kind of holiday within a holiday, a paradise on earth. The title's "terrible boredom" is captured in the strange quality of desolation and the static beauty that pervades them. There are no people, nothing messy or living. They form, in frieze, a perfect utopia and its perfect lifelessness.

Paradise is a garden in which everything is perfect in order and beauty. It is the physical and spatial embodiment of divine perfection. It is a place of perfect formal unity: nothing is out of order or ugly, nothing is unexpected. But when everything is perfect, everything is predictable. And when everything is predictable, there is a strong possibility that boredom will follow. In his book-length philosophy of boredom, Lars Svendsen observes that "all utopias seem to be deadly boring, because only that which is imperfect is interesting." For this reason, "Boredom constitutes a boundary for a utopia. A utopia can never be completely accomplished, for that would be synonymous with boredom—and this boredom would eat up any utopia from the inside."[26]

Indeed, there's a long and robust history of thought on the boredom of Paradise, which includes Friedrich Schlegel's assertion (in a chapter of *Lucinde* entitled "An Idyll of Idleness") that "the highest, most fulfilled form of life would . . . be nothing else than *pure vegetating*,"[27] Blaise Pascal's warning against having everything one needs or desires fulfilled,[28] and Arthur Schopenhauer's observation of the endless cycle of desire-fulfillment (embodied as total perfect formal unity) and the emergence of boredom, which sparks new desires, and so on.[29] Kant suggested that Adam and Eve would have suffered tremendous boredom had they stayed on in Eden, and Nietzsche writes that God himself was bored on the seventh day, faced with his perfect creation.[30] Kierkegaard summed up the chain of perfect boredoms in this way: "The gods were bored; therefore they created human beings. Adam was bored because he was alone; therefore Eve was created. Since that moment, boredom entered the world and grew in quantity in exact proportion to the growth of the population."[31] Svendsen connects the boredom of paradise to the modern boredom of postindustrial affluence, claiming that "the utopia we are living in [today] can satisfy practically any need. The utopia does not lack anything—except meaning. When this meaning is looked for, the utopia begins to crack,"[32] echoing

Tocqueville's observation of the "strange melancholy which often haunts the inhabitants of democratic countries in the midst of their abundance."[33] Turning to the play of perfection in a work of art, we must ask whether it is possible for an aesthetic or poetic form to be *too perfect* to capture the attention—or whether, the closer human-made forms get to divine or ideal form, they inevitably court a certain kind of boredom. In the words of Novalis, the question is this: "How can one avoid boredom in the presentation of Perfection?"[34]

Certainly the notion of a figure or form being "too perfect" is familiar in human beauty. For example, it is not uncommon for someone to speak of an individual as "classically handsome" or "beautiful," but not necessarily *attractive*, not necessarily alluring. But what is it about perfection that slackens the line of interest and stalls attention into boredom? How can we think about this perfect boredom of the perfect form in the poetic context? To explore this question, I would like to consider an example of the deliberate employment of static, perfect forms—and the particular kind of boredom they produce and embody—in the early poems of Thom Gunn. In Gunn's first published volume, *Fighting Terms* (1954), this tight formal control is played up, to a point where one must consider that formal perfection may be the aesthetic driver of the work, creating what might be thought of as a kind of formally produced boredom in which the attention, confronted with such static beauty, cannot get purchase or traction on the poetic object and stalls out.

While most scholarship on Gunn has focused on his later work, particularly the powerful AIDS-related elegies of *The Man with Nightsweats* (1992), and on his bolder, more urban poetry dealing with homosexuality and the heavy drug use (which would take his life in 2004) permeating his Haight-Ashbury life, I would like to focus on his early, pre-emigration poetry.[35] This work offers an important contribution to an understanding of the uses of imposed form in modern verse. Traditional form can in some ways be seen as Gunn's natural register, as he writes candidly about the difficulty of transitioning to free verse at Stanford, under the mentorship of "arch-formalist" Yvor Winters,[36] and the ungainliness of writing without rhythmic constraint: "I was thinking iambically, rhythmically, yes: and when I broke the rhythm, it was just chopped-up prose, of the worst kind—I know that was boring, and not rhythmically interesting in itself. The difficult thing about learning to write free verse is that you have to improvise what you consider to be interesting enough rhythms to exist on their own, and they have to be different for each line. So I think it's easier to write well in metrical poetry, when you can: but it's difficult changing from one to another."[37] Gunn's description of bad free verse as "boring" here is important, because it signals two different kinds of boredom in poetry: the unintentional and the formally crafted. In bad free verse of the kind Gunn claims to have written in his first forays into the "new form," the poetry is boring because it doesn't come together, isn't alive on the page. It has no unity as an organism because there is no formal necessity holding its parts together, so they cannot attain the movement and internally defined integrity that gives a poem presence in the attention.

In Gunn's early work, the poem *does* come together, but with such completeness and unity that its poetic effect is one of static perfection: a nonporous, airtight structure yielding a reading experience in which nothing seems to move. Emphasizing a variety of formal repetitions and rigors during a time when free verse, fragmentation, and more disrupted forms were in vogue, Gunn's first collection deployed a quality of verse that would have stood out from the work of most of his contemporaries. Instead of emphasizing fragmentation and free play, these poems emphasize meter, rhyme, and repetition. Gunn takes advantage of the out-of-key nature of conventional form in the literary moment that surrounded these poems' original reception to produce forms that embody a mechanization of the attention and a stalling out of life within a tightly controlled system. *Boring* becomes in these perfect forms an active—and, paradoxically, fascinating—verb. To be quite clear, the works themselves are not *symptomatically* boring. In interesting and even daring ways, they actively investigate and ultimately transpose the internal structures of boredom into poetic form. In their untimely emphasis on imposed form, these poems can be seen to produce a kind of temporal doldrum, one of the defining characteristics of boredom. This attentional effect bolsters the themes of taedium vitae, repetition, control, and the absence of change or happening that runs through the collection, underlining an important connection between the mechanistic, externally imposed control of time and the deadening or stalling out of the natural movements of attention and interest: that is, the perfect form itself forms a commentary on the emergence of boredom within a life of order and material abundance that is poor in meaning and purpose.

The poem "Wind in the Streets," offers a useful starting place because it melds a formal enactment of the temporal doldrums of boredom with a semantic and thematic occupation with the same; there is almost no space between form and semantic content:

> The same faces, and then the same scandals
> Confront me inside the talking shop which I
> Frequent for my own good. So the assistant
> Points to the old cogwheels, the old handles
> Set in machines which to buy would be to buy
> The same faces, and then the same scandals.
>
> I climb by the same stairs to a square attic.
> And I gasp, for surely this is something new!
> So square, so simple. It is new to be so simple.
> Then I see the same sky through the skylight, static
> Cloudless, the same artificial toylike blue.
> The same stairs led to the same attic.
>
> I only came, I explain, to look round,
> To the assistant who coos while I regain the street.
> Searching thoroughly, I did not see what I wanted.
> What I wanted would have been what I found.
> My voice carries, his voice blows to his feet:
> I only came, I explain, to look round.
>
> I may return, meanwhile I'll look elsewhere:
> My want may modify to what I've seen.
> So I smile wearily, though even as I smile
> A purposeful gust of wind tugs at my hair;
> But I turn, I wave, I am not sure what I mean.
> I may return, meanwhile I'll look elsewhere.[38]

In the poem, the speaker walks into a shop "to look around," an aimless act we understand to be both habitual and vaguely medicinal from the repetition of "same" in line 1, from the description of the shop as one "I / Frequent for my own good" in line three. The form of the poem is a rigorous study in habitude: the last line of each sestet a reiteration of the first, and the rhyme scheme following a tight ABCABA structure (with the first and last A's being the same word). With the interesting exception of stanza two, the C of each sestet ("assistant," "simple," "wanted," "smile") opens a narrow window of variation in each sestet, like the attic discovered above the shop—"surely this is something new!," though that square of newness is short-lived in the poem, its square repeated in the square of the skylight's view of the same blue of the same sky. Rhymes and near-rhymes proliferate within each line, and often the same word is repeated several times within a sestet (in the third sestet, we see this in "came," "explain," "regain," "explain").

The "I" of the poem becomes increasingly, claustrophobically pervasive in the second two sestets, repeated nine times in stanza 3 and eleven times in stanza 4. Structurally and semantically, the poem seems to enact an increasingly tight loop of mind in a self-reiterative pattern: uncertain what is sought or what might be found, and unable to find anything of interest in its surroundings, the I returns to its own uneasy loudness. In the poem's penultimate line, "I" occupies a third of the sonic space, surrounded by monosyllabic verbs without object. The quality of objectless and fruitless searching through a shop-world of sames evokes an unsettled and unsettling quality that is at once recursive and tautological: "Searching thoroughly, I did not see what I wanted. / What I wanted would have been what I had found." It is a quality of obsessive efforts to engage or to "discover" the world, continually "confronted" by its failure to do so, resulting in a return to "square" one to "look elsewhere." Here the subject can be seen as a part missing a whole, a piece of a relation that lacks connection to the rest of the mechanism of action. At the same time, the mechanism itself (though broken) is itself a mechanism of reproduction and reiteration, and to connect would be to connect to more of the social and industrial/commercial same: "the old cogwheels, the old handles / Set in machines which to buy would be to buy / The same faces, and then the same scandals."

We find another example of Gunn's formal monotony (this time round, not square) in "Round and Round," in which the poem's structural effect is already present in its title. The form of this poem echoes that of "Wind in the Streets," with the first and last line of each nine-line stanza the same. In "Round and Round," however, the form is even tighter: only slight variation in repeated lines and a more regular iambic tetrameter maintained, with only a few exceptions, throughout.

> The lighthouse keeper's world is round,
> Belongings skipping in a ring—

> All that a man may want, therein,
> A wife, a wireless, bread, jam, soap,
> Yet day by night his straining hope
> Shoots out to live upon the sound
> The spinning waves make while they break
> For their own endeavor's sake—
> The lighthouse keeper's world is round.
>
> . . .
>
> When it is calm, the rocks are safe
> To take a little exercise
> But all he does is fix his eyes
> On that huge totem he has left
> Where thoughts dance round what will not shift—
> His secret inarticulate grief.
> Waves have no sun, but are beam-caught
> Running below his feet, wry salt,
> When, in a calm, the rocks are safe.[39]

"What will not shift," the center of the rotational form of the poem's thinking, is this "inarticulate grief"—objectless, or at least object-unknown—and generalizing outward in centripetal motion without end. The objects in the keeper's round world are also round, "skipping in a ring," their words almost the only breaks (or skips) in the poem's iambic meter: "A wife, a wireless, bread, jam, soap." The weight of these objects and the way they jut out from the formal weave of the poem indicates a degree of strangeness between subject and objects, a lack of familiarity or closeness in the poem's replication of perception. They are, in this sense, "belongings" without belonging. So is their keeper, though the speaker's estrangement is more of a lock-in: he cannot leave the axle of unidentified grief and so is caught in the stasis of its spin. He might "take a little exercise," venturing out among the calm, safe rocks, but even then cannot take his eyes from the lighthouse, "that huge totem he has left." Thus even diversion cannot take him out of the doldrums produced by the endless rotation of the mind around the buried kernel of its suffering. The world turns around this central source of unease, and, because the unease has no name, and the world (even the house, even language and thinking) has taken shape around it, cannot move in any other way.

Gunn also describes love in this way—or rather, describes the way love is subsumed under the desire to control. In the poem "La Prisonnière," this control informs the rigid mastery of language that forms the poem itself:

> Now I will shut you in a box
> With massive sides and a lid that locks.
> Only by that I can be sure
> That you are still mine and mine secure,
> And know where you are when I'm not by,
> No longer needing to wonder and spy.
> I may forget you at party or play
> But do not fear I shall keep away
> With any Miss Brown or any Miss Jones.
> If my return finds a heap of bones—
> Too dry to simper, too dry to whine—
> You will still be mine and only mine.[40]

The tight, almost singsong meter and AABBCCDD rhyme scheme that run through the poem, their regularity calling up the lilt of nursery rhymes, embody the rigidity of control driving this love-poem-turned-master-poem. This poem moves from imprisonment to a promise of faithfulness to a declaration of possession even at the cost of the beloved's life. Any sweetness that might have survived the first two lines vanishes in the last three. The formal regularity of this poem is exaggerated to the point of mechanical strictness, offering an interesting self-critical insight on the part of Gunn regarding his tendency toward formal control that would stay with him even in his later efforts at free verse. This verse is very much not free—it is bound, both formally and semantically—to the point of lifelessness.

This poem is vital in understanding the strange formal effect of *Fighting Terms* as a whole, because it signals a high degree of self-awareness on Gunn's part, not only of the unique formal rigor of the poems but also of the qualities of mind this degree of formal perfectness produces and reflects. This poem stands as a kind of self-reflective commentary on the others—signaling an acknowledgment (through critical deployment) of the ways in which the life of a poem can be suffocated by formal control. The locking-down of the poem formally enacts a kind of imprisonment and mastery that suggests the killing of the poem itself. Yet it also *uses* formal control as a tool for the production of this quality. Paradoxically, the ability of the poem to both kill itself and comment formally on this act of self-murder brings it back to life, but also indicates yet another level of mastery, and so the cycle continues.

All of this comes back to boredom when we consider the kind of attention the poem produces. The lines are crafted toward what I have been calling the boredom of perfect form, in that there is a high degree of mechanical regularity. The attention itself becomes lulled into mechanical head-bobbing (with subtle formal fractures signaling below-ground shocks to the system). At the same time, the vacant or vacuous quality of the verse yields a dulling of attention that *renders* the poem a "heap of bones." The poem is not raised—it is the body of a beloved, not her or his spirit. It does not take flight and so is rendered the perfect formal embodiment of taedium vitae—the result, also, of the locking-down and overcontrolling of attention so that it does not wander or play. The poetics of the static, unenlivened form takes on deeper and broader significance in the poem "Lazarus Not Raised," where, as in Stevens's "The Worms at Heaven's Gate," the body is "bodied forth" as mere flesh, the spirit not rising, the "scheduled miracle" of poetic transfiguration "not taking place":

> He was not changed. His friends around the grave
> Stared down upon his gray placid face
> Bobbling on shadows; nothing it seemed could save
> His body now from the sand below their wave,
> The scheduled miracle not taking place.
>
> He lay inert beneath those outstretched hands
> Which beckoned him to life. Though coffin case
> Was ready to hold life and winding bands
> At his first stir would loose the frozen glands,
> The scheduled miracle did not take place.
>
> . . .
>
> Abruptly the corpse blinked and shook his head
> Then sank again, sliding without a trace

> From sight, to take slime on the deepest bed
> Of vacancy. He had chosen to stay dead,
> The scheduled miracle did not take place.
>
> Nothing else changed. I saw somebody peer,
> Stooping, into the oblong box of space.
> His friends had done their best: without such fear,
> Without that terrifying awakening glare,
> The scheduled miracle would have taken place.[41]

It is difficult in this presentation of the distended body of the poem in "Lazarus Not Raised" not to think of Blanchot's essay "Literature and the Right to Death," to which I also made reference at the end of my discussion of desire. In that essay, Blanchot writes of the particular "deceit" of both "imaginative literature" and the "literature of action." The first, in presenting itself as imaginary, in fact "only puts to sleep those who want to go to sleep." The second, however, is deceitful because it suggests a form of command (urging people "to do something") that betrays the work of literature:

> The language of the writer . . . does not command; it presents; and it does not present by causing whatever it portrays to be present, but by portraying it behind everything, as the meaning and the absence of this everything. The result is either that the appeal of the author to the reader is only an empty appeal, and expresses only the effort which a man cut off from the world makes to reenter the world, as he stands discreetly at its periphery—or that "something to do," which can only be recovered by starting from absolute values, appears to the reader precisely as that which cannot be done or as that which requires neither work nor action in order to be done.[42]

Instead of a literature that seeks "something to do," Blanchot urges a literature that stays with Lazarus, as Gunn's poem does, in nonrisen form, even if this formal stasis is painful—it is painful because it is all that is rejected in existence or defined out of the kind of attention that "must be paid" to things: "The language of literature is a search for this moment which precedes literature. Literature usually calls it existence; it wants the cat as it exists, the pebble *taking the side of things*, not man, but the pebble, and in this pebble what man rejects by saying it, what is the foundation of speech and what speech excludes in speaking, the abyss, Lazarus in the tomb and not Lazarus brought back into daylight, the one who already smells bad, who is Evil, Lazarus lost and not Lazarus saved and brought back to life."[43] In Blanchot's reading of literature as Lazarus "not raised," we find a common thread in articulating the empty claim (the miracle that does not take place) in literature's efforts to be more than language—that is, to find "something to do." And in this common thread we find also something of the focus on material form, a mode of attention stuck in the "merely this," that might in fact take us out of boredom's "unhappy consciousness" by stepping *into it*. Gunn's early poems perform, in their highly composed attention to form over what lives therein, a formal parallel of the turn to the corpse, to the poem's body rather than its mind, to the form of tedious days *as form*, *as the form of tedium*. In presenting boredom as form, Gunn's early poems call attention to the material structure of stopped time, thrown mind, stalled life, and world inertia—and at the same time offer a commentary on the boredom that wells up in the "paradise" of postindustrial materialism. This is the boredom of the perfect form.

From Social Symptom to Spiritual Practice: Boredom and Acedia in Eliot

So far we have seen boredom's slackened attentional line acted out as attitudinal stance in Bukowski and deployed as formal perfection in Gunn. In this last section, let us fall back a bit in time, digging into the roots of the modernist articulation of boredom in the poems of T. S. Eliot, clearly forecasting the kind of contemporary wreckage in which Bukowski's poems take place—and also prefiguring the passivity of his "Zen-dropout" poetics of intentional boredom. Images and tonal qualities of modern boredom proliferate in both "The Love Song of J. Alfred Prufrock" and *The Waste Land*. In the former, these evocations remain in the self-attributed mode of "observations." In the latter, they move to the level of world-form, a commentary that is at once social, historical, and theological. By the time Eliot wrote *Four Quartets*, however, we see a transformation in his engagement with the poetics of boredom, from a symptom of modernity and a twilight of the soul to a modern revision of acedia. What is interesting in this development, and what I will attempt to draw out in the readings that follow, is that this symptom of modernity becomes, in Eliot's later work, also its solution—the only way *through* boredom is a practice of meditative endurance in acedia, so that getting through the condition is reframed as a kind of generative suffering-through into presence and ultimately into a form of nondirected and even unintentional love. Here boredom becomes a site of challenge in the way it confronts the subject, with its position in relation to time, death, and selfhood, and at the same time becomes a teacher of presence through its painful temporal suspension. In other words, in the course of his major works, Eliot transforms boredom from symptomatic description into a prescription for attentional practice.

In "Prufrock," a certain quality of sluggishness and bogged-down time, paired with contentless diversions, is captured in voice, image, and form—in "half-deserted streets / The muttering retreats / Of restless nights in one-night cheap hotels," in "Streets that follow like a tedious argument," in the "yellow fog that rubs its back upon the window-panes," and, most notably, in the absent refrain that punctuates the poem in at once observation and enactment of vacuous time-filling, "In the room the women come and go / Talking of Michelangelo."[44] The observation of boredom as a quality and condition running through urban life, with its drab exteriors and cheap thrills, its mechanical measuring of time, its empty diversions and social niceties, offers a preview of the starker portrayal of this condition in *The Waste Land*.

At the same time, the *voice* of "Prufrock"—arguably the poem's defining element—both inhabits and embodies boredom's uniquely alienated relation to the world. Things happen around, but without particular felt connection or attachment to the implied speaking subject. The voice behind self-descriptive lines such as "Politic, cautious, and meticulous; / Full of high sentence, but a bit obtuse; / At times, indeed, almost ridiculous— / Almost, at times, the Fool" seems to be trapped in its own air-tight jar, filling the space with snatches of days and recursively anxious questions about what to do next, all shot through with a quality of tiredness and repetition, as though all of the circles of thought might be repeated endlessly over the course of one afternoon or many. And indeed the snatches of days we catch in the poem underscore this quality of clockwork lives—the circulation of ladies through a room, the circulations of trends in hairstyles, the tired "butt-ends of . . . days and ways" that all look alike.[45] Sometimes, for a moment, the doldrums give way to distraction, and the mind lifts off a little and gains some temporary relief from lingering for a moment in daydream, hearing the music of the mermaids and catching glimpses in imagination of their blowing hair—or even just in a simpler dream of an imagined life, walking the shore with rolled trouser legs, eating a peach. But distraction is only a momentary respite from boredom. Inevitably the conversation breaks in the way live voices sometimes blend with a dream before waking. The subject awakes to the airless chamber of the real day, as "human voices wake us and we drown." Here, drowning is another form of suffocation. "Prufrock" offers us the sound of the mind in this airless chamber, in a mode of attention that does not "breathe," does not inhale of the world or exhale into it and so produces the sealed-off quality of suffocation.

In *The Waste Land*, Eliot takes "Prufrock"'s interiority of mind and both externalizes and pluralizes it into a fragmentary collective. Voices cut in and out, their assemblage of particulars and layered references forming a textual terrain at once teeming and desolate. The lack of ease or embeddedness of mind and world is still present, but magnified, as there is not one singular speaking subject but many. Even Tiresias, whom Eliot identifies as the primary seer of the poem, and whose blind and pluralized vision forms "the substance of the poem," is not-one. At once blind and too-much-seeing, he inhabits a body made monstrous by combination. Many of the poem's evocations of modern boredom, and its engagement with Baudelairean concepts of "spleen" and "ennui," echo those of "Prufrock," particularly in lines like "Under the brown fog of a winter dawn," "staring forms / Leaned out, leaning, hushing the room enclosed,"[46] and the one-sided conversation of "A Game of Chess":

"What shall I do now? What shall I do?
"I shall rush out as I am, and walk the street
"With my hair down, so. What shall we do tomorrow?
"What shall we ever do?"[47]

The lines just following these emphasize the automatization of time down to a "withered stump" and call forth an important element of the attentional quality of boredom, that of a certain kind of directionless and objectless waiting, for something—anything—to happen: "The hot water at ten. / And if it rains, a closed car at four. / And we shall play a game of chess, / Pressing lidless eyes and waiting for a knock upon the door." All of this is couched in a room lushly but datedly furnished with the wreckage of the aristocracy, its "burnished throne," its marble and glass, its branching candelabra and laquearia, swimming in the nouveau riche odor of synthetic perfume. Writing on the identification of some of these running themes in the context of one of Eliot's primary influences, Walter Benjamin observes that "Baudelaire envisions readers to whom the reading of lyric would present difficulties. . . . Willpower and the ability to concentrate are not their strong points. What they prefer is sensual pleasure; they are familiar with 'spleen' which kills interest and receptiveness. . . . If conditions for a positive reception of lyric poetry have become less favorable, it is reasonable to assume that only in rare instances does lyric poetry accord with the experience of its readers. This may be due to a change in the structures of their experience."[48] Importantly, in his reading of Baudelaire, Benjamin links what he describes in the same essay as "the standardized, denatured life of the civilized masses" to a decline in the attentional capacities of both interest and receptiveness, yielding a pervasive condition of boredom that cannot be separated from the kind of loss of aura through the rise in the "mechanical reproducibility" (of both art and experience) he identifies elsewhere.[49]

Yet while "A Game of Chess" emphasizes the relationship of sensual and material indulgence with modern boredom (an important element in Baudelaire's thinking of both ennui and the flaneur), in "The Fire Sermon" we find the condition also in the lives of poorer working-class characters (as Eliot noted, all the women in the poem are in some way, for better or worse, indistinguishable). The attentional doldrum of the "violet hour" is not a phenomenon of a certain class, but civilizational, embodied even in the land itself, in the broken tent of the river (173), the sinking of leaf into mud (173–74), and in the rat, creeping "softly through the vegetation / dragging its slimy belly on the bank" as the fisher king fishes (174–75). The most evocative description of the play of boredom, and the most strikingly evident of this condition as a particular mode of attention, comes when the typist, home from typing, goes through the mindless motions of setting out "food in tins." The description of her lover's arrival and her indifferent reception of his advances captures the quality of a mind worn past the ability or desire to engage by day upon day (presumably) of typing things up—an act of disinterested but directed, narrow-focus attention, the kind capitalized upon in the new attention economy of the modern workplace:

> The time is now propitious, as he guesses,
> The meal is ended, she is bored and tired,
> Endeavors to engage her in caresses
> Which still are unreproved, if undesired.
> Flushed and decided, he assaults at once;
> Exploring hands encounter no defense;
> His vanity requires no response,
> And makes a welcome of indifference.
> . . .
> She turns and looks a moment in the glass,
> Hardly aware of her departed lover;
> Her brain allows one half-formed thought to pass:
> "Well, now that's done: and I'm glad it's over."
> When lovely woman stoops to folly and
> Paces about her room again, alone,
> She smoothes her hair with automatic hand,
> And puts a record on the gramophone.
>
> (236–56)

The automatization of human pleasures like food, love, and sex and the portrayal of a woman too bored and tired to resist unwanted entry emerge as signs and symptoms of a world gone wrong, and at the heart of this commentary is a reminder that this impoverishment of the mind is the result of the overtapping of one attentional resource and the neglect of all others, with the flattening of attention (in interest, intentionality, apprehension, and subjective presence) into this its most negative mode.

Boredom as Attentional Practice: Acedia, *Askesis,* and *Agape* in the *Four Quartets*

The metaphysical implications of this flattening of the attention come to the fore in "What the Thunder Said," but without solution. In this final section of the poem, Eliot positions the crisis of metaphysical boredom in terms of a failure of grace in the Christian theological sense (a failure of resurrection of the soul, which has turned its gaze to the ground before its feet): "He who was living is now dead / We who were living are now dying / With a little patience" (322–30). The barrenness of the terrain in this section embodies the stasis and dissatisfaction of the soul-bored world:

> Here one can neither stand nor lie nor sit
> There is not even silence in the mountains
> But dry sterile thunder without rain
> There is not even solitude in the mountains
> But red sullen faces sneer and snarl
> From doors of mudcracked houses.
> (340–45)

Yet the response comes from a time before, or a voice before and farther away, bringing in the imperative that, for Eliot, tied together both Christian and Buddhist forms of asceticism as a path through and against the misguided and soul-deadening indulgences of modern life. What the thunder utters, *datta, dayadhvam, damyata* (encapsulated in the refrain *DA*), form three imperatives that provide an ethics of austerity through what amounts to a meditative bolstering and self-giving of the attentional capacity: give, compassion, control. It is here that we find a casting-forward toward the *Four Quartets*, which takes up the problem of modern boredom not as social symptom but as spiritual illness in the form of the sin of acedia. It is also here that Eliot provides the kernel of what the *Quartets* develop as solution: acedia is overcome through a practice of attentional *askesis* in which meditation on presence without attachment yields a kenotic release of self into *agape*, or selfless love.

"Human kind / Cannot bear very much reality,"[50] Eliot writes, in one of the most oft-quoted lines of the *Quartets*. And, indeed, over the course of the decades since the publication of *The Waste Land*, the overmuchness of a certain kind of "reality" and its discontents only increased in both the U.S. and the UK. One world war had passed and a second was already underway. The quality of newness in *The Waste Land*'s description of modern life and the sense of energy in its breaking of conventional form to get at the broken world to which it responded have, in the *Quartets*, shifted to a simpler, slower, more pensive response—perhaps out of an increase in wisdom, perhaps out of an increase in readings in sacred texts, perhaps out of a world-worn fatigue. It seems that in this later work Eliot has decided to counter the noise, speed, and fragmentation of "this twittering world" with an almost medicinal antidote.[51] While the themes of the urban wasteland are still present in this work, they are presented from what feels like emotional, temporal, or philosophical distance. In fact, all these distances are present as elements of a particular practice of boredom transformed to meditative detachment.

"Distracted from distracted by distraction," Eliot writes in "Burnt Norton," echoing Aristotle's formulation of God in *De Anima* as a "thinking on thinking." And it is only proper that this formulation of the modern soul should be in terms of a fragmentation of attention and that this should be formally opposite from the soul close to God, a communion of attention. The lines here reflect the kind of suffocation palpable in "Prufrock," this time with the benefit of reflective distance from which to contemplate this place and time:

> Here is a place of disaffection
> Time before and time after
> In a dim light: neither daylight
> Investing form with lucid stillness
> Turning shadow into transient beauty
> With slow rotation suggesting permanence
> Nor darkness to purify the soul
> Emptying the sensual with deprivation
> Cleansing affection from the temporal.
> Neither plenitude nor vacancy. Only a flicker
> Over the strained time-ridden faces
> Distracted from distraction by distraction
> Filled with fancies and empty of meaning
> Tumid apathy with no concentration . . .[52]

Importantly, this passage describes the condition of this "place of disaffection" in terms of a series of neither/nors, in which the soul benefits from the tonic effects of neither end of any experiential spectrum: neither past nor future, neither form-giving "daylight" "nor darkness" with its soul-purifying deprivation training, "Neither plenitude nor vacancy." It would be difficult to express the emotional texture of boredom and its particular constellation of attention's dynamic coordinates more clearly than "tumid apathy with no concentration." The line of interest is slack, and there is no directing or orienting of the concentration toward any particular object of engagement. Without any sustained engagement, without the ability either to rest the mind in idled awareness or to direct it in concentrated attention, it is, like the daydreaming mind in "Prufrock," able to escape only into "fancies," "empty of meaning."

> And cold the sense and lost the motive of action.
> And we all go with them, into the silent funeral,
> Nobody's funeral, for there is no one to bury.
> I said to my soul, be still, and let the dark come upon you
> Which shall be the darkness of God.[53]

What has been lost is the capacity where perception and intentionality meet in the attention: in modern mechanization of this faculty, the soul becomes alienated from itself, becomes thrown out of both its sensual connection to the world and its relation of proximity to God. The soul is, in a sense, unsouled in the alienating, temporally mechanized, internally stalled mode of boredom. When boredom is thought metaphysically, in terms of the health of the soul and its degree of mindfulness (or mindlessness) of God, the word then is *acedia*, attentional torpor. Acedia can be understood as the sin of boredom with prayer or boredom with existence that comes through fatigue with the routinized nature of daily life, especially in monastic contexts.

Askesis and Kenosis: Deconstituting the Bored Subject

What is interesting about the *Quartets*' response to the condition of acedia is that, instead of attempting to pull the self out of its blighted temporal and intentional senses (trying to *escape* this metaphysical boredom by investing more concerted interest in work, a more fervent mustering of reverence in prayer and duty, or by seeking companionship or diversion), the poem seems to suggest that the path through acedia is simple perseverance, simply suffering boredom until the soul's thrownness out-of-ease in world and with God is released in a giving way of the self itself, a giving over of preference, attachment, and the insatiability of sensual desires. In Eliot's very Schopenhauerian terms, this takes place through a starving out (a deprivation, a desiccation, an evacuation) of "appetency," the root of boredom's existential dissatisfaction:

> Descend lower, descend only
> Into the world of perpetual solitude,
> World not world, but that which is not world,
> Internal darkness, deprivation
> And destitution of all property,
> Desiccation of the world of sense,
> Evacuation of the world of fancy,
> Inoperancy of the world of spirit;
> This is the one way, and the other
> Is the same, not in movement
> But abstention from movement; while the world moves
> In appetency, on its metalled ways . . .[54]

We find here not only the description of a human condition, but the prescription of a path through it. Interestingly, in his articulation of a "middle way,"[55] itself the name for the path of Buddhist practice, Eliot brings together Christian and Buddhist forms of monastic askesis into a kind of eightfold path for modern enlightenment. That he shares this fusion of spiritual influences with Schopenhauer, the Western philosophical guru on the subject of modern boredom and nonattachment, only underscores this fascinating emergence of intentional attention practice, or meditation, as an antidote to the modern attention economy's "metalled ways" and their by-products, boredom and distraction.

Grace, in this view, involves a renunciation even of the desire to get out of acedia, and an emptying of the self into a particular kind of "concentration without elimination," or what I have elsewhere gestured toward as nonselective or open-focus attention:

> The inner freedom from the practical desire,
> The release from action and suffering, release from the inner
> And the outer compulsion, yet surrounded
> By a grace of sense, a white light still and moving,
> *Erhebung* without motion, concentration
> Without elimination . . .[56]

Later in the *Quartets*, the language involves more and more paradox and self-contradiction, suggesting a movement from teaching to practice or from description to formal training. Consider the following koanlike passage:

> To arrive where you are, to get from where you are not,
>   You must go by a way wherein there is no ecstasy.
> In order to arrive at what you do not know
>   You must go by a way which is the way of ignorance.
> In order to possess what you do not possess
>   You must go by the way of dispossession.[57]

Or this one:

> I said to my soul, be still, and wait without hope
> For hope would be hope for the wrong thing; wait without love
> For love would be love of the wrong thing; there is yet faith
> But the faith and the love and the hope are all in the waiting.
> Wait without thought, for you are not ready for thought:
> So the darkness shall be the light, and the stillness the dancing.[58]

The imperative, here, goes beyond a simple overcoming of restlessness by simplifying one's focus, or overcoming greed by renouncing one's wealth. It concerns the suspension of the part of the soul that is connected to the world of industry and its artificial parsing of time. At stake, it would seem, is the possibility that, in contemplating passages like these, the subject might cease spinning, stop chasing the objects of its desire (in the case of the paradox, a single fixed object of meaning), and be still. Stillness—not the stillness of the fixed form but the stillness of waiting—emerges[59] as the "point" of the poem itself and the effect of its dance of paradox:

> At the still point of the turning world. Neither flesh nor fleshless;
> Neither from nor towards; at the still point, there the dance is,
> But neither arrest nor movement. And do not call it fixity,
> Where past and future are gathered. Neither movement from nor
>   towards,

> Neither ascent nor decline. Except for the point, the still point,
> There would be no dance, and there is only the dance.[60]

What exactly the nature of the "dance" is in the context of the work or in the context of Eliot's thinking remains undefined. However, when we connect the destitution of the self and its possessions (including emotion in the personal affective sense) to the concept of impersonality developed as early as 1919 in his essay "Tradition and the Individual Talent,"[61] a way forward emerges. "The point of view which I am struggling to attack," writes Eliot, "is perhaps related to the metaphysical theory of the substantial unity of the soul: for my meaning is, that the poet has, not a 'personality' to express, but a particular medium, which is only a medium and not a personality, in which impressions and experiences combine in peculiar and unexpected ways. Impressions and experiences which are important for the man may take no place in the poetry, and those which become important in the poetry may play quite a negligible part in the man, the personality."[62] Of importance in the work of poetry is not the poet (the expression of his feelings and desires, for example), but the work of the poem itself—its formal processes, what it sets moving, the changes it makes possible. In Eliot's rethinking of poetry itself not as "a turning loose of emotion, but an escape from emotion, . . . not the expression of personality, but an escape from personality,"[63] it follows that he thus sees Wordsworth's definition of poetry as "emotion recollected in tranquility" as "an inexact formula," "For it is neither emotion, nor recollection, nor, without distortion of meaning, tranquility. It is a *concentration*, and a new thing resulting from the concentration, of a very great number of experiences which to the practical and active person would not seem to be experiences at all; it is a concentration which does not happen consciously or of deliberation. These experiences are not 'recollected' and they finally unite in an atmosphere which is 'tranquil' only in that it is a *passive attending upon the event*." This "concentration," this "passive attending," can only be reached through a form of self-emptying, or kenosis: "the poet cannot reach this impersonality without surrendering himself wholly to the work to be done. And he is not likely to know what is to be done unless he lives in what is not merely the present, but the present moment of the past, unless he is conscious, not of what is dead, but of what is already living."

This surrendering of self to work, this concentration and passive attending in the present moment in which the work unfolds (for the work can *only* unfold in the present) is for Eliot an act of love that is the result of meditative endurance, of *suffering through* profound boredom. It is a form of love that has neither subject nor object, that has no direction, aim, or purpose, and in which the horizon of present experience expands to include and thus dissolve the boundaries marking our false division of "time past," "time present," and "time future,"[64] for "love is most nearly itself / When here and now cease to matter."[65] This description of agape resonates, in turn, with Kant's description of the aesthetic moment as one of disinterested contemplation in which neither subject nor object is involved in any external motivation (desire), through entrance into a suspended temporality occupied only by the work of the work. In the terms offered by the poem, "Not the intense moment / Isolated, with no before and after, / But a lifetime burning in every moment / And not the lifetime of one man only / But of old stones that cannot be deciphered."[66] Returning to the "dance" Eliot finds in stillness, it seems this might be the "burning of the moment" in the movement of the work itself—the dance of the work of the poem itself, which plants a lotus in the heart and exists only in the moment of love or of selfless, passive attending:

> Dry the pool, dry concrete, brown edged,
> And the pool was filled with water out of sunlight,
> And the lotus rose, quietly, quietly,
> The surface glittered out of heart of light,
> And they were behind us, reflected in the pool.
> Then a cloud passed, and the pool was empty.[67]

Coda

Toward a Practice of Poetic Attention

This pen is where the writing flows in sight
the measuring eye follows line by line,
mouth set in the mind's movement throughout attentive, tentative—let the numbers fall
into the hands   one drawing the letters   one
by one   holds the count at bay,   the other
keeps the time of an inner wave in sway.

All is enfolded in a body of thought
the body occupies.   The taut bow bends over
this work in words   studious as a lover
caught up on this telling of a tale the ear
attends the wary listening of,   as if to hear
as that reader   entirely his   other
hears the ring of truth in the sound of it
the writing is mute witness to.

—ROBERT DUNCAN, "ILLUSTRATIVE LINES"

It is April. The room in which I write now is quite different from the one in which I began: a windowless five-by-five carrel in the basement of a university library. One wall is lined with metal-rack shelves populated by stacks of spines, and overhead is a long fluorescent light. I have taken to this more hermetic writing location in order to get done the particular kinds of work that accompany the final stretch of a long project: proofreading, paring down, bibliographic notes, and thinking about how (and whether) to "conclude." Because it is too gloriously beautiful outside to do this kind of work. This is, in itself, a small but intentional act of attention: carving out, even with a kind of self-inflicted violence, a space without much sensory input, without the lure of sunlight and benches and walks with friends, to write. Outside, on this the first truly hot day of spring, I might be tempted to engage mostly in the kind of poetic attention Ammons's poems embody—long meanders, noticing things, afternoons without agenda. But a more Dickinsonian study affords (and even seems to require) a different kind of attention. And on the page before me is a poem that seems carved out, too, by attention—in which attention is both the bow and the lyre string, both form and theme, pulled into tension.[1]

The poem, Robert Duncan's "Illustrative Lines," inhabits a single suspended moment: the act of writing. The pen poised, the bow bent "over / this work in words."[2] The "studious" work of measuring, drawing out, and keeping time takes place in several senses at once: in "measuring eye," in "wary listening," and, in "the hands," one "hold[ing] the count at bay," the other "keep[ing] the time of an inner wave in sway." The act is both "inner" and "embodied" in a "body of thought," a body on which and through which time plays out and is made form. The in-line gaps and suspensive syntax draw the "tension of attention" tight through delays, so that time is felt not only in unmetered rhythmic swells and strong rhyme but in silences and distances that evoke the strange relation between the hermetic moment of composition and the undefined space of

   that reader   entirely his   other.

The poem's "mute witness" thus points to the tension between singularity and relation, between solitary utterance and reception's indeterminate potentiality that surrounds any work written in solitude and shared with an unknowable and equally solitary potential readership. The "ring of truth" is a sounding made possible only in reception, a sounding whose resonance is the result of "bending the bow" of language tight across intervals of distance and spaces of silence. In this way, Duncan's poem embodies the act of poetic attention, its form the expression of a suspended and attenuated moment, stretched formally to become a soundable string In his introduction to *Bending the Bow*, Duncan writes of "drawing the lines of attention beyond war into music where the flint strikes fire from the rock."[3] The poem "Bending the Bow" puts the poetic act between music and archery, the drawing-taut of a string toward a sending, in both evocations: "bend back the bow in dream as we may / til the end rimes in the taut string / with the sending."[4] Drawn taut are the "lines of attention" in the production, out of language's raw material, of a formed line in the "mind's movement." This is the "work of words."

What, then, is formed, tensed, in poetic form? Attention. Once we begin to think through what this means for an understanding of poetry, several things happen. We begin to see how poems of diverse form, style, convention, period, and even sensory location, take shape, and what is shaped in their taking shape. At the same time, we begin to see attention not as effect, not as trend, not as mandate, but rather as *medium*, a medium that can be formed in a variety of ways, and which makes up the structures and terrains of inner experience where it meets sensual perception. And, going a step further, we begin to see "the poetic" not as a narrow set of qualities or ideals but as a process through which the material of language forms—dynamically and fundamentally—the very shape and texture of inner life. In returning language to its nature as formed material (whether written, performed, or coded), poetry gathers attention into a medium shaping inner and outer perception, feeling-tones, pattern recognition, and, perhaps above all, the sense of time.

In these closing thoughts, I will not go through the motions of summarizing and restating each of the steps this exploration of poetic attention has taken. Rather, I would like to close by opening it again onto a few veins of slightly wider implication that have emerged in its course and by directing our joint attention outward toward questions that lie ahead.[5] I would like to consider first the relationship between attention and spatiotemporal presence—a vein that has coursed through both part 1's investigation of transitive attention and part 2's of intransitive attention. Thinking about poetic attention as always a *present* act, however temporally inflected, leads to a consideration of what the *practice* of poetic attention might look like and what (if any) effects or implications it might have beyond the domain of the page.

In its formation as physical, embodied structure, poetry places language most pressingly in the senses, grounding the "movement of the mind" in the sensing body and thus in physical presence. This presence is at once spatial, sensorial, and temporal. The breath of the body that forms the workable, stretchable horizon of the lyric line locates the act of poetic attention in the present. Attention takes place always and only in the "now" of the breathing body in which the mind moves. This holds, however, that the thematic content of attention's field might be temporally inflected, as in the modes of recollection or vigilance. In his speech "The Meridian," delivered in Darmstadt on the occasion of receiving the Büchner Prize in

1960, Paul Celan spoke of poetry as signifying "an *Atemwende*, a Breathturn": "Who knows, perhaps poetry follows its path—also the path of art—for the sake of such a breathturn?"[6] The movement or turning or pausing of the breath in the poem was for Celan, as for Duncan, the site of a potential encounter—an opening for relation between strangers, between others, and what is "wholly Other."[7] This possibility for poetry is never guaranteed, only dimly glimpsable in the kind of "attentiveness" poetic language embodies and produces. "No one can say," Celan reminds us, "how long the breath-pause—the longing and the thought—will last. . . . A poem knows this; but it makes straight for that 'Other' which it deems reachable, free-able, perhaps empty and thus turned . . . toward it, toward the poem."[8]

Celan's emphasis on potentiality is important for an understanding of poetic attention because it underlines that events of attention are not *promised*, not *inevitable* in any act of reading or writing—from person to person and even, in a single individual, from reading to reading or from day to day. This is built into the very nature of poetry's medium—that its acts of attention are the result of tuning language (itself, in spoken form, only a combination of vibrations and stops) in an interval between two or more minds, or between one mind and itself, and set in the moving terrain of time. The precariousness, the contingency of this form's emergence out of silence, or out of nonbeing, is important, and is part of what makes events of attentional resonance in reading or writing a poem so charged and so impactful. The poem is never firmly *there* and certainly not *ours* to count on. It is always carved out at the edge of silence: "The poem unmistakably shows a strong bent toward falling silent. It holds on . . . the poem holds on at the edge of itself; so as to exist, it ceaselessly calls and hauls itself from its Now-no-more back into its Ever-yet."[9] The "holding on" of the poem, its ushering-out from nonbeing or from silence, is for Celan always an act of attentiveness. Importantly, this attention takes the form of the living medium of the poem itself. It is not simply a measure of perfect mastery of a set of conventions or turns of phrase, "is not attained by an eye vying (or conniving) with constantly more perfect instruments." It is rather in the material of the poem itself, and the way form moves and reaches in attention's interval between mind and a world of others: "The attentiveness a poem devotes to all encounters, with its sharper sense of detail, outline, structure, color, but also of 'quivering' and 'intimations.' . . . It is a concentration that stays mindful of all our dates."

Celan's emphasis of "our dates" places the act of poetic attention (as the "natural prayer of the soul," recalling Benjamin recalling Malebranche) not in some removed hermetic study,[10] and not "out there" in an abstract plane, but very much *in the world*: in the body, in the body of history, in relation to other bodies, in relation to those who have been lost, in relation to ongoing human conditions in the world.[11] When Celan writes of "others," he has at hand the "vanished others" who did not survive what he (for a while longer) survived. When Duncan bends a weapon of war into Eros's bow, his act cannot be removed from its worldly position as a response to the war in Vietnam. Of this position, he writes: "Cities laid waste, villages destroyd, men, women and children hunted down in their fields, forests poisond, herds of elephants screaming under our fire— . . . When in moments of vision I see back of the photographt details and the daily body counts actual bodies in agony and hear—what I hear now is the desolate bellowing of some ox in a ditch—madness starts up in me. The pulse of this sentence beats before and beyond all proper bounds and we no longer inhabit what we thought properly our own."[12] Attention is always embodied and thus always embedded in a historical moment and in a sociopolitical weave. In orienting the mind in its spatiotemporal present, drawing out certain things and leaving others either in the background or off frame, attention is always at once a historical and a political act. It is also always creaturely, bound up with the limitations and pains of the body, the limits of perception, the vagaries of relation and judgment in a condition of contingencies. Celan writes of "a poem's lingerings and longings" as "related to the creatures" because, while language is often thought of as that which distinguishes human from animal—that which, in the Cartesian dichotomy, separates *res cogitans* from *res extensa*—the bodilyness and thingliness of poetic utterance points back to the body,[13] to the human as suffering, feeling animal in the world, among others.

In her terrain-changing, book-length poem *Citizen: An American Lyric*, African American poet Claudia Rankine speaks to the creatureliness of the voice in the "moan" and "sigh" brought out by the ongoing and systemic racial violence that plagues contemporary America: "To live through the days sometimes you moan like deer. Sometimes you sigh. The world says stop that. Another sigh. Another stop that. Moaning elicits laughter, sighing upsets. Perhaps each sigh is drawn into existence to pull in, pull under, who knows; truth be told, you could no more control those sighs than that which brings the sighs about."[14]

Rankine's poem uses both sound and image to capture the force and form of the voice sounded from a place before language's orderings, a response that escapes through the fabric of what should and should not be said in social discourse, in everyday speech: "The sighing is a worrying exhale of an ache. You wouldn't call it an illness; still it is not the iteration of a free being. What else to liken yourself to but an animal, the ruminant kind?"[15] At the same time, even unformed language—even these sighs—are public acts. As soon as a sound is voiced it positions its subject among others, in a body marked out by sex, by color, and by class. The formal, material density of poetic language calls out this fact of the body. It "bodies forth." For Rankine, this bodily presence is the site of both poetry's resistant potential and language's capacity to harm, to dehumanize: "you begin to understand yourself as rendered hypervisible in the face of such language acts. Language that feels hurtful is intended to exploit all the ways that you are present. Your alertness, your openness, and your desire to engage actually demand your presence, your looking up, your talking back, and, as insane as it is, saying please."[16] Her response is to *use* the bodily presence of her poetry to stand and call out, draw attention, make visible, *be* visible.

Writing on the position of writing within a condition of sociopolitical and national brokenness, Duncan observes:

> We enter again and again the last days of our own history, for everywhere living and productive forms in the evolution of forms fail, weaken, or grow monstrous, destroying the terms of their existence. . . . Now, where other nations before us have floundered, we flounder. To defend a form that our very defense corrupts. We cannot rid ourselves of the form to which we now belong. . . . We must begin where we are. Our own configuration entering and belonging to a configuration of what "we" means.[17]

Writing into the present, bodying forth in the present, means "entering" into history, into the systems of attention, neglect, and mindlessness that shape a particular moment in a particular social framework. The turning of the breath in the poem is, for both Rankine and Celan, the site of survival and, perhaps, an opening for relation between living others. The survival of poetic making and of song must be fought for, guarded, cultivated. The precariousness of poetry's survival is thus central to its continual invention and reinvention. As breath or even as the trace of breath, the poem is carved out at the edge of silence from the mortal medium of embodied language itself. Perhaps one "value" of a poetic act in this particular historical moment might be the standing of the poem as a living organ of attention—of which breath and pulse (line and rhythm) are the signs of life. The body of the poem, in its perceptions, tunings, and composition of time and space, has then an orientative power.

Writing on Celan's poetry—a poetry that, like Rankine's, also "moans," also "sighs" with personal and historical ache—Allen Grossman describes the recuperative potential of this "orientative possibility" of poetic attention. Celan's poems, writes Grossman, "engage in the recovery of orientative possibility—the mother's body, let us say, which has disappeared—by putting language (the competence for which is the specifying difference of humanity) in service of *Richtung*, orientation in space and time."[18] Extending this possibility to poetic language more broadly, he asserts that "*all poems begin with a reestablishment of relation reorientation within space and time.*"[19] The specifically recuperative capacity of orienting in space and time has to do with coming to reality through the body—through the human body and its language.[20] "Only language, the reality-wounded hero hand," insists Grossman, "can signify the direction, recover time and space. And what will constitute that recovery? It will be encounter with another (*Entgegnung,* reply), a second person who makes reason, communicative relationship, possible—response to the need of reason." The "reality-wound" of which Grossman speaks is reason itself or the subjugation of the human by logical systems that go under the heading of post-Enlightenment reason.[21]

To value, or love, the human—to experience human life and human others in a way that includes difference, that enables embodied relation rather than logic's monologue, requires a language that itself has a body, and whose very "wounds" serve as an opening for exposure, encounter, and relation, as attention itself is an opening, a site of porosity between subject and object, between subject and subject. Charles Bernstein sees this porosity as taking place in the acts of reading and writing, in the poem's "articulation of contemplation": "the articulation of contemplation is an example of how (a technique) words can be brought into one's more total awareness in reading, where in reading you are brought up short to the point of the text becoming viscerally present to you, the 'content' and the 'experience of reading' are collapsed onto each other, the content being the experience of reading, the consciousness of the language and its movement and sound, the page."[22] Bringing us back round to the breathing, rhythmic, perceiving body as the site of poetic contemplation, he writes, "the music and rhythm of contemplation become the form of the life, a life, as it is being lived in a body."[23]

This convergence, in attention, of perception with subjective acts of "valuing" brings us to judgment. Attention is the ground of any judgment, and the quality of attention determines, in part, the capacity to judge. As Gérard Genette points out in his *Essays in Aesthetics*, "the word *value* is inseparable from the word *judgment*, to which it is always explicitly or implicitly linked in the notion of 'value judgment.' . . . Every value is only, can only be, judged; to be valued is to be judged. To say it in a still different way, there is value only *of* something (or someone) *for* someone."[24] In challenging and training our capacity to attend, and in pushing our attention to make ever finer and more nuanced readings and selections in perception, poetic attention also challenges and trains what might be thought of as the insufficient preconditions for judgment. Preconditions because the capacity to attend (to another, to a situation, to a problem) precedes necessarily the ability to judge. Insufficient because judgment also depends on things outside of the capacity to attend: things like character, conscience, competing priorities, and one's personal or culturally prevailing moral framework. Yet, every time we attend, we are in one way or another navigating and putting into practice our values. And every time something *acts* on our attention in unexpected or challenging ways, our values are likewise challenged and posed in question. Because the pure act of reading and writing poems falls outside of or works, at least to a degree, independently of surrounding economies of interest and utility,[25] the kind of attentional challenge offered by poetic language offers an invitation to value, or an invitation to place one's valuing in the way of a question.[26]

Given that poetic attention brings about an event that positions us in spatial, physical, and temporal presence, given that it positions us *in relation* (to at least one object in the world and to the space inhabited by others, readers and writers), the necessary question is this: what are the ethical implications of the kind of training that takes place in poetic attending? I do think that the practice of poetic attention affects the conditions for ethical relation, but perhaps not in the way or to the extent that one might expect. Specifically, I would argue that reading and writing poems—particularly poems that engage actively with the attention, that require something more from us or produce an unexpected mode, since poems that do only what we expect of them should not bear the title—both require and produce intensified modes of attention. By intensified, I mean formally and experientially rich, whether narrow or open in focus, whether endogenous or exogenous in intentionality. Moreover, I would suggest that doing so frequently in the course of one's life might have the capacity to cultivate and pluralize one's attentive faculty: sharpening and honing one's ability to attend and increasing the mind's ability to attend in a greater variety of ways. One might think of this pluralization of available modes as a kind of attentional polydexterity.

When first embarking on this project, I anticipated that perhaps poetry might have, in general, one single primary effect on the attention, such as focused contemplation or meditation. I found instead that, while attention constitutes the raw material of the poem, the possibilities for how a given poem shapes the reader's attentional "clay" are boundless. Thus where some scholars of attention (poetic and otherwise) have jumped from the cultivation of attention to an assertion that cultivating attention leads necessarily to *moral* improvement, I part ways.[27] While some (Martha Nussbaum in particular) have made convincing arguments for a heightening of the capacity to feel responsibility through the cultivation of empathetic awareness in richly descriptive studies of characters such as those in Henry James's novels, I am not convinced that increasing one's ability to perceive attentively, or even to feel and understand what others experience, necessarily leads everyone to the same moral outcome. This is not even to take up the problem that there are as many differing moral codes as there are populations and indeed individuals. Even if "we all" held the same basic qualities to be morally good, as I suspect many of "us" do, becoming better at paying attention might not make everyone act upon those morals. Indeed, being more "finely aware," to use Nussbaum's phrase, might serve other ends as well—such as becoming better at manipulating others by observing and anticipating their reactions or knowing precisely how to inflict pain. Moreover, not all literature resembles a Henry James novel, much less all poems. As I hope to have shown in the chapters of this study, poems produce not one single form of pure and reverent attention but *many*, many of which are decidedly *ir*reverent, *im*pure, and *a*moral. And this amorality of poetry (its capacity to be many things and therefore to be, in many senses, *alive*) is not something to be simply accepted, but to rather celebrated, as ecocritics hope that one might celebrate the complexity of a living thing, a working ecosystem. The amorality of poetic attention is crucial to its livingness.

What I *would* venture is a more modest proposal: that poetic attention can cultivate the *necessary but insufficient grounds* for ethical response. That is, practicing poetic attention—cultivating attention in the diverse and complex ways good poems demand and encourage—might lead to a refinement of perception or a honing of our capacities for judgment, pattern-recognition, and discernment, requisite preconditions for compassion and responsibility in relation, though one might not choose ultimately to put these faculties into practice toward moral ends. Thus the practice of poetic attention might make us more adept at perception and judgment, but might not necessarily make us more reverent, respectful, or charitable people. Poetry can sharpen our cognitive and emotional tools, but it can't determine whether we use those tools for good.

Returning to the *livingness* of the poem's attention, Hayden Carruth captures the 'bare minimum' ethics I have tried to draw out and, more important, the complex life of attention as it wells in poetic language across publics, conventions, and occasions: "Let the poem be conventional, public, and occasional, since that is the mask one must wear—so she might have spoken—but let each poem reveal just enough of a private inner violence to make the surface move without breaking. A passionate austerity, a subtle balance; and only perfect poetic attention, far beyond technique, could attain it."[28]

This work is not finished. It is an invitation to think in a new way about how poems work and how we might work differently with them. It is my hope that this book might offer more opening than closing, and that it might prove useful in raising questions others might push forward, and problematize, in diverse fields of literary studies. Because, in Agha Shahid Ali's words, "rooms are never finished,"[29] I will close with a poem that, opening with a knock at the door, invites us to "see the earth again":

ANGEL SURROUNDED BY PAYSANS

One of the Countrymen:
                              There is
   A welcome at the door to which no one comes?
The angel:
   I am the angel of reality,
   Seen for a moment standing in the door.

   I have neither ashen wing nor wear of ore
   And live without a tepid aureole,

   Or stars that follow me, not to attend,
   But, of my being and its knowing, part.

   I am one of you and being one of you
   Is being and knowing what I am and know.

   Yet I am the necessary angel of earth,
   Since, in my sight, you see the earth again,

   Cleared of its stiff and stubborn, man-locked set,
   And, in my hearing, you hear its tragic drone

   Rise liquidly in liquid lingerings,
   Like watery words awash; like meanings said

   By repetitions of half-meanings. Am I not,
   Myself, only half of a figure of a sort,

   A figure half seen, or seen for a moment, a man
   Of the mind, an apparition appareled in

   Apparels of such lightest look that a turn
   Of my shoulder and quickly, too quickly, I am gone?[30]

Notes

Introduction

1. James Wright, *Above the River: The Complete Poems* (New York: Farrar, Straus and Giroux, 1990), 121.
2. For a thoughtful take on contemporary attention culture, see Malcolm McCullough, *Ambient Commons: Attention in the Age of Embodied Information* (Cambridge, MA: MIT Press, 2013). Tim Wu's *The Attention Merchants* (New York: Knopf, 2016) offers a historical account of the capture and resale of attention leading to the contemporary "attention economy"—a term coined by Thomas H. Davenport and John C. Beck in *The Attention Economy: Understanding the New Currency of Business* (Cambridge, MA: Harvard Business Review Press, 2002). For a sideways entry point to fragmented attention (distraction) in the context of normative pressures on productivity and concentration, see Joseph R. Urgo, *In the Age of Distraction* (Jackson: University Press of Mississippi, 2000). See also N. Katherine Hayles, "Hyper and Deep Attention: The Generational Divide in Cognitive Modes," *Profession* (2007): 187–99.
3. In the brief introduction to his (substantial) volume, *A Little Book on Form: An Exploration into the Formal Imagination of Poetry* (New York: Ecco, 2017), Robert Hass gives examples of some of the ways "form," has been incorporated ("traditional form," "rules of composition," "external shape," and "the arrangement and relationship of basic elements in a work of art, through which it produces a coherent whole") before offering, almost in passing, a definition that comes closest to what I am suggesting in this book: "The way a poem embodies the energy of the gesture of its making" (3). The underlying "energy" is attention, and its "gesture of making" is both produced and embodied in the object, act, and event of the poem. In another deeply resonant work, Caroline Levine has both theorized and modeled a vibrant (and necessary) rethinking form as

dynamic, relational, and historically embedded, in her book *Forms: Whole, Rhythm, Hierarch, Network* (Princeton: Princeton University Press, 2015).

4. Important examples of recent and forthcoming work in the emerging field of literary and aesthetic attention studies include Andrew Epstein, *Attention Equals Life: The Pursuit of the Everyday in Contemporary Poetry and Culture* (Oxford: Oxford University Press, 2016); Elaine Scarry, *Dreaming by the Book* (Princeton: Princeton University Press, 1999); Richard B. Lanham, *The Economics of Attention* (Chicago: University of Chicago Press, 2006); Joshua Cohen, *Attention! A (Very) Short History* (London: Notting Hill, 2013); Patrick Jagoda, *Network Aesthetics* (Chicago: University of Chicago Press, 2016); Yves Citton, *The Ecology of Attention*, trans. Barnaby Norman (Cambridge: Polity, 2017); Jonathan Crary, *Suspensions of Perception: Attention, Spectacle, and Modern Culture* (Cambridge, MA: MIT Press, 1999); Margaret Koehler, *Poetry of Attention in the Eighteenth Century* (New York: Palgrave Macmillan, 2012); Andrew Lee DuBois, *Ashbery's Forms of Attention* (Tuscaloosa: University of Alabama Press, 2006); Lily Gurton-Wachter, *Watchwords: Romanticism and the Poetics of Attention* (Stanford: Stanford University Press, 2016); David Marno, *Death Be Not Proud: The Art of Holy Attention* (Chicago: University of Chicago Press, 2016); Lisbeth Lipari, *Listening, Thinking, Being: Toward an Ethics of Attunement* (University Park: Penn State University Press, 1014); Sven Birkerts, *Changing the Subject: Art and Attention in the Internet Age* (Minneapolis: Graywolf, 2015); and N. Katherine Hayles, *Unthought: The Power of the Cognitive Nonconscious* (Chicago: University of Chicago Press, 2017).

5. Virginia Jackson, *Dickinson's Misery: A Theory of Lyric Reading* (Princeton: Princeton University Press, 2005). See especially chapters 1 ("Dickinson Undone") and 2 ("Lyric Reading").

6. Jonathan Culler, *Theory of the Lyric* (Cambridge, MA: Harvard University Press, 2015), 7–8.

7. Jahan Ramazani, *Poetry and Its Others: News, Prayer, Song, and the Dialogue of Genres* (Chicago: University of Chicago Press, 2014). See especially 6–9.

8. Husserl writes, "*attention* is a tending of the ego toward an intentional object, toward a unity which appears continually in the change of the modes of its givens.... It is a tending toward realization." Edmund Husserl, *Experience and Judgment; Investigations in a Genealogy of Logic,* trans. James Spencer Churchill and Karl Ameriks (Evanston, IL: Northwestern University Press, 1973), 80.

9. In his discussion of the roots of phenomenology in the work of Edmund Husserl's teacher Franz Brentano, Wilhelm Baumgartner describes the movement of the mind as follows: "Each act, whilst directed towards an object is at the same time and besides this directed towards itself. Being presented with a 'primary object,' e.g., a sound, we are aware of being presented with something. A psychological phenomenon as such always includes the consciousness of itself as the 'secondary object of perception.'" Wilhelm Baumgartner, "On the Origins of Phenomenology: Franz Brentano," in Elisabeth Baumgartner, ed., *Handbook—Phenomenology and Cognitive Science* (Dettelbach: J. H. Röll, 1996), 32. Baumgartner describes the stages of phenomenological investigation as *noticing, fixation, generalization,* and *deduction* (33–34).

10. Methodologically, I have been both encouraged and inspired by the work of Hans Ulrich Gumbrecht, particularly on the concepts of presence, historical latency, and *Stimmung* (mood, atmosphere), which have contributed to this book's approach in subtle but profound ways. See especially *Production of Presence: What Meaning Cannot Convey* (Stanford: Stanford University Press, 2004); *After 1945: Latency as Origin of the Present* (Stanford: Stanford University Press, 2013); and *Atmosphere, Mood, Stimmung: On a Hidden Potential of Literature* (Stanford: Stanford University Press, 2012). Additionally, I am grateful to Gumbrecht for his generous engagement with an early version of this book's central argument in his article "How to Approach 'Poetry as a Mode of Attention,'" *Eutomia* 16, no. 1 (December 2015): 192-207.
11. As Susi Ferrarello has written, "receptive activity creates a horizon of apprehending attention that modifies the structure of the not-yet-I, into a tension, meaning the I *tendens ad* (stretching toward) its object." Susi Ferrarello, *Husserl's Ethics and Practical Intentionality* (New York: Bloomsbury Academic, 2015), 165.
12. I develop this conception of the subject, or *subject-space*, of poetic attention in greater detail in part 1, on the dynamics of object-oriented or "transitive" attention. The same concept of subjectivity holds in the context of "intransitive attention" as well (part 2).
13. I address the difference between these two kinds of attentional objects in the introduction to part 1, in the section on endogenous and exogenous (active and passive) attention.
14. For a more extensive exploration of how figure and ground play out in literary language, see Peter Stockwell, "Surreal Figures," in *Cognitive Poetics in Practice*, ed. Joanna Gavins and Gerard Steen (London: Routledge, 2003), 15; and Stockwell, *Cognitive Poetics: An Introduction* (London: Routledge, 2002). See in particular the chapter entitled "Figures and Grounds," 26–39.
15. In "Surreal Figures," Stockwell outlines the progressive development of the concepts and characteristics of figure and ground from classical gestalt psychology, to attention studies of the visual field, to the emergent work on specifically linguistic and more specifically literary attention.
16. Several studies have considered the multisensory nature of poetry, most notably Susan Stewart, *Poetry and the Fate of the Senses* (Chicago: University of Chicago Press, 2002). See also Laura U. Marks, *Touch: Sensuous Theory and Multisensory Media* (Minneapolis: University of Minnesota Press, 2002), 107, 109, 181; Geraldine Shaw, "The Multisensory Image and Emotion in Poetry," *Psychology of Aesthetics, Creativity, and the Arts* 2 (August, 2008): 175–78; and Paul Fraisse, "Multisensory Aspects of Rhythm," in *Intersensory Perception and Sensory Integration*, ed. Richard D. Walk and Herbert L. Pick (Boston: Springer, 1981). Juhani Pallasmaa has noted that "artistic expression is engaged with preverbal meanings of the world, meanings that are incorporated and lived rather than simply intellectually understood. In my view, poetry has the capacity of bringing us momentarily back to the oral and enveloping world. The re-oralised world of poetry brings us back to the centre of an interior world. The poet speaks not only 'on the threshold of being,' as Gaston Bachelard notes, but also on the threshold of language." Juhani Pallasmaa, *The Eyes of the Skin: Architecture and the Senses* (Chichester: Wiley, 2012), 28.

17. Stockwell, "Surreal Figures," 16.
18. Stockwell, 15–16. Stockwell emphasizes that "we can describe any stylistic feature that draws our attention as an *attractor*. Attractors function to *distract* our attention, while by contrast the rest of the ground is characterised by cognitive *neglect*."
19. Wolfgang Iser, *The Fictive and the Imaginary: Charting Literary Anthropology* (Baltimore: Johns Hopkins University Press, 1993), 5. Stockwell calls this latent presence of what is not spotlighted the "present absence."
20. Stockwell, "Surreal Figures," 20.
21. Iser writes: "Out of this operation [of selection] arises the intentionality of the text, which is to be identified neither with the system in question nor with the imaginary as such (for its conditioning depends largely on those extratextual systems to which reference is made). It is, rather, a 'transitional object' between the real and the imaginary, and it has the all-important quality of actuality." By "actuality," Iser means the "constitutive feature of an event" (*The Fictive and the Imaginary*, 5–6). A note of lexical clarification: While I refer to the degree of intentionality that characterizes the specific form(s) of attention, Iser uses this term to designate something more akin to the life of the text—its movement within the sphere of experience and its ability to lift off from external referents, operating directly on the attention. Iser stresses this notion to discourage reading for authorial intent, focusing instead on the dynamics of the text where it meets the active attention of the engaged reader.
22. Roman Jakobson, "Linguistics and Poetics," in *Style in Language*, ed. Thomas Sebeok (Cambridge, MA: MIT Press, 1960), 350–77. One of the early formalist readers, Jakobson defines the "poetic function of language" as "the set (*Einstellung*) toward the message as such, focus on the message for its own sake" as opposed to focus on the addresser or addressee, the context, or the content of the message (25). This definition of the poetic function is helpful even as we move beyond a formalist approach to the poetic text, for it helps us to draw loose outlines around the "poetic" even as the outlines of the "poem" itself grow faint, and even as literary prose is increasingly recognized for its poetic dimensions, and even as nonliterary texts enter into the conversation, regardless of their intentional role, "as poetry." I maintain this formalist conception of the poetic as a way of holding onto the subject of inquiry even as we then engage it with context, historical sensitivity, and the manifold other attentional angles we might bring to the "poetic work."
23. Just as aesthetics may be read as a history of aesthetic attention. See Gérard Genette, *The Aesthetic Relation* (Ithaca, NY: Cornell University Press, 1999), 7–11.
24. Accounting for the *why* of this swell would far exceed this book's focal lens and would suggest a narrative-historical arc that I would not wish to assume.
25. Alexander Gottlieb Baumgarten, *Metaphysics: A Critical Translation with Kant's Elucidations, Selected Notes, and Related Materials*, ed. and trans. Courtney D. Fugate and John Hymers (London: Bloomsbury, 2004); originally *Metaphysica Alexandri Gottlieb Baumgarten, Professoris Philosophiae*, editio 4 (Halae, Magdebvrgicae, impensis C. H. Hemmerde, 1779); and *Aesthetica* (Hildesheim: G. Olms, 1961 [1750]).
26. Genette, *The Aesthetic Relation*. This resonates with the notions of disinterestedness and "purposiveness without purpose," which Kant uses to describe the qualities of aesthetic

judgment in the third critique. Immanuel Kant, *Critique of the Power of Judgment,* trans. Paul Guyer (Cambridge: Cambridge University Press, 2000), 111–13.

27. In his introduction to *Close Reading: The Reader,* Andrew Dubois sums up what he sees as the central attentional problem of close reading: "Paying attention: almost anyone can do it; and it's not requisite for reading, but for reading well. . . . As a term, *close reading* hardly seems to leave the realm of so-called common sense, where it would appear to mean something understandable and vague like 'reading with special attention;' but it is also jargon, albeit jargon of a not uninviting variety." Andrew Dubois and Frank Lentricchia, eds., *Close Reading: The Reader* (Durham, NC: Duke University Press, 2003), 2.

28. See, for example, Graham Harman, *Guerrilla Metaphysics: Phenomenology and the Carpentry of Things* (Peru, IL: Open Court, 2005); and Harman, *Object-Oriented Ontology: A New Theory of Everything* (London: Penguin, 2018); John Searle, *Seeing Things as They Are: A Theory of Perception* (Oxford: Oxford University Press, 2015); Loraine Daston and Peter Galison, *Objectivity* (New York: Zone, 2007); Bill Brown, *A Sense of Things* (Chicago: University of Chicago Press, 2003); and Brown, *Other Things* (Chicago: University of Chicago Press, 2015); Peter Stockwell, *Cognitive Poetics: An Introduction* (London: Routledge, 2002); and Nikki Skillman, *The Lyric in the Age of the Brain* (Cambridge, MA: Harvard University Press, 2016).

29. See Gabrielle Starr, "Poetic Subjects and Grecian Urns: Close Reading and the Tools of Cognitive Science," *Modern Philology* 105 (August 2007): 48–61.

30. Roland Greene, "Not Works but Networks: Colonial Worlds in Comparative Literature," in *Comparative Literature in an Age of Globalization,* ed. Haun Saussy (Baltimore: Johns Hopkins University Press, 2006), 214.

31. I. A. Richards, *How to Read a Page: A Course in Effective Reading, with an Introduction to a Hundred Great Words* (New York: Norton, 1942), 20.

32. Ezra Pound, *How to Read* (London: D. Harmsworth, 1931).

33. Richards, *How to Read a Page.*

34. In close reading's place, Franco Moretti, David Damrosch, and Roland Greene have explored the possibilities in distant reading. Understanding distance as itself "*a condition of knowledge,*" Moretti has focused on units both much smaller and much larger than the text, tracking themes, formal conventions, genres, and systems of exchange. "And if," in the distance of systems, "the text itself disappears, well, it is one of those cases when one can justifiably say, Less is more. If we want to understand the system in its entirety, we must accept losing something." Franco Moretti, *Distant Reading* (London: Verso, 2013), 48–49. Without arguing to do away with close reading, Greene has made a compelling case for thinking literature in terms of comparative and overlapping "networks," embodying collectively a wide web of cultural, historical, and intellectual currents, the model for which he finds in comparative literature's concern not with the isolated corpus but with "the exchanges out of which literatures are made: the economies of knowledge, social relations, power, and especially art that make literature possible. Not literature but literatures; not works but networks" (Greene, "Not Works but Networks," 214).

35. Epstein, *Attention Equals Life,* 40.

36. I am indebted, here and throughout this project, to the work of Susan Stewart, especially *Poetry and the Fate of the Senses* (Chicago: University of Chicago Press, 2002) and *A Poet's Freedom: A Notebook on Making* (Chicago: University of Chicago Press, 2011).
37. Genette (I think rightly) positions aesthetic attention as the necessary precondition for aesthetic judgment or appreciation. Joshua Landy's *How to Do Things with Fictions* (Oxford: Oxford University Press, 2014) has been invaluable on this point by refining the distinction between moral improvement and the *formative* capacities of literature—between "teaching" and "training" (10).
38. Simon Critchley, *Things Merely Are: Philosophy in the Poetry of Wallace Stevens* (London: Routledge, 2005), 2.
39. Ed Roberson, "To See the Earth Before the End of the World," in *To See the Earth Before the End of the World* (Wesleyan, CT: Wesleyan University Press, 2010), 3.

1. Modes of Transitive Attention

1. Valerie Worth, *All the Small Poems,* illustrations by Natalie Babbit (London: Faber Children's, 1989).
2. A great deal of cognitive research has been devoted to understanding the dynamics of attending to objects of the imagination through mental representation. See in particular Michael Pendlebury, "The Role of Imagination in Perception," *South African Journal of Philosophy* 15, no. 4 (1996): 133–38; Simon G. Gosling and Duncan E. Astle, "Directing Spatial Attention to Locations Within Remembered and Imagined Mental Representations," *Frontiers in Human Neuroscience* 7 (April 2013): 154; Jöran Lepsien, Ivan C. Griffin, Joseph T. Devlin, and Anna C. Nobre, "Directing Spatial Attention in Mental Representations: Interactions Between Attentional Orienting and Working-Memory Load," *NeuroImage* 26, no. 3 (March 2005): 733–43; Jöran Lepsien and Anna C. Nobre, "Cognitive Control of Attention in the Human Brain: Insights From Orienting Attention to Mental Representations," *Brain Research* 1105, no. 1 (September 2006): 20–31; Jöran Lepsien and Anna C. Nobre, "Attentional Modulation of Object Representations in Working Memory," *Cerebral Cortex* 17, no. 9 (September 2007): 2072–83; Duncan E. Astle, Jennifer Summerfield, Ivan Griffin, and Anna C. Nobre, "Orienting Attention to Locations in Mental Representations," *Attention, Perception, and Psychophysics* 74, no. 1 (January 2012): 146–62; and Duncan E. Astle, Anna C. Nobre, and Gaia Scerif, "Subliminally Presented and Stored Objects Capture Spatial Attention," *Journal of Neuroscience: The Official Journal of the Society for Neuroscience* 30, no. 10 (March 2010): 3567–71. For a philosophical perspective linking cognitive research on mental representation with the question of abstract thinking, see Eric Margolis and Stephen Laurence, "The Ontology of Concepts—Abstract Objects or Mental Representations," *NOÛS* 41, no. 4 (October 2007): 561–93; and Margot D. Lasher, John T. Carroll, and Thomas G. Bever, "The Cognitive Basis of Aesthetic Experience," *Leonardo* 16, no. 3 (Summer 1983): 196–99.
3. For a thoughtful discussion of Kant's thinking on imagination and beauty in the third critique as it relates to the attentional demands of literary objects, see Peggy Ann

Knapp, "Aesthetic Attention and the Chaucerian Text," *Chaucer Review* 39, no. 3 (2005): 245.
4. Nietzsche raises the problem of truth in the *Beyond Good and Evil*, writing "Suppose we want truth: why not rather untruth? and uncertainty? even ignorance? . . . Why insist on the truth?" He critiques the moral and scientific "will to truth" in the *Gay Science* and proposes art's capacity for uniting the Dionysian and Apollonian impulses, and to reflect the tragic world as a beautiful illusion, as a salutary alternative to the rigidity of the rule of truth and knowledge in the *Birth of Tragedy* ("Knowledge kills action; action requires the veil of illusion"). See Friedrich Nietzsche, *Beyond Good and Evil: On the Genealogy of Morality,* trans. Adrian Del Caro (Stanford: Stanford University Press, 2014), sections 1 and 16; Nietzsche, *The Gay Science,* trans. Josefine Naukhoff and Adrian Del Caro (Cambridge: Cambridge University Press, 2001), section 344; and *Beyond Good and Evil,* 7.
5. Wallace Stevens, "Imagination as Value," in Wallace Stevens, *Collected Poetry and Prose* (New York: Library of America, 1997), 737–38.
6. Stevens, 728.
7. While this idea is given flesh in Stevens's long poem, "Notes Toward a Supreme Fiction," in the same essay we find the following sketch: "Nietzsche walked in the Alps in the caresses of reality. We ourselves crawl out of our offices and classrooms and become alert at the opera. Or we sit listening to music as in an imagination in which we believe. If the imagination is the faculty by which we import the unreal into what is real, its value is the value of the way of thinking by which we project the idea of God into the idea of man" (735–36).
8. For research on exogenous versus endogenous attention, see Jan Theeuwes, "Exogenous and Endogenous Control of Attention: The Effect of Visual Onsets and Offsets," *Perception and Psychophysics* 49 (January 1991): 83–90; Michael I. Posner and Steven E. Petersen, "The Attention System of the Human Brain," *Annual Review of Neuroscience* 13 (March 1990): 25–42; updated by Petersen and Posner as "The Attention System of the Human Brain: Twenty Years After," *Annual Review of Neuroscience* 35 (July 2012): 73–85); Michael I. Posner and Mary K. Rothbart, "Attention, Self-Regulation and Consciousness," *Philosophical Transactions of the Royal Society of London B: Biological Sciences* 353 (December 1998): 1915–27; and Michael I. Posner, "Orienting of Attention," *Quarterly Journal of Experimental Psychology* 32, no. 1 (February 1980): 3–25; updated as Posner, "Orienting of Attention: Then and Now," 69, no. 10 (August 2016): 1864–75. For research on the relationship between endogenous attention and working memory, see Duncan E Astle and Gaia Scerif, "Using Developmental Cognitive Neuroscience to Study Behavioral and Attentional Control," *Developmental Psychobiology* 51, no. 2 (March 2009): 107–18.
9. For a discussion of the critical rejection of Kantian aesthetics—and the concept of disinterestedness in particular—as well as a detailed exploration of four key aspects of Kantian aesthetics as they relate to an aesthetics of attention, see Knapp, "Aesthetic Attention and the Chaucerian Text," 241–42 and 245–47.
10. "I feel my way in fiddling a little, or then sometimes more, on the roof of the burning or rusting world / '. . . to care and not to care . . . to sit still' / Careful of earth and air

and water mainly perhaps, and other lives, but some (how many?) other things too. Walden, ah! The dancer and the dance." Larry Eigner, "Approaching Things: Some Calculations How Figure It of Everyday Life Experience," L=A=N=G=U=A=G=E 1 (February 1978): 2.
11. Sappho, *If Not, Winter: Fragments of Sappho,* trans. Anne Carson (New York: Vintage, 2003), 63.
12. Derek Mahon, "A Disused Shed in Co. Wexford," in Jahan Ramazani, Richard Ellmann, and Robert O'Clair, eds., *The Norton Anthology of Modern and Contemporary Poetry* (New York: Norton, 2003), 802–3. Source: Derek Mahon, *New Collected Poems* (Oldcastle: Gallery, 2011).
13. For empirical studies of endogenous and exogenous attentional modes, see Theeuwes, "Exogenous and Endogenous Control of Attention." For an account of the neurological location and workings of the endogenous faculty, see Posner and Petersen, "The Attention System of the Human Brain"; Posner and Rothbart, "Attention, Self-Regulation, and Consciousness"; and Posner, "Orienting of Attention."
14. In general, ancient and premodern thought (most notably Plato, Democritus, Homer, Hesiod, Cicero, Lucan, Ficino, and Poliziano) leaned more in the direction of inspiration and madness, attributing the poet's genius to external influence of a muse or, later, to Christian rapture. Starting in the eighteenth century, we see increasing skepticism regarding the role of inspiration and greater emphasis on rational intentionality. However, this historical arc is far from clean. Homer makes clear that Demodokos is a conscious "maker" of his art. The elder Seneca and Philip Sidney, in *Astrophil and Stella,* both reject a totalizing role of inspiration (or, in Sidney's language, "poetic fury") in favor of a more tempered combination of inspiration and agency or passive and active intentionalities. The importance of exogenous intentionality in the suspension of subjective intentionality through madness, transportation, or inspiration remains significant in romanticism as well as in modern and contemporary poetry such as that of Walt Whitman, Charles Baudelaire, Allen Ginsberg, Yves Bonnefoy, and Nathaniel Mackey. The sources of these shifts into passive intentionality are often located in an interest in madness, drunkenness and delirium, or, as in the case of Mackey, immersion in musical flow, particularly jazz. See Eugène Napoléon Tigerstedt, "Furor Poeticus: Poetic Inspiration in Greek Literature Before Democritus and Plato," *Journal of the History of Ideas* 31 (April-June 1970): 163–78; William O. Scott, "Perotti, Ficino, and Furor Poeticus," *Res Publica Litterarum* 4 (1981): 273–84; Frederick Burwick, *Poetic Madness and the Romantic Imagination* (University Park: Pennsylvania State University Press, 1996); Robert Von Hallberg, *Lyric Powers* (Chicago: University of Chicago Press, 2008), 20–21; George MacLennan, *Lucid Interval: Subjective Writing and Madness in History* (Leicester: Leicester University Press, 1992), 42; and Stephen Murphy, *The Gift of Immortality: Myths of Power and Humanist Poetics* (Madison, NJ: Fairleigh Dickinson University Press, 1997), 168–78.
15. Walt Whitman, "Song of Myself" in *Leaves of Grass* (New York: New York University Press, 1965), section 51, lines 1324–26.
16. Stevens, "Theory," in *Collected Poetry and Prose,* 70.
17. 'Abd al-Wahhāb al-Bayātī, *Abārīq Muhashshamah: Shi'r* (Beirut: Dar Bayrūt, 1955).

18. For a discussion of the influence of Eliot in the imagination of a modern Arabic poetics, see H. N. Khadim, "Rewriting 'The Waste Land:' Badr Shakir al-Sayyab's 'Fi al-Maghrib al-Arabi'" (Influences of T. S. Eliot on modern Arabic poetry), *Journal of Arabic Literature* 30 (1999): 128–70.
19. See Muḥammad Muṣṭafā Badawī, *A Critical Introduction to Modern Arabic Poetry* (Cambridge: Cambridge University Press, 1975); and Shmuel Moreh, *Modern Arabic Poetry, 1800–1970: The Development of Its Forms and Themes Under the Influence of Western Literature* (Leiden: Brill, 1976). In Moreh, see especially chapter 7: "The Influence of Western Poetry, Particularly That of T. S. Eliot on Modern Arabic Poetry (1947–70)." See also Muḥammad 'Abd al-Ḥayy, *Tradition and English and American Influence in Arabic Romantic Poetry* (Reading: Ithaca, 1982); and Salma Khadra Jayyusi, *Trends and Movements in Modern Arabic Poetry* (Leiden: Brill, 1977), in particular vol. 2, chapter 5, on the rise of symbolism in Arabic poetry, which looks at the influences that contributed to the adaptation of French symbolism in Lebanon.
20. Moreh offers an excellent analysis of the formal explorations of modern Arabic poets, and a detailed discussion of the formal influence of Eliot, with particular emphasis on metrical developments and the significance of rhythmic instability in mid-twentieth-century Arabic poetry, in *Modern Arabic Poetry*. For a discussion of the publication culture surrounding the development of the new poetry, see F. M. Corrao, "ŠI'R": Poetics in Progress," *Quaderni di Studi Arabi* 18 (2000): 97–104.
21. For a discussion of the links between modernist poetic form and political change in the Arabic-speaking world, see Khaled Furani, "Rhythms of the Secular: The Politics of Modernizing Arab Poetic Forms," *American Ethnologist* 35, no. 2 (May 2008): 290–307.
22. Li-Young Lee, "Persimmons," *Rose* (Rochester, NY: BOA, 1986), 17–19, 17.
23. Stevens, *Collected Poetry and Prose*, 46.
24. Stevens, 49.
25. Stevens, "The Noble Rider and the Sound of Words," in *Collected Poetry and Prose*, 650. Stevens is summarizing Bateson's *English Poetry and the English Language: An Experiment in Literary History* (Oxford: Clarendon, 1943).
26. Stevens, 649–50.
27. Stevens, 654. Fleshing out what he saw as the historical and sociological significance of the pressure of reality, Stevens writes, "The way we live and the way we work alike cast us out on reality. . . . We no longer live in homes but in housing projects and this is so whether the project is literally a project or a club, a dormitory, a camp or an apartment in River House. It is not only that there are more of us and that we are actually close together. We are close together in every way. We lie in bed and listen to a broadcast from Cairo, and so on. There is no distance. We are intimate with people we have never seen and, unhappily, they are intimate with us."
28. Stevens, 659.
29. Philip Sidney, "The Defense of Poesy," in William Harmon, ed., *Classic Writings on Poetry* (New York: Columbia University Press, 2003), 149.
30. Seamus Heaney, "Death of a Naturalist," in *Opened Ground: Selected Poems, 1966–1996* (New York: Farrar, Straus and Giroux, 1998), 5.
31. Heaney, 7.

32. Jahan Ramazani, "E. E. Cummings," in Ramazani, Ellmann, and O'Clair, *The Norton Anthology of Modern and Contemporary Poetry*, 545.
33. Gottfried Benn, "Astern," trans. Robert M. Browning, in *Prose, Essays, Poems*, ed. Volkmar Sander (New York: Continuum, 1987), 215–17 (translation modified).
34. Emily Dickinson, Poem 962, in *The Complete Poems* (Boston: Little, Brown, 1960), 450.
35. Stevens, *Collected Poetry and Prose*, 45.
36. Stevens, 47.
37. Thomas Merton, *New Seeds of Contemplation* (New York: New Directions, 1961), 14. For a scholarly approach resonant with Merton's notion of right soil, see Joshua Landy, *How to Do Things with Fictions* (Oxford: Oxford University Press, 2012). See especially chapter 2 on Jesus's parables in the gospel of Mark, in which Landy argues that the parables were in fact designed to separate their listeners into those prepared to received them and those unprepared—the unique work tailored to a unique capacity of the individual soul. This meeting and matching of object to subject in the right moment of reception, and under the right conditions of openness or faith and cognitive/perceptive acuity, offers an analogue to the dynamic element I call apprehension in the poetic context.
38. Stevens, *Collected Poetry and Prose*, 652.

2. Contemplation

Sources for epigraph 1: George Rostrevor Hamilton, *Poetry and Contemplation: A New Preface to Poetics* (Cambridge: Cambridge University Press, 1937), p. 81; and epigraph 2: George Washington Carver, Incomplete letter, box 62, George Washington Carver Papers, Tuskegee University Archives, Tuskegee, Alabama; "Carver Quotes," box 62, George Washington Carver Papers, Tuskegee University Archives, Tuskegee, Alabama. Manuscripts cited in Mark D. Hersey, *My Work Is That of Conservation: An Environmental Biography of George Washington Carver* (Environmental History and the American South Series) 187, ftn. p. 270. Athens: University of Georgia Press, 2011. This quotation also serves as epigraph to Harryette Mullen's *Urban Tumbleweed*.

1. Writing on "holy attention" in the poetry of John Donne, David Marno has described the relationship between attention and prayer in this way: "Attention is the cultivation of a passive disposition, a solicitous waiting for a conversation to happen. . . . It is by attending that the subject can fill up the confined but still existing space of agency in thinking and prayer: indeed, it is by attending that he can probe the boundaries of this space." For Marno, the "holy attention" cultivated in Christian spiritual exercises (including Donne's *Holy Sonnets*) can be seen as a "regulative ideal"—a practice toward an unattainable oneness of attention to God. In prayer, attention can be directed to text, to the verbal recitation of scripture, or, in the case of mental payer, on the inward thought toward God. See David Marno, *Death Be Not Proud: The Art of Holy Attention* (Chicago: University of Chicago Press, 2016), 1–2.

2. For a philosophical approach to Buddhist concentration, nirvāna, non-self, and emptiness, see Mark Siderits, *Buddhism as Philosophy: An Introduction* (Indianapolis: Hackett, 2007).
3. Nicolas Malebranche, *The Search After Truth: Elucidations of the Search After Truth,* ed. and trans. Thomas M. Lennon and Paul J. Olscamp (Cambridge: Cambridge University Press, 1997), 529, 559. Simone Weil, *Gravity and Grace,* trans. Emma Crawford and Mario von der Ruhr (London: Routledge, 2002 [1952]), 117. Originally published as *La Pesanteur et la grâce* (Paris: Plon, 1947).
4. Weil's ethics of ascetic attention can be seen as a form of spiritual and philosophical anticonsumerism that, taken to physical extremes, led to her death by starvation, but also underpinned her split allegiances to Marxism and Catholicism. Françoise Meltzer argues convincingly that Weil's writings on attention and work reveal a surprising synthesis between the seemingly irreconcilable strains of religious and Marxist thought in "The Hands of Simone Weil," *Critical Inquiry* 27 (Summer 2001): 611–28. On Weil and Marxist politics, see Louis Patsouras, *Simone Weil and the Socialist Tradition* (San Francisco: EMText, 1991); Lawrence A. Blum and Victor Seidler, *A Truer Liberty: Simon Weil and Marxism* (London: Routledge, 1989); Eugène Fleur, "Le 'Social' dans *La Condition ouvrière,*" *Cahiers Simone Weil* 7 (December 1984): 341–46; Mamadi Keita, "Critique de l'état-nation dans 'l'enracinement' de Simone Weil," *CLA Journal* 46 (June 2003): 543–61; Thomas Dommange, "Simone Weil: Le Marxisme hors de soi," *Études philosophiques* 3 (July 2007): 207–22; and Robert Sparling, "Theory and Praxis: Simone Weil and Marx on the Dignity of Labor," *Review of Politics* 74 (Winter 2012): 87–107.
5. Simone Weil, *Waiting for God,* trans. Emma Craufurd (New York: Perennial, 2001 [1951]), 27. For more detailed accounts of Herbert's influence on Weil's thought, see Diogenes Allen, "George Herbert and Simone Weil," *Religion and Literature* 17 (Summer 1985): 17–34; and Michael Vander Weele, "Simone Weil and George Herbert on the Vocations of Reading and Writing," *Religion and Literature* 32 (Autumn 2000): 69–102.
6. Francis Ponge, *Le parti pris des choses* (Paris: Gallimard, 1942). English translation: *Partisan of Things,* trans. Joshua Corey and Jean-Luc Garneau (Chicago: Kenning, 2016).
7. Ponge, *Le parti pris des choses,* 37; *Partisan of Things,* 6 (translation modified).
8. Francis Ponge, *The Voice of Things,* ed. and trans. Beth Archer Brombert (New York: McGraw-Hill, 1972), 109.
9. Joshua Corey, "The Challenge of Francis Ponge," introduction to *Partisan of Things,* x.
10. Italo Calvino, *Six Memos for the Next Millennium,* trans. Patrick Creagh (Cambridge, MA: Harvard University Press, 1988), 76.
11. Seamus Heaney, *Opened Ground: Selected Poems 1966–1996* (New York: Farrar, Straus and Giroux, 1998), 139.
12. Wallace Stevens, *The Collected Poems of Wallace Stevens* (New York: Knopf, 1954), 534.
13. Wallace Stevens, *Collected Poetry and Prose* (New York: Library of America, 1997), 180–81.
14. Charles Altieri, "Why Stevens Must Be Abstract, or, What Poets Can Learn from Painting," in Albert Gelpi, ed., *Wallace Stevens: The Poetics of Modernism* (Cambridge: Cambridge University Press, 1990), 97. Altieri offers transformative readings of Stevens and the relationship between poetry and painterly abstraction in *Painterly Abstraction in Modernist American Poetry: The Contemporaneity of Modernism* (New York: Cambridge

University Press, 1989); *The Art of Modern American Poetry* (Oxford: Blackwells, 2005); and *Wallace Stevens and the Demands of Modernity: Toward a Phenomenology of Value* (Ithaca, NY: Cornell University Press, 2013).

15. B. J. Leggett, *Wallace Stevens and Poetic Theory: Conceiving the Supreme Fiction* (Chapel Hill: University of North Carolina Press, 1987), 125.
16. Bonnie Costello, *Planets on Tables: Poetry, Still Life, and the Turning World* (Ithaca, NY: Cornell University Press, 2008), 47.
17. Altieri, "Why Stevens Must Be Abstract," 97–98.
18. Mark Doty, *Still Life with Oysters and Lemon* (Boston: Beacon, 2001), 4.
19. Jane Hirshfield, *Ten Windows: How Great Poems Transform the World* (New York: Knopf, 2017), 5.
20. Costello, *Planets on Tables*, 14.
21. Hirshfield, *Ten Windows*, 20.
22. Elizabeth Bishop, *Poems* (New York: Farrar, Straus and Giroux, 2011), 43–44.
23. Stephen Cushman has traced a relationship between syntax and attentional orientation in this poem, in which the paratactical skeleton signals shifts in attention or emotion, and hypotaxis "signals the journey to the interior." Stephen Cushman, "Elizabeth Bishop's Winding Path," in *Fictions of Form in American Poetry* (Princeton: Princeton University Press, 1993), 131.
24. Susan McCabe, "Artifices of Independence," in *Elizabeth Bishop: Her Poetics of Loss* (University Park: Pennsylvania State University Press, 1994), 95.
25. James Longenbach has observed the quality of discovery in this poem's unfolding: "the poem seems to discover its direction only as we read it." He goes on to point out that the fish is not "imaginary" (its "brute otherness" is emphasized in visceral terms) but "imagined": "it makes sense—tentatively—only as values are attributed to it. By its very otherness the fish seems to teach the speaker how to imagine and therefore appreciate her world." James Longenbach, *Modern Poetry After Modernism* (Oxford: Oxford University Press, 1997), 27. In James McCorkle's reading, "The power of observation and looking resides in and rises with the power of imagining. We move closer to the certainty we believe lies in the tactility of physical presence—be it fish or rhetoric. At each of these liminal moments, transformation takes place, since we cross the abyss between the two halves of a metaphor or simile." James McCorkle, *The Still Performance: Writing, Self, and Interconnection in Five Postmodern American Poets* (Charlottesville: University Press of Virginia, 1989), 14.
26. McCabe observes that, at this point, "the poem takes us two ways: into recognizing difference and into apprehending unity, into perceiving connection and its frailty. But to comprehend, to totalize would be to underrate. We recall that this is a poem about a visionary moment: it can't keep, but must be let go" ("Artifices of Independence," 96). C. K. Doreski notes that, "as in the Christian parable, the oil upon the waters brings peace. It also engenders communication with the otherworldly. Through a rare Wordsworthian 'spot of time,' a genuine epiphany, the poet admits, somewhat reluctantly, a momentary conventional wisdom. This leap from perception to wisdom signals the arbitrariness so characteristic of the epiphany." C. K. Doreski, *Elizabeth Bishop: The Restraints of Language* (Oxford: Oxford University Press, 1993), 40.

27. Cautioning against a too-easy reading of this moment of ecstasy as suggesting a mutual recognition or synthesis between speaker and fish (or between all things), McCorkle argues that, "instead, the materiality of language and time comes to be emphasized; the poem lets go of the symbolic, and reinvents the relational. The poem moves toward transcendent closure with "rainbow, rainbow, rainbow," but opens up and initiates a new, though unfigured, process that subverts closure and death: 'And I let the fish go'" (*The Still Performance*, 17).
28. Doty, *Still Life with Oysters and Lemon*, 9–10.
29. "*Stilleven*, in Dutch; *la vie coite*, quiet or immobile life, in Old French; later, *nature morte*. *Stilstaende dingehn*, still-standing things. Still life. The deep pun hidden in the term: life with death in it, life after the knowledge of death, is, after all, still life. The darkness behind these gathered things—a living darkness, almost breathing, almost a pressure against us—is the not-here, the not-now; what we can see are the illuminated things right before us, our good company. The space looming behind them is the unknown of everything else—is, in other words, a visible form of death, and therefore what stands before that darkness stands close together" (Doty, 69–70).
30. Doty, 48.
31. Anne Carson, "Sappho Shock," in *Dwelling in Possibility: Woman Poets and Critics on Poetry*, ed. Yopie Prins and Maeera Shreiber (Ithaca, NY: Cornell University Press, 1997), 23.
32. Harryette Mullen, *Urban Tumbleweed: Notes from a Tanka Diary* (Minneapolis: Graywolf, 2013).
33. Mullen, viii.
34. Mullen, vii.
35. Alan Golding, "Between the News and the Dews: A Review of Harryette Mullen's *Urban Tumbleweed: Notes from a Tanka Diary*," *Iowa Review* 44 (Fall 2014): 174–77, 175.
36. Mullen, *Urban Tumbleweed*, ix.
37. Andrew Epstein, *Attention Equals Life: The Pursuit of the Everyday in Contemporary Poetry and Culture* (Oxford: Oxford University Press, 2016), p. 267.
38. Mullen, *Urban Tumbleweed*, 94.
39. Mullen, 102.
40. Mullen, 13.
41. Mullen, viii.
42. Mullen, viii.
43. Mullen, ix.
44. Mullen, 6.
45. Mullen, 122.
46. Josef Pieper, *Only the Lover Sings: Art and Contemplation*, trans. Lothar Krauth (San Francisco: Ignatius, 1990). German original: *Nur der Liebende singt* (Ostfildern: Schwabenverlag, 1988), p. 23. For a fuller discussion of Pieper's thought on contemplation and art, see Christopher A. Dustin and Joanna E. Ziegler, eds., *Practicing Mortality: Art, Philosophy, and Contemplative Seeing* (Palgrave Macmillan, 2005), pp. 1–12, 20–25, 37–47.
47. Pieper, *Only the Lover Sings*, 23.
48. Pieper, 73.
49. Hirshfield, *Ten Windows*, 11–12.

50. Søren Kierkegaard, *The Lily of the Field and the Bird of the Air: Three Godly Discourses*, trans. Bruce H. Kirmmse (Princeton: Princeton University Press, 2016), 33–34.
51. Kierkegaard, 16–38.
52. Kierkegaard, 46–70.
53. Kierkegaard, 47, 84.
54. Eliot, *Burnt Norton* III, lines 23–24, *The Four Quartets,* in *The Poems of T. S. Eliot*, ed. Christopher Ricks and Jim McCue (London: Faber and Faber, 2015).

3. Desire

1. Roland Barthes, *Le Plaisir du texte* (Paris: Seuil, 1973).
2. Wallace Stevens, "Imagination as Value," in Stevens, *Collected Poetry and Prose* (New York: Library of America, 1997), 734 (my emphasis).
3. David Schalkwyk, "Love and Service in Twelfth Night and the Sonnets," *Shakespeare Quarterly* 56 (Spring 2005): 76–77. Schalkwyk's distinction between love and desire resonates with my own, focusing on the characteristic of spatiotemporal remove or lack: "Love is concerned not just with the absences and inequities of desire but also with the pleasures of intimacy and the demands of reciprocity."
4. Rābi'a al-'Adawiyya al-Qaysiyya (also referred to as Rabi'a al-Basri), أحبك حبين ("I Love You with Two Loves"), in Abdullah al-Udhari, ed., *Classical Poems by Arab Women* (London: Saqi, 1999), 104–5 (translation modified). For an alternative translation, see Martin Lings, ed., *Sufi Poems: A Mediaeval Anthology* (Cambridge: Islamic Texts Society, 2004), 2–3.
5. Translation by Sam Hamill, in *The Erotic Spirit* (Boston: Shambhala, 1996), 1. An earlier translation can be found in Samivel, *The Glory of Egypt* (New York: Vanguard, 1955), 99. Because my language abilities do not include ancient Egyptian, I have limited my reading to Hamill's translation of this poem, focusing primarily on the semantic content and sequencing in the poem and not on those formal features that depend on reference to the original language, such as musicality, syntactic arrangement, and lexical and idiomatic choices. I work instead with Hamill's translation as a poem in its own right and as a suggestion of how desire was composed at this earliest stage of lyric history.
6. Writing about this relationship between desire and not-having in poetic language, Allen Grossman notes, "Insofar as true-love imports a simultaneity (consistent with predication), it appears to intend a violation of what appears to be the logic of signification by language. As evidence of this, consider the following very simple observation: there are many poems of not yet having (petitional poems, as it were, or poems of seduction), and there are also poems (though proportionally to the first type many fewer) of having had (doxological poems as it were, e.g., the aubade). But there are no poems (certainly no Western poems) situated upon the zero point of having, of union just so. At that moment, the coincidence of consciousness and experience, language disappears and with it representation as depiction—for the same reasons, no doubt, that there are no private languages nor for that matter perfectly public languages." Allen Grossman,

True-Love: Essays on Poetry and Valuing (Chicago: University of Chicago Press, 2009), 34. Grossman goes on to claim that at a more essential level, "poetry, *like language itself*, does not reach to the real."

7. Emily Dickinson, *The Poems of Emily Dickinson* (Cambridge, MA: Belknap Press of Harvard University Press, 1999), 203.
8. Shakespeare, *Twelfth Night*, 2.3.50. In his annotated edition of the plays, Samuel Johnson noted that the line is a play on the saying "In *decay* there lies no plenty:" "A reproof of avarice, which stores up perishable fruits till they *decay*. To these fruits the Poet, humorously, compares youth or virginity; which, he says, is a *stuff will not endure.*" *The Plays of William Shakespeare*, ed. Samuel Johnson and George Steevens, vol. 2 (London: J. and R. Tonson, 1765), 381.
9. Petronius Arbiter, "Fragmentum," translated by Ben Jonson in *The Works of Ben Jonson* (London: Edward Moxon, 1938), 740. Jonson's translation is reprinted in Hamill: "Doing, a filthy pleasure is, and short; / And done, we straight repent us of the sport: / Let us not rush blindly on unto it; / Like lustful beasts, that only know to do it: / For lust will languish, and that heat decay. / Be thus, thus, keeping endless holiday, / Let us together closely lie and kiss, / There is no labour, nor no shame in this; / This hath pleased, doth please, and long will please; never / Can this decay, but is beginning ever" (*The Erotic Spirit*, 33).
10. Marcus Argentarius, in A. S. F. Gow and D. L. Page, eds., *The Greek Anthology: The Garland of Philip and Some Contemporary Epigrams*, vol. 1 (Cambridge: Cambridge University Press, 1968), 154. Hamill has translated this poem as follows: "Her perfect naked breast / Upon my breast, / Her lips between my lips, / I lay in perfect bliss / With lovely Antigone, / Nothing caught between us. / I will not tell the rest. / Only the lamp bore witness" (*The Erotic Spirit*, 24).
11. Peter Stockwell, "Surreal Figures," in *Cognitive Poetics in Practice*, ed. Joanna Gavins and Gerard Steen (London: Routledge, 2003), 15–16.
12. William Shakespeare, "Sonnet 18," in *Shakespeare's Sonnets* (Nashville, TN: Thomas Nelson, 1997), 18.
13. Helen Vendler, *The Art of Shakespeare's Sonnets* (Cambridge, MA: Harvard University Press, 1997), 120.
14. Vendler, 28.
15. Vendler, 14.
16. Vendler, 17 (my emphasis).
17. Vendler, 32–33. In an impish turn to contemporary love lyric, Vendler quips that "Frank O'Hara had a better sense for the essential semantic emptiness of love lyrics when he represented them . . . as 'saying' 'I need you, you need me, yum, yum,'" concluding that "the appeal of lyric lies somewhere else than in its paraphrasable statement" (14).
18. Sandra L. Bermann, "Love Poetry," in Roland Greene and Stephen Cushman, eds., *The Princeton Encyclopedia of Poetry and Poetics*, 4th ed. (Princeton: Princeton University Press, 2012), 814–820, 814.
19. See Audre Lorde's essays "Poetry Is Not a Luxury" and "The Uses of the Erotic: The Erotic as Power," collected in *Sister Outsider: Essays and Speeches* (Berkeley: Crossing,

2007 [1984]), 36–39, 53–59. See also Lorde, *Zami: A New Spelling of My Name—a Biomythography* (Berkeley: Crossing, 1982).
20. Audre Lorde, *The Collected Poems of Audre Lorde* (New York: Norton, 2000), 51.
21. Amy Lowell, "The Blue Scarf," in *Sword Blades and Poppy Seed* (Boston: Houghton Mifflin, 1914), 236–37.
22. George Oppen, "Psalm," in *New Collected Poems* (New York: New Directions, 2008), 99. The poem first appeared in *Poetry Magazine* 102 (July 1963) and in Oppen's third collection, *This in Which* (1965).
23. Oren Izenberg, *Being Numerous: Poetry and the Ground of Social Life* (Princeton: Princeton University Press, 2011), 99.
24. Charles Tomlinson, "Cézanne at Aix" in Jahan Ramazani, Richard Ellmann, and Robert O'Clair, eds., *The Norton Anthology of Modern and Contemporary Poetry*, vol. 2: *Contemporary Poetry* (New York: Norton, 2003), 376–77.
25. Izenberg, *Being Numerous*, 106.
26. See Richard Swigg, ed., *Speaking with George Oppen: Interviews with the Poet and Mary Oppen, 1968–1987* (Jefferson, NC: McFarland, 2012), 82–23. On Pound's use of the phrase in Canto 90, see James J. Wilhelm, *Ezra Pound: The Tragic Years (1925–1972)* (Pennsylvania: Pennsylvania State University Press, 1994), 297. For a discussion of the phrase in the contemplative writings of Richard and Dante, see Vallentina Atturo, "Contemplating Wonder: 'Ad-miratio' in Richard of St. Victor and Dante," *Dante Studies, with the Annual Report of the Dante Society* 129 (2011): 99–124.

Returning to Pieper, we find this mutual necessity between contemplation and love echoed and elaborated: "even the most intensive seeing and beholding may not yet be true contemplation . . . Rather, the ancient expression of the mystics applies here: *ubi amor, ibi oculus*—the eyes see better when guided by love; a new dimension of 'seeing' is opened up by love alone! And this means contemplation is visual perception prompted by loving acceptance! I hold that this is the specific mark of seeing things in contemplation: it is motivated by loving acceptance, by affectionate affirmation." Pieper, *Only the Lover Sings: Art and Contemplation*, trans. Lothar Krauth (San Francisco: Ignatius, 1990), 73–74.
27. Robert Hass, "Meditation at Lagunitas," in *Praise* (New York: Ecco, 1979), 4–5.
28. Maurice Blanchot, "Literature and the Right to Death," in *The Station Hill Blanchot Reader: Fiction and Literary Essays*, ed. George Quasha, trans. Lydia Davis, Paul Auster, and Robert Lamberton (Barrytown, NY: Station Hill/Barrytown, 1999), 379.
29. "I say, 'This woman.' Hölderlin, Mallarmé, and all poets whose theme is the essence of poetry have felt that the act of naming is disquieting and marvelous. A word may give me its meaning, but first it suppresses it. For me to be able to say, 'This woman' I must somehow take her flesh and blood reality away from her, cause her to be absent, annihilate her. The word gives me the being, but it gives it to me deprived of being. The word is the absence of that being, its nothingness, what is left of it when it has lost being—the very fact that it does not exist" (Blanchot, 379). Blanchot also brought attention to Hegel's phrase: "Adam's first act, which made him master of the animals, was to give them names, that is, he annihilated them in their existence (as existing creatures)," from a collection of essays entitled *System of 1803–1804*, written prior to the *Phenomenology of*

Spirit. In a note Blanchot points out that "[Alexandre] Kojève, in his *Introduction à la lecture de Hegel*, interpreting a passage from *The Phenomenology*, demonstrates in a remarkable way how for Hegel comprehension was equivalent to murder" (n379).
30. Blanchot, 383.
31. Stevens, "The Worms at Heaven's Gate," in Stevens, *Collected Poetry and Prose*, 40.
32. Blanchot, *The Station Hill Blanchot Reader*, 383.
33. Audre Lorde, "Recreation," in *The Collected Poems of Audre Lorde*, 296.

4. Recollection

1. Sigmund Freud, "Mourning and Melancholia," in *General Psychological Theory: Papers on Metapsychology*, ed. Philip Rieff (New York: Collier, 1963), 164. This term's significance in the context of the particular "work" of elegy is taken up and deepened by Peter Sacks in *The English Elegy: Studies in the Genre From Spenser to Yeats* (Baltimore: Johns Hopkins University Press, 1985), 1.
2. I borrow this term from Slavoj Žižek's *Tarrying with the Negative: Kant, Hegel, and the Critique of Ideology* (Durham, NC: Duke University Press, 1993). While Žižek's book is not explicitly concerned with the work of recollection, his reading of subjectivity in philosophy's sequential rejections of itself (from Kant to Hegel to Kierkegaard to Heidegger to Lacan) enacts, through the work of memory, a dissolution of the subject itself—so that acts of recollection call up not only the essential absence of the object but also of the attending subject, constituted by the nature of that to which it attends. In a reading of noir cinema of the eighties, he asks, "How, then, are we to diagnose the position of the hero at the end of his quest, after the recovery of memory deprives him of his very identity?" (11). Interestingly for our purposes, this simultaneous ungraspability of subject and object opens onto other acts of apperception, not only those of recollection.
3. Carolyn Forché, "An Interview by David Montenegro," *American Poetry Review* 17, no. 6 (1988): 36. Well worth considering in this context, Forché's collection *Angel of History* (New York: Harper Collins, 1994) offers a dark meditation on the "work of incessant reminding" and the question of what can survive the twentieth-century cataclysms that shape the terrain of her poems, from war-scarred rural Europe to the death camps to the Chernobyl nuclear disaster.
4. Forché, "An Interview by David Montenegro," 38.
5. Ingeborg Bachmann, "[Immerzu in den Worten sein]," in *Darkness Spoken: The Collected Poems*, trans. Peter Filkins (Brookline, MA: Zephyr, 2006), 518/519.
6. Geoffrey Hill, *New and Collected Poems, 1952–1992* (Boston: Houghton Mifflin, 1994), 55.
7. Jahan Ramazani, *Poetry of Mourning: The Modern Elegy from Hardy to Heaney* (Chicago: University of Chicago Press, 1994), 8. Langdon Hammer has observed, in Hill's references to soldiers (including Isaac Rosenberg, Siegfried Sassoon, Charles Péguy, and Ivor Gurney), victims (including Robert Desnos), and survivors (including Paul Celan) of the two world wars in other poems, a vexed combination of identification, advocacy, and separation. Langdon Hammer, "The American Poetry of Thom Gunn and

Geoffrey Hill," *Contemporary Literature* 43 (Winter 2002): 657–58. The convergence of elegy with historical account and moral witnessing in Hill's poems charges his poem's sites with the relentless work of an obligatory yet self-consciously insufficient, morally entangled act of recollection.
8. Hammer, 660.
9. Hammer, 661. Hammer also points to the pressurized nature of Hill's speech in this "broken sonnet," and to the way in which the whittled and highly crafted syntax leads to morally laden moments of semantic doubling: "for example, does the phrase 'it / is true' confirm Hill's admission of self-interest (an apology that falsifies, or greatly complicates, the poem's pathos), or does it convert that admission into something like a boast ("I have written this for my own satisfaction, and I say it is true")? Typically, Hill does not allow us to decide in favor of one or the other reading but forces us to include both" (Hammer, 660–61). Neil Corcoran has written of this moment in "September Song," "The poem can be given its permission only by the scrupulous skepticism of its unease before its own powers of appropriation and exploitation." Neil Corcoran, "September Song," in *English Poetry Since 1940* (London: Routledge, 2013 [1993]), 122. Speaking of Hill's meticulous attention to form, and the peculiar disjunction in his oeuvre between "absolute control within each poem (or form)" and the "variety of form over the spread of his work so far," Jon Silkin has concluded that "each fragment of absoluteness represents a pragmatic concession to the intractable nature of the matter and response to it in each poem," reflecting an "on-going struggle between form, expressiveness, and the scrupulous attention Hill usually gives to his material, even when it is struggling against that oppressive attention so as to retain an existence (in life) independent of his own." Jon Silkin, "The Poetry of Geoffrey Hill," *Iowa Review* 3 (Summer 1972): 109.
10. Peter Sacks, *The English Elegy: Studies in the Genre from Spenser to Yeats* (Baltimore: Johns Hopkins University Press, 1885), 1.
11. Ramazani, *The Poetry of Mourning*, 3.
12. Ramazani, 8.
13. Ramazani, ix–x. Ramazani goes on to contend that "in becoming anti-elegiac, the modern elegy more radically violates previous generic norms than did earlier phases of elegy: it becomes anti-consolatory and anti-encomiastic, anti-Romantic and anti-Victorian, anti-conventional and sometimes even anti-literary" (2).
14. R. Clifton Spargo, *The Ethics of Mourning: Grief and Responsibility in Elegiac Literature* (Baltimore: Johns Hopkins University Press, 2004), 11.
15. Spargo, 13.
16. Ḥamdū Ṭammās, ed., *Dīwān Al-Khansā'* (Beirutt: Dār al-Ma'rifah, 2003), 25. These lines are from an elegy to her brother Sakhr, circa 613 (my translation).
17. Indeed, the *marthiya* as a genre is thought to have its cultural roots in the rhythmic laments of female tribal members' public mourning of male relatives, so the raw sonic wail of Al-Khansā''s language may well signal her adaptation of the form's Bedouin roots. See Rebecca Dyer, "Poetry of Politics and Mourning: Mahmoud Darwish's Genre-Transforming Tribute to Edward W. Said," *PMLA* 122, no. 5 (2007): 1453; and Charles Pellat, "Marthiya (1)," in P. J. Bearman, ed., *The Encyclopaedia of Islam* (Leiden:

E. J. Brill, 1998), 602–7. Pellat also notes that pre-Islamic poets (male and female) did not traditionally grieve for female relatives. However, Leor Halevi points out that elegies for women may well have been "selected out of the Islamic canon." Halevi notes that Jarir devoted some of his elegiac verses to his wife Khalida. Leor Halevi, *Muhammad's Grave: Death Rites and the Making of Islamic Society* (New York: Columbia University Press, 2007), 292n19).

18. Primo Levi, *Se questo è un uomo*, completed in 1946, twenty-five hundred copies published by the small press De Silva in 1947. Translation: *Survival in Auschwitz*, trans. Stuart Woolf (New York: Touchstone, 1995).

19. Levi, *Survival in Auschwitz*, 11.

20. See Thomas H. Davenport and John C. Beck, *The Attention Economy: Understanding the New Currency of Business* (Boston: Harvard Business School Press, 2001); and Richard A. Lanham, *The Economics of Attention: Style and Substance in the Age of Information* (Chicago: University of Chicago Press, 2006).

21. Lyn Hejinian, "The Rejection of Closure," in *The Language of Inquiry* (Berkeley: University of California Press, 2000).

22. Examples of this faith in unity or the discovery of essence through poetic attention can be found in Cleanth Brooks, "The Heresy of Paraphrase," in *The Well Wrought Urn* (New York: Houghton Mifflin Harcourt, 1947), 192–201; and Denise Levertov's revelation of the underlying form of objects and experiences through poetic form in "Some Notes on Organic Form," in *The Poet in the World* (New York: New Directions, 1973), 7–13. Both center on a notion of poetic experience as capable of altering, charging, or exposing our experience of things through the charging, disrupting, and forming of language. In Levertov, the act of poetic listening promises a kind of ecstatic revelation that is nowhere in *Nox*. Carson's text is relentless, even cold, in its refusal to seek an underlying meaning or form (in which form is an intrinsic unity or essence, resonant with Levertov and Brooks) to her brother's life. If Carson's aesthetic practice of irrecuperative attention resonates with anyone, perhaps it would be Victor Shklovsky's concept of aesthetic defamiliarization, which finds value in the experience of unsettlement, in the strangeness and unassimilability of aesthetic experience. Yet Carson's text doesn't go so far as to offer the transformative power of defamiliarization's perceptual making-new.

23. Ramazani's treatment of what he sees as a specifically modern set of problems and demands on the nature of elegy offers a good example of this kind of historicism. He cites the decreased time allotted to social rituals of mourning (Ramazani, *Poetry of Mourning,* 11) and the "multitude of new deaths" experienced in the twentieth century ("war victims," "God," "the sanctity of the dead," "traditional consolation" and "even—in the age of the visual media and psychology—the death of the poet") as uniquely modern phenomena leading to elegy's redirection toward the mourning of mourning itself.

24. Examples include pre- and post-Islamic Arabic poetry, Renaissance and Reformation poetries, and pre- and postrevolutionary American literature. While opting for a historically defined lens, Ramazani acknowledges that "the modern elegy may really elaborate one set of transhistorical tendencies long embedded in the form" (*Poetry of*

Mourning, 9). These tendencies, passed over perhaps too quickly by most scholars, necessitate a serious exploration into the transhistorical nature of the poetry of recollection, and the traceable dynamics and challenges it poses, across traditions and time periods.
25. John Felstiner has called "Engführung" Celan's "follow-up" to "Todesfuge," a movement "deeper into inaccessible terrain." Felstiner, *Paul Celan: Poet, Survivor, Jew* (New Haven: Yale University Press, 2001), 118.
26. Paul Celan, *Selected Poems and Prose of Paul Celan*, ed. John Felstiner (New York: Norton, 2001), 118. Henceforth referred to as *PC*. For this stanza, however, the version that appears in the English translation of Peter Szondi's article "Reading 'Engführung'" better captures these lines exilic violence: "Driven into the / terrain." Peter Szondi, "Reading 'Engführung': An Essay on the Poetry of Paul Celan," trans. D. Caldwell and S. Esh, *Boundary 2* 11, no. 3, "The Criticism of Peter Szondi" (Spring 1983): 231–64, 231.
27. Szondi observes that "the repeated use of the definite article presumes that the reader already knows which 'terrain' and which 'trace' are meant. For this reason, then, at the beginning of 'Engführung,' the (possible) sense of the words employed is of less importance than the fact that the reader is led into an unfamiliar context, one in which he is nevertheless treated as someone who knows it or, more precisely, as one not permitted to know" (Szondi, 232).
28. *PC* 118.
29. In *Paul Celan,* Felstiner notes biblical resonances with the cry of Isaiah: "Surely the people is grass!" (40:7) and the Hebrew psalm: "My days are like a shadow that declineth, and I am withered like grass" (102:11). Also Deuteronomy: "Your children who follow you in later generations and foreigners who come from distant lands will see the calamities that have fallen on the land and the diseases with which the lord has afflicted it. The whole land will be a burning waste of salt and sulfur—nothing planted, nothing sprouting, no vegetation growing on it" (29:22–23).
30. *PC* 121.
31. *PC* 126–27.
32. The word "Saying" here invokes Emmanuel Levinas's writing on the essence of language that precedes language and exceeds representation (the said): "To say is to approach a neighbor, 'dealing him signifyingness' . . . prior to all objectification"; "Saying is . . . a condition for all communication, as exposure [to another]." Emmanuel Levinas, *Otherwise Than Being; or, Beyond Essence*, trans. Alphonso Lingis (Pittsburgh: Duquesne University Press, 1981), 48.
33. *PC* 126–27: "the / world sets its inmost / at stake with the new / hours."
34. *PC* 128–29.
35. *PC* 131.
36. "At owl's flight" (*PC* 128–29, 130–31).
37. "Only when the dusk starts to fall does the owl of Minerva spread its wings and fly." Georg Wilhelm Fredrich Hegel, "Preface," in *Hegel: Elements of the Philosophy of Right,* ed. Allen W. Wood, trans. H.B. Nisbet (Cambridge: Cambridge University Press, 1991).
38. Heidegger, too, called for the change of hands, in which philosophy was in the final hour set aside for a more originary (poietic) language. Critiquing calculative reasoning,

he suggests the return of humans to their origin through language—not as system of representation but as that through which humankind encounters existence by entering into relation (*Mitsein*). See Christopher Fynsk's analysis of Heidegger's thinking on language and the human in *Language and Relation . . . That There Is Language* (Stanford: Stanford University Press, 1996), 75, 19.

39. Wittgenstein tried to think ethical experience from a sense of wonder at the fact of existence (what Heidegger phrases as the miracle "Dass es Seiendes ist—und nicht Nichts") and located this experience in the miracle of language: "Now I am tempted to say that the right expression in language for the miracle of the world, though it is not any proposition *in* language, is the existence of language itself." Ludwig Wittgenstein, "A Lecture on Ethics," *Philosophical Review,* 74 (January 1965): 3–12.
40. *PC* 118.
41. Szondi, "Reading 'Engführung,'" 234: "The hour that has no more sisters is the last hour, death. Whoever is there is 'at home.'"
42. *PC* 131.
43. *PC* 411. On the same page we find the lines: "Here too in your presence, I've taken this path. It was a circle." John Felstiner points to the asterisks not only between stanzas but also just before the first line, dividing it from what? Perhaps from the breath of the last line before we begin the poem again, in the manner of Joyce's novel, connecting last word to first, "last hour" to "new hour," "to set out again, *da capo*" (Felstiner, *Paul Celan,* 125).
44. Felstiner, 125 (translation modified).
45. Anne Carson, *Nox* (New York: New Directions, 2010).
46. "Multas per gentes et multa per aequora vectus / advento has miseras, frater, ad inferias / ut te postremo donatem munere mortis / et mutam nequiquam alloquerer cinerem. / quandoquidem fortuna mihi tete abstulit ipsum, / heu miser indigne frater adempte mihi, / munc tamen interea haec, prisco quae more parentum / tradita sunt tristi munere ad inherias, / accipe fraterno multum manantia fletu / atque in perpetuum, frater, ave atque vale." "Many the peoples many the oceans I crossed—/ I arrive at these poor, brother, burials / so I could give you the last gift owed to death /and talk (why?) with mute ash. / Now that Fortune tore you from me, you / oh poor (wrongly) brother (wrongly) taken from me, / now still anyway this—what a distant mood of parents / handed down as the sad gift for burials—/ accept! soaked with the tears of a brother / and into forever, brother, farewell and farewell" (translation by Anne Carson).
47. Mandy Bloomfield develops this term to describe resonant practices in the work of such poets as Theresa Hak Kyung Cha, Kamau Brathwaite, and M. NourbeSe Philip in *Archaeopoetics: Word, Image, History* (Tuscaloosa: University of Alabama Press, 2016).
48. Ramazani notes that in contemporary writing "every elegy is an elegy for elegy—a poem that mourns the diminished efficacy and legitimacy of poetic mourning." Going further, "As poets mourn not only dead individuals but mourning itself, elegize not only the dead but elegy itself, the genre develops by feeding off a multitude of new deaths, including the body of its own traditions. Intruding into modern laments for war victims, public figures, relatives, and friends are many extraneous deaths—the death of mourning ritual, of God, of traditional consolation, of recuperative elegy, of the

sanctity of the dead, of 'healthy' mourning, and even perhaps—in the age of the visual media and psychology—the death of the poet" (Ramazani, *Poetry of Mourning*, 8).

49. In Ramazani's terms, "God may have died, but the dead have turned to gods for many modern poets. Always a favorite muse, death has outstripped most rivals by the time that Stevens declares it "the mother of beauty" (Ramazani, 1).

50. We can see this understanding of translation as an open latticework informed as much by absence and incompletion as by assimilation in Carson's translation of Sappho's fragments in *If Not, Winter* (New York: Vintage, 2003). There, rather than glossing over the missing pieces and untranslatable aspects of Sappho's remains, Carson chooses to bracket them, letting the syntax gape, a "barking web."

51. This process of poetic valuing, in which the significance is placed on the language object itself, rather than on its communicative or pragmatic functions, resonates with Roman Jakobson's definition of the poetic function of language as "the set (*Einstellung*) toward the message as such, focus on the message for its own sake" (Roman Jakobson, "Linguistics and Poetics," in *Style in Language*, ed. Thomas Sebeok (Cambridge, MA: MIT Press, 1960), 350–77, 356.)

52. Theresa Hak Kyung Cha, *Dictee* (Berkeley: University of California Press, 2001).

53. Kun Jong Lee describes Cha's style in *Dictee* as "nonlinear, cyclical, nonprogressive, fluid, open, fragmented, and surreal." Kun Jong Lee, "Rewriting Hesiod, Revisioning Korea: Theresa Hak Kyung Cha's *Dictee* as a Subversive Hesiodic 'Catalogue of Women,'" *College Literature* 33 (Summer 2006): 77. Anne Anlin Cheng describes it as an "aesthetic of the montage." Anne Anlin Cheng, "Memory and Anti-Documentary Desire in Theresa Hak Kyung Cha's Dictée," *MELUS* 23, no. 4 (1998): 125.

54. Cheng, "Memory and Anti-Documentary Desire," 122–23.

55. Cha, *Dictee*, 38.

56. Lisa Lowe, "Unfaithful to the Original: The Subject of Dictée," in Elaine Kim and Norma Alarcón, eds., *Writing Self/Writing Nation: A Collection of Essays on Dictée by Theresa Hak Kyung Cha* (Berkeley: Third Woman, 1994), 35–69, 39.

57. Shelly Sunn Wong, "Unnaming the Same: Theresa Hak Kyung Cha's DICTEE," in Kim and Alarcón, *Writing Self/Writing Nation*, 103–40, 113.

58. Sue J. Kim, "Narrator, Author, Reader: Equivocation in Theresa Hak Kyung Cha's Dictee," *Narrative* 16 (May 2008): 168–69. Likewise, Cheng argues that, "By not allowing for the mobility and complacency of translation, Cha suggests that it is precisely the radical contingency of terms such as 'alien' and 'original'—the mobility of their signification—that forms that basis for and finally offers a critique for both colonial and nationalist discourses of origin" (Cheng, "Memory and Anti-Documentary Desire," 128).

59. Marjorie Perloff, *Differentials: Poetry, Poetics, Pedagogy* (Tuscaloosa: University of Alabama Press, 2004), 100.

60. Cha, *Dictee*, 155. Later she urges: "*Render voices to meet the weight of stone with the / weight of voices*" (162). What emerges is a meditation on the transformative capacities of this transposition of remnants into written marks: "Words cast each by each to weather / avowed indisputably, to time. / . . . make fossil trace of word, / residue of word, stand as a ruin stands, / simply, as mark" (177).

61. Cha, 33.

62. Reznikoff writes, "to name and to name and to name—and to name in such a way that you have rhythm, since music . . . is also part of the meaning." L. S. Dembo and Charles Reznikoff, "Charles Reznikoff," *Contemporary Literature* 10 (Spring 1969): 193–202, 193–94.
63. Cha, *Dictee*, 179.
64. *PC* 402.
65. *PC* 409.

5. Imagination

1. See, for example, Jöran Lepsien, Ivan C. Griffin, Joseph T. Devlin, and Anna C. Nobre, "Directing Spatial Attention in Mental Representations: Interactions Between Attentional Orienting and Working-Memory Load," *NeuroImage* 26, no. 3 (2005): 733–43; and Ivan C. Griffin and Anna C. Nobre, "Orienting Attention to Locations in Internal Representations," *Journal of Cognitive Neuroscience* 15, no. 8 (2003): 1176–94.
2. For research on attention's spatial navigation of recalled objects of mental representation, see Duncan E. Astle, Anna C. Nobre, and Gaia Scerif, "Subliminally Presented and Stored Objects Capture Spatial Attention," *Journal of Neuroscience: The Official Journal of the Society for Neuroscience* 30, no. 10 (2010): 3567–71; and Simon G. Gosling and Duncan E. Astle, "Directing Spatial Attention to Locations Within Remembered and Imagined Mental Representations," *Frontiers in Human Neuroscience* 7 (2013): 154. Ruth M. J. Byrne has suggested that imaginative thinking and the generation of counterfactual or fictive objects and narratives may involve identical cognitive processes as those of "rational" thoughts rooted in factual events. Ruth M. J. Byrne, *The Rational Imagination: How People Create Alternatives to Reality* (Cambridge, MA: MIT Press, 2007).
3. S. Foley, "Imagination," in Roland Greene and Stephen Cushman, eds., *The Princeton Encyclopedia of Poetry and Poetics,* 4th ed. (Princeton: Princeton University Press, 2012), 667. See also Richard Kearney, *The Wake of Imagination: Toward a Postmodern Culture* (Minneapolis: University of Minnesota Press, 1988), 669.
4. Kearney, *The Wake of the Imagination,* 667.
5. For detailed accounts of the development of these terms in classical, medieval and Renaissance poetic theory, see Murray W. Bundy, *The Theory of Imagination in Classical and Mediaeval Thought* (Urbana: University of Illinois Press, 1927); and Bundy, " 'Invention' and 'Imagination' in the Renaissance," *Journal of English and Germanic Philology* 29, no. 4 (1930): 535–45. See also William Rossky, "Imagination in the English Renaissance: Psychology and Poetic," *Studies in the Renaissance* 5 (1958): 49–73.
6. In his study of Al-Farabi's theory of poetic imagination, Nabil Matar points to the confusion over the plurality of terms for imagination, including divergent forms from the root *khal*: *takhayyulat, khuyyil, yukhayyal, takhayyal, yukhayyil, tukhayyil,* and *mukhayyil*. At the same time, Matar notes that some of these terms (notably *khayal* and *wahm*, both of which were used in the translations of Aristotle by Alkindi, Qusta bin Luqa, and Ishaq bin Hunayn in the ninth century) were associated with undisciplined sensuality

and lunacy—paralleling the associative differences between "fantasy" and "imagination." Nabil Matar, "Alfārābī on Imagination: With a Translation of His 'Treatise on Poetry,'" *College Literature* 23 (February 1996): 100–10.

7. See Alethea Hayter, *Opium and the Romantic Imagination* (Berkeley: University of California Press, 1968); Jürgen Klein, "Genius, Ingenium, Imagination: Aesthetic Theories of Production from the Renaissance to Romanticism," in *The Romantic Imagination: Literature and Art in England and Germany,* ed. Frederick Burwick and Jürgen Klein (Amsterdam: Rodopi, 1996), 19–62; and Mario L. D'Avanzo, *Keats's Metaphors for the Poetic Imagination* (Durham, NC: Duke University Press, 1967), 3–5.

8. M. H. Abrams named this phenomenon in *Natural Supernaturalism: Tradition and Revolution in Romantic Literature* (New York: Norton, 1973).

9. See Samuel Taylor Coleridge, *Biographia Literaria* (Edinburgh: Edinburgh University Press, 2014), chapter 14.

10. This plan did not work out so well, as Coleridge describes at some length and with a mix of regret and irritation in chapter 14 of the *Biographia*.

11. James Vaughn describes Wordsworth's classifications as "confusing and inexact," and notes that it is difficult to discern which poems fall under which heading; cited in James Scoggins, *Imagination and Fancy: Complementary Modes in the Poetry of Wordsworth* (Lincoln: University of Nebraska Press, 1966), 23. Scoggins also observes the failure of most critics to distinguish sufficiently between Coleridge's and Wordsworth's uses of the terms, and their "habit of looking to Coleridge for explanations of Wordsworth's distinction between these faculties" (24).

12. Coleridge, *Biographia Literaria, or Biographical Sketches of My Literary Life and Opinions,* ed. James Engell and W. Jackson Bate (Princeton: Princeton University Press, 1983), 82.

13. Coleridge, 82–83.

14. Coleridge, 302.

15. Coleridge, 305 (Coleridge's emphasis).

16. For an early but detailed account of the development of theories and lexicons of imagination, fancy and invention during the medieval and Renaissance periods, see Bundy, "'Invention' and 'Imagination' in the Renaissance." For a consideration of the social psychological roots of attitudes toward the imaginative faculty in the English Renaissance, including how specifically poetic imagination was shaped, constrained, and challenged to counter distinguish itself from other imaginative modes considered more pathological in nature, see Rossky, "Imagination in the English Renaissance."

17. See Klein, "Genius, Ingenium, Imagination."

18. This is not to suggest, of course, that *The Prelude should* have been written in prose. There are moments of intense poetic embodiment throughout the work. Yet long stretches of *The Prelude,* particularly in books 12 and 13, "Imagination and Taste, How Impaired and Restored," offer more in the way of commentary and lessons, their focus on delivering semantic messages rather than on bodying forth poetic experience or imagination. The ascent to Mount Snowden in book 13 "rises up" so dramatically in part because of the shift in language from description to formal embodiment. In this sense, perhaps the flatter terrain of the surrounding sections can be seen as formally effective by offering contrast. Mount Snowden is particularly interesting in this regard

because it opens book 13, thus falling right in the middle of the surrounding descriptive valleys. One could read this as Wordsworth actively engaging both poetry *on* and poetry *of* imagination, using the former mode to intensify the latter. We see a resonant moment in the passage through the Simplon Pass, where imagination itself rises from the mind "Like an unfathered vapor" (6:527), interrupting Wordsworth's disappointment over missing the anticipated Alpen crossing-point—simultaneously transforming both the speaker's perspective and the poem's formal register.

19. While I use the term *mental representation* here in accordance with the term's meaning in the ongoing psychological and cognitive research, there's an inherent tension in *re*-presentation's suggestion of a prior presented object, particularly in the context of this second mode of *productive* or purely creative imagination, whose presentation before the attending inner eye is (or at least *feels*) wholly new.

20. The suggestion that even direct perception takes place through an act of the imagination or mental representation has been made by Aristotle in *De Anima*, by both Abu-Sinna and Al-Farabi in the ninth century and by later philosophical approaches such as that of Fichte.

    Kant aimed to recognize the gradation between "reproductive" and "pure" or "productive" imagination in the third critique by suggesting a "tertium medium,' an intermediary synthesis of the two.

21. I draw this distinction primarily from Kant's writings on imagination in the *Anthropology* as well as in both the first and the third critiques. While Kant's earlier works dismiss the imagination (*Einbildung*), perhaps due to lingering cultural wariness of the imagination's potential to supplant reason and morality, and the *Critique of Practical Reason* does not explicitly address the concept, Kant's writings in the first and third critiques in particular not only originate a clear distinction between productive and reproductive imagination, but situate the imagination (particularly in its former mode) as a central element in transcendental cognition. For a more thorough analysis of Kant's thinking on these forms of imagination, see Béatrice Longuenesse, *Kant and the Capacity to Judge: Sensibility and Discursivity in the Transcendental Analytic of the Critique of Pure Reason,* trans. Charles T. Wolfe (Princeton: Princeton University Press, 1998), part 3.

22. Aristotle, *The Basic Works of Aristotle* (New York: Random House, 1941), 427b, 16. See "Imagination," in Howard Caygill, *A Kant Dictionary* (Oxford: Blackwell Reference, 1995). Caygill underscores the "peculiar, intermediate status of imagination" in philosophical and aesthetic conceptualizations since Aristotle, and further notes that "in the synthesis of Plato and Aristotle ventured by the Renaissance philosophers Ficino and Pico della Mirandola, imagination featured as the vehicle of participation between human sensation and the ideas, with the art of genius featuring prominently as the perfect expression of their unity."

23. Longuenesse notes the pre-Kantian circulation of both Wolff and Baumgarten in empirical psychology textbooks of the time, both strongly resonant with Kant's definition of imagination in *Anthropology from a Pragmatic Standpoint* as the "faculty of representing an object of intuition even when it is not present" (*Kant and the Capacity to Judge,* 205), and in the *Transcendental Deduction* (section 24), where he distinguishes imagination's figurative synthesis from the rational synthesis of the intellect: "the figurative

synthesis . . . must, in order to be distinguished from the merely intellectual combination, be called the *transcendental synthesis of imagination.* Imagination is the faculty of representing in intuition an object *even when it is not present* [*auch ohne dessen Gegenwart*]" (B151, translation modified by Longuenesse).

24. Immanuel Kant, *Anthropology from a Pragmatic Point of View,* trans. Robert B. Louden and Manfred Kuehn (Cambridge: Cambridge University Press, 2006), §28, Ak. VII, 167.

25. Immanuel Kant, *Metaphysical Foundations of Natural Science,* trans. Michael Friedman (Cambridge: Cambridge University Press, 2004), 191, 229; Immanuel Kant, *Critique of Pure Reason,* trans. Paul Guyer and Allen W. Wood (Cambridge: Cambridge University Press, 1998), A 141/B 181.

26. Almost, because even the wildest and most unearthly dreams fantasies must have some connection to experience in order to be conceived and visualized. These mark a kind of limit to the creative stretch of perceptional material beyond the domain of experience. The degree of this stretch in any individual might be seen as a measure of what has been called creative genius.

27. Wordsworth, "Lines Written a Few Miles Above Tintern Abbey," in *Lyrical Ballads and Other Poems, 1797–1800,* ed. James Butler and Karen Green (Ithaca, NY: Cornell University Press, 1992), 116–20. All subsequent citations from the poems in *Lyrical Ballads* refer to this edition and are cited in the text by lines.

28. Harold Bloom, "Tintern Abbey," in Harold Bloom, ed., *William Wordsworth* (Philadelphia: Chelsea House, 2003), 118.

29. Rainer Maria Rilke, *New Poems,* trans. Edward Snow (New York: North Point, 2001), 160.

30. Elaine Scarry, *Dreaming by the Book* (New York: Farrar, Straus and Giroux, 1999), 53. Scarry explains that "the imaginability of the flower can in part be attributed to its size, which lets it sit in the realm in front of our faces and migrate into the interior of what Aristotle called 'our large moist brains.' It can in part be attributed to the flower's cuplike shape, breaking over the curve of our eyes, whether in actual acts of seeing or in mimetic seeing. A third feature is its intense localization. . . . If one closes one's eyes and pictures, say, a landscape that encompasses the imaginative equivalent of our visual field, it is very hard to fill in its entirety with concentrated colors and surfaces. If, instead, one imagines the face of a flower . . . the concentration of color and surface comes into reach."

31. This is particularly striking in comparison to Coleridge's other poems as well as in his notebooks, the imaginative workings of which are richly considered in John Felstiner's chapter on Coleridge in John Felstiner, *Can Poetry Save the Earth?: A Field Guide to Nature Poems* (New Haven: Yale University Press, 2009), 39–45.

32. Wallace Stevens, *Collected Poetry and Prose* (New York: Library of America, 1997), 919.

33. Stevens, "The Noble Rider and the Sound of Words," in Stevens, 644.

34. Speaking about the experience of the figure post-imaginative-lapse, Stevens explained that, "While we are moved by it, we are moved as observers. We recognize it perfectly. We do not realize it. We understand the feeling of it, the robust feeling, clearly and fluently communicated. Yet we understand it rather than participating in it" (645).

35. Stevens, 644.

36. Stevens.

37. "The poet makes silk dresses out of worms" ("Adagia," Stevens, 900).

38. Stevens, 903.
39. Stevens, 914.
40. Stevens, 909.
41. John Burnside, "The Fair Chase," in John Burnside, *Black Cat Bone* (London: Cape Poetry, 2011), 1–13, 1.
42. Burnside, 3.
43. Burnside.
44. Burnside, 6.
45. Burnside, 4.
46. Burnside, 6.
47. Burnside, 9.

6. Modes of Intransitive Attention

1. Mirabai, "*bhaja mana charana kamval,*" in *For Love of the Dark One: Songs of Mirabai,* trans. Andrew Schelling (Boston: Shambhala, 1993), 9.
2. Shakespeare, *Macbeth,* ed. Stephen Orgel (New York: Penguin, 2000), 1.5.30–33.
3. See Warren F. Motte, ed. *Oulipo: A Primer of Potential Literature,* trans. Warren F. Motte (Normal, IL: Dalkey Archive, 1998).
4. I consider these dynamics in more depth in my reading of Joan Retallack in the chapter on idleness.
5. Emily Dickinson, *The Poems of Emily Dickinson* (Cambridge, MA: Belknap Press of Harvard University Press, 1999), 215.
6. Anne Carson, "Decreation: How Women Like Sappho, Simone Weil, and Marguerite Porete Tell God," *Common Knowledge* 8, no. 1 (2002): 190.
7. Carson, 191.
8. Robert Pogue Harrison, *Gardens: An Essay on the Human Condition* (Chicago: University of Chicago Press, 2008), 115.
9. Jonathan Crary has offered a strong account of the dominance of vision and visibility in modern art and culture in *Techniques of the Observer: On Vision and Modernity in the Nineteenth Century* (Cambridge, MA: MIT Press, 1990).

7. Vigilance

1. For an in-depth discussion of vigilance as a mode of "antinatural" or intentionally cultivated mode of attention and a positioning of this mode within both phenomenology and cognitive science, see Natalie Depraz, *Attention et vigilance: À la croisée de la phénoménologie et des sciences cognitives* (Paris: Presses Universitaires de France, 2014).
2. A number of psychological studies have found this state of prolonged alert to be particularly sapping for attentional resources, triggering a higher output of cortisol or stress response. See Joel S. Warm, Raja Parasuraman, and Gerald Matthews, "Vigilance Requires Hard Mental Work and Is Stressful," *Human Factors* 50 (June 2008): 433–41.

Vigilance has been the subject of systematic research since Norman Mackworth's study of sonar and radar operators during World War II. His 1948 study examined the operators' vigilance decrement, or the breakdown of vigilant attention over time. H. N. Mackworth, "The Breakdown of Vigilance During Prolonged Visual Search," *Quarterly Journal of Experimental Psychology* 1 (1948): 6–21.
3. Simone Weil, *Waiting for God*, trans. Emma Craufurd (New York: HarperCollins, 2009; *Attente de Dieu* (Paris: Fayard, 1966), 62.
4. Maurice Blanchot, *The Infinite Conversation*, trans. Susan Hanson (Minneapolis: University of Minnesota Press, 1993), 121. On the play of vigilance in Blachot's writings, see Lars Iyers, *Blanchot's Vigilance: Literature, Phenomenology, and the Ethical* (London: Palgrave Macmillan, 2005).
5. Blanchot, 121.
6. Françoise Meltzer, "The Hands of Simone Weil," *Critical Inquiry* 27, no. 4 (Summer 2001): 611–29.
7. Simone Weil, "Attention and Will," trans. Richard Rees, in *Simone Weil: An Anthology*, ed. Siân Miles (New York, 1986), 213.
8. Simone Weil, *Gravity and Grace*, trans. Arthur Wills (Lincoln: University of Nebraska Press, 1997), 10.
9. Simone Weil, *The Notebooks of Simone Weil*, trans. Arthur Wills (London: Routledge, 2004 [1956]), 130.
10. See David Marno, *Death Be Not Proud: The Art of Holy Attention* (Chicago: University of Chicago Press, 2016), 1–2. As noted in my chapter on contemplation, because imperfect (desirous and distractable) human beings are incapable of perfect attention to God, Marno proposes that attention serves for both thinkers as a "regulative ideal"—prayer then becomes spiritual exercise toward an impossible vanishing point, grace.
11. I draw both the original poem and, except where noted, the translation from Friedrich Hölderlin, *Poems and Fragments: English and German Edition*, trans. Michael Hamburger (London: Carcanet, 2004), 462–67.
12. Maurice Blanchot, *The Infinite Conversation*, trans. Susan Hanson (Minneapolis: University of Minnesota Press, 1993), 39.
13. "A great destiny ponders, / made ready, on the residual site" (Hölderlin, *Poems and Fragments*, 459).
14. Blanchot, *The Infinite Conversation*, 40.
15. Blanchot, 38–39.
16. William S. Allen, *Ellipsis: Of Poetry and the Experience of Language After Heidegger, Hölderlin, and Blanchot* (Albany: State University of New York Press, 2012).
17. See Steve McCaffery, *Prior to Meaning: The Protosemantic and Poetics* (Evanston, IL: Northwestern University Press, 2001); and Julia Kristeva, *Revolution in Poetic Language*, trans. Margaret Waller (New York: Columbia University Press, 1984).
18. Hölderlin, *Poems and Fragments*, 318–29.
19. Hölderlin, 318/319 (translation modified).
20. Hölderlin, 320/321 (translation modified).
21. The seminal work on this concept is Karl Heinz Bohrer, *Plötzlichkeit: Zum Augenblick Des Ästhetischen Scheins* (Frankfurt: Suhrkamp, 1981), translated as Karl Heinz Bohrer,

Suddenness: On the Moment of Aesthetic Appearance, trans. Ruth Crowley (New York: Columbia University Press, 1994). For perspectives on suddenness, moments, and temporal disruption in the modern context, see Heidrun Friese, ed., *The Moment: Time and Rupture in Modern Thought* (Liverpool: Liverpool University Press, 2001).
22. Hölderlin, *Poems and Fragments,* 320/321 (translation modified).
23. For my discussion of the Angel of History, see chapter 3 in part 1.
24. Writing about the proliferation of contradictions in Mallarmé's poetry, Blanchot emphasizes the lack of resolution or synthesis: "If I speak of contradictions, it is to better experience their necessity. . . . Contradictions without conciliation: it is not a question of dialectics." Maurice Blanchot, "Enigma," *Yale French Studies* 79 (1991): 8–10.
25. Stéphane Mallarmé, "Crise de vers," in *Igitur; Divagations; Un Coup De Dés* (Paris: Gallimard, 2003), 241. Translation from *Divagations,* trans. Barbara Johnson (Cambridge, MA: Harvard University Press, 2007), 205.
26. "Monument en ce désert, avec le silence loin; dans une crypte, la divinité ainsi d'une majestueuse idée inconsciente" / "A monument in the desert, surrounded by silence; in a crypt, the divinity of a majestic unconscious idea." Mallarmé, 241/202.
27. Mallarmé, 249/208.
28. Mallarmé, 241/202.
29. Blanchot, "Enigma," 9.
30. Henry Weinfield evokes this as, "With nothing else for speech / than . . ." in his translation of Mallarmé's *Collected Poems: A Bilingual Edition,* trans. Henry Weinfield (Berkeley: University of California Press, 1994), 49.
31. Building on his work in *Unfolding Mallarmé: The Development of a Poetic Art* (Oxford: Oxford University Press, 1997), Roger Pearson has written an astonishingly lucid analysis of Mallarméan circumstance and abyssal contingencies in *Mallarmé and Circumstance: The Translation of Silence* (Oxford: Oxford University Press, 2004).
32. Weinfield's translation reads: "Though it be / the / Abyss" (Mallarmé, *Collected Poems,* 129).
33. "Le Mystère dans les Lettres" (Mallarmé, 278/234–235).
34. Mallarmé, 242/203.
35. "Crise de vers" (Mallarmé, 251/210). On the same page we find: "À quoi bon la merveille de transposer un fait de nature en sa presque disparition vibratoire selon le jeu de la parole, cependant; si ce n'est pour qu'en émane, sans la gêne d'un proche ou concret appel, la notion pure" ("What good is the marvel of transposing a fact of nature into its vibratory near disappearance according to the play of language, however: if it is not, in the absence of the cumbersomeness of a near or concrete reminder, the pure notion").
36. Translated as "keeping vigil / doubting / rolling / shining and meditating" (Mallarmé, *Collected Poems,* 144/145).

8. Resignation

1. J. Hillis Miller, "Wallace Stevens' Poetry of Being," *ELH* 31 (1964): 92. An expanded version of this essay forms the chapter "Wallace Stevens" in J. Hillis Miller, *Poets of*

Reality: Six Twentieth-Century Writers (Cambridge: Belknap Press of Harvard University Press, 1965). Stevens continues: "we return / To a plain sense of things," and "it is as if / We had come to an end of imagination." Wallace Stevens, *Collected Poetry and Prose* (New York: Library of America, 1997), 502.

2. T. S. Eliot, *The Waste Land: Authoritative Text, Contexts, Criticism* (New York: Norton, 2001), 5, lines 19–26.
3. Wallace Stevens, *The Collected Poems of Wallace Stevens* (New York: Knopf, 1954), 487.
4. Paul Celan, "Was Geschah?" in *Selected Poems and Prose of Paul Celan*, trans. John Felstiner (New York: Norton, 2000), 186.
5. Stevens experienced this not so much as death, but as the chilly realization that god had never been there at all, that man had always been alone in a world of objects: "The death of one god is the death of all" (*The Collected Poems of Wallace Stevens*, 381).
6. As elsewhere, I use this term to denote the Kantian meaning in the context of aesthetic contemplation, not in the sense of indifference.
7. Northrop Frye came perhaps the closest to identifying modernism's resignative turn in locating the roots of modernism in the paradigm shift from "the nominal world of Fichte" to the "sinister world-as-will of Schopenhauer"—a shift in which "Romanticism's drunken boat is tossed from ecstasy to ironic despair." Northrop Frye, foreword to "Romanticism Reconsidered," in *Northrop Frye's Writings on the Eighteenth and Nineteenth Centuries* (Toronto: University of Toronto Press, 2005), 74. It is then not surprising that, elaborating on Frye's account, Alan Grob identifies "the first and perhaps the fullest exposition" of this paradigm shift in Matthew Arnold's "Resignation" (1909), which he sees as the "only substantial poem of the age to express truly this special and indispensable moment in that intellectual process Arnold knew to be 'the main line of modern development.'" Alan Grob, "The Poetry of Pessimism: Arnold's 'Resignation,'" *Victorian Poetry* 26 (Spring/Summer 1988): 25–26.
8. Writing on Brecht's *Hollywood Songbook*, Stathis Gourgouris has described a lyricism shorn of conventional sentimental expression, producing a quality of alienation from the lyrical tradition itself. See Stathis Gourgouris, "The Lyric in Exile (Meditations on the Hollywooder Liederbuch)," *Qui Parle* 14 (Spring/Summer 2004): 145–75.

See Susan Sontag, "Notes on 'Camp,'" *Partisan Review* 31 (Fall 1964): 515–30.

Vattimo makes an etymological link between postmodern *Verwindung* and the act of resignation, pointing out that the lexical root suggests two dimensions: "that of convalescence ('*eine Krankheit verwinden*' means to cure or heal, to recover from an illness) and that of distortion (tied secondarily to *winden*, to wind or twist) and 'deviating alteration,' one of the meanings of the prefix *ver-*. 'Resignation' is also tied to the connotation of convalescence; one overcomes, recovers from, gets over (*verwindet*) not only an illness but also a loss or a defeat, sorrow or pain . . . [metaphysics] is something one retains within oneself, like the traces of an illness or a sorrow to which one is resigned. One might say . . .'de la métaphysique on se remet' (one recovers from metaphysics); 'à la métaphysique on se remet' (one entrusts oneself to metaphysics as to a destiny, one resigns oneself to it) . . . a suggestion of distortion persists which, moreover, can also be found in the notion of convalescence/resignation." Gianni Vattimo, "'Verwindung': Nihilism and the Postmodern in Philosophy," *SubStance* 16, no. 2 (1987): 7–17, 11–12.

9. Svetlana Boym has recited some for us: "end of history, end of art, end of literary theory . . . (Fukuyama 1992, Danto 1997, Tihanov 2004)." Svetlana Boym, "Poetics and Politics of Estrangement: Victor Shklovsky and Hannah Arendt," *Poetics Today* 26, no. 4 (2005): 581.
10. Jameson reframes Heidegger's understanding of the "drift" of "world" and "earth" in modernity in the materialist terms of "history/society" and "nature/matter." Whereas Heidegger had argued that the vocation of the artwork is to disclose this rift and allow us to witness it, Jameson thinks there is no longer a vantage available to us from which such a witnessing could occur. See Fredric Jameson, "Baudelaire as Modernist and Postmodernist: The Dissolution of the Referent and the Artificial Sublime," in *The Modernist Papers* (London: Verso, 2007): 223–37, 225–27.
11. Gourgouris, 379.
12. Brian Crews, "Martin Amis and the Postmodern Grotesque," *Modern Language Review* (2010): 659.
13. Philippe Lacoue-Labarthe, "Poetry as Experience: Two Poems by Paul Celan," in Virginia Jackson and Yopi Prins, ed., *The Lyric Theory Reader: A Critical Anthology* (Baltimore: Johns Hopkins University Press, 2014): 399–417, 409.
14. Lacoue-Labarthe, 412.
15. While *Une Saison* is considered Rimbaud's official "adieu" to poetry writing, some of the poems in *Les Illuminations* are thought to have been written after its publication, during Rimbaud's London years after the break with Verlaine. The manuscript of *Les Illuminations* was handed off by Rimbaud to Verlaine during their last meeting in Stuttgart, before Rimbaud's departure for Africa.
16. Ross Posnock includes a discussion of Rimbaud's work and resignation from poetry in his sweeping and deeply thoughtful volume, *Renunciation: Acts of Abandonment By Writers, Philosophers, and Artists* (Cambridge, MA: Harvard University Press, 2016). As spiritual, psychological, and aesthetic act, renunciation and resignation can be seen to share a number of common themes, tensions, and significances.
17. Arthur Rimbaud, *Rimbaud: Complete Works, Selected Letters—a Bilingual Edition,* trans. Wallace Fowlie (Chicago: University of Chicago Press, 2005), 276: "Why! the clock of life stopped just now. I am no longer in the world" (277).
18. Rimbaud, 277. "Decidedly we are out of the world. No more sound. My touch has gone. Ah! my castle, my Saxony, my willow grove. The evenings, mornings, nights, days. How tired I am!" (277).
19. Rimbaud, 296: "—I was right to despise those fellows who never lost the chance of caress . . . I was right in my scorn since I am escaping! / I am escaping!" (297).
20. Rimbaud, 300: "My life is worn out" (301).
21. Rimbaud, 278: "I am dying of weariness. It is the tomb. I am going to the worms, horror of horrors! Satan, joker, you are trying to dissolve me with your charms. I object. I object! Give me a poke with your pitchfork! A drop of fire" (279).
22. Rimbaud, 288–89: "If I have any taste, it is for hardly /Anything but earth and stones. / I always feed on air, / Rock, coal, and iron. // My hungers, turn about. Graze, hungers, / On the meadow of bran. / Suck the bright poison / Of the bindweed. // Eat the rocks that are broken, / The old stones of churches; / The pebbles of old floods, / Bread scattered in gray alleys."

23. Rimbaud, 296: "Is there not real torture in the fact that, since the declaration of science, and Christianity, man deludes himself, proving obvious truth, puffing up with the pleasure of repeating his proofs, and living only in this way."
24. Rimbaud, 296: "A subtle, ridiculous torture; source of my spiritual meanderings. Nature might be bored, perhaps!"
25. Rimbaud, 298: "Isn't it because we cultivate fog? We eat fever with our watery vegetables. And drunkenness! and tobacco! and ignorance! and devotedness!"
26. Rimbaud, 292: "Morality is a weakness of the brain."
27. Rimbaud, 198: "—But I see my spirit is sleeping. / If it were always wide awake from this moment on, we would soon reach truth, who perhaps surrounds us with her weeping angels! . . . If it had been awake until this moment, I would not have given in to my deleterious instincts at an immemorial time! . . . —If it had always been awake, I would be sailing in full wisdom!"
28. Rimbaud, 302/303: "Autumn. Our boat, in the motionless mist, turns toward the harbor of wretchedness, the huge city under a sky stained with fire and mud. [. . .] We must be absolutely modern. / No hymns. I must hold what has been gained. Hard night! The dried blood smokes on my face, and I have nothing behind me except that horrible tree!"
29. Rimbaud, 326/327: "I am an ephemeral and not-too-discontented citizen of a metropolis obviously modern because every known taste has been avoided in the furnishing and in the outsides of the houses as well as in the layout of the city. Here you would not discover the least sign of any monument of superstition. In short, morals and speech are reduced to their simplest expression."
30. Rimbaud, "Solde," in Rimbaud, *Rimbaud: Complete Works*, 356.
31. Georges Bataille, *L'Expérience intérieure* (Paris: Gallimard, 1943), 82; Georges Bataille, *Inner Experience,* trans. Leslie Anne Boldt (Albany: State University of New York Press, 1988), 50.
32. Bataille, 82/50.
33. Bataille, 33/15.
34. Bataille, 77. "The imitation of Jesus:. . . we must imitate in God (Jesus) the fall from grace, the agony, the moment of 'non-knowledge' of the 'lama sabachtani'; drunk to the lees, Christianity is absence of salvation, the despair of God" (*Inner Experience,* 47).
35. Rimbaud, "Enfance," in *Rimbaud: Complete Works,* 310. "The boredom of saying 'dear body,' 'dear heart'" (311).
36. Rimbaud, 320. "Seen enough. The vision met itself in every kind of air. / Had enough. Noises of cities in the evening, in the sunlight, and forever. / Known enough. The haltings of life.—Oh! Noises and visions! / Departure into new affection and sound?" (321).
37. Rimbaud, 312. "The pathways are rough. The slopes are covered with broom. The air is still. How far away are the birds and the springs of water! This must be the end of the world, lying ahead" (313).
38. Rimbaud, 320. "It all began with feelings of disgust and it ended—since I could not seize its eternity on the spot—it ended with a riot of perfumes" ("Morning of Drunkenness," 321).
39. Rimbaud, 377, from a letter to Paul Demeny, Charleville, May 15, 1871.
40. Rimbaud, 379.

41. Bataille, *L'Expérience intérieure/Inner Experience*, 29/13.
42. "[Il] est vrai que les mots, leur dédales, l'immensité épuisante de leurs possibles, enfin leur traîtrise, ont quelque chose des sables mouvants" (Bataille, 31).
43. For a concise description of objectless contemplation and the cultivation of "bare attention," see Thera Nyanaponika, *The Heart of Buddhist Meditation: The Buddha's Way of Mindfulness* (San Francisco: Weiser, 2014), chapter 2, 30–45.
44. Bataille, *L'Expérience Intérieure/Inner Experience* 31–32/14.
45. Bataille, 79.
46. Interestingly, the words *meditation* and *meditative* run almost reflexively through the abundant criticism on Wright's work, yet, to my knowledge, nowhere do we find an account of what exactly meditation means, how it functions in Wright's poetry, or why it seems to be the intuitive mot juste for both form and subject matter. See, for example, Langdon Hammer, "The Latches of Paradise: Charles Wright's Meditations and Memories at Year's End," *American Scholar* 74 (Autumn 2005): 73–74; Helen Vendler on "the realm of meditation which Wright has made his own" in her review of *Zone Journals*, "'Travels in Time' (1988)," in Adam Gianelli, ed., *High Lonesome: On the Poetry of Charles Wright* (Oberlin, OH: Oberlin College Press, 2006), 29–35, 33; Carol Muske-Dukes, "Guided by Dark Stars," review of *Black Zodiac*, in the *New York Times Book Review*, August 31, 1997, 11–12, reprinted in Giannelli, 83–86; James Longenbach, "From 'Earned Weight' (1995)," in Gianelli, 79–82, 81; and David Baker, "From 'On Restraint' (1996)," in Gianelli, 76–87, 76.
47. Charles Wright, "Stray Paragraphs in April, Year of the Rat," in *Negative Blue: Selected Later Poems* (New York: Farrar, Straus and Giroux, 2000), 146.
48. Mark Jarman, "The Pragmatic Imagination and the Secret of Poetry," *Gettysburg Review* 1, no. 4 (1988). Reprinted in Gianelli, *High Lonesome*, 25–28, 27.
49. Charles Wright, "Apologia Pro Vita Sua," in Wright, *Negative Blue*, 72.
50. Charles Wright, "Tennessee Line," in Wright, *Negative Blue*, 17.
51. Charles Wright, "Easter 1989," Wright's stubbornly antiglory response to Yeats (Wright, *Negative Blue*, 8–9).
52. Wright, *Negative Blue*, 9.
53. Wright, *Negative Blue*, 3.
54. Wright, *Halflife: Improvisations and Interviews, 1977–87* (Ann Arbor: University of Michigan Press, 1988), 83.
55. Wright, *Halflife*, 108.
56. Skip James, "Hard Times Killing Floor Blues," Paramount Records, 1931; *"I'm So Glad": The Complete 1931 Paramount Recordings*, Document Records, 1990.
57. Wright sees the dropped line as a way of introducing space into the poem: "Using the dropped line, the 'low rider,' you are able to use both sides of the page, use both left- and right-hand margins, and you can carry the long line on as an imagistic line rather than a rhetorical or discursive line." Charles Wright, *Halflife*, 33.
58. Wright, *Halflife*, 85.
59. "Like Mallarmé (more or less), I want to hang in the center of myself like a sacred spider, radiating out, axle by silken axle, then encircling it with a glittering wheel" (Wright, *Halflife*, 29.)

60. Consider these lines and titles from poems spanning the later volumes *Chickamauga, Black Zodiac, Appalachia,* and *North American Bear,* gathered in *Negative Blue: Selected Later Poems* (New York: Farrar, Straus and Giroux, 2000): "Those two dark syllables, *begin /* offer no sustenance" (41): "Thinking of Winter at the Beginning of Summer" (116); "High / Spring light through new green, / a language, it seems, I have forgotten" (179); "Spring like smoke in the fruit trees" (30); "Summer's crepuscular, rot and wrack, / Rain-ravaged, root-ruined" (33).
61. Wright, *Halflife,* 93.
62. Wright, "Sitting Outside at the End of Autumn," in *Negative Blue,* 3.
63. Wright, *Negative Blue,* 4.
64. Wright, *Halflife,* 37. He develops this "ongoing argument" more fully in a 1985 interview with Elizabeth McBride, speaking about poetry as a substitution, an act of prayer, in the absence of or as substitution for religious belief: "I play with words and try to use them as little prayer wheels, as little wafers. . . . Yes, they are sacraments. Poems are sacred texts" (129). Wright sees the idea of god in patterns and connections in the world: "I don't think He exists other than in a harmony, the geometry and physics of whatever it is that holds the universe together." (109).
65. Langdon Hammer has insightfully compared Wright's "almanac" meditations in "Appalachian Autumn," to Stevens's "Auroras of Autumn" in "The Latches of Paradise," 74.
66. Wright, "Interview at Oberlin College, 1977," in *Halflife,* 83.
67. Charles Wright, "Night Journal," in Charles Wright, *The World of the Ten Thousand Things: Poems, 1980–1990* (New York: Farrar, Straus and Giroux, 1990), 149.
68. Wright, *Negative Blue,* 4. "Poetry is just the shadow of the dog. . . . The dog is elsewhere, and constantly on the move," Wright, *Halflife,* 5.
69. Wright, *Halflife,* 82.
70. Charles Wright, "Miles Davis and Elizabeth Bishop Fake the Break," in Wright, *Negative Blue,* 41.
71. Charles Wright, "Disjecta Membra," in *Negative Blue,* 133.
72. Wright, *Negative Blue,* 131.
73. Wallace Stevens wrote that "the major poetic idea in the world is and has always been the idea of God—The figures of the essential poets should be spiritual figures"—quoted by Wright in the commonplace book (29). In interviews, Wright lists three things as the central questions in his poetry: language, landscape, and the idea of God.
74. Wright, *Halflife,* 38.
75. Wright, *Halflife,* 35.
76. Wright, "Disjecta Membra," 130.
77. Vendler, "Travels in Time," 30.
78. James McCorcle, "Things That Lock Our Wrists to the Past," in Gianelli, *High Lonesome,* 180–81.
79. Wright, *Halflife,* 128.
80. Charles Wright, "A Journal of English Days," in Wright, *The World of the Ten Thousand Things,* 131.

81. Wright, *Halflife*, 128–29. Wright's "angels" here include "the ghost of Thomas Hardy and Hart Crane, . . . Emily Dickinson and Arthur Rimbaud." Charles Wright, "A Journal of the Year of the Ox," in Wright, *The World of the Ten Thousand Things*, 176.

9. Idleness

Epigraph: Robert Hass, "Measure," in *The Apple Trees at Olema* (New York: HarperCollins, 2010), p. 64.

1. Brian O'Connor has written thoughtfully on the interplay of idleness and boredom in chapter 3 of *Idleness: A Philosophical Essay* (Princeton: Princeton University Press, 2018), 100–34.
2. See Andrew C. Papanicolaou, "The Default Mode and Other Resting State Networks," in *The Oxford Handbook of Functional Brain Imaging in Neuropsychology and Cognitive Neurosciences*, ed. Andrew C. Papanicolaou (Oxford: Oxford University Press, 2017); and Dennis Ramirez, *Default Mode Network (DMN): Structural Connectivity, Impairments, and Role in Daily Activities*, Neuroscience Research Progress Series (Hauppauge, NY: Nova Biomedical, 2015).
3. Lutz P. Koepnick, *On Slowness: Toward an Aesthetic of the Contemporary* (New York: Columbia University Press, 2014). For an earlier formulation of Koepnick's thinking on aesthetic attention in the context of windows and frames in German television and film, see *Framing Attention: Windows on Modern German Culture* (Baltimore: Johns Hopkins University Press, 2007). For a discussion of ambient attention in contemporary life, see McCullough, *Ambient Commons: Attention in the Age of Embodied Information*.
4. For cross-disciplinary perspectives on the terminological history of boredom in all its forms, see Ian Irvine, "Acedia, Tristitia and Sloth: Early Christian Forerunners to Chronic Ennui," *Humanitas* 12, no. 1 (Spring 1999): 89–103; Peter Toohey, "Some Ancient Forms of Boredom," *Illinois Classical Studies* 13 (Spring 1988): 151–64; Toohey, *Melancholy, Love, and Time: Boundaries of the Self in Ancient Literature* (Ann Arbor: University of Michigan Press, 2004); Michael L. Raposa, *Boredom and the Religious Imagination* (Charlottesville: University of Virginia Press, 1999); Raposa, "Boredom and the Religious Imagination," *Journal of the American Academy of Religion* 53 (March 1985): 75–91; and John P. Sisk, "The End of Boredom," *Georgia Review* 39 (Spring 1985): 25–34.
5. Latin text from D. F. S. Thomson, ed., *Catullus* (Toronto: University of Toronto Press, 1997), p. 130.
6. Monika Fludernik and Miriam Nandi have edited an excellent volume of scholarly perspectives on idleness in English literature from a variety of historical periods, late medieval to contemporary, *Idleness, Indolence, and Leisure in English Literature* (Basingstoke: Palgrave Macmillan, 2014).
7. Looking ahead into these developments' profound impact on twentieth- and twenty-first-century values, Bertrand Russell wrote, "I think that there is far too much work done in the world, that immense harm is caused by the belief that work is virtuous."

Bertrand Russell, *In Praise of Idleness: And Other Essays* (London and New York: Routledge, 2004), 1.

8. For two theological perspectives on acedia in the contemporary context, see Jean-Charles Nault, *The Noonday Devil: Acedia, the Unnamed Evil of Our Times*, trans. Michael J. Miller (San Francisco: Ignatius, 2015), originally published as Jean-Charles Nault, *Le Démon de midi—l'acédie, mal obscur de notre temps* (Dijon: L'Échelle de Jacob, 2013); and R. J. Snell, *Acedia and Its Discontents: Metaphysical Boredom in an Empire of Desire* (Kettering, OH: Angelico, 2015). Theologian Tim Lilburn includes a discussion of acedia in the context of a meditation on ascesis, eros, and epektasis in *Living in the World as If It Were Home: Essays* (Dunvegan: Cormorant, 1999), 64–65.
9. For a rich case study in how this last effect plays out in the context of Beckett, see Joshua Landy, *How to Do Things with Fictions* (Oxford: Oxford University Press, 2012), 124–44.
10. Stephen Arata, "On Not Paying Attention," *Victorian Studies* 46 (Winter 2004): 193–205, 193.
11. I have made this distinction in previous chapters—especially concerning the poetries of imagination and resignation—but it bears repeating because of the temptation of equating poems' subject matter with their underlying attentional form.
12. The political value of idleness is in its resistance to instrumentalization and "productivity," where productivity is driven, as it has been increasingly in the modern period, by market value, the time-is-money philosophy of capitalism. "Laziness," for Bernstein, "is a kind of stubbornness—at one's own pace, my own measure, and not doing anything, just doing. . . . Instrumentality in contrast is labor done to produce a product, the means for an end." Charles Bernstein, "Thought's Measure," in Charles Bernstein, *Content's Dream* (Evanston, IL: Northwestern University Press, 1986), 84, 83.
13. Bernstein, 84.
14. John Ashbery, introduction to *The Collected Poems of Frank O'Hara,* ed. Donald Allen (Berkeley: University of California Press, 1995), viii.
15. Ashbery, ix.
16. Simone Weil writes, "Friendship cannot be separated from reality any more than the beautiful. It is a miracle, like the beautiful. And the miracle consists simply in the fact that it *exists*." Simone Weil, *Gravity and Grace,* trans. Emma Crawford and Mario von der Ruhr (London: Routledge Classics, 2002 [1952]), 67.
17. O'Hara, *The Collected Poems of Frank O'Hara*, 135–36.
18. Srikanth Reddy, *Changing Subjects: Digressions in Modern American Poetry* (Oxford: Oxford University Press, 2012), 114, 109.
19. Reddy, 111.
20. Perloff, *Unoriginal Genius.*
21. For two compelling accounts of the roots of "cool" in American arts and idiom, see Joel Dinerstein, *The Origins of Cool in Postwar America* (Chicago: University of Chicago, 2017); and Peter Stearns, *American Cool: Constructing a Twentieth-Century Emotional Style* (New York: New York University Press, 1994).
22. A. R. Ammons, *Bosh and Flapdoodle: Poems* (New York: Norton, 2005), 13.
23. Ammons. 13.

24. Patricia Parker has written insightfully on circulation, movement, and flow in Ammons's work in her essay "Configurations of Shape and Flow," *diacritics* 3 (Winter 1973): 25–33.
25. A. R. Ammons, *Briefings: Poems Small and Easy* (New York: Norton, 1971).
26. A. R. Ammons, *Collected Poems, 1951–1971* (New York: Norton, 1972), 219, 237, 222.
27. A. R. Ammons, *The Complete Poems of A. R. Ammons*, vol. 1, ed. Robert M. West (New York: Norton, 2017), 450. Originally published in *Briefings: Poems Small and Easy* (New York: Norton, 1971).
28. From "Fasting," in Ammons, *Bosh and Flapdoodle*. The thematic and formal centrality of walking in Ammons's poems has been widely acknowledged. Harold Bloom has written extensively on Ammons's place in the lineage of romantics like Wordsworth and transcendentalists like Emerson, Whitman, and Thoreau, for whom walking was a primary mode of contemplation. Harold Bloom, "The New Transcendentalism: The Visionary Strain in Merwin, Ashbery, and Ammons," *Chicago Review* 24 (Winter 1972): 25–43. Thomas Greene observes of the poem "Corsons Inlet" that, "as the naming of description turns into the naming of metaphor, the dunes the speaker is moving through become symbols of his mind's movements, so that he seems to be taking a walk through his own consciousness. The mind is mirroring not only as a receptive vehicle, but its activity of wandering follows rather the indeterminate shapes of the beach. . . . The walk through the dunes seems to lead to a kind of poetics or rudimentary epistemology, in which the mind has to settle for the temporary emergent shapes constantly reforming in the wind of consciousness." Thomas M. Greene, *Calling from Diffusion: Hermeneutics of the Promenade* (Northampton: Smith College Press, 2002), 7–8.
29. Bataille's description of meditative ecstasy in *Inner Experience* is useful here, for its emphasis on a dissolution, through the rhythms of the breath, of the subject-object distinction: "And above all *no more object*. Ecstasy is not love: love is possession for which the object is necessary, and at the same time possession of the subject, possessed by it. There is no longer subject-object, but a 'yawning gap' between the one and the other and, in the gap, the subject, the object are dissolved; there is passage, communication, but not from one to the other: *the one* to *the other* have lost their separate existence. The questions of the subject, its will to know are suppressed: the subject is no longer there, its interrogation no longer has either meaning or a principle which introduces it." Georges Bataille, *Inner Experience*, trans. Leslie Anne Boldt (Albany: State University of New York Press, 1988), 59–60.
30. One could also say "wonder," or in David Lehman's terms, "a triumph of wonderment," in his introduction to Ammons's *Selected Poems* (New York: Library of America, 2006), xvii. *Wonder*, as an out-of-self openness or awe before the world, captures Ammons's place in the lineage of Romanticism and the American transcendentalism of Emerson, Whitman, and Thoreau. Yet, in Ammons, *insight* is more apt, given the centrality of vision to his thinking and given the closeness of the kind of meditation his poems enact and the tradition of insight or Vipassana meditation, which Ammons encountered during the Vietnam War. Stephen Cushman has noted that the poem "Pray Without Ceasing" recalls a period in May of 1966 when at least ten monks soaked themselves in gasoline and set themselves on fire, burning to death in the lotus position. Stephen Cushman, "'Pray Without Ceasing' and the Postmodern Canon," in Steven P.

Schneider, ed., *Complexities of Motion: New Essays on A. R. Ammons's Long Poems* (Madison, NJ: Fairleigh Dickinson University Press, 1999), 263–64. Cushman notes that, while ripples and images of the war reached the poet, its distance lends anxiety to influence.

31. A. R. Ammons, *Tape for the Turn of the Year* (Ithaca, NY: Cornell University Press, 1965), 54–55.
32. A. R. Ammons, *Garbage* (New York: Norton, 1993).
33. Ammons, 3.
34. Ammons places a period once at the end of part 10 (68) and again after 11 (73) till it full-stops book's end, the flood nipped off at a seemingly arbitrary point that syntactically could have been a question: "if I reap the peripheries will I / get hardweed seed and dried roughage, roughage // like teasel and cattail and brush above snow in / winter, pure design lifeless in a painted hold" (121).
35. A. R. Ammons, "Gravelly Run," in *Corsons Inlet: A Book of Poems* (Ithaca, NY: Cornell University Press, 1965), 64.
36. Frederick Buell, "'To Be Quiet in the Hands of the Marvelous': The Poetry of A. R. Ammons," *Iowa Review* 8, no. 1 (Winter 1977): 67–68.
37. David Lehman, "God Is the Sense the World Makes Without God," *American Poetry Review* 35, no. 2 (May/June 2006): 19–21.
38. Ammons, *Garbage*, 67–68.
39. Harold Bloom, "A. R. Ammons: The Breaking of the Vessels," *Salmagundi* 31/32, 10th anniversary issue (Fall 1975–Winter 1976): 185–203.
40. J. T. Barbarese, "Theology for Atheists: Reading Ammons," *Journal of Modern Literature* 26, nos. 3/4 (Spring 2003): 73–83. Barbarese rightly points out that Ammons's meditative immersion in "stuff" yields a practice that suggests both romanticism and Greek and Roman visions of self-world unity: "Not just every day but at every moment in its 'thinning sheaf of days' consciousness is bridging the gap between the self and the abyss. . . . The result is a kind of natural theology for atheists, a stance toward phenomena that echoes the philosophical doubts of Greek skepticism but also leaves room for the more traditionally essentialist responses of post-Enlightenment poets" (78).
41. Parker, "Configurations of Shape and Flow," 27.
42. Marius Bewley, "Modes of Poetry," *Hudson Review* (1968/1969): 713.
43. Hyatt H. Waggoner, "Notes and Reflections," in Harold Bloom, ed., *A. R. Ammons* (New York: Chelsea House, 1986), 63–71, 70; Helen Vendler, *The Music of What Happens: Poems, Poets, Critics* (Cambridge, MA: Belknap Press of Harvard University Press, 1988), 338; Frank J. Lepkowski, "'How Are We to Find Holiness?': The Religious Vision of A. R. Ammons," *Twentieth Century Literature* 40 (Winter 1994): 477–98.
44. M. H. Abrams, *Natural Supernaturalism: Tradition and Revolution in Romantic Literature* (New York: Norton, 1973), 65. Robert Kirschten describes what he sees as Ammons's mythopoetic mode in his book, *Approaching Prayer: Ritual and the Shape of Myth in A. R. Ammons and James Dickey* (Baton Rouge: Louisiana State University Press, 1998).
45. Joan Qionglin Tan, *Han Shan, Chan Buddhism, and Gary Snyder's Ecopoetic Way* (Brighton: Sussex Academic, 2009), 69; Donald H. Reiman, "A. R. Ammons: Ecological Naturalism and the Romantic Tradition," *Twentieth Century Literature* 31 (Spring 1985):

22–54; Kevin McGuirk, "A. R. Ammons and the Whole Earth," *Cultural Critique* 37 (Autumn 1997): 131–58; John Felstiner, *Can Poetry Save the Earth?: A Field Guide to Nature Poems* (New Haven: Yale University Press, 2009), 294–300.
46. Buell, "'To Be Quiet in the Hands of the Marvelous,'" 71, 72.
47. In the yoga sutras of Patanjali, we find a useful distinction between three modes of attention relevant to Ammons's practice, as well as to the other intentional practices I've considered thus far. In *dharana*, imperfectly translated as "concentration," a single locus of attention (flame, breath, mantra) is isolated to the exclusion of other perceptual input. The process of whittling attention down to so singular a point, which is then not observed out of interest in the thing itself, but rather for the purpose of concentration itself, has two effects: the training of attention away from the narrative tangents of the mind's attachments and the opening up of space, or emptiness, through the process of evacuation. I have referred to this use of focal objects as indirect objects of attention. In *dhyana*, the subject enters more fully into a state of absorbed meditation in which the foothold of focalization (the indirect object of attention) is released and the attention is fully immersed in the perceptual present without any point of fixity. The first modality is most associated with beginning meditation instruction, and with Zen's highly structured focus toward emptiness, while the second is closer to what in Western adaptations is referred to as "mindfulness" or, in my nonspiritual attentional terms, nonselective receptivity. This is where we find Ammons practicing most often. *Samadhi* represents a final stage of intransitive awareness as attention moves deeper and beyond absorption toward an ultimate withdrawal from the senses wholesale, falling "out of mind," in the sense of releasing from the sensual attachments that demarcate the boundaries between things and between self and other. A classic explanation of these modes can be found in B. K. S. Iyengar, *Light on Yoga: Yoga Dipika* (New York: Schocken, 1979), 21–31, 48–53. See also Śāntideva, *The Bodhicaryāvatāra,* trans. Kate Crosby and Andrew Skilton (Oxford: Oxford University Press, 1995), 20–22, 30–33, and 75–87. Śāntideva notes that "the classic account of Buddhist meditation, common to Mahayana and non-Mahayana forms of Buddhism, enjoins a judicious balance of these two kinds of meditation. For western audiences, these instructions and modalities have been condensed, collapsed and translated into a set of relatively consistent basic instructions under the heading of 'mindfulness.'" See Nyanaponika, *The Heart of Buddhist Meditation: The Buddha's Way of Mindfulness*; Thich Nhat Hanh, *The Heart of the Buddha's Teaching* (New York: Broadway, 1999); Joseph Goldstein and Jack Kornfield, *Seeking the Heart of Wisdom: The Path of Insight Meditation* (Boston: Shambhala, 2001).
48. Retallack defines the essay form as an "urgent and aesthetically aware thought experiment." Joan Retallack, *The Poethical Wager* (Berkeley: University of California Press, 2003), 4.
49. Joan Retallack, *Errata 5uite* (Washington, DC: Edge, 1993).
50. *The Chicago Manual of Style*'s definition of the errata sheet underscores these material and poetic features nicely: "Errata, lists of errors and their corrections, may take the form of loose, inserted sheets or bound-in pages. An errata sheet is definitely not a usual part of a book. It should never be supplied to correct simple typographical errors (which may be rectified in a later printing) or to insert additions to, or revisions of, the printed text (which should wait for the next edition of the book). It is a device to be used only in

extreme cases where errors severe enough to cause misunderstanding are detected too late to correct in the normal way but before the finished book is distributed. Then the errors may be listed with their locations and their corrections on a sheet that is tipped in, either before or after the book is bound, or laid in loose, usually inside the front cover of the book. (Tipping and inserting must be done by hand, thus adding considerably to the cost of the book)." *The Chicago Manual of Style: The Essential Guide for Writers, Editors, and Publishers,* 14th ed. (Chicago: University of Chicago Press, 1993), 42, section 1.107.

51. Retallack, *The Poethical Wager,* 4.
52. Andrew Epstein discusses Retallack's poetics of attention, with reference to Cage and others, in *Attention Equals Life: The Pursuit of the Everyday in Contemporary Poetry and Culture* (Oxford: Oxford University Press, 2016), 66–69.
53. Walter Benjamin, *Origin of the German Trauerspiel,* trans. Howard Eiland (Cambridge, MA: Harvard University Press, 2019), 2–3.
54. For a rich account of the role of Buddhist thinking in Cage's life and work, see Kay Larson, *Where the Heart Beats: John Cage, Zen Buddhism, and the Inner Life of Artists* (New York: Penguin, 2012). Some of Cage's own written meditations on Zen Buddhism and the role of silence in his work can be found in John Cage, *Silence: Lectures and Writings* (Middletown, CT: Wesleyan University Press, 1961).
55. Retallack collaborated with Cage on the publication of a series of conversations that took place near the end of his life.
56. Christopher Shultis, "Silencing the Sounded Self: John Cage and the Intentionality of Nonintention," *Musical Quarterly* 79 (Summer 1995): 312–16. Shultis provides an insightful and nuanced analysis of how intentional nonintentionality functions in Cage's musical compositions and in Cage's theoretical work.

10. Boredom

1. See John Eastwood, Alexandra Frischen, Mark J. Fenske, and Daniel Smilek, "The Unengaged Mind: Defining Boredom in Terms of Attention," *Perspectives on Psychological Science* 7, no. 5 (September 2012): 482–95.
2. For example, see Erik Ringmar, "Attention and the Cause of Modern Boredom," in *Boredom Studies: Postdisciplinary Inquiries,* ed. Michael E. Gardiner and Julian Jason Haladyn (New York: Routledge, 2016).
3. Eastwood et al., "The Unengaged Mind."
4. Seneca, *Epistulaemorales* 24.26, in Peter Toohey, *Melancholy, Love, and Time: Boundaries of the Self in Ancient Literature* (Ann Arbor: University of Michigan Press, 2004), 120.
5. Martin Heidegger, *The Fundamental Concepts of Metaphysics: World, Finitude, Solitude,* trans. William McNeill and Nicholas Walker (Bloomington: Indiana University Press, 1995), 93.
6. Giorgio Agamben, *The Open: Man and Animal* (Stanford: Stanford University Press, 2004), 64.
7. Eastwood et al., "The Unengaged Mind," 482.

8. Rasmus Johnsen, "On Boredom: A Note on Experience Without Qualities," *Ephemera: Theory and Politics in Organization* 11, no. 4 (November 2011): 485.
9. Johnsen, 484–85.
10. Patricia Meyer Spacks, *Boredom: The Literary History of a State of Mind* (Chicago: University of Chicago Press, 1995), 163.
11. Elizabeth S. Goodstein, *Experience Without Qualities: Boredom and Modernity* (Stanford: Stanford University Press, 2004), 3. In a resonant literary-period analysis, Lee Anna Maynard addresses the role of boredom and idleness as a site of "feminine self-realization" in the Victorian novel: Lee Anna Maynard, *Beautiful Boredom: Idleness and Feminine Self-Realization in the Victorian Novel* (Jefferson, NC: McFarland, 2009).
12. Saikat Majumdar, *Prose of the World: Modernism and the Banality of Empire* (New York: Columbia University Press, 2013), 19.
13. Majumdar, 1–4.
14. Goodstein, *Experience Without Qualities*, 1.
15. Andrew Epstein, *Attention Equals Life: The Pursuit of the Everyday in Contemporary Poetry and Culture* (Oxford: Oxford University Press, 2016), 45.
16. Charles Simic, "To Boredom," *New Yorker*, December 10, 2007, accessed March 22, 2016, http://www.newyorker.com/magazine/2007/12/10/to-boredom.
17. Margaret Atwood, "Bored," *Atlantic Monthly* 274 (December 1994): 102.
18. See, in particular, "out of the mainstream," in Charles Bukowski, *Dangling in the Tournefortia* (Santa Barbara: Black Sparrow, 1981), 87–88.
19. Charles Bukowski, "the old big time," unpublished MS, 1982, https://bukowski net/manuscripts/displaymanuscript.php?show=poem1982-06-11-the_old_big_time.jpg.
20. Charles Bukowski, *Come On In!* (New York: Ecco, 2007), 94.
21. Charles Bukowski, *The Pleasures of the Damned: Poems, 1951–1993* (New York: Ecco, 2008), 261.
22. Bukowski, 82–83.
23. Bukowski, 334–35.
24. Bukowski, 112.
25. Derek Henderson, "The Terrible Boredom of Paradise," accessed March 24, 2016, http://www.derekhenderson.net/tbop.html.
26. Lars Svendsen, *A Philosophy of Boredom* (London: Reaktion, 2005), 138.
27. Friedrich von Schlegel, *Friedrich Schlegel's Lucinde and the Fragments,* trans. Peter Firchow (Minneapolis: University of Minnesota Press, 1971), 66. Just prior to this quotation, Schlegel observes that "the more divine a man or a work of man is, the more it resembles a plant; of all the forms of nature, this form is the most moral and the most beautiful." This connection of divine form to the forms of plant life adds an interesting hinge in Schlegel's thinking on boredom and idleness: the first is a result of the human's striving for a perfection that is outside of or separated from the natural. The second, which Schlegel encourages, is a mode that Firchow describes, in his introduction, as "passive and purposeless" (26).
28. Blaise Pascal, *Pensées,* trans. A. J. Krailsheimer (London: Penguin, 1995), 137, 42.
29. Schopenhauer's most extensive discussion of the cyclical dynamics of boredom and desire can be found in Arthur Schopenhauer, *Parerga and Paralipomena: Short Philosophical*

Essays, ed. and trans. Sabine Roehr and Christopher Janaway (Cambridge: Cambridge University Press, 2014).
30. Immanuel Kant, *Immanuel Kant: Gesammelte Schriften (Akademie-Ausgabe), i–xxiii. Band 9. Logik. Physische Geographie, Pädagogik* (Charlottesville, VA: InteLex, 1999), 471. Cf. Svendsen 138. For an in-depth discussion of the relationship between perfect beauty and boredom in Kant, particularly as it pertains to the concept of the good, see Rachel Zuckert, "Boring Beauty and Universal Morality: Kant on the Ideal of Beauty," *Inquiry* 48, no. 2 (2005): 107–30.
31. Søren Kierkegaard, *Either/Or,* trans. Howard V. Hong and Edna H. Hong (Princeton: Princeton University Press, 1987), 286.
32. Svendsen, *A Philosophy of Boredom,* 138.
33. Alexis de Tocqueville, *Democracy in America* (New York: Knopf, 1945), 147; cf. Svendsen, 138.
34. Novalis, "Das allgemeine Brouillon," in *Werke, Tagebücher und Briefe Friedrich von Hardenbergs,* vol. 2 (Munich: C. Hanser, 1978), 676.
35. See, for example, Deborah Landau, "'How to Live. What to Do': The Poetics and Politics of Aids," *American Literature* 68 (Spring 1996): 193–225; Tyler B. Hoffman, "Representing Aids: Thom Gunn and the Modalities of Verse," *South Atlantic Review* 65 (Spring 2000): 13–39; and Colin Gillis, "Rethinking Sexuality in Thom Gunn's *The Man with Night Sweats,*" *Contemporary Literature* 50 (Spring 2009): 156–82.
36. David Orr, "Too Close to Touch: Thom Gunn's Selected Poems," *New York Times Book Review,* July 10, 2009, accessed March 22, 2016, http://www.nytimes.com/2009/07/12/books/review/Orr-t.html?_r=0.
37. Robert Potts, "Moving Voice," *Guardian,* September 26, 2003, accessed March 22, 2016, http://www.theguardian.com/books/2003/sep/27/featuresreviews.guardianreview13.
38. Thom Gunn, *Collected Poems* (New York: Farrar, Straus and Giroux, 1994), 6.
39. Gunn, 11.
40. Gunn, 14.
41. Gunn, 7–8.
42. Maurice Blanchot, "Literature and the Right to Death," in *The Station Hill Blanchot Reader: Fiction and Literary Essays,* ed. George Quasha, trans. Lydia Davis, Paul Auster, and Robert Lamberton (Barrytown, NY: Station Hill/Barrytown, 1999), 374.
43. Blanchot, 383.
44. T. S. Eliot, *Prufrock, and Other Observations* (New York: Knopf, 1920), lines 4–6, 8, 13–14.
45. Eliot, line 60.
46. T. S. Eliot, *The Waste Land: Authoritative Text, Contexts, Criticism* (New York: Norton, 2001), 5–26, lines 61, 106–7. Hereafter all Eliot citations will refer to lines, not pages.
47. Eliot, 131–34.
48. Walter Benjamin, "On Some Motifs in Baudelaire," in Virginia Jackson and Yopi Prins, eds., *The Lyric Theory Reader: A Critical Anthology* (Baltimore: Johns Hopkins University Press, 2014), 327–28.
49. Walter Benjamin, "The Work of Art in the Age of Mechanical Reproduction," in Walter Benjamin, *Illuminations,* ed. Hannah Arendt, trans. Harry Zohn (New York: Schocken, 1969), 217–52.

50. T. S. Eliot, "Burnt Norton," I: lines 42–43, in *The Poems of T. S. Eliot,* vol. 1: *Collected and Uncollected Poems,* ed. Christopher Ricks and Jim McCue (London: Faber and Faber, 2015).
51. Eliot, lines 23–24.
52. Eliot, lines 1–14.
53. Eliot, "East Coker," III: lines 9–13.
54. Eliot, "Burnt Norton," III: lines 25–36.
55. Eliot, "East Coker," V: lines 1–6. "So here I am, in the middle way, having had twenty years— / Twenty years largely wasted, the years of *l'entre deux guerres*— / Trying to learn to use words, and every attempt / Is a wholly new start, and a different kind of failure / Because one has only learnt to get the better of words / For the thing one no longer has to say."
56. Eliot, "Burnt Norton," II: lines 24–29.
57. Eliot, "East Coker," III: lines 36–41.
58. Eliot, "East Coker," III: lines 13–28.
59. Kevin Hood Gary makes the important connection between Eliot's treatment of boredom and Simone Weil's theory of attention: "Detachment from the captivity of interests requires what Simone Weil describes as a posture of waiting, of being patient in the true sense of that word, deriving from the Latin *pati*, meaning to suffer, doing so calmly, without complaint. Such suffering involves undergoing an ascesis or purgation from external and internal stimuli and engagement, resisting what John Keats describes as the itch for certainty, and what T. S. Eliot diagnoses as the temptation to flee the present moment, seeking refuge in time future or time past." Kevin Hood Gary, "Boredom, Contemplation, and Liberation," *Philosophy of Education Society Yearbook Archive* (2014): 427–35, 433.
60. Eliot, "Burnt Norton," II: lines 16–21.
61. T. S. Eliot, "Tradition and the Individual Talent," in *The Sacred Wood: Essays on Poetry and Criticism* (London: Faber and Faber, 1997 [1920]), 39–49.
62. Eliot, 46.
63. Eliot, 48.
64. "Time past and time future / What might have been and what has been / Point to one end, which is always present" (Eliot, "Burnt Norton," I: lines 44–46).
65. Eliot, "East Coker," V: lines 29–30.
66. Eliot, "East Coker," V: lines 21–25.
67. Eliot, "Burnt Norton," I: lines 34–39.

Coda

Epigraph: Robert Duncan, "Illustrative Lines," in Duncan, *Selected Poems* (New York: New Directions, 1997), pp. 163–64.

1. In Husserl, attention is a physical act of tending- or, more aptly, *tensing*-toward. He writes, "In general, *attention* is a tending of the ego toward an intentional object, toward a unity which appears continually in the change of the modes of its givens . . . it is a

tending toward realization." Edmond Husserl, *Experience and Judgment: Investigations in a Genealogy of Logic,* ed. Ludwig Landgrebe, trans. James Spencer Churchill and Karl Ameriks. Evanston, IL: Northwestern University Press, 1973), 80. Susi Ferrarello points out that "the receptive activity creates a horizon of apprehending attention that modifies the structure of the not-yet-I, into a tension, meaning the I *tendens ad* (stretching toward) its object." Susi Ferrarello, *Husserl's Ethics and Practical Intentionality* (New York: Bloomsbury Academic, 2015), 165.

2. These lines echo the title of Duncan's 1968 collection. Of this volume, Jim Harrison wrote, "*Bending the Bow* is for the strenuous, the hyperactive reader of poetry; to read Duncan with any immediate grace would require Norman O. Brown's knowledge of the arcane mixed with Ezra Pound's grasp of poetics. Though Duncan avows himself a purely derivative poet, his capacities are monstrous and have taken a singular direction: in Duncan the range of affection is great and nothing is barred entrance into the 'field' of composition. . . . Form in [these poems] is a four-dimensional process, constantly active, never passive, moving through time with the poet. The poems are music-based rather than ideational, the rhythms concentrated in time, avoiding any strict sense of measure." Jim Harrison, *Just Before Dark: Collected Nonfiction* (Boston: Houghton Mifflin/S. Lawrence, 1991), 222. Some of the thematic and attentional qualities of his later, more distilled verse are evoked in Duncan's introduction to *Bending the Bow*: "The poem is not a stream of consciousness, but an area of composition in which I work with whatever comes into it. . . . The poet works with a sense of parts fitting in relation to a design that is larger than the poem. The commune of Poetry becomes so real that he sounds each particle in relation to parts of a great story that he knows will never be completed. A word has a weight of an actual stone in his hand. The tone of a vowel has the color of a wing." Robert Duncan, *Bending the Bow* (New York: New Directions, 1968), ii.

3. Duncan, vii.

4. Duncan, 7.

5. Joint attention is the phenomenon of shared attention, in which two or more subjects direct their attention toward a common object, and, moreover, know that they are doing so. I glance at you, then toward some object ahead, then back at you, and your gaze follows mine, and we are aware of sharing an act of attention, even from slightly (or vastly) different perspectives. For a significant collection of perspectives on joint attention, see Axel Seemann, ed., *Joint Attention: New Developments in Psychology, Philosophy of Mind, and Social Neuroscience* (Cambridge, MA: MIT Press, 2011).

6. Paul Celan, "The Meridian," in Paul Celan, *Selected Poems and Prose of Paul Celan*, ed. and trans. John Felstiner (New York: Norton, 2000), 407–8.

7. "Perhaps even a meeting between this 'wholly Other' . . . and a not all that distant, quite near "other" becomes thinkable—thinkable again and again" (Celan, 408.). Later, Celan develops this reach of the poem more fully, "The poem wants to reach an Other, it needs this Other, it needs an Over-against. It seeks it out, speaks toward it. For the poem making toward an Other, each thing, each human being is a form of this Other" (409).

8. Celan, 408–9.

9. Celan, 409.

10. Celan, 410.
11. Christopher Fynsk offers an important account of "the realities at stake" in Celan's work in his book, *Language and Relation:. . . That There Is Language* (Stanford, CA: Stanford University Press, 1996), 135–60.
12. Duncan, *Bending the Bow*, i.
13. In his essay, "Thought's Measure," Charles Bernstein relates the "wordness," or materiality, of poetic language to the crafting of attention therein in this way: "the wordness of the poem is foregrounded, as a way of concretizing the language, making it visible on the page, sounding it at the level of each phoneme, so that the phonemes turning to morphemes turning to words turning to phrases turning to 'poems' is felt, heard, made tangible, palpable. . . . Rather than making the language as transparent as possible . . . the movement is toward opacity/denseness—visibility of language through the making translucent of the medium. To actually map the fullness of thought and its movement. . . . Poem becoming a perceptual field/experience 'independent' of 'author.' " And further, "The antihabitual ordering of attentions so that attention can be vivid, including order of sound/syllable/phonemes. . . . To make language opaque so that writing becomes more and more conscious of itself as world generating, object generating. This goes not only for making palpable the process of the mind and heart (inseparable) but for revealing the form and structure in which writing occurs, the plasticity of form/shape. So that writing may be an experience in which the forms and object of the world may seem to be coming into being." Charles Bernstein, "Thought's Measure," in *Content's Dream* (Evanston, IL: Northwestern University Press, 1986): 61–86, 70–71.
14. Claudia Rankine, *Citizen: An American Lyric* (Minneapolis: Graywolf, 2014), 59.
15. Rankine, 60.
16. Rankine, 49.
17. Duncan, *Bending the Bow*, i–ii.
18. Allen Grossman, *True-Love: Essays on Poetry and Valuing* (Chicago: University of Chicago Press, 2009), 10.
19. Grossman, 12 (my emphasis).
20. Grossman is careful to specify that this is not merely a question of the physical senses, or the body in a material sense, but the body in which attention's capacities of orientation, recognition, and meaning-making converge in the human: "I am not talking about the body of the senses, but about the body that makes human, is orientative, recognitional, hermeneutic—the body that grounded Kant's confident orientation or Whitman's *confiance au monde*" (Grossman, 11).
21. "Enlightenment has inflicted upon language a wound—a reality wound (*Wirklichkeitswund*—wound, trauma of knowledge, darkness inflicted by light)" (Grossman, 10).
22. Bernstein, "Thought's Measure," 68–69. Bernstein's examples of this reading experience include Creeley's "A Piece," Brian McInerney's "The World," and Zukofsky's "It's a Gay Li-ife."
23. Bernstein, 67.
24. Gérard Genette, *Essays in Aesthetics,* trans. Dorrit Cohn (Lincoln: University of Nebraska Press, 2005), 29.

25. This also bears on the peculiar freedom of aesthetic judgments. because they are not ruled by a "objective" or "universal" norm—they move in a kind of "safe zone" of personal experience, voluntary exchange, and the relativity of taste: "[Aesthetic judgment's] autonomy results from the fact that no norm of obligation weighs on it, no norm dictated by any collective or superior interest: an aesthetic judgment, extravagant as it may seem in the eyes of another, is *in itself* of a nature that hurts no one, neither individuals nor groups; it can distress only on account of its possible intolerance" (Genette, 34).
26. I do not speak of a "universal" or "objective" value of a given poem, but rather of the poem as a site for a more active, subjective, and fraught terrain in which knowing what and how to value is brought to the fore. I am on board with Genette's assessment of value when he writes: "We can . . . state as a principle that no value of any sort is objective and absolute because nothing, by definition, can present 'value,' can be valuable, except in the eyes of one or several persons; to be valuable is inevitably *to be valuable for;* every value is, in this sense, relative. An object can have a high value for a subject, a much lesser value or no value at all for another. It can happen, by chance or by necessity . . . that an object is equally valuable for all, but it cannot happen that it is valuable (whatever its nature) *in itself*, independently of one or several subjects that evaluate it—or give it value" (Genette, 29). I am also "with him" in the assertion that the "pretension to universality, which cannot be founded on the myth of thus universal community of sensibilities, bases itself more today on a confusion between aesthetic values, by definition autonomous and relative, and ethical values, which owe their 'absolute,' that is to say obligatory, character to essentially social reasons (possibly sacralized by religious motives). . . . It leans on a confusion between norms of conformity and norms of obligation" (36).
27. I am thinking in particular of the work of ecocritical works such as John Felstiner, *Can Poetry Save the Earth?: A Field Guide to Nature Poems* (New Haven: Yale University Press, 2009); Don McKay's discussion of a narrower and ethically charged version of poetic attention in his essay "Baler Twine: Thoughts on Ravens, Home, and Nature Poetry," *Studies in Canadian Literature/Études en littérature canadienne* 18, no. 1 (January 1993); and Tim Lilburn, *Living in the World as If It Were Home: Essays* (Dunvegan: Cormorant, 1999); as well as arguments from moral philosophy such as Martha Nussbaum, "'Finely Aware and Richly Responsible': Moral Attention and the Moral Task of Literature," *Journal of Philosophy* 82 (October 1985): 516–29; and from continental philosophy, such as Lisbeth Lipari, *Listening, Thinking, Being: Toward an Ethics of Attunement* (University Park, Penn.: Pennsylvania State University Press, 2014).
28. Hayden Carruth, "A Balance Exactly Struck," *Poetry* 114 (August 1969): 330–31, 330.
29. Agha Shahid Ali, *Rooms Are Never Finished: Poems* (New York: Norton, 2002).
30. Wallace Stevens, "Angel Surrounded by Paysans," in Wallace Stevens, *Collected Poetry and Prose* (New York: Library of America, 1997), 423.

Bibliography

'Abd al-Ḥayy, Muḥammad. *Tradition and English and American Influence in Arabic Romantic Poetry.* Reading: Ithaca, 1982.

Abrams, M. H. *Natural Supernaturalism: Tradition and Revolution in Romantic Literature.* New York: Norton, 1973.

Agamben, Giorgio. *The Open: Man and Animal.* Stanford: Stanford University Press, 2004.

Al-Bayātī, 'Abd al-Wahhāb. *Abārīq Muhashshamah: Shi'r.* Beirut: Dar Bayrūt, 1955.

Ali, Agha Shahid. *Rooms Are Never Finished: Poems.* New York: Norton, 2002.

Allen, Diogenes. "George Herbert and Simone Weil." *Religion and Literature* 17 (Summer 1985): 17–34.

Allen, William S. *Ellipsis: Of Poetry and the Experience of Language After Heidegger, Hölderlin, and Blanchot.* Albany: SUNY Press, 2012.

Allison, John. *A Way of Seeing: Perception, Imagination, and Poetry.* Great Barrington, MA: Lindisfarne, 2003.

Altieri, Charles. *The Art of Modern American Poetry.* Oxford. Blackwell, 2005.

———. *Painterly Abstraction in Modernist American Poetry: The Contemporaneity of Modernism.* Cambridge: Cambridge University Press, 1989.

———. *The Particulars of Rapture: An Aesthetics of the Affects.* Ithaca, NY: Cornell University Press, 2003.

———. *Postmodernism Now: Essays on Contemporaneity in the Arts.* University Park: Penn State University Press, 1998.

———. *Subjective Agency: A Theory of First-Person Expressivity and Its Social Implications.* Oxford: Blackwell, 1994.

———. *Wallace Stevens and the Demands of Modernity: Toward a Phenomenology of Value.* Ithaca, NY: Cornell University Press, 2013.

Al-Udhari, Abdullah, ed. *Classical Poems By Arab Women* London: Saqi, 1999.

Ammons, A. R. *Bosh and Flapdoodle: Poems.* New York: Norton, 2005.
———. *Briefings: Poems Small and Easy.* New York: Norton, 1971.
———. *Collected Poems, 1951–1971.* New York: Norton, 1972.
———. *The Complete Poems of A. R. Ammons.* Edited by Robert M. West. 2 vols. New York: Norton, 2017.
———. *Corsons Inlet: A Book of Poems.* Ithaca, NY: Cornell University Press, 1965.
———. *Garbage.* New York: Norton, 1993.
———. *Selected Poems.* New York: Library of America, 2006.
———. *Tape for the Turn of the Year.* Ithaca, NY: Cornell University Press, 1965.
Aristotle. *The Basic Works of Aristotle.* Edited by Richard McKeon. New York: Random House, 1941.
Arpaly, Nomi, and Timothy Schroeder. *In Praise of Desire.* Oxford: Oxford University Press, 2013.
Astle, Duncan E., Anna C. Nobre, and Gaia Scerif. "Subliminally Presented and Stored Objects Capture Spatial Attention." *Journal of Neuroscience: The Official Journal of the Society for Neuroscience* 30, no. 10 (March 2010): 3567–71.
Astle, Duncan E., and Gaia Scerif. "Using Developmental Cognitive Neuroscience to Study Behavioral and Attentional Control." *Developmental Psychobiology* 51, no. 2 (March 2009): 107–18.
Astle, Duncan E., Gaia Scerif, Bo-Cheng Kuo, and Anna C. Nobre. "Spatial Selection of Features Within Perceived and Remembered Objects." *Frontiers in Human Neuroscience* 3 (April 2009): 6.
Astle, Duncan E., Jennifer Summerfield, Ivan Griffin, and Anna C. Nobre. "Orienting Attention to Locations in Mental Representations." *Attention, Perception, and Psychophysics* 74, no. 1 (January 2012): 146–62.
Atturo, Vallentina. "Contemplating Wonder: 'Ad-miratio' in Richard of St. Victor and Dante." *Dante Studies, with the Annual Report of the Dante Society* 129 (2011): 99–124
Atwood, Margaret. "Bored." *Atlantic Monthly* 274 (December 1994): 102.
Bachmann, Ingeborg. *Darkness Spoken: The Collected Poems.* Translated and introduced by Peter Filkins. Brookline, MA: Zephyr, 2006.
Badawī, Muḥammad Muṣṭafá. *A Critical Introduction to Modern Arabic Poetry.* Cambridge and New York: Cambridge University Press, 1975.
Baker, David. "On Restraint." *Poetry* 168, no. 1 (April 1996): 33–47. Reprinted as "*From* 'On Restraint' (1996)," in *High Lonesome: On the Poetry of Charles Wright,* ed. Adam Gianelli, 76–87. Oberlin, OH: Oberlin College Press, 2006.
Barbarese, J. T. "Theology for Atheists: Reading Ammons." *Journal of Modern Literature* 26, nos. 3/4 (Spring 2003): 73–83.
Barthes, Roland. *Le Plaisir du texte.* Paris: Seuil, 1973.
Bataille, Georges. *L'Expérience intérieure.* Paris: Gallimard, 1943.
———. *Inner Experience.* Translated by Leslie Anne Boldt. Albany: State University of New York Press, 1988.
Baumgarten, Alexander Gottlieb. *Aesthetica.* Hildesheim: G. Olms, 1961 [1750].
———. *Metaphysica Alexandri Gottlieb Baumgarten, Professoris Philosophiae, editio 4. Halae, Magdebvrgicae, impensis C. H. Hemmerde, 1779.*

———.*Metaphysics: A Critical Translation with Kant's Elucidations, Selected Notes, and Related Materials*. Edited and translated by Courtney D. Fugate and John Hymers. London: Bloomsbury, 2004.

Baumgartner, Elisabeth, ed. *Handbook—Phenomenology and Cognitive Science*. Dettelbach, Germany: Röll, 1996.

Bearman, P. J., ed. *The Encyclopaedia of Islam*. Leiden: Brill, 1998.

Benjamin, Walter. *Illuminations*. Edited by Hannah Arendt. Translated by Harry Zohn. New York: Schocken, 1969.

Benn, Gottfried. *Prose, Essays, Poems*. Translated by Volkmar Sander. New York: Continuum, 1987.

Bernstein, Charles. *Content's Dream*. Evanston, IL: Northwestern University Press, 1986.

———. "Thought's Measure." In *Content's Dream*, 61–86. Evanston, IL: Northwestern University Press, 1986.

Bewley, Marius. "Modes of Poetry." *Hudson Review* (Winter 1969): 713–18.

Birkerts, Sven. *Changing the Subject: Art and Attention in the Internet Age*. Minneapolis: Graywolf, 2015.

Bishop, Elizabeth, *Poems*. New York: Farrar, Straus, and Giroux, 2011.

Blanchot, Maurice. "Enigma." *Yale French Studies* 79 (1991): 8–10.

———. *L'Entretien infini*. Paris: Gallimard, 1971 [1969].

———. *The Infinite Conversation*. Translated by Susan Hanson. Minneapolis: University of Minnesota Press, 1993.

———. *The Station Hill Blanchot Reader: Fiction and Literary Essays*. Edited by George Quasha. Translated by Lydia Davis, Paul Auster, and Robert Lamberton. Barrytown, NY: Station Hill/Barrytown, 1999.

Blasing, Mutlu Konuk. *Lyric Poetry: The Pain and the Pleasure of Words*. Princeton: Princeton University Press, 2007.

Bloom, Harold. "A. R. Ammons: The Breaking of the Vessels." *Salmagundi* 31/32 (Fall 1975–Winter 1976): 185–203.

———. "The New Transcendentalism: The Visionary Strain in Merwin, Ashbery, and Ammons." *Chicago Review* 24 (Winter 1972): 25–43.

Bloom, Harold, ed. *A. R. Ammons*. New York: Chelsea House, 1986.

———. *William Wordsworth*. Philadelphia: Chelsea House, 2003.

Bloomfield, Mandy. *Archaeopoetics: Word, Image, History*. Tuscaloosa: University of Alabama Press, 2016.

Blum, Lawrence A., and Victor Seidler. *A Truer Liberty: Simon Weil and Marxism*. New York: Routledge, 1989.

Bohrer, Karl Heinz. *Plötzlichkeit: Zum Augenblick des Ästhetischen Scheins*. Frankfurt: Suhrkamp, 1981.

———. *Suddenness: On the Moment of Aesthetic Appearance*. Translated by Ruth Crowley. New York: Columbia University Press, 1994.

Boym, Svetlana. "Poetics and Politics of Estrangement: Victor Shklovsky and Hannah Arendt." *Poetics Today* 26, no. 4 (Winter 2005): 581–611.

Brinkmann, Rolf Dieter. *An Unchanging Blue: Selected Poems, 1962–1975*. Translated by Mark Terrill. Anderson, SC: Parlor, 2011.

Brooks, Cleanth. *The Well Wrought Urn*. New York: Houghton Mifflin Harcourt, 1947.
Brown, Bill. *Other Things*. Chicago: University of Chicago Press, 2015.
———. *A Sense of Things*. Chicago: University of Chicago Press, 2003.
Buell, Frederick. "'To Be Quiet in the Hands of the Marvelous': The Poetry of A. R. Ammons." *Iowa Review* 8, no. 1 (Winter 1977): 67–85.
Bukowski, Charles. *Come On In!* (New York: Ecco, 2007).
———. *Dangling in the Tournefortia*. Santa Barbara, CA: Black Sparrow, 1981.
———. *Living on Luck: Selected Letters, 1960s–1970s*. Santa Rosa, CA: Black Sparrow, 1995.
———. "The Old Big Time." In *Charles Bukowski poem and letter manuscripts*. Accessed February 24, 2015. http://bukowski.net/manuscripts/displaymanuscript.php?show=poem1982-06-11-the_old_big_time.jpg&workid=3360.
———. *The Pleasures of the Damned: Poems, 1951–1993*. New York: Ecco, 2007.
———. *Sifting Through the Madness for the Word, the Line, the Way: New Poems*. New York: Ecco, 2003.
Bundy, Murray W. *The Theory of Imagination in Classical and Mediaeval Thought*. Urbana: University of Illinois Press, 1927.
———. "'Invention' and 'Imagination' in the Renaissance." *Journal of English and Germanic Philology* 29, no. 4 (October 1930): 535–45.
Burnside, John. *Black Cat Bone*. London: Cape Poetry, 2011.
Burt, Stephanie. *The Poem Is You: Sixty Contemporary American Poems and How to Read Them*. Cambridge, MA: Harvard University Press, 2016.
Burwick, Frederick. *Poetic Madness and the Romantic Imagination*. University Park: Pennsylvania State University Press, 1996.
Byrne, Ruth M. J. *The Rational Imagination: How People Create Alternatives to Reality*. Cambridge, MA: MIT Press, 2007.
Byron, George Gordon Lord. *Lord Byron: The Major Works*. Edited by Jerome J. McGann. Oxford: Oxford University Press, 2008.
Cage, John. *Empty Words*. Middletown, CT: Wesleyan University Press, 1979.
———. *Silence: Lectures and Writings*. Middletown, CT: Wesleyan University Press, 1961.
Cage, John, and Joan Retallack. *Musicage: Cage Muses on Words, Art, Music*. Middletown, CT: Wesleyan University Press, 2011.
Calvino, Italo. *Six Memos for the Next Millennium*. Translated by Patrick Creagh. Cambridge, MA: Harvard University Press, 1988.
Carruth, Hayden. "A Balance Exactly Struck." *Poetry* 114 (August 1969): 330–31.
———. "A Failure of Contempt." *Poetry* 107, no. 6 (March 1966): 396–97.
Carson, Anne. "Decreation: How Women Like Sappho, Simone Weil, and Marguerite Porete Tell God." *Common Knowledge* 8, no. 1 (Winter 2002): 188–203.
———. *Nox*. New York: New Directions, 2010.
Cartmill, Erica A., Sian Beilock, and Susan Goldin-Meadow. "A Word in the Hand: Action, Gesture and Mental Representation in Humans and Non-Human Primates." *Philosophical Transactions: Biological Sciences* 367, no. 1585 (January 2012): 129–43.
Caygill, Howard. *A Kant Dictionary*. Oxford: Blackwell Reference, 1995.
Celan, Paul. *Selected Poems and Prose of Paul Celan*. Edited and translated by John Felstiner. New York: Norton, 2000.

Cha, Theresa Hak Kyung. *Dictee*. Berkeley: University of California Press, 2001.
Cheng, Anne Anlin. "Memory and Anti-Documentary Desire in Theresa Hak Kyung Cha's *Dictee*." *MELUS* 23, no. 4 (Winter 1998): 119–33.
The Chicago Manual of Style: The Essential Guide for Writers, Editors, and Publishers. 14th ed. Chicago: University of Chicago Press, 1993.
Citton, Yves. *The Ecology of Attention*. Cambridge: Polity, 2017.
Clark, T. J. *The Sight of Death: An Experiment in Art Writing*. New Haven: Yale University Press, 2006.
Cohen, Joshua. *Attention! A (Short) History*. London: Notting Hill, 2013.
———. *ATTENTION: Dispatches from a Land of Distraction*. New York: Random House, 2018.
Coleridge, Samuel Taylor. *Biographia Literaria*. Edited by Adam Roberts. Edinburgh: Edinburgh University Press, 2014.
———. *Biographia Literaria, or Biographical Sketches of My Literary Life and Opinions*. Edited by James Engell and W. Jackson Bate. London: Routledge & Kegan Paul, 1983.
Cook, Eleanor. *Elizabeth Bishop at Work*. Cambridge, MA: Harvard University Press, 2016.
Corbetta, Maurizio, and Gordon L. Shulman. "Control of Goal-Directed and Stimulus-Driven Attention in the Brain." *Nature Reviews: Neuroscience* 3, no. 3 (March 2002): 201–15.
Corcoran, Neil. *Poetry and Responsibility*. Liverpool: Liverpool University Press, 2014.
———. "September Song." In *English Poetry Since 1940*. London: Routledge, 2013 [1993].
Corey, Joshua. "The Challenge of Francis Ponge." Introduction to *Partisan of Things*. Chicago: Kenning, 2016.
Corrao, F. M. "'ŠI'R:' Poetics in Progress." *Quaderni di Studi Arabi* 18 (2000): 97–104.
Costello, Bonnie. *Planets on Tables: Poetry, Still Life, and the Turning World*. Ithaca, NY: Cornell University Press, 2008.
Crary, Jonathan. *Suspensions of Perception: Attention, Spectacle, and Modern Culture*. Cambridge, MA: MIT Press, 1999.
———. *Techniques of the Observer: On Vision and Modernity in the Nineteenth Century*. Cambridge, MA: MIT Press, 1990.
Crews, Brian. "Martin Amis and the Postmodern Grotesque." *Modern Language Review* 105, no. 3 (July 2010): 641–59.
Critchley, Simon. *Things Merely Are: Philosophy in the Poetry of Wallace Stevens*. London: Routledge, 2005.
Culler, Jonathan. *Theory of the Lyric*. Cambridge, MA: Harvard University Press, 2015.
Cushman, Stephen. *Fictions of Form in American Poetry*. Princeton: Princeton University Press, 1993.
Daston, Lorraine, ed. *Things That Talk: Object Lessons from Art and Science*. New York: Zone, 2004.
Daston, Lorraine, and Peter Galison. *Objectivity*. New York: Zone, 2007.
D'Avanzo, Mario L. *Keats's Metaphors for the Poetic Imagination*. Durham, NC: Duke University Press, 1967.
Davenport, Thomas H., and John C. Beck. *The Attention Economy: Understanding the New Currency of Business*. Boston: Harvard Business School Press, 2001.

Dembo, L. S., and Charles Reznikoff. "Charles Reznikoff." *Contemporary Literature* 10 (Spring 1969): 193–202.
Depraz, Natalie. *Attention et vigilance: À la croisée de la phénoménologie et des sciences cognitives.* Paris: Presses Universitaires de France, 2014.
Dickinson, Emily. *The Complete Poems.* Boston: Little, Brown, 1960.
———. *The Poems of Emily Dickinson.* Cambridge, MA: Belknap Press of Harvard University Press, 1999.
Dinerstein, Joel. *The Origins of Cool in Postwar America.* Chicago: University of Chicago, 2017.
Dommange, Thomas. "Simone Weil: Le Marxisme hors de soi." *Études philosophiques* 3 (July 2007): 207–22.
Doreski, C. K. *Elizabeth Bishop: The Restraints of Language.* Oxford: Oxford University Press, 1993.
Doty, Mark. *Still Life with Oysters and Lemon.* Boston: Beacon, 2001.
DuBois, Andrew Lee. *Ashbery's Forms of Attention.* Tuscaloosa: University of Alabama Press, 2006.
DuBois, Andrew, and Frank Lentricchia, eds. *Close Reading: The Reader.* Durham, NC: Duke University Press, 2003.
Duncan, Robert. *Bending the Bow.* New York: New Directions, 1968.
———. *Selected Poems.* New York: New Directions, 1997.
Dustin, Christopher A., and Joanna E. Ziegler, eds. *Practicing Mortality: Art, Philosophy, and Contemplative Seeing.* Palgrave Macmillan, 2005.
Dyer, Rebecca. "Poetry of Politics and Mourning: Mahmoud Darwish's Genre-Transforming Tribute to Edward W. Said." *PMLA* 122, no. 5 (October 2007): 1447–62.
Eastwood, John, Alexandra Frischen, Mark J. Fenske, and Daniel Smilek. "The Unengaged Mind: Defining Boredom in Terms of Attention." *Perspectives on Psychological Science* 7, no. 5 (September 2012): 482–95.
Eigner, Larry. "Approaching Things: Some Calculations How Figure It of Everyday Life Experience." *L=A=N=G=U=A=G=E* 1 (February 1978): 2.
Eliot, T. S. *The Poems of T. S. Eliot,* vol. 1: *Collected and Uncollected Poems.* Edited by Christopher Ricks and Jim McCue. London: Faber and Faber, 2015.
———. *Prufrock, and Other Observations.* New York: Knopf, 1920.
———. *The Sacred Wood: Essays on Poetry and Criticism* (London: Faber and Faber, 1997 [1920]).
———. *The Waste Land: Authoritative Text, Contexts, Criticism.* Edited by Michael North. New York: Norton, 2001.
Epstein, Andrew. *Attention Equals Life: The Pursuit of the Everyday in Contemporary Poetry and Culture.* Oxford: Oxford University Press, 2016.
Ezrahi, Sidra DeKoven. *By Words Alone: The Holocaust in Literature.* Chicago: University of Chicago Press, 1980.
Fehmi, Les, and Jim Robbins. *The Open-Focus Brain.* Boston: Trumpeter, 2008.
Felstiner, John. *Can Poetry Save the Earth?: A Field Guide to Nature Poems.* New Haven: Yale University Press, 2009.
———. *Paul Celan: Poet, Survivor, Jew.* New Haven: Yale University Press, 2001.
Ferrarello, Susi. *Husserl's Ethics and Practical Intentionality.* New York: Bloomsbury Academic, 2015.

Fleur, Eugène. "Le 'Social' dans *La Condition ouvrière.*" *Cahiers Simone Weil* 7 (December 1984): 341–46.

Fludernik, Monika, and Miriam Nandi, eds. *Idleness, Indolence, and Leisure in English Literature.* Basingstoke: Palgrave Macmillan, 2014.

Forché, Carolyn. "An Interview by David Montenegro." *American Poetry Review* 17, no. 6 (November/December 1988): 35–40.

Fraisse, Paul. "Multisensory Aspects of Rhythm," In *Intersensory Perception and Sensory Integration,* edited by Richard D. Walk and Herbert L. Pick, 217–45. Boston: Springer, 1981.

Franciosi, Robert. "'Detailing the Facts:' Charles Reznikoff's Response to the Holocaust." *Contemporary Literature* 29, no. 2 (Summer 1988): 241–64.

Freud, Sigmund. "Mourning and Melancholia," In *General Psychological Theory: Papers on Metapsychology,* edited by Philip Rieff, 164–79. New York: Collier, 1963.

Fried, Michael. *Absorption and Theatricality: Painting and Beholder in the Age of Diderot.* Chicago: University of Chicago Press, 1980.

———. *Art and Objecthood.* Chicago: University of Chicago Press, 1998.

Friese, Heidrun, ed. *The Moment: Time and Rupture in Modern Thought.* Liverpool: Liverpool University Press, 2001.

Frye, Northrop. *Collected Works of Northrop Frye: Northrop Frye on Milton and Blake.* Edited by Angela Esterhammer. Toronto: University of Toronto Press, 2005.

———. *Northrop Frye's Writings on the Eighteenth and Nineteenth Centuries.* Edited by Imre Salusinszky. Toronto: University of Toronto Press, 2005.

Furani, Khaled. "Rhythms of the Secular: The Politics of Modernizing Arab Poetic Forms." *American Ethnologist* 35, no. 2 (May 2008): 290–307.

Fynsk, Christopher. *Language and Relation: . . . That There Is Language.* Stanford: Stanford University Press, 1996.

Gary, Kevin Hood. "Boredom, Contemplation, and Liberation." *Philosophy of Education Society Yearbook Archive* (2014): 427–35.

Gelpi, Albert, ed. *Wallace Stevens: The Poetics of Modernism.* Cambridge: Cambridge University Press, 1990.

Genette, Gérard. *The Aesthetic Relation.* Translated by G. M. Goshgarian. Ithaca, NY: Cornell University Press, 1999.

———. *Essays in Aesthetics.* Translated by Dorrit Cohn. Lincoln: University of Nebraska Press, 2005.

Gianelli, Adam, ed. *High Lonesome: On the Poetry of Charles Wright.* Oberlin, OH: Oberlin College Press, 2006.

Gillis, Colin. "Rethinking Sexuality in Thom Gunn's *The Man with Night Sweats.*" *Contemporary Literature* 50 (Spring 2009): 156–82.

Goethe, Johann Wolfgang von. *Wilhelm Meisters Lehrjahre.* Dusseldorf: Artemis & Winkler, 2006.

Golding, Alan. "Between the News and the Dews. A Review of Harryette Mullen's *Urban Tumbleweed: Notes from a Tanka Diary.*" *Iowa Review* 44 (Fall 2014): 174–77.

Goldstein, Joseph, and Jack Kornfield. *Seeking the Heart of Wisdom: The Path of Insight Meditation.* Boston: Shambhala, 2001.

Goodstein, Elizabeth S. *Experience Without Qualities: Boredom and Modernity*. Stanford: Stanford University Press, 2004.

Gosling, Simon G., and Duncan E. Astle. "Directing Spatial Attention to Locations Within Remembered and Imagined Mental Representations." *Frontiers in Human Neuroscience* 7 (April 2013): 154.

Gourgouris, Stathis. "The Lyric in Exile." In *The Lyric Theory Reader: A Critical Anthology*, edited by Virginia Jackson and Yopi Prins, 368–81. Baltimore: Johns Hopkins University Press, 2014.

Gow, A. S. F., and D. L. Page, eds. *The Greek Anthology: The Garland of Philip and Some Contemporary Epigrams*, vol. 1. Cambridge: Cambridge University Press, 1968.

Greene, Roland. *Five Words: Critical Semantics in the Age of Shakespeare and Cervantes*. Chicago: University of Chicago Press, 2013.

———. "Not Works But Networks: Colonial Worlds in Comparative Literature." In *Comparative Literature in an Age of Globalization*, edited by Haun Saussy, 212–23. Baltimore: Johns Hopkins University Press, 2006.

———. *Post-Petrarchism: Origins and Innovations of the Western Lyric Sequence*. Princeton: Princeton University Press, 1991.

Greene, Roland, and Stephen Cushman, eds. *The Princeton Encyclopedia of Poetry and Poetics*, 4th ed. Princeton: Princeton University Press, 2012.

Greene, Thomas M. *Calling from Diffusion: Hermeneutics of the Promenade*. Northampton: Smith College, 2002.

Griffin, Ivan C., and Anna C. Nobre. "Orienting Attention to Locations in Internal Representations." *Journal of Cognitive Neuroscience* 15, no. 8 (November 2003): 1176–94.

Grob, Alan. "The Poetry of Pessimism: Arnold's 'Resignation.'" *Victorian Poetry* 26 (Spring-Summer 1988): 25–44.

Grossman, Allen. *True-Love: Essays on Poetry and Valuing*. Chicago: University of Chicago Press, 2009.

Grünbein, Durs. *Ashes for Breakfast; Selected Poems*. Translated by Michael Hofmann. New York: Farrar, Straus, and Giroux, 2005.

———. *Grauzone Morgens: Gedichte*. Frankfurt: Suhrkamp, 1988.

Gumbrecht, Hans Ulrich. *After 1945: Latency as Origin of the Present*. Stanford: Stanford University Press, 2013.

———. *Atmosphere, Mood, Stimmung: On a Hidden Potential of Literature*. Stanford: Stanford University Press, 2012.

———. "How to Approach 'Poetry as a Mode of Attention.'" *Eutomia* 16, no. 1 (December 2015): 192–207.

———. *Production of Presence: What Meaning Cannot Convey*. Stanford: Stanford University Press, 2004.

Gumbrecht, Hans Ulrich, and K. Ludwig Pfeiffer, eds. *Materialities of Communication*. Translated by William Whobrey. Stanford: Stanford University Press, 1994.

Gunn, Thom. *Collected Poems*. New York: Farrar, Straus and Giroux, 1994.

Gurton-Wachter, Lily. *Watchwords: Romanticism and the Poetics of Attention*. Stanford: Stanford University Press, 2016.

Halevi, Leor. *Muhammad's Grave: Death Rites and the Making of Islamic Society.* New York: Columbia University Press, 2007.

Hamill, Sam, ed. *The Erotic Spirit.* Boston: Shambhala, 1996.

Hammer, Langdon. "The American Poetry of Thom Gunn and Geoffrey Hill." *Contemporary Literature* 43 (Winter 2002): 644–66.

———. "The Latches of Paradise: Charles Wright's Meditations and Memories at Year's End." *American Scholar* 74 (Autumn 2005): 73–74.

Hampl, Patricia. *The Art of the Wasted Day.* New York: Viking, 2018.

Harman, Graham. *Guerrilla Metaphysics: Phenomenology and the Carpentry of Things.* Peru, IL: Open Court, 2005.

———. *Object-Oriented Ontology: A New Theory of Everything.* London: Penguin, 2018.

Harmon, William, ed. *Classic Writings on Poetry.* New York: Columbia University Press, 2003.

Harrison, Jim. *Just Before Dark: Collected Nonfiction.* Boston: Houghton Mifflin/S. Lawrence, 1991.

Harrison, Robert Pogue. *Gardens: An Essay on the Human Condition.* Chicago: University of Chicago Press, 2008.

Hartman, Geoffrey. "The Romance of Nature and the Negative Way," In *William Wordsworth*, edited by Harold Bloom, 37–54. Philadelphia: Chelsea House, 2003.

Hass, Robert. *The Apple Trees at Olema: New and Selected Poems.* New York: Ecco, 2010.

———. *A Little Book on Form: An Exploration Into the Formal Imagination of Poetry.* New York: Ecco, 2017.

———. *Praise.* New York: Ecco, 1979.

Hayles, N. Katherine. "Hyper and Deep Attention: The Generational Divide in Cognitive Modes." *Profession* (2007): 187–99.

———. *Unthought: The Power of the Cognitive Nonconscious.* Chicago: University of Chicago Press, 2017.

Hayter, Alethea. *Opium and the Romantic Imagination.* Berkeley: University of California Press, 1968.

Heaney, Seamus. *Opened Ground: Selected Poems, 1966–1996.* New York: Farrar, Straus and Giroux, 1998.

Hegel, Georg Wilhelm Fredrich. *Hegel: Elements of the Philosophy of Right.* Edited by Allen W. Wood. Translated by H.B. Nisbet. Cambridge: Cambridge University Press, 1991.

Heidegger, Martin. *Basic Writings: From Being and Time (1927) to the Task of Thinking (1964).* Translated by David Krell. San Francisco: Harper and Row, 1993.

———. *The Fundamental Concepts of Metaphysics: World, Finitude, Solitude.* Translated by William McNeill and Nicholas Walker. Bloomington: Indiana University Press, 1995.

———. *Wegmarken.* Frankfurt: Vittorio Klostermann, 1976.

Heiti, Warren. "Eros and Necessity." *New Quarterly* 125 (Winter 2013): 46–53.

Hejinian, Lyn. *The Language of Inquiry.* Berkeley: University of California Press, 2000.

———. *My Life.* Providence: Burning Deck, 1980.

Henderson, Derek. "The Terrible Boredom of Paradise." Accessed March 24, 2016. http://www.derekhenderson.net/tbop.html.

Herbert, Zbigniew. *Raport Z Oblężonego Miasta I Inne Wiersze.* Paris: Instytut Literacki, 1983.

———. *Report from the Besieged City and Other Poems.* New York: Ecco, 1985.
Heuvig, Jeanne. *The Transmutation of Love and Avant-Garde Poetics.* Tuscaloosa: University of Alabama Press, 2016.
Hill, Geoffrey. *New and Collected Poems, 1952–1992.* Boston: Houghton Mifflin, 1994.
Hirshfield, Jane. *Ten Windows: How Great Poems Transform the World.* New York: Knopf, 2017.
Hochhuth, Rolf. *The Deputy.* New York: Grove, 1964.
Hoffman, Tyler B. "Representing Aids: Thom Gunn and the Modalities of Verse." *South Atlantic Review* 65 (Spring 2000): 13–39.
Hölderlin, Friedrich. *Poems and Fragments: English and German Edition.* Translated by Michael Hamburger. London: Carcanet, 2004.
hooks, bell. *all about love: new visions.* New York: Harper Perennial, 2001.
Husserl, Edmund. *Experience and Judgment: Investigations in a Genealogy of Logic.* Edited by Ludwig Landgrebe. Translated by James Spencer Churchill and Karl Ameriks. Evanston, IL: Northwestern University Press, 1973.
———. *Wahrnehmung und Aufmerksamkeit: Texte aus dem Nachlass (1893–1912).* Edited by Thomas Vongehr and Regula Giuliani. Dordrecht: Springer, 2004.
Irvine, Ian. "Acedia, Tristitia, and Sloth: Early Christian Forerunners to Chronic Ennui." *Humanitas* 12, no. 1 (Spring 1999): 89–103.
Iser, Wolfgang. *The Fictive and the Imaginary: Charting Literary Anthropology.* Baltimore: Johns Hopkins University Press, 1993.
Iyengar, B. K. S. *Light on Yoga: Yoga Dipika.* New York: Schocken, 1979.
Iyers, Lars. *Blanchot's Vigilance: Literature, Phenomenology, and the Ethical.* London: Palgrave Macmillan, 2005.
Izenberg, Gerald. *Identity: The Necessity of a Modern Idea.* Philadelphia: University of Pennsylvania Press, 2016.
Izenberg, Oren. *Being Numerous: Poetry and the Ground of Social Life.* Princeton: Princeton University Press, 2011.
Jabès, Edmond. *Le Livre des questions I.* Paris: Gallimard, 1900.
Jackson, Virginia. *Dickinson's Misery: A Theory of Lyric Reading.* Princeton: Princeton University Press, 2005.
Jackson, Virginia, and Yopi Prins, eds. *The Lyric Theory Reader: A Critical Anthology* Baltimore: Johns Hopkins University Press, 2014.
Jagoda, Patrick. *Network Aesthetics.* Chicago: University of Chicago Press, 2016.
Jakobson, Roman. "Linguistics and Poetics." In *Style in Language*, edited by Thomas Sebeok, 350–77. Cambridge, MA: MIT Press, 1960.
James, Skip. "Hard Times Killing Floor Blues." Paramount Records, 1931.
———. *"I'm So Glad": The Complete 1931 Paramount Recordings.* Document Records, 1990.
Jameson, Fredric. "Baudelaire as Modernist and Postmodernist: The Dissolution of the Referent and the Artificial Sublime." In *The Modernist Papers,* 223–37. London: Verso, 2007. Reprinted in *The Lyric Theory Reader: A Critical Anthology,* edited by Virginia Jackson, and Yopi Prins, 350–60. Baltimore: Johns Hopkins University Press, 2014.
Jarman, Mark. "The Pragmatic Imagination and the Secret of Poetry," *Gettysburg Review* 1, no. 4 (1988). Reprinted in *High Lonesome: On the Poetry of Charles Wright,* ed. Adam Gianelli, 25–28. Oberlin, OH: Oberlin College Press, 2006.

Jayyusi, Salma Khadra. *Trends and Movements in Modern Arabic Poetry.* Leiden: Brill, 1977.
Johnsen, Rasmus. "On Boredom: A Note on Experience Without Qualities." *Ephemera: Theory and Politics in Organization* 11, no. 4 (November 2011): 482–89.
Johnson, Addie, and Robert W. Proctor. *Attention: Theory and Practice.* SAGE Publications, 2004.
Jonson, Ben. *The Works of Ben Jonson.* London: Edward Moxon, 1938.
Kabat-Zinn, Jon. *Coming to Our Senses: Healing Ourselves and the World Through Mindfulness.* New York: Hyperion, 2005.
———. *Full Catastrophe Living: Using the Wisdom of Your Body and Mind to Face Stress, Pain, and Illness.* New York: Delta, 1990.
———. *Wherever You Go, There You Are: Mindfulness Meditation in Everyday Life.* New York: Hyperion, 2005.
Kamenetz, Rodger. "Rediscovering 'Family Chronicle' by Charles Reznikoff." *Georgia Review* 47 (Winter 1993): 709–13.
Kant, Immanuel. *Anthropology from a Pragmatic Point of View.* Edited by Robert B. Louden and Manfred Kuehn. Translated by Robert B. Louden and Manfred Kuehn. Cambridge: Cambridge University Press, 2006.
———. *Critique of Pure Reason*, Edited by Paul Guyer and Allen W. Wood. Translated by Paul Guyer and Allen W. Wood. Cambridge: Cambridge University Press, 1998.
———. *Critique of the Power of Judgment.* Edited by Paul Guyer. Translated by Paul Guyer. Cambridge: Cambridge University Press, 2000.
———. *Immanuel Kant: Gesammelte Schriften (Akademie-Ausgabe), i–xxiii. Band 9. Logik. Physische Geographie, Pädagogik.* Charlottesville, VA: InteLex, 1999.
———. *Metaphysical Foundations of Natural Science.* Edited by Michael Friedman. Translated by Michael Friedman. Cambridge: Cambridge University Press, 2004.
Kearney, Richard. *The Wake of Imagination: Toward a Postmodern Culture.* Minneapolis: University of Minnesota Press, 1988.
Keita, Mamadi. "Critique de l'état-nation dans 'l'enracinement' de Simone Weil." *CLA Journal* 46 (June 2003): 543–61.
Khadim, H. N. "Rewriting 'The Waste Land': Badr Shākir al-Sayyāb's 'Fī al-Maghriɔ al-'Arabī,'" *Journal of Arabic Literature* 30, no. 2 (1999): 128–70.
Dīwān Al-Khansā'. Edited by Ḥamdū Ṭammās. Beirut: Dār al-Ma'rifah, 2003.
Kierkegaard, Søren. *Either/Or.* Translated by Howard V. Hong and Edna H. Hong. Princeton: Princeton University Press, 1987.
———. *The Lily of the Field and the Bird of the Air: Three Godly Discourses.* Translated by Bruce H. Kirmmse. Princeton: Princeton University Press, 2016.
Kim, Elaine, and Norma Alarcón, eds. *Writing Self/Writing Nation: A Collection of Essays on Dictee by Theresa Hak Kyung Cha.* Berkeley: Third Woman, 1994.
Kim, Sue J. "Narrator, Author, Reader: Equivocation in Theresa Hak Kyung Cha's *Dictee.*" *Narrative* 16 (May 2008): 163–77.
Kirschten, Robert. *Approaching Prayer: Ritual and the Shape of Myth in A. R. Ammons and James Dickey.* Baton Rouge: Louisiana State University Press, 1998.
Klein, Jürgen. "Genius, Ingenium, Imagination: Aesthetic Theories of Production from the Renaissance to Romanticism." In *The Romantic Imagination: Literature and Art in*

England and Germany, 19–62. Edited by Frederick Burwick and Jürgen Klein. Amsterdam: Rodopi, 1996.

Knapp, Peggy Ann. "Aesthetic Attention and the Chaucerian Text." *Chaucer Review* 39, no. 3 (2005): 241–58.

Koehler, Margaret. *Poetry of Attention in the Eighteenth Century.* New York: Palgrave Macmillan, 2012.

Koepnick, Lutz P. *Framing Attention: Windows on Modern German Culture.* Baltimore: Johns Hopkins University Press, 2007.

———. *On Slowness: Toward an Aesthetic of the Contemporary.* New York: Columbia University Press, 2014.

Kraft, Ulrich. "Train Your Brain: Mental Exercises With Neurofeedback May Ease Symptoms of Attention-Deficit Disorder, Epilepsy and Depression—and Even Boost Cognition in Healthy Brains." *Scientific American* (February 2006): 58–63.

Kristeva, Julia. *Revolution in Poetic Language.* Translated by Margaret Waller. New York: Columbia University Press, 1984.

Lacoue-Labarthe, Philippe. "Poetry as Experience: Two Poems by Paul Celan," In *The Lyric Theory Reader: A Critical Anthology,* edited by Virginia Jackson and Yopi Prins, 399–418. Baltimore: Johns Hopkins University Press, 2014.

Landau, Deborah. "'How to Live. What to Do': The Poetics and Politics of Aids." *American Literature* 68 (Spring 1996): 193–225.

Landy, Joshua. *How to Do Things with Fictions.* Oxford: Oxford University Press, 2012.

Langer, Susanne. *Feeling and Form: A New Theory of Art Developed from Philosophy in a New Key.* New York: Scribners, 1977.

Lanham, Richard A. *The Economics of Attention: Style and Substance in the Age of Information.* Chicago: University of Chicago Press, 2006.

Larson, Kay. *Where the Heart Beats: John Cage, Zen Buddhism, and the Inner Life of Artists.* New York: Penguin, 2012.

Lasher, Margot D., John T. Carroll, and Thomas G. Bever. "The Cognitive Basis of Aesthetic Experience." *Leonardo* 16, no. 3 (Summer 1983): 196–99.

Lee, Kun Jong. "Rewriting Hesiod, Revisioning Korea: Theresa Hak Kyung Cha's *Dictee* as a Subversive Hesiodic 'Catalogue of Women.'" *College Literature* 33 (Summer 2006): 77–99.

Lee, Li-Young. "Persimmons." In *Rose,* 17–19. Rochester, NY: BOA, 1986.

Leggett, B. J. *Wallace Stevens and Poetic Theory: Conceiving the Supreme Fiction.* Chapel Hill: University of North Carolina Press, 1987.

Lehman, David. "God Is the Sense the World Makes Without God." *American Poetry Review* 35, no. 2 (May/June 2006): 19–21.

———. Introduction to *A. R. Ammons: Selected Poems,* ed. David Lehman, xiii–xxv. New York: Library of America, 2006.

Lepkowski, Frank J. "'How Are We to Find Holiness?': The Religious Vision of A. R. Ammons." *Twentieth Century Literature* 40 (Winter 1994): 477–98.

Lepsien, Jöran, Ivan C. Griffin, Joseph T. Devlin, and Anna C. Nobre. "Directing Spatial Attention in Mental Representations: Interactions Between Attentional Orienting and Working-Memory Load." *NeuroImage* 26, no. 3 (March 2005): 733–43.

Lepsien, Jöran, and Anna C. Nobre. "Attentional Modulation of Object Representations in Working Memory." *Cerebral Cortex* 17, no. 9 (September 2007): 2072–83.
———. "Cognitive Control of Attention in the Human Brain: Insights from Orienting Attention to Mental Representations." *Brain Research* 1105, no. 1 (September 2006): 20–31.
Levertov, Denise. *The Poet in the World*. New York: New Directions, 1973.
Levinas, Emmanuel. *Otherwise Than Being; or, Beyond Essence*. Translated by Alphonso Lingis. Pittsburgh: Duquesne University Press, 1981.
Levine, Caroline. *Forms: Whole, Rhythm, Hierarchy, Network*. Princeton: Princeton University Press, 2015.
Lilburn, Tim. *Living in the World as If It Were Home: Essays*. Dunvegan: Cormorant, 1999.
Lings, Martin, ed. *Sufi Poems: A Mediaeval Anthology*. Cambridge: Islamic Texts Society, 2004.
Lipari, Lisbeth. *Listening, Thinking, Being: Toward an Ethics of Attunement*. University Park: Pennsylvania State University Press, 2014.
Locklin, Gerald. *Charles Bukowski: A Sure Bet*. Sudbury, MA: Water Row, 1996.
Longenbach, James. *Modern Poetry After Modernism*. Oxford: Oxford University Press, 1997.
———. "Poetry in Review." *Yale Review* 83, no. 4 (October 1995): 148–51. Reprinted as "*From* 'Earned Weight' (1995)," in *High Lonesome: On the Poetry of Charles Wright*, ed. Adam Gianelli, 79–82. Oberlin, OH: Oberlin College Press, 2006.
———. *The Virtues of Poetry*. Minneapolis: Graywolf, 2013.
Longuenesse, Béatrice. *Kant and the Capacity to Judge: Sensibility and Discursivity in the Transcendental Analytic of the Critique of Pure Reason*. Translated by Charles T. Wolfe. Princeton: Princeton University Press, 1998.
Lorde, Audre: *The Collected Poems of Audre Lorde*. New York: Norton, 1997.
———. *Sister Outsider: Essays and Speeches*. Berkeley: Crossing, 2007 [1984].
———. *Zami: A New Spelling of My Name*. Berkeley: Crossing, 1982.
Lowe, Lisa. "Unfaithful to the Original: The Subject of Dictée." In Elaine Kim and Norma Alarcón, eds., *Writing Self/Writing Nation: A Collection of Essays on Dictée by Theresa Hak Kyung Cha*, 35–69. Berkeley: Third Woman, 1994.
Lowell, Amy. *Sword Blades and Poppy Seed*. Boston: Houghton Mifflin, 1914.
Mackworth, H. N. "The Breakdown of Vigilance During Prolonged Visual Search." *Quarterly Journal of Experimental Psychology* 1 (April 1948): 6–21.
MacLennan, George. *Lucid Interval: Subjective Writing and Madness in History*. Leicester: Leicester University Press, 1992.
Majumdar, Saikat. *Prose of the World: Modernism and the Banality of Empire*. New York: Columbia University Press, 2013.
Malebranche, Nicolas. *The Search After Truth: Elucidations of the Search After Truth*. Edited and translated by Thomas M. Lennon and Paul J. Olscamp. Cambridge: Cambridge University Press, 1997.
Mallarmé, Stéphane. *Collected Poems: A Bilingual Edition*. Translated by Henry Weinfield. Berkeley: University of California Press, 1994.
———. *Divagations*. Translated by Barbara Johnson. Cambridge, MA: Harvard University Press, 2007.
———. *Igitur; Divagations; Un Coup de Dés*. Paris: Gallimard, 2003.

Margolis, Eric, and Stephen Laurence. "The Ontology of Concepts—Abstract Objects or Mental Representations." *NOÛS* 41, no. 4 (October 2007): 561–93.

Marks, Laura U. *Touch: Sensuous Theory and Multisensory Media.* Minneapolis: University of Minnesota Press, 2002.

Marno, David. *Death Be Not Proud: The Art of Holy Attention.* Chicago: University of Chicago Press, 2016.

Matar, Nabil. "Alfārābī on Imagination: With a Translation of His 'Treatise on Poetry.'" *College Literature* 23 (February 1996): 100–10.

Maynard, Lee Anna. *Beautiful Boredom: Idleness and Feminine Self-Realization in the Victorian Novel.* Jefferson, NC: McFarland, 2009.

McCabe, Susan. *Elizabeth Bishop: Her Poetics of Loss.* University Park: Pennsylvania State University Press, 1994.

McCaffery, Steve. *Prior to Meaning: The Protosemantic and Poetics.* Evanston, IL: Northwestern University Press, 2001.

McCorkle, James. *The Still Performance: Writing, Self, and Interconnection in Five Postmodern American Poets.* Charlottesville: University Press of Virginia, 1989.

McCullough, Malcolm. *Ambient Commons: Attention in the Age of Embodied Information.* Cambridge, MA: MIT Press, 2013.

McGuirk, Kevin. "A. R. Ammons and the Whole Earth." *Cultural Critique* 37 (Autumn 1997): 131–58.

McKay, Don. "Baler Twine: Thoughts on Ravens, Home, and Nature Poetry." *Studies in Canadian Literature/Études en littérature canadienne* 18, no. 1 (January 1993).

Meltzer, Françoise. "The Hands of Simone Weil." *Critical Inquiry* 27 (Summer 2001): 611–29.

Merton, Thomas. *New Seeds of Contemplation.* New York: New Directions, 1961.

Miller, J. Hillis. *Poets of Reality: Six Twentieth-Century Writers.* Cambridge: Belknap Press of Harvard University Press, 1965.

———. "Wallace Stevens' Poetry of Being." *ELH* 31, no. 1 (March 1964): 86–105.

———. "Wallace Stevens' Poetry of Being." In *Tropes, Parables, Performatives: Essays on Twentieth-Century Literature.* Durham, NC: Duke University Press, 1991.

Mīrābāī. *For Love of the Dark One: Songs of Mirabai.* Translated by Andrew Schelling. Boston: Shambhala, 1993.

Montemayor, Carlos, and Harry Haroutioun Haladjian. *Consciousness, Attention, and Conscious Attention.* Cambridge, MA: MIT Press, 2015.

Moreh, Shmuel. *Modern Arabic Poetry, 1800–1970: The Development of Its Forms and Themes Under the Influence of Western Literature.* Leiden: Brill, 1976.

Moretti, Franco. *Distant Reading.* London: Verso, 2013.

———. *Graphs, Maps, Trees: Abstract Models for a Literary History.* London: Verso, 2005.

Morgan, Benjamin. *The Outward Mind: Materialist Aesthetic in Victorian Science and Literature.* Chicago: University of Chicago Press, 2017.

Motte, Warren F., ed. *Oulipo: A Primer of Potential Literature.* Translated by Warren F. Motte. Normal, IL: Dalkey Archive, 1998.

Mullen, Harryette. *Urban Tumbleweed: Notes from a Tanka Diary.* Minneapolis: Graywolf, 2013.

Murphy, Stephen. *The Gift of Immortality: Myths of Power and Humanist Poetics.* Madison, NJ: Fairleigh Dickinson University Press, 1997.

Muske-Dukes, Carol. "Guided by Dark Stars." *New York Times Book Review,* August 31, 1997, 11–12. Reprinted as "From 'Guided by Dark Stars' (1997)," in *High Lonesome: On the Poetry of Charles Wright,* ed. Adam Gianelli, 83–86. Oberlin, OH: Oberlin College Press, 2006.

Nault, Jean-Charles. *Le Démon de midi—l'acédie, mal obscur de notre temps.* Dijon: L'Échelle de Jacob, 2013.

———. *The Noonday Devil: Acedia, the Unnamed Evil of Our Times.* Translated by Michael J. Miller. San Francisco: Ignatius, 2015.

Ngai, Sianne. *Our Aesthetic Categories: Zany, Cute, Interesting.* Cambridge, MA: Harvard University Press, 2012.

Nhat Hanh, Thich. *The Heart of the Buddha's Teaching: Transforming Suffering Into Peace, Joy, and Liberation: The Four Noble Truths, the Noble Eightfold Path, and Other Basic Buddhist Teachings.* New York: Broadway, 1999.

Nietzsche, Friedrich Wilhelm. *Beyond Good and Evil: On the Genealogy of Morality.* Translated by Adrian Del Caro. Stanford: Stanford University Press, 2014.

———. *The Gay Science,* Edited by Bernard Williams. Translated by Josefine Naukhoff and Adrian Del Caro. Cambridge: Cambridge University Press, 2001.

Novalis. *Werke, Tagebücher Und Briefe Friedrich Von Hardenbergs.* Munich: C. Hanser, 1978.

North, Paul. *The Problem of Distraction.* Stanford: Stanford University Press, 2012.

Nussbaum, Martha. "'Finely Aware and Richly Responsible': Moral Attention and the Moral Task of Literature." *Journal of Philosophy* 82 (October 1985): 516–29.

Nyanaponika, Thera. *The Heart of Buddhist Meditation: The Buddha's Way of Mindfulness.* San Francisco: Weiser, 2014.

O'Connor, Brian. *Idleness: A Philosophical Essay.* Princeton: Princeton University Press, 2018.

O'Hara, Frank. *The Collected Poems of Frank O'Hara.* Edited by Donald Allen. Berkeley: University of California Press, 1995.

Oppen, George. *New Collected Poems.* New York: New Directions, 2002.

Orr, David. "Too Close to Touch: Thom Gunn's *Selected Poems.*" *New York Times Book Review,* July 10, 2009. Accessed March 22, 2016. http://www.nytimes.com/2009/07/12/books/review/Orr-t.html?_r=0.

Pallasmaa, Juhani. *The Eyes of the Skin: Architecture and the Senses.* Chichester: Wiley, 2012.

Palva, Satu, and J. Matias Palva. "New Vistas for Alpha-Frequency Band Oscillations." *Trends in Neurosciences* 30, no. 4 (February 2007): 150–58.

Papanicolaou, Andrew C., ed. *The Oxford Handbook of Functional Brain Imaging in Neuropsychology and Cognitive Neurosciences.* Oxford: Oxford University Press, 2017.

Parker, Patricia A. "Configurations of Shape and Flow." *diacritics* 3 (Winter 1973): 25–33.

Pascal, Blaise. *Pensées.* Translated by A. J. Krailsheimer. London: Penguin, 1995.

Patsouras, Louis. *Simone Weil and the Socialist Tradition.* San Francisco: EMText, 1991.

Pendlebury, Michael. "The Role of Imagination in Perception." *South African Journal of Philosophy* 15, no. 4 (1996): 133–38.

Perloff, Marjorie. *Differentials: Poetry, Poetics, Pedagogy.* Tuscaloosa: University of Alabama Press, 2004.

———. *Unoriginal Genius: Poetry by Other Means in the New Century.* Chicago: University of Chicago Press, 2010.

Petersen, Steven E. and Michael I. Posner. "The Attention System of the Human Brain: Twenty Years After." *Annual Review of Neuroscience* 35 (July 2012): 73–85.

Phillips, Natalie M. *Distraction: Problems of Attention in Eighteenth-Century Literature.* Baltimore: Johns Hopkins University Press, 2016.

Pieper, Josef. *Nur der Liebende singt.* Ostfildern: Schwabenverlag, 1988.

———. *Only the Lover Sings: Art and Contemplation.* Translated by Lothar Krauth. San Francisco: Ignatius, 1990.

Ponge, Francis. *Le parti pris des choses.* Paris: Gallimard, 1942.

———. *Partisan of Things.* Translated by Joshua Corey and Jean-Luc Garneau. Chicago: Kenning, 2016.

———. *The Voice of Things.* Edited and translated by Beth Archer Brombert. New York: McGraw-Hill, 1972.

Posner, Michael I. "Attention as a Cognitive and Neural System." *Current Directions in Psychological Science* 1, no. 1 (February 1992): 11–14.

———. "Orienting of Attention." *Quarterly Journal of Experimental Psychology* 32, no. 1 (February 1980): 3–25.

———. "Orienting of Attention: Then and Now." *Quarterly Journal of Experimental Psychology* 69, no. 10 (October 2010): 1864–75.

Posner, Michael I., and Steven E. Petersen. "The Attention System of the Human Brain." *Annual Review of Neuroscience* 13 (March 1990): 25–42.

Posner, Michael I., and Mary K. Rothbart. "Attention, Self-Regulation, and Consciousness." *Philosophical Transactions of the Royal Society of London B: Biological Sciences* 353 (December 1998): 1915–27.

Posnock, Ross. *Renunciation: Acts of Abandonment by Writers, Philosophers, and Artists.* Cambridge, MA: Harvard University Press, 2016.

Potts, Robert. "Moving Voice." *Guardian,* September 26, 2003. Accessed March 22, 2016. http://www.theguardian.com/books/2003/sep/27/featuresreviews.guardianreview13.

Pound, Ezra. *How to Read.* London: D. Harmsworth, 1931.

Ramazani, Jahan. *Poetry and Its Others: News, Prayer, Song, and the Dialogue of Genres.* Chicago: University of Chicago Press, 2014.

———. *Poetry of Mourning: The Modern Elegy from Hardy to Heaney.* Chicago: University of Chicago Press, 1994.

Ramazani, Jahan, Richard Ellmann, and Robert O'Clair, eds. *The Norton Anthology of Modern and Contemporary Poetry,* vol. 1: *Modern Poetry.* New York: Norton, 2003.

Ramazani, Jahan, Richard Ellmann, and Robert O'Clair, eds. *The Norton Anthology of Modern and Contemporary Poetry,* vol. 2: *Contemporary Poetry.* New York: Norton, 2003.

Ramirez, Dennis. *Default Mode Network (DMN): Structural Connectivity, Impairments and Role in Daily Activities.* Neuroscience Research Progress Series. Hauppauge, NY: Nova Biomedical, 2015.

Rankine, Claudia. *Citizen: An American Lyric.* Minneapolis: Graywolf, 2014.

Raposa, Michael L. "Boredom and the Religious Imagination." *Journal of the American Academy of Religion* 53 (March 1985): 75–91.

———. *Boredom and the Religious Imagination.* Charlottesville: University of Virginia Press, 1999.

Reddy, Srikanth. *Changing Subjects: Digressions in Modern American Poetry.* Oxford: Oxford University Press, 2012.

Reiman, Donald H. "A. R. Ammons: Ecological Naturalism and the Romantic Tradition." *Twentieth Century Literature* 31 (Spring 1985): 22–54.

Retallack, Joan. *Errata 5uite.* Washington, DC: Edge, 1993.

———. *The Poethical Wager.* Berkeley: University of California Press, 2003.

Richards, I. A. *How to Read a Page: A Course in Effective Reading, with an Introduction to a Hundred Great Words.* New York: Norton, 1942.

Rilke, Rainer Maria. *New Poems.* Translated by Edward Snow. New York: North Point, 2001.

Rimbaud, Arthur. *Rimbaud: Complete Works, Selected Letters—a Bilingual Edition.* Translated by Wallace Fowlie. Chicago: University of Chicago Press, 2005.

Ringmar, Erik. "Attention and the Cause of Modern Boredom," In *Boredom Studies: Postdisciplinary Inquiries,* edited by Michael E. Gardiner and Julian Jason Haladyn. New York: Routledge, 2016.

Roberson, Ed. *To See the Earth Before the End of the World.* Middletown, CT: Wesleyan University Press, 2010.

Rossky, William. "Imagination in the English Renaissance: Psychology and Poetic." *Studies in the Renaissance* 5 (1958): 49–73.

de Rougemont, Denis. *L'Amour et l'occident.* Paris: Plon, 1972 [1940].

———. *Love in the Western World.* Translated by Montgomery Belgion. Princeton: Princeton University Press, 1983 [1956].

Russell, Bertrand. *In Praise of Idleness: And Other Essays.* London: Routledge, 2004.

Sacks, Peter M. *The English Elegy: Studies in the Genre from Spenser to Yeats.* Baltimore: Johns Hopkins University Press, 1985.

Samivel. *The Glory of Egypt.* New York: Vanguard, 1955.

Śāntideva. *The Bodhicaryāvatāra.* Translated by Kate Crosby and Andrew Skilton. Oxford: Oxford University Press, 1995.

Sappho. *If Not, Winter: Fragments of Sappho.* Translated by Anne Carson. New York: Vintage, 2003.

Scarry, Elaine. *Dreaming by the Book.* New York: Farrar, Straus and Giroux, 1999.

Schalkwyk, David. "Love and Service in Twelfth Night and the Sonnets." *Shakespeare Quarterly* 56 (Spring 2005): 76–100.

Schlegel, Friedrich von. *Friedrich Schlegel's Lucinde and the Fragments.* Translated by Peter Firchow. Minneapolis: University of Minnesota Press, 1971.

Schneider, Steven P. *A. R. Ammons and the Poetics of Widening Scope.* Rutherford, NJ: Fairleigh Dickinson University Press, 1994.

———, ed. *Complexities of Motion: New Essays on A. R. Ammons's Long Poems.* Madison, NJ: Fairleigh Dickinson University Press, 1999.

Schopenhauer, Arthur. *Parerga and Paralipomena: Short Philosophical Essays.* Edited and translated by Sabine Roehr and Christopher Janaway. Cambridge: Cambridge University Press, 2014.

Scoggins, James. *Imagination and Fancy: Complementary Modes in the Poetry of Wordsworth*. Lincoln: University of Nebraska Press, 1966.

Scott, William O. "Perotti, Ficino, and Furor Poeticus." *Res Publica Litterarum* 4 (1981): 273–84.

Searle, John. *Seeing Things As They Are: A Theory of Perception*. Oxford: Oxford University Press, 2015.

Seemann, Axel, ed. *Joint Attention: New Developments in Psychology, Philosophy of Mind, and Social Neuroscience*. Cambridge, MA: MIT Press, 2011.

Schroeder, Timothy. *Three Faces of Desire*. Oxford: Oxford University Press, 2004.

Shakespeare, William. *The Plays of William Shakespeare*, vol. 2. Edited by Samuel Johnson and George Steevens. London: J. and R. Tonson, 1765.

———. *Shakespeare's Sonnets*. Edited by Katherine Duncan-Jones. Nashville, TN: Thomas Nelson, 1997.

Shaw, Geraldine. "The Multisensory Image and Emotion in Poetry." *Psychology of Aesthetics, Creativity, and the Arts* 2 (August 2008): 175–78.

Shultis, Christopher. "Silencing the Sounded Self: John Cage and the Intentionality of Nonintention." *Musical Quarterly* 79 (Summer 1995): 312–50.

Siderits, Mark. *Buddhism as Philosophy: An Introduction*. Indianapolis: Hackett, 2007.

Silkin, Jon. "The Poetry of Geoffrey Hill." *Iowa Review* 3 (Summer 1972): 108–28.

Simic, Charles. "To Boredom." *New Yorker,* December 10, 2007. Accessed March 22, 2016. http://www.newyorker.com/magazine/2007/12/10/to-boredom.

Sisk, John P. "The End of Boredom." *Georgia Review* 39 (Spring 1985): 25–34.

Skillman, Nikki. *The Lyric in the Age of the Brain*. Cambridge, MA: Harvard University Press, 2016.

Sloterdijk, Peter. *Du mußt dein Leben ändern*. Frankfurt: Suhrkamp, 2009.

———. *You Must Change Your Life: On Anthropotechnics*. Cambridge: Polity, 2013.

Snell, R. J. *Acedia and Its Discontents: Metaphysical Boredom in an Empire of Desire*. Kettering, OH: Angelico, 2015.

Spacks, Patricia Meyer. *Boredom: The Literary History of a State of Mind*. Chicago: University of Chicago Press, 1995.

Spargo, R. Clifton. *The Ethics of Mourning: Grief and Responsibility in Elegiac Literature*. Baltimore: Johns Hopkins University Press, 2004.

Sparling, Robert. "Theory and Praxis: Simone Weil and Marx on the Dignity of Labor." *Review of Politics* 74 (Winter 2012): 87–107.

Starr, Gabrielle. "Poetic Subjects and Grecian Urns: Close Reading and the Tools of Cognitive Science." *Modern Philology* 105 (August 2007): 48–61.

Stearns, Peter. *American Cool: Constructing a Twentieth-Century Emotional Style*. New York: New York University Press, 1994.

Stevens, Wallace. *The Collected Poems of Wallace Stevens*. New York: Knopf, 1954.

———. *Collected Poetry and Prose*. New York: Library of America, 1997.

Stewart, Susan. "Discandied: On Women and Elegy." *Nation,* September 12, 2011. Accessed April 16, 2016. http://www.thenation.com/article/162953/discandied-women-and-elegy?page=0,2.

———. *Poetry and the Fate of the Senses*. Chicago: University of Chicago Press, 2002.

———. *The Poet's Freedom: A Notebook on Making*. Chicago: University of Chicago Press, 2011.

Stockwell, Peter. *Cognitive Poetics: An Introduction*. Abingdon: Routledge, 2002.

———. "Surreal Figures," In *Cognitive Poetics in Practice*, edited by Joanna Gavins and Gerard Steen, 13–26. London: Routledge, 2003.

Svendsen, Lars. *A Philosophy of Boredom*. London: Reaktion, 2005.

Swigg, Richard, ed. *Speaking with George Oppen: Interviews with the Poet and Mary Oppen, 1968–1987*. Jefferson, NC: McFarland, 2012.

Szondi, Peter. "Reading 'Engführung': An Essay on the Poetry of Paul Celan." Trans. D. Caldwell and S. Esh. *Boundary 2* 11, no. 3, "The Criticism of Peter Szondi" (Spring 1983): 231–64.

Tan, Joan Qionglin. *Han Shan, Chan Buddhism, and Gary Snyder's Ecopoetic Way*. Brighton: Sussex Academic, 2009.

Theeuwes, Jan. "Exogenous and Endogenous Control of Attention: The Effect of Visual Onsets and Offsets." *Perception and Psychophysics* 49 (January 1991): 83–90.

Thomson, D.F.S. *Catullus*. Toronto and Buffalo: University of Toronto Press, 1997.

Tigerstedt, Eugène Napoléon. "Furor Poeticus: Poetic Inspiration in Greek Literature Before Democritus and Plato." *Journal of the History of Ideas* 31 (April-June 1970): 163–78.

Tocqueville, Alexis de. *Democracy in America*. New York: Knopf, 1945.

Toohey, Peter. *Melancholy, Love, and Time: Boundaries of the Self in Ancient Literature*. Ann Arbor: University of Michigan Press, 2004.

———. "Some Ancient Forms of Boredom." *Illinois Classical Studies* 13 (Spring 1988): 151–64.

Urgo, Joseph R. *In the Age of Distraction*. Jackson: University Press of Mississippi, 2000.

Vander Weele, Michael. "Simone Weil and George Herbert on the Vocations of Reading and Writing." *Religion and Literature* 32 (Autumn 2000): 69–102.

Vattimo, Gianni. "'Verwindung': Nihilism and the Postmodern in Philosophy." *SubStance* 16, no. 2 (1987): 7–17.

Vendler, Helen. *The Art of Shakespeare's Sonnets*. Cambridge, MA: Harvard University Press, 1997.

———. *The Breaking of Style: Hopkins, Heaney, Graham*. Cambridge, MA: Harvard University Press, 1995.

———. "Charles Wright." In *The Music of What Happens: Poems, Poets, Critics*. Cambridge, MA: Belknap Press of Harvard University Press, 1988. Reprinted as "'Travels in Time' (1988)," in *High Lonesome: On the Poetry of Charles Wright*, ed. Adam Gianelli, 29–35. Oberlin, OH: Oberlin College Press, 2006.

———. "Lowell's Persistence: The Forms Depression Makes." *Kenyon Review* 22 (Winter 2000): 216–33.

———. *The Music of What Happens: Poems, Poets, Critics*. Cambridge, MA: Belknap Press of Harvard University Press, 1988.

———. *The Ocean, the Scholar, the Bird*. Cambridge, MA: Harvard University Press, 2015.

von Hallberg, Robert. *Lyric Powers*. Chicago: University of Chicago Press, 2008.

Warm, Joel S., Raja Parasuraman, and Gerald Matthews. "Vigilance Requires Hard Mental Work and Is Stressful." *Human Factors* 50 (June 2008): 433–41.

Weil, Simone. *Attente de Dieu*. Paris: Fayard, 1966.

———. *Cahiers, tomes I, II, et III*. Rev. ed. Paris: Plon, 1970–1974.
———. *Gravity and Grace*. Translated by Arthur Wills. Lincoln: University of Nebraska Press, 1997.
———. *The Notebooks of Simone Weil*. Translated by Arthur Wills. Abingdon: Routledge, 2004 [1956].
———. *La Pesanteur et la grâce*. Paris: Plon, 1947.
———. *Simone Weil: An Anthology*, ed. Siân Miles. New York: Grove, 1986.
———. *Waiting for God*. Translated by Emma Craufurd. New York: HarperCollins, 2009.
Weiss, Peter. *Die Ermittlung: Oratorium in 11 Gesängen*. Frankfurt: Suhrkamp, 2005.
White, Gillian. *Lyric Shame: The "Lyric" Subject of Contemporary American Poetry*. Cambridge, MA: Harvard University Press, 2014.
Whitman, Walt. *Leaves of Grass*. Edited by Harold W. Blodgett and Sculley Bradley. New York: New York University Press, 1965.
Wilhelm, James J. *Ezra Pound: The Tragic Years (1925–1972)*. University Park: Pennsylvania State University Press, 1994.
Willard, Nancy. *Swimming Lessons: New and Selected Poems*. New York: Knopf, 1996.
Wittgenstein, Ludwig. "A Lecture on Ethics," *Philosophical Review* 74 (January 1965): 3–12.
Wong, Shelly Sunn. "Unnaming the Same: Theresa Hak Kyung Cha's DICTEE." In Kim and Norma Alarcón, eds., *Writing Self/Writing Nation: A Collection of Essays on Dictée by Theresa Hak Kyung Cha*, 103–40. Berkeley: Third Woman, 1994.
Wordsworth, William. *The Complete Poetical Works of William Wordsworth*. New York: Macmillan, 1893.
———. *Lyrical Ballads and Other Poems, 1797–1800*. Edited by James Butler and Karen Green. Ithaca, NY: Cornell University Press, 1992.
———. *The Prelude. Wordsworth's Major Works Including The Prelude*, 375–590. Ed. Stephen Gill. New York: Oxford University Press, 2008.
———. *The Prelude of 1850*. In *The Prelude: 1799, 1805, 1850*, 29–483, edited by Jonathan Wordsworth, M. H. Abrams, and Stephen Gill. New York: Norton, 1979.
Wright, Charles. *Halflife: Improvisations and Interviews, 1977–87*. Ann Arbor: University of Michigan Press, 1988.
———. *Negative Blue: Selected Later Poems*. New York: Farrar, Straus and Giroux, 2000.
———. *The World of the Ten Thousand Things: Poems, 1980–1990*. New York: Farrar, Straus and Giroux, 1990.
Wright, James. *Above the River: The Complete Poems*. New York: Farrar, Straus and Giroux, 1990.
Wu, Tim. *The Attention Merchants: The Epic Scramble to Get Inside Our Heads*. New York: Knopf, 2016.
Zagajewski, Adam. *A Defense of Ardor: Essays*. Translated by Clare Cavanaugh. New York: Farrar, Straus and Giroux, 2004.
Žižek, Slavoj. *Tarrying with the Negative: Kant, Hegel, and the Critique of Ideology*. Durham, NC: Duke University Press, 1993.
Zuckert, Rachel. "Boring Beauty and Universal Morality: Kant on the Ideal of Beauty." *Inquiry* 48, no. 2 (April 2005): 107–30.

Permission Credits

Anonymous, "Women's Love Song," translated by Sam Hamill, from *The Erotic Spirit: An Anthology of Poems of Sensuality, Love, and Longing*, edited by Sam Hamill, copyright ©1996 by Sam Hamill. Reprinted by arrangement with the Permissions Company, Inc., on behalf of Shambhala Publications Inc., Boulder, Colorado, www.shambhala.com.

Marcus Argentarius, a text extract from not exceeding 50 words on page 155 from A. S. F. Gow, *The Greek Anthology 2 Volume Set, The Garland of Philip and some Contemporary Epigrams* copyright © Cambridge University Press 1968. Reprinted with permission from Cambridge University Press.

Ingeborg Bachmann, excerpts from ["Immerzu in den Worten sein" / "Always to live among words"] translated by Peter Filkins, from Darkness Spoken: The Collected Poems of Ingeborg Bachmann. Copyright © 1978, 2000 by Piper Verlag GmbH, München. Translation copyright © 2006 by Peter Filkins. Reprinted with the permission of The Permissions Company LLC on behalf of Zephyr Press, www.zephyrpress.org.

John Burnside, "The Fair Chase" from Black Cat Bone. Copyright © 2011 by John Burnside. Reprinted with the permission of the Permissions Company LLC on behalf of Graywolf Press, www.graywolfpress.org.

Poetry and translations from Anne Carson, NOX, copyright © 2010 by Anne Carson. Reprinted by permission of New Directions Publishing Corp.

THE POEMS OF EMILY DICKINSON: READING EDITION, edited by Ralph W. Franklin, Cambridge, Mass.: The Belknap Press of Harvard University Press, Copyright © 1998, 1999 by the President and Fellows of Harvard College. Copyright © 1951, 1955 by the President and Fellows of Harvard College. Copyright © renewed 1979, 1983 by the President and Fellows of Harvard College. Copyright © 1914, 1918, 1919, 1924, 1929, 1930, 1932, 1935, 1937, 1942 by Martha Dickinson Bianchi. Copyright © 1952, 1957, 1958, 1963, 1965 by Mary L. Hampson.

Seamus Heaney, "Oysters," and "Blackberry Picking" from *Opened Ground* © 1998 by Seamus Heaney. Reprinted with the permission of Faber and Faber, Ltd. and Farrar, Straus, and Giroux.

"September Song" from *New and Collected Poems, 1955–1992* by Geoffrey Hill. Copyright © 1994 by Geoffrey Hill. Reprinted by permission of Houghton Mifflin Harcourt Publishing Company. All rights reserved.

Poems from Friedrich Hölderlin, *Friedrich Hölderline: Poems and Fragments,* translated by Michael Hamburger, copyright © 1966, 1980, 1994, 2004 by Michael Hamburger. Reprinted with permission of Carcanet Press, Ltd.

Li-Young Lee, "Eating Alone" from Rose. Copyright © 1986 by Li-Young Lee. Reprinted with the permission of The Permissions Company, Inc., on behalf of BOA Editions, Ltd., www.boaeditions.org.

"The Blue Scarf" by Amy Lowell from THE COMPLETE POETICAL WORKS OF AMY LOWELL. Copyright © 1955 by Houghton Mifflin Company. Copyright © renewed 1983 by Houghton Mifflin Company, Brinton P. Roberts, and G. D'Andelot, Esquire. Reprinted with the permission of Houghton Mifflin Company. All rights reserved.

Derek Mahon, "A Disused Shed in Co. Wexford," from *New Collected Poems* © 2011 by Derek Mahon. Reprinted with the permission of The Gallery Press, Loughcrew, Oldcastle, Co Meath, Ireland. www.gallerypress.com

Lines from Mirabai in *For Love of the Dark One* reprinted by permission of the translator, Andrew Schelling.

Excerpts from *Urban Tumbleweed: Notes from a Tanka Diary.* Copyright © 2013 by Harryette Mullen. Reprinted with the permission of The Permissions Company, Inc., on behalf of Graywolf Press, www.graywolfpress.org.

"Psalm" By George Oppen, from NEW COLLECTED POEMS, copyright ©1965 by George Oppen. Reprinted by permission of New Directions Publishing Corp. UK permission granted by Carcanet Press, Ltd.

Quotations from Joan Retallack, *Errata 5uite,* copyright © 1993 by Joan Retallack. Reprinted with the permission of the author.

Claudia Rankine, excerpts from *Citizen: An American Lyric*. Copyright © 2014 by Claudia Rankine. Reprinted with the permission of The Permissions Company, Inc., on behalf of Graywolf Press, www.graywolfpress.org.

Quotations from Arthur Rimbaud, *Complete Works, Selected Letters: A Bilingual Edition*, translated by Wallace Fowlie. University of Chicago Press, reprint edition, 2005. Approximately 480 words from pages 198, 256, 276, 277, 278, 279, 280, 292, 296, 297, 298, 301, and 377; "Farewell": half of poem (page 303); and "City" (page 327), reprinted with permission from University of Chicago Press.

Wallace Stevens, "Study of Two Pears," and "Angel Surrounded by Paysans" from THE COLLECTED POEMS OF WALLACE STEVENS by Wallace Stevens, copyright © 1954 by Wallace Stevens and copyright renewed 1982 by Holly Stevens. Used by permission of Alfred A. Knopf, an imprint of the Knopf.

Doubleday Publishing Group, a division of Penguin Random House LLC. All rights reserved.

James Wright, "Autumn Begins in Martins Ferry, Ohio" from *Above the River: The Complete Poems* copyright © 1990 by Anne Wright. Reprinted with permission of Wesleyan University Press.

Index

abîme. See blanks
Abrams, M. H., 230
acedia, in Eliot, 256–57, 260–65
active passivity, 153–55
"Adieu" (Rimbaud), 199–200
Adorno, Theodor, 107
aesthetics, 16
Agamben, Giorgio, 239
agape, in *Four Quartets*, 260–61, 267
aimlessness, 215–16
alertness, 167; *Un Coup de dés* and, 181; Hölderlin and, 176; stress and, 305*n*2
Alexandrines, in *Un Coup de dés*, 186, 189
Ali, Agha Shahid, 277–78
Allen, William, 174
Altieri, Charles, 61, 65
ambient attention, 213–15
Ammons, A. R., 268–69, 314*n*24; "Attention," 225–26, 315*n*34; banter in, 224; Bloom on, 314*n*28; *Bosh and Flapdoodle*, 224; Buell on, 228, 230; ecopoetics and, 230; "Fasting," 224–25; friendship in, 228; *Garbage*, 227–30; God and, 226, 228; "Gravelly Run," 227–28; idleness in, 6, 218, 224–31, 314*n*28; insight in, 315*n*30; meditative practice in, 224–31, 315*n*30, 316*n*40, 316*n*47; revelation absent in, 226; *Tape for the Turn of the Year*, 225–26; walking and, 224–31, 314*n*28; wonder in, 315*n*30
anti-elegy, 102–5, 296*n*13
anxiety, temporal inflection of, 160
apprehension, 5, 28–29, 288*n*37; Benn and, 46–48; capture and, 43, 71; Heaney and, 44–46; narrative and, 46; *Nox* and, 44; "Of the Surface of Things" and, 48–49; Poem 962 and, 48; Ponge and, 45–46; reader, as dependent on, 49–50; resolution and, 44, 46–48
"Approaching Things: Some Calculations How Figure It of Everyday Life Experience" (Eigner), 285*n*10

Aquinas, Thomas, 92
Arata, Stephen, 217–18
Argentarius, Marcus, 83, 293*n*10
Aristotle, 4; God and, 262; imagination and, 125, 127, 134, 303*n*20, 303*n*22, 304*n*30; mimesis and, 16
Arnold, Matthew, 308*n*7
Ashbery, John, 219–20, 223
askesis, in *Four Quartets*, 260–64
"As on a Holiday. . . ." *See* "Wie wenn am Feiertage . . ."
"Astern" (Benn), 46–48
attention. *See specific topics*
"Attention" (Ammons), 225–26, 315*n*34
attentional polydexterity, 276
attention economy, 107
attention studies, 4
attractors, 282*n*18
Atwood, Margaret, 242
"Autumn Begins in Martins Ferry, Ohio" (Wright, C.), 1–3

Bachmann, Ingeborg, 100
banter, 220–23, 224
Barbarese, J. T., 316*n*40
Barthes, Roland, 77
Bashō, Matsuo: *Oku no Hosomichi*, 72; selectivity and, 36
Basri, Rābi'a al-, 78–79
Bataille, Georges, 246, 311*n*42, 315*n*29; God and, 200–1, 310*n*34; Rimbaud and, 200–4
Bateson, Frederick Wilse, 41
Baudelaire, Charles: Benjamin on, 259; resignation and, 191, 196
Baumgarten, Alexander Gottlieb, 303*n*23; taste and, 16
Baumgartner, Wilhelm, 280*n*9
Bayāti, 'Abd al-Wahhab Al-, 38
Bending the Bow (Duncan), 269, 272, 322*n*2

Benjamin, Walter, 16, 180, 233; Baudelaire and, 259; history and, 108; lyric and, 259
Benn, Gottfried, 46–48
Bermann, Sandra. L., 88
Bernstein, Charles, 323*n*13; contemplation and, 274–75; idleness and, 218, 314*n*12
Berryman, John, 242
bint 'Amr, Tumadir. *See* Al-Khansā'
Bishop, Elizabeth, 55–56, 67–69, 290*n*23, 290*nn*25–26
"Blackberry-Picking" (Heaney), 45
Blanchot, Maurice, 95, 97, 203, 255–56, 294*n*29; Hölderlin and, 172–173; Mallarmé and, 184–85, 307*n*24; vigilance and, 168–69, 172–73
blanks (*l'abîme*): *Un Coup de dés* and, 181–85, 189; Retallack and, 232, 234–35; C. Wright and, 207
Bloom, Harold: Ammons and, 314*n*28; "Tintern Abbey" and, 137
"Blue, Scarf, The" (Lowell), 90–91
blues: Bukowski and, 245; S. James and, 206, 311*n*56
the body, 11–13, 269–75, 323*n*20; as corpse, 96, 254–56; materiality of language and, 96–97
boredom, 6, 152, 164–65, 237, 319*n*29, 321*n*59; *acedia* and, 256–57, 260–64; Agamben on, 239; Atwood and, 242; Bukowski and, 242–46, 256; colonialism and, 240; Eastwood on, 238–39; Epstein on, 242; form, perfect, of, 246–56; *Four Quartets* and, 243, 256, 260–67; Goodstein on, 240–41; Gunn and, 243, 246, 248–56; Heidegger on, 239; idleness versus, 212–13; intentionality (intransitive) and, 155, 213; Kant on, 247; "The Love Song of J. Alfred Prufrock"

and, 256–58; modernity and, 214–15, 239–41, 247–48, 256–64; Nietzsche and, 247; paradise and, 246–48, 256; perfection and, 246–56, 319*n*27; photography and, 246–47; poetry on, 241–43; productivity and, 242; resignation and, 196–202; Rimbaud and, 196–202; Schopenhauer on, 247, 264–65, 319*n*29; secularization and, 240; self-realization, feminine, and, 319*n*11; Seneca on, 238–39; temporal suspension and, 238–39, 256; transhistoricity and, 238, 243; *The Waste Land* and, 243, 256–61; Weil and, 321*n*59

Bosh and Flapdoodle (Ammons), 224
"Bowl of Roses." *See* "Rosenschale, Die"
Boym, Svetlana, 309*n*9
breath, 270–71, 273–74
Brentano, Franz, 280*n*9
"Brod und Wein" (Hölderlin), 174–80
Buddhism, 203, 233, 264, 316*n*47; contemplation in, 54
Buell, Frederick, 228, 230
Bukowski, Charles: boredom in, 242–46, 256; desire in, 245–46; effort in, 243–46; intentionality (intransitive) and, 244–46; love in, 245–46; sexual violence in, 245
Burnside, John, 126, 145–47
Byrne, Ruth M. J., 301*n*2
Byron (Lord), 215–16

Cage, John, 318*n*55; idleness and, 234–35; intentionality (intransitive) and, 318*n*56
Cahier d'un retour au pays natal (Césaire), 35
Calvino, Italo, 59

capture, 43; contemplation and, 71
Carruth, Hayden, 277
Carson, Anne, 70–71, 142; *If Not, Winter,* 300*n*50; Sappho and, 162–63, 300*n*50. *See also Nox*
Carver, George Washington, 71
catastrophe, 191; "Engführung" and, 108–14; recollection and, 108–14, 295*n*3
Catullus: in *Nox*, 115, 119, 299*n*46; *otium* and, 216–17; poem 51, 216–17; poem 101, 115, 119, 299*n*46
Caygill, Howard, 303*n*22
Celan, Paul, 191, 203, 322*n*7; embodiment and, 271–74; "The Meridian," 124, 270–72; orientative possibility in, 274; potentiality and, 270–71; "Todesfuge," 108. *See also* "Engführung"
Césaire, Aimé, 35
Cha, Theresa Hak Kyung, 121–24, 300*n*53, 300*n*58, 300*n*60
chance. *See* contingency
chaos, in *Un Coup de dés,* 186–87
Chase, William Merritt, 66
Cheng, Anne Anlin, 121–22, 300*n*58
Christianity, contemplation in, 54
Citizen: An American Lyric (Rankine), 73, 272–74
close reading, 17, 282*n*27; formalism and, 17
Coleridge, Samuel Taylor, 302*n*10, 304*n*31; fancy and, 129–32; imagination and, 126, 128–32; "Kubla Khan," 142–43; *Lyrical Ballads* and, 129–30, 136
colonialism, boredom and, 240
concentration. *See* selectivity
connotation, resolution and, 41
constitution, subjectivity and, 161–64

contemplation, 5, 52, 53, 274; Bernstein and, 274–75; Buddhism and, 54; capture and, 71; Christianity and, 54; Croce on, 50; desire and, 77–79; "The Fish" and, 55–56, 67–69; *Gelassenheit* and, 77; Hölderlin and, 174–75, 177; intentionality (transitive) and, 54, 74; interest and, 51; "L'Huître" and, 58–60; love and, 91–94, 294n26; metaphorization and, 57–60; "The Necessary Angel" and, 50; object-oriented poetry and, 56–57; Oppen and, 91–94; "Oysters" and, 59–60; painting and, 64–71; privilege and, 59–60, 71–74; "Die Rosenschale" and, 139–40; silence and, 75; spatiotemporal remove and, 51; spiritual practice and, 54–55; "A Study of Two Pears" and, 56–57, 61–65; *Urban Tumbleweed* and, 56, 71–74

contingency: chaos as, 186–87; *Un Coup de dés* and, 181–90; form and, 19–20; postmodernism and, 195; resignation and, 195; Retallack and, 234

conversation. *See* banter; friendship

Corcoran, Neil, 296n9

Costello, Bonnie: Bishop and, 67; Stevens and, 65

Coup de dés jamais n'abolira le hasard, Un (throw of the dice will never abolish chance, A) (Mallarmé): alertness in, 181; Alexandrines in, 186, 189; blanks in, 181–85, 189; chaos in, 186–87; contingency in, 181–90; event in, 188–89; Hegel and, 187, 189; nonrevelatory vigilance in, 170, 181–90; practice in, 181, 190; presence in, 188; temporal inflection in, 188

Crary, Jonathan, 306n9

Crews, Brian, 195

Crise de vers (Mallarmé), 183, 186, 307n35

Critchley, Simon, 20

Croce, Benedetto, 50

Culler, Jonathan, 9

Cummings, E. E., 46

"Curtains in the House of the Metaphysician, The" (Stevens), 40–41

Cushman, Stephen, 315n30

Damrosch, David, 283n34

Dante Alighieri, 142–43

death, 300n49; desire and, 80–81, 96; "Engführung" and, 108–14; of God, 191, 299–300nn48–49; Gunn and, 254–56; of Hugo, 183–84; Mallarmé and, 183–84; *Nox* and, 115–16, 118–20; Stevens and, 96, 308n5; C. Wright and, 208–10

"Death of a Naturalist" (Heaney), 44–45

deconcentration, 36; Hölderlin and, 171

decreation: ecstasy and, 162–63; kenosis and, 161, 263–67; Miller on, 191; Sappho and, 162–63; subjectivity and, 161–64; Weil on, 169

defamiliarization, 297n22; Hölderlin and, 176–77

default mode network, 213

"Defense of Poesy, The" (Sidney), 44

deintegration, 37–38

denotation, resolution and, 41

desire, 33, 50, 52, 292n6, 293n9, 293n10; Barthes and, 77; Bukowski and, 245–46; contemplation and, 77–79; death and, 80–81, 96; figure-ground relationship and, 84; *Four Quartets* and, 260–67; Hass and, 78, 94–95; Hölderlin and, 172–73; "I had been Hungry all the Years" and, 5, 81–82; imagination and, 84, 88, 90; intentionality (intransitive) and, 154–55; interest and, 51, 76–84;

lesbian love poems and, 88–91; Lorde and, 88–89; Lowell and, 90–91; Mahon and, 32; "Meditation at Lagunitas" and, 78, 94–95; Sappho and, 31; selectivity and, 84; Shakespeare and, 82; spatiotemporal remove and, 78–84, 88–91, 95–97, 292n3; vigilance and, 169–70; *The Waste Land* and, 259–60; Weil on, 169–70
despair, 196, 199–204
Deuteronomy, 298n29
devotional poems, 154
Dickinson, Emily, 269; grace and, 159; "I had been Hungry all the Years," 5, 81–82; poem 76, 159; poem 466, 158–59; poem 962, 48; scope and, 158–59; selectivity and, 36; subjectivity in, 163–64
Dictee (Cha), 300n53, 300n60; Cheng on, 121–22, 300n58; Hesiod in, 122; hope in, 123; memoir and, 121–24; photography in, 121–22; recollection in, 121–24
"Dinggedichte" (Rilke), 136, 139–41
direct perception, 26–28
disinterest. *See* interest
distant reading, 17, 283n34
distraction, 53–54
"Disused Shed in Co. Wexford, A" (Mahon), 32–33
divinity, in C. Wright, 208–11
documentary: *Dictee* as, 121–24; *Nox* as, 115–16, 118–20
Donne, John, 288n1
Doreski, C. K., 290n26
Doty, Mark, 66, 69–70, 291n29
double transitivity, of poetry, 14, 26–28
"Dreamsong 14" (Berryman), 242
dropped lines, in C. Wright, 207, 311n57
Dryden, John, 127

Dubois, Andrew, 282n27
Duncan, Robert, 269, 272, 322n2

Eastwood, John, 238–39
ecopoetics, 230
ecstasy: decreation and, 162–63; "The Fish" and, 69, 291n27; Lowell and, 90–91; meditative practice and, 315n29; Sappho and, 162–63
effort, 20, 153–55; in Bukowski, 243–46; "Engführung" and, 108; imagination and, 147–48; spatiotemporal remove and, 78. *See also* intentionality
Egyptian love poems, 76, 79–81, 292n5
Eigner, Larry, 285n10
ekphrasis, 66, 70; "A Study of Two Pears" and, 61
elaboration, imagination and, 134–36
elegiac attention, 43
elegy, 42, 297n22, 297n24; anti-, 102–5, 296n13; history and, 98–99, 101–2, 120, 295n7; *marthiya* as, 104, 296n17; melancholia and, 103; modern, 102–3, 106–8, 297n23, 299n48; mourning and, 99–108, 299n48; negative, 115; *Nox* as, 115–16, 118–20; Ramazani on, 101–3, 296n13, 297nn23–24, 299–300nn48–49; silence as enemy of, 124; transhistoricity and, 102
Eliot, T. S., 287n20, 321n59; acedia in, 256–57, 260–65; *Four Quartets*, 243, 256, 260–67, 321n55, 321n64; God and, 262–63; impersonality and, 266; kenosis and, 263–67; "The Love Song of J. Alfred Prufrock," 256–58; meditative practice in, 256–57, 260–65; resignation and, 191–92; selectivity and, 38; "Tradition and the Individual Talent," 266; *The Waste Land*, 38, 88, 108, 113, 243, 256–61; Wordsworth and, 266

embodiment, 323*n*20; Celan and, 271–74; Rankine and, 272–74

endogenous attention, 29, 33–35; imagination and, 131, 139, 148; intentionality (intransitive) and, 153–55; subjectivity and, 161. *See also* effort

"Engführung" (Celan): catastrophe and, 108–14; death and, 108–14; effort in, 108; Felstiner on, 298*n*25, 298*n*29, 299*n*43; prayer in, 111–13; recollection and, 108–14, 124; spectatorship in, 110; Szondi on, 109, 114, 298*nn*26–27, 299*n*41; *The Waste Land* and, 108, 113

ennui: boredom and, 214, 313*n*4; in Eliot, 258–59; resignation and, 191, 196; in Rimbaud, 201

Epicurus, 233

epiphany, in "The Fish," 290*n*26

Epstein, Andrew, 19; boredom and, 242; *Urban Tumbleweed* and, 73

errata, 317*n*50

Errata 5uite (Retallack), 232–35

"Essay as Wager" (Retallack), 232

ethics, poetic attention relationship with, 276–77

event: *Un Coup de dés* and, 188–89; Hölderlin and, 172–73, 180

eventfulness, of imagination, 147

"Everything That Acts Is Actual" (Levertov), 132

exclusivity, scope and, 157–59

exogenous attention, 29, 33–35; imagination and, 131, 139, 148; intentionality (intransitive) and, 153, 155; subjectivity and, 161–62. *See also* active passivity; effort

"Faim" (Rimbaud), 198

"Fair Chase, The" (Burnside), 126, 145–47

fancy, 134; Coleridge on, 129–32; *Four Quartets* and, 262–63

"Fasting" (Ammons), 224–25

Felstiner, John: "Engführung" and, 298*n*25, 298*n*29, 299*n*43; Hölderlin and, 174

Ferrarello, Susi, 281*n*11, 321*n*1

fictionality, imagination and, 134

Fighting Terms (Gunn), 248

figure-ground relationship, 12, 281*n*15; attractors and, 282*n*18; desire and, 84; graded depth and, 13; intentionality (transitive) and, 13–14; love and, 84; spotlight model and, 13

"Fish, The" (Bishop), 290*n*23; contemplation in, 55–56, 67–69; ecstasy in, 69, 291*n*27; epiphany in, 290*n*26; imagination in, 290*n*25; McCabe on, 68, 290*n*26

flaneur, *Urban Tumbleweed* and, 73

flowers, imagination and, 140–41, 304*n*30

Fludernik, Monika, 313*n*6

focalization: Hölderlin and, 171; imaginative, 27–28; Kant and, 27; object, attentional stance directed toward, 51; scope and, 157–58

focus, 53–54

Forché, Carolyn, 99, 120, 295*n*3

form, 3–4, 279*n*3; boredom and, 246–56; contingency and, 19–20

formalism, historicism and, 12, 15, 17, 282*n*22

Four Quartets (Eliot), 321*n*55, 321*n*64; *agape* in, 260–61, 267; *askesis* in, 260–64; boredom in, 243, 256, 260–67; desire in, 260–67; fancy in, 262–63; grace in, 264

Fragment 31 (Sappho), 30–31, 216

freedom, 19, 99; aesthetic judgment, 324*n*25; *Un coup de dés* and, 184; in

Four Quartets, 264; imagination and, 129, 147. *See also* contingency
free verse, Gunn on, 248–49
friendship: Ammons and, 228; idleness and, 216, 220–22, 228; O'Hara and, 220–23; Weil on, 314*n*16
Frye, Northrop, 308*n*7
future experience, in "Tintern Abbey," 138

Garbage (Ammons), 227–30
"Garden, The" (Marvell), 217
Gary, Kevin Hood, 321*n*59
Gelassenheit, 77
Genette, Gérard, 17, 275, 324*nn*25–26
God, 247, 288*n*1, 306*n*10; Ammons and, 226, 228; Aristotle and, 262; Bataille and, 200–1, 310*n*34; death of, 191, 299–300*nn*48–49; Eliot and, 262–63; Hölderlin and, 179–80; intentionality (transitive) and, 54; Rimbaud and, 200–1; Stevens and, 28, 196, 285*n*7, 308*n*5, 312*n*73; C. Wright and, 205, 208, 210–11, 312*n*64
Goodstein, Elizabeth, 240–41
Gourgouris, Stathis, 195, 308*n*8
grace, 55; Dickinson and, 159; Eliot and, 261, 264; *Four Quartets* and, 264; imagination (Burnside) and, 246–47; Weil on, 170; C. Wright and, 210
graded depth, 13
"Gravelly Run" (Ammons), 227–28
Greene, Roland, 17, 283*n*34
Greene, Thomas, 314*n*28
grief, in Gunn, 252
Grob, Alan, 308*n*7
Grossman, Allen, 274, 292*n*6, 323*n*20
Gumbrecht, Hans Ulrich, 281*n*10
Gunn, Thom: boredom in, 243, 246, 248–56; death in, 254–56; *Fighting Terms*, 248; free verse and, 248–49; grief in, 252; "Lazarus Not Raised," 254–56; love in, 253–54; *The Man with Nightsweats*, 248; "La Prisonnière," 253–54; repetition in, 250–51; "Round and Round," 251–53; "Wind in the Streets," 249–51

haibun, 72
haiku, 72
Halevi, Leor, 296*n*17
Hamburger, Michael, 172
Hammer, Langdon, 102, 295*n*7
Harrison, Jim, 322*n*2
Harrison, Robert, 165
hasard. See contingency
Hass, Robert, 279*n*3; "Meditation at Lagunitas," 78, 94–95, 97; presence in, 94–95; spatiotemporal remove in, 78, 94–95
Heaney, Seamus, 56–57; apprehension and, 44–46; "Blackberry-Picking," 45; "Death of a Naturalist," 44–45; "Oysters," 59–60
Hegel, G. W. F., 294*n*29, 298*n*37; *Un Coup de dés* and, 187, 189
Heidegger, Martin, 11, 298*n*38, 309*n*10; boredom and, 239; *Gelassenheit* and, 77; resignation and, 194–95; *Verwindung* and, 194–95, 308*n*8
Henderson, Derek, 246–47
Herbert, George, 55
Hesiod, 122
Hill, Geoffrey, 101–2, 295*n*7, 296*n*9
Hirshfield, Jane, 66–67, 74
historical inflection of poetic attention, 6–8
historicism, 17
historicity, of idleness, 6, 235
history: Benjamin on, 108; elegy and 98–99, 101–2, 120, 295*n*7; *Nox* and, 118, 119–20

Hölderlin, Friedrich: alertness in, 176; Blanchot on, 172–73; "Brod und Wein," 174–80; contemplation in, 174–75, 177; deconcentration in, 171; defamiliarization in, 176–77; desire in, 172–73; event in, 172–73, 180; Felstiner on, 174; focalization in, 171; God and, 179–80; hypotaxis in, 171; presence in, 172–76; revelatory vigilance in, 170–80, 209; suspense in, 161, 171, 173–75, 178; temporal inflection in, 171–72, 177–78, 180; "Wie wenn am Feiertage . . . ," 170–74; "Der Winkel von Hahrdt," 173

Holocaust: "Engführung" and, 108–14; recollection and, 101–2, 108–14

holy attention, 288n1

Homer, 286n14

hope, in *Dictee*, 123

Hopkins, Gerard Manley, 11

Hosanna in excelsis, 112

Hours of Idleness (Byron), 215–16

Hugo, Victor, 183–84

"L'Huître" (Ponge), 58–60

hunger, Rimbaud and, 198

Husserl, Edmund, 10, 16, 239, 321n1; intentionality (transitive) and, 33

hypotaxis: Hölderlin and, 171; temporal inflection and, 160–61

idleness, 164, 313n6; aimlessness and, 215–16; ambient attention and, 213–15; Ammons and, 6, 218, 224–31, 314n28; banter and, 220–23, 224; Bernstein and, 218, 314n12; boredom versus, 212–13; Byron and, 215–16; Cage and, 234–35; default mode network and, 213; friendship and, 216, 220–22, 228; historicity of, 6, 235; *imitatio* and, 215–16; intentionality (intransitive) and, 213, 234; Marvell and, 217; modernity and, 214–15, 217, 235; O'Hara and, 6, 218–24; *otium* and, 214–17, 233–34; postmodernism and, 233; productivity, as resistance to, 213, 217, 234, 314n12; Retallack and, 6, 218, 231–36; transhistoricity of, 6, 235

If Not, Winter (Carson), 300n50

"I had been Hungry all the Years" (Dickinson), 5, 81–82

Illuminations, Les (Rimbaud), 196–200, 309n15

imaginatio, 128, 130

imagination, 5, 50–52, 301n2, 301n6; Aristotle on, 125, 127, 134, 303n20, 303n22, 304n30; "Bowl of Roses" and, 126, 139–41; Coleridge on, 126, 128–32; desire and, 84, 88, 90; Dryden on, 127; effort and, 147–48; elaboration and, 134–36; endogenous attention and, 131, 139, 148; eventfulness of, 147; exogenous attention and, 131, 139, 148; "The Fair Chase" and, 126, 145–47; fancy as, 129–32, 134, 262–63; fictionality and, 134; "The Fish" and, 290n25; flowers and, 140–41, 304n30; *imaginatio* as, 128, 130; imagism and, 134; intentionality (transitive) and, 148; inventive, 141–48, 303n19, 304n26; Kant on, 125, 134–36, 303nn20–21; Keats and, 132; Levertov and, 132; literary vertigo and, 134; Lorde and, 88; Lowell and, 90; *Lyrical Ballads* and, 129–30, 136; metaphor and, 134; perception and, 125, 128, 130–48, 303n20; *phantasia* as, 128, 130; Plato on, 143–44; poetry on, 127–32, 302n18; *poiesis* and, 134; recombination and, 134–36;

referentiality and, 133, 142–43; reproductive, 134–36; resolution and, 141; "Die Rosenschale," 126, 139–41; Sartre on, 147–48; Scarry on, 140–41, 304n30; selectivity and, 141; spatiotemporal remove and, 51; Stevens on, 125, 127, 143–45, 304n34; symbolism and, 134; "Tintern Abbey" and, 126, 132, 136–38; value of, 285n7; verisimilitude and, 134; Wordsworth on, 129–30, 132, 302n11

"Imagination as Value" (Stevens), 28, 285n7

imaginative focalization, 27–28

imagism, 134

imitatio, 215–16

impersonality, Eliot on, 266

"L'impossible" (Rimbaud), 197

inclusivity, scope and, 157–58

indirect objects, 6, 151, 153; interest and, 156; meditative practice and, 151, 157; as tools, 157

Inferno (Dante), 142–43

insight, 315n30

inspiration: intentionality (transitive) and, 34–35, 286n14; madness and, 286n14

integrity, selectivity and, 37–38

intentionality (intransitive), 6, 152; active passivity and, 153–55; boredom and, 155, 213; Bukowski and, 244–46; Cage and, 318n56; desire and, 154–55; devotional poems and, 154; endogenous attention and, 153–55; exogenous attention and, 153, 155; idleness and, 213, 234; *Macbeth* and, 154; practice and, 154–55

intentionality (transitive), 5, 28, 282n21; Césaire and, 35; contemplation and, 54, 74; figure-ground relationship and, 13–14; God and, 54; Husserl on, 33; imagination and, 148; inspiration and, 34–35, 286n14; Plato on, 34; Pound and, 35; spiritual practice and, 54; Stein and, 35; "A Study of Two Pears" and, 35; as subject-oriented dynamic, 29

interest, 5, 28; contemplation and, 51; desire and, 51, 76–84; indirect objects and, 156; Kant on, 30, 32, 77, 267, 282n26, 308n6; love and, 76–84; Mahon and, 32–33; *Nox* and, 120; recollection and, 120; Sappho and, 30–31; at semantic level, 30–31; Stevens and, 77; as subject-oriented dynamic, 29; Weil on, 79

intransitive attention: Arata on, 217–18; indirect objects and, 6, 151, 153, 156–57; in modern age, 165–66; scope and, 6, 153, 157–59. *See also* boredom; intentionality (intransitive); temporal inflection

invention: imagination and, 141–48, 303n19, 304n26; presence and, 142–43; Stevens on, 143–45

Isaiah, 298n29

Iser, Wolfgang, 13, 282n21

Izenberg, Oren, 92, 94

Jackson, Virginia, 9

Jakobson, Roman, 14, 282n22, 300n51

James, Henry, 276

James, Skip, 206, 311n56

James, William, 16

Jameson, Fredric, 195, 309n10

Jarman, Mark, 205

Johnsen, Rasmus, 239

Johnson, Samuel, 293n8

joint attention, 270, 322n5

Jonson, Ben, 82–83, 293n9

judgment, 20, 275–77, 324nn25–26

Kant, Immanuel, 16, 187; boredom and, 247; focalization and, 27; imagination and, 125, 134–36, 303nn20–21; interest and, 30, 32, 77, 267, 282n26, 308n6

Keats, John, 132

kenosis: decreation and, 161, 263–67; Eliot and, 263–67

Al-Khansā' (Tumadir bint 'Amr), 103–5, 296n17

Kierkegaard, Søren, 75, 247

Kim, Sue, 122

Koepnick, Lutz, 213, 313n3

Korean War, 121–24

"Kubla Khan" (Coleridge), 142–43

Lacoue-Labarthe, Philippe, 195

Landy, Joshua, 284n37, 288n37

"Lazarus Not Raised" (Gunn), 254–56

Lee, Kun Jong, 122, 300n53

Lee, Li-Young, 39

Leggett, B. J., 65

Lehman, David, 315n30

lesbian love poems, 88–91

Levertov, Denise, 12, 297n22; "Everything That Acts Is Actual," 132

Levi, Primo, 106

Levinas, Emmanuel, 298n32

Levine, Caroline, 279n3

literary vertigo, imagination and, 134

livingness, of poems, 277

Longenbach, James, 290n25

Longuenesse, Béatrice, 303n23

Longus, 220, 222

Lorde, Audre, 97; desire and, 88–89; "Sowing," 88–89

love, 292n6, 293n9, 293n10; agape as, 260–61, 267; Bermann and, 88; Bukowski and, 245–46; contemplation and, 91–94, 294n26;
Egyptian love poems and, 76, 79–81, 292n5; figure-ground relationship and, 84; Gunn and, 253–54; interest and, 76–84; learning to, 20–21; lesbian love poems and, 88–91; Lowell and, 90–91; O'Hara on, 293n17; Oppen and, 91–94; selectivity and, 84; Sonnet 18 and, 84–88; spatiotemporal remove and, 78–84, 88–91, 95–97, 292n3; *The Waste Land* and, 88

"Love Song of J. Alfred Prufrock, The" (Eliot), 256–58

Lowe, Lisa, 122

Lowell, Amy, 46, 90–91

lyric, 8–11, 77; Benjamin on, 259; Bermann and, 88; inner life represented by, 86; novels and, 15; O'Hara on, 293n17

Lyrical Ballads, 129–30, 136

lyrical novels, 15

Macbeth (Shakespeare), 154

madness, inspiration and, 286n14

Mahon, Derek: desire and, 32; "A Disused Shed in Co. Wexford," 32–33; interest and, 32–33

Majumdar, Saikat, 240

Mallarmé, Stéphane, 307n26, 307n31; Blanchot on, 184–85, 307n24; *Un Coup de dés jamais n'abolira le hasard*, 170, 181–90; *Crise de vers*, 183, 186, 307n35; death in, 183–84; Hugo and, 183–84; suspense in, 161

Man with Nightsweats, The (Gunn), 248

Marno, David, 288n1, 306n10

marthiya, 104, 296n17

Marvell, Andrew, 217

Matar, Nabil, 301n6

Maynard, Lee Anna, 319n11

McCabe, Susan, 68, 290n26

McCorkle, James, 210, 290n25, 291n27
"Meditation at Lagunitas" (Hass), 78, 94–95, 97
meditative practice, 233; *acedia* as, 256–57, 260–65; Ammons and, 224–31, 315n30, 316n40, 316n47; ecstasy and, 315n29; Eliot and, 256–57, 260–65; indirect objects and, 151, 157; Rimbaud and, 201, 204; vigilance as, 167; C. Wright and, 196, 204–11, 311n46; yoga as, 201, 316n47
medium, attention as, 270
melancholia, 103
Meltzer, Françoise, 169, 288n1
memoir, *Dictee* as, 121–24
memory. *See* recollection
mental representation, transitive attention and, 26–28
"Meridian, The" (Celan), 124, 270–72
Merton, Thomas, 50
metaphor, imagination and, 134
metaphorization, contemplation and, 57–60
Miller, J. Hillis, 191
mimesis, Aristotle on, 16
Mirabai, 154
modernism, resignation and, 191–95, 308n7
modernity, 309n10; boredom and, 214–15, 239–41, 247–48, 256–64; idleness and, 214–15, 217, 235; intransitive attention and, 165–66; recollection and, 102–3, 106–8, 297n23, 299n48; selectivity and, 166
Moreh, Shmuel, 287n20
Moretti, Franco, 283n34
Morris, William, 217–18
mourning, 296n17; elegy and, 99–108, 299n48; recollection and, 99–108, 297n23

Mullen, Harryette, 56, 71–74
"Mûres" (Ponge), 58
music: Duncan and, 269; Retallack and, 231–32, 233–35. *See also* blues
Musil, Robert, 193
"My Creative Method" (Ponge), 59

Nandi, Miriam, 313n6
narrative, apprehension and, 46
Narrow Road to the Interior. See Oku no Hosomichi
"Necessary Angel, The" (Stevens), 50
negative elegy, *Nox* as, 115
Nietzsche, Friedrich, 27, 285n7; boredom and, 247; truth and, 285n4
Nijinsky, Vaslav, 222
nonrevelatory vigilance, 168; *Un Coup de dés* and, 170, 181–90
North River Shad (Chase), 66
nostalgia, temporal inflection of, 160
Novalis, 248
novels, 14; lyrical, 15
Nox (Carson), 98; apprehension and, 44; Catullus in, 115, 119, 299n46; death and, 115–16, 118–20; documentary and, 115–16, 118–20; history and, 118, 119–20; interest in, 120; as negative elegy, 115; photography in, *116, 117*; *poiesis* and, 120; prayer in, 119; recollection and, 115–16, 118–24, 297n22
Nussbaum, Martha, 276

object of poetic attention, 12; focalization directed toward, 51; spoken versus written poems as, 11
object-oriented poetry, twentieth century, contemplation in, 56–57
"Of the Surface of Things" (Stevens), 40, 48–49

O'Hara, Frank: Ashbery on, 219–20, 223; banter in, 220–23; friendship in, 220–22; idleness in, 6, 218–24; love and, 293*n*17; lyric and, 293*n*17; originality and, 223; practice in, 223–24; Vendler on, 293*n*17; "Very rainy light, an eclogue," 220–23

Oku no Hosomichi (*Narrow Road to the Interior*) (Bashō), 72

Oppen, George, 91–94, 97

"L'Orange" (Ponge), 58

orientative possibility, in Celan, 274

originality, in O'Hara, 223

otium, 214–17, 233–34

Oulipo (Ouvroir de littérature potentielle), 155

"Oysters" (Heaney), 59–60

painting: contemplation and, 64–71; Doty on, 66, 69–70, 291*n*29; "A Study of Two Pears" and, 64–65

Pallasmaa, Juhani, 281*n*16

paradise, boredom and, 246–48, 256

parataxis, temporal inflection and, 160

Parker, Patricia, 314*n*24

Parti pris des choses, Le (Ponge), 58–59

Pascal, Blaise, 247

Pearson, Roger, 307*n*31

Pellat, Charles, 296*n*17

perception: direct, 26–28; imagination and, 125, 128, 130–48, 303*n*20; "Die Rosenschale" and, 139–41; Stevens on, 144–45

perfection, boredom and, 246–56, 319*n*27

Perloff, Marjorie, 123, 223

"Persimmons" (Lee, L.), 39

Petronius Arbiter, 82–83, 293*n*9

phantasia, 128, 130

photography: boredom and, 246–47; *Dictee* and, 121–22; *Nox* and, 116, 117

Pieper, Josef, 74, 292*n*26

"Place of the Solitaires, The" (Stevens), 49

Plato, 16; imagination and, 143–44; intentionality (transitive) and, 34

poem 51 (Catullus), 216–17

poem 76 (Dickinson), 159

poem 101 (Catullus), 115, 119, 299*n*46

poem 466 (Dickinson), 158–59

poem 962 (Dickinson), 48

poetic attention. *See specific topics*

poetic function, 14, 282*n*22, 300*n*51

poetic responsibility, Rimbaud on, 202–3

poetic theory, as critical attention, 15–19

poiesis, 9, 19; imagination and, 134; *Nox* and, 120; recollection and, 120

Ponge, Francis, 11–12, 56–57; apprehension and, 45–46; Calvino on, 59; "L'Huître," 58–60; "L'Orange," 58; "Mûres," 58; "My Creative Method," 59; *Le Parti pris des choses*, 58–59

Ponticus, Evagrius, 217

Posnock, Ross, 309*n*16

postmodernism: contingency and, 195; idleness and, 233; resignation and, 193–95, 308*n*8

potentiality, Celan on, 270–71

Pound, Ezra, 46, 207; intentionality (transitive) and, 35

practice: *Un Coup de dés* and, 181, 190; intentionality (intransitive) and, 154–55; O'Hara and, 223–24; spiritual, 54–55, 193; vigilance and, 167–68. *See also* meditative practice

prayer, 55, 306*n*10; "Engführung" and, 111–13; holy attention and, 288*n*1; *Hosanna in excelsis* and, 112; *Nox* and, 119; Oppen and, 92; Weil on, 168–70, 193, 210; C. Wright and, 312*n*64

Prelude, The (Wordsworth), 132, 302*n*18

presence, 97, 270, 294*n*29; *Un Coup de dés* and, 188; Hass and, 94–95; Hölderlin and, 172–76; invention and, 142–43; resignation and, 192–93
"Prisonnière, La" (Gunn), 253–54
privilege: contemplation and, 59–60, 71–74; "Oysters" and, 59–60; *Urban Tumbleweed* and, 56, 71–74
productivity: boredom and, 242; idleness as resistance to, 213, 217, 234, 314*n*12
Proust, Marcel, 90
"Psalm" (Oppen), 91–94, 97
Psalm 137, 105–6

Ramazani, Jahan, 9; Cummings and, 46; elegy and, 101–3, 296*n*13, 297*nn*23–24, 299–300*nn*48–49; recollection and, 101–3, 296*n*13, 297*nn*23–24, 299–300*nn*48–49
Rankine, Claudia, 73; breath in, 273–74; embodiment in, 272–74
recollection, 5, 50–52; attention economy and, 107; Bachmann and, 100; catastrophe and, 108–14, 295*n*3; *Dictee* and, 121–24; documentary and, 115–16, 118–24; "Engführung" and, 108–14, 124; Hill and, 101–2, 295*n*7, 296*n*9; Holocaust and, 101–2, 108–14; interest and, 120; Al-Khansā' and, 103–5, 296*n*17; Korean War and, 121–24; Levi and, 106; memoir and, 121–24; modernity and, 102–3, 106–8, 297*n*23, 299*n*48; mourning and, 99–108, 297*n*23; *Nox* and, 115–16, 118–24, 297*n*22; *poiesis* and, 120; Psalm 137 and, 105–6; Ramazani on, 101–3, 296*n*13, 297*nn*23–24, 299–300*nn*48–49; "Die Rosenschale" and, 139–40; spatiotemporal remove and, 51; testimony and, 98, 107, 121; "Tintern Abbey" and, 137; transhistoricity and, 108, 297*n*24; trauma and, 99–108; Žižek on, 295*n*2. *See also* elegy
recombination, imagination and, 134–36
Reddy, Srikanth, 222–23
referentiality, imagination and, 133, 142–43
repetition: Gunn and, 250–51; C. Wright and, 206
reproduction, imagination and, 134–36
resignation, 6, 164–65; Baudelaire and, 191, 196; boredom and, 196–202; contingency and, 195; despair and, 196, 199–204; Eliot and, 191–92; Heidegger on, 194–95; Lacoue-Labarthe on, 195; modernism and, 191–95, 308*n*7; poetry on, 196; postmodernism and, 193–95, 308*n*8; presence and, 192–93; Rimbaud and, 196–204, 309*n*16; silence and, 196, 199–203; spiritual practice and, 193; Stevens and, 191–92; temporal inflection of, 192–93; *Verwindung* and, 194–95, 308*n*8; C. Wright and, 196, 204–11
resistance, 75; to productivity, 213, 217, 234, 314*n*12; "A Study of Two Pears" and, 61–65
resolution: apprehension and, 44, 46–48; Benn and, 46–48; connotation and, 41; denotation and, 41; imagination and, 141; selectivity and, 38–40; spatiotemporal remove and, 42–43
Retallack, Joan, 318*n*55; blanks in, 232, 234–35; contingency in, 234; Epicurus and, 233; *Errata 5uite*, 232–35; "Essay as Wager," 232; idleness in, 6, 218, 231–36; music in, 231–32, 233–35; *otium* in, 233–34; swerves in, 232–34

revelation: Ammons lacking, 226; "Tintern Abbey" as, 136
revelatory vigilance, 167–68; Hölderlin and, 170–80, 209
Reznikoff, Charles, 123, 300n62
Richard of St. Victor, 94
Richards, I. A., 18
Rilke, Rainer Maria, 165; "Dinggedichte," 136, 139–41; "Die Rosenschale," 126, 139–41
Rimbaud, Arthur: "Adieu," 199–200; Bataille on, 200–4; boredom in, 196–202; despair in, 196, 199–204; "Faim," 198; God and, 200–1; hunger in, 198; *Les Illuminations*, 196–200, 309n15; "L'impossible," 197; meditative practice and, 201, 204; poetic responsibility and, 202–3; resignation in, 196–204, 309n16; *Une Saison en enfer*, 196–202, 309–10nn18–29, 309n15, 310nn36–38; silence of, 196, 199–203; temporal inflection of, 202; vigilance in, 199
Roethke, Theodore, 210
"Rosenschale, Die" ("Bowl of Roses") (Rilke): contemplation in, 139–40; imagination in, 126, 139–41; perception in, 139–41; recollection in, 139–40
"Round and Round" (Gunn), 251–53
"Ruined Cottage, The" (Wordsworth), 132
Russell, Bertrand, 313n7

Sacks, Peter, 102
sacred, as set apart, 19
Saison en enfer, Une (Rimbaud), 196–202, 309–10nn18–29, 309n15, 310nn36–38
Santideva, 316n47
Sappho, 2; Carson and, 162–63, 300n50; decreation in, 162–63; desire and, 31; ecstasy and, 162–63; Fragment 31, 30–31, 216; interest and, 30–31; spatiotemporal remove and, 42
Sartre, Jean-Paul, 147–48
Scarry, Elaine, 140–41, 304n30
Schalkwyk, David, 77, 292n3
Schlegel, Friedrich, 247, 319n27
Schopenhauer, Arthur, 247, 264–65, 319n29
Scoggins, James, 302n11
scope, 6, 153; Dickinson and, 158–59; exclusivity of, 157–59; focalization and, 157–58; inclusivity of, 157–58; Whitman and, 158
"Second Coming" (Yeats), 114
secularization, boredom and, 240
selectivity, 5, 28; Bashō and, 36; "The Curtains in the House of the Metaphysician" and, 40–41; deconcentration and, 36; desire and, 84; Dickinson and, 36; Eliot and, 38; imagination and, 141; integrity and, 37–38; love and, 84; modernity and, 166; as object-oriented coordinate, 29; resolution and, 38–40; scope as, 6, 153, 157–59; Sonnet 18 and, 37; "A Study of Two Pears" and, 37, 40; Whitman and, 36–37; C. Wright and, 36
self-realization, feminine, boredom as, 319n11
Seneca, 286n14; boredom and, 238–39
the senses, 11–13, 269–75, 323n20
"September Song" (Hill), 101–2, 295n7, 296n9
sexual violence, in Bukowski, 245
Shakespeare, William: desire in, 82; *Macbeth*, 154; Sonnet 18, 7, 37, 84–88, 93, 96; *Twelfth Night*, 82, 293n8
Shklovsky, Victor, 297n22
Shultis, Christopher, 234, 318n56

Sidney, Philip, 44, 286n14
silence: contemplation and, 75; elegy, as enemy of, 124; resignation and, 196, 199–203; of Rimbaud, 196, 199–203
Silicon Valley, 2
Silkin, Jon, 296n9
Simic, Charles, 242
"Sitting Outside at the End of Autumn" (Wright, C.), 206
"Song of Myself" (Whitman), 37
Sonnet 18 (Shakespeare), 7, 93, 96; love and, 84–88; selectivity and, 37; Vendler on, 86–87
"Sowing" (Lorde), 88–89
Spacks, Patricia Meyers, 240
Spargo, R. Clifton, 103
spatiotemporal remove, 5, 28; contemplation and, 51; desire and, 78–84, 88–91, 95–97, 292n3; effort and, 78; Egyptian love poems and, 79–81; Hass and, 78, 94–95; imagination and, 51; love and, 78–84, 88–91, 95–97, 292n3; as object-oriented coordinate, 29; recollection and, 51; resolution and, 42–43; Sappho and, 42
spectatorship, in "Engführung," 110
spiritual practice: contemplation in, 54–55; intentionality (transitive) and, 54; resignation and, 193. *See also* prayer
spoken poems, as object of attention, 11
spotlight model, 13
Stein, Gertrude, 11; intentionality (transitive) and, 35
Stevens, Wallace, 60, 287n27; Altieri on, 61, 65; Costello on, 65; "The Curtains in the House of the Metaphysician," 40–41; death in, 96, 308n5; God and, 28, 196, 285n7, 308n5, 312n73; imagination and, 125, 127, 143–45, 304n34; "Imagination as Value" and, 28, 285n7; interest and, 77; invention and, 143–45; "The Necessary Angel," 50; "Of the Surface of Things," 40, 48–49; perception and, 144–45; "The Place of the Solitaires," 49; resignation and, 191–92; "A Study of Two Pears," 35, 37, 40, 56–57, 61–65
Stevenson, Robert Louis, 217–18
Stockwell, Peter, 281n15, 282n18
stress, alertness and, 305n2
"Study of Two Pears, A" (Stevens): contemplation in, 56–57, 61–65; ekphrasis and, 61; intentionality (transitive) in, 35; painting in, 64–65; resistance in, 61–65; selectivity in, 37, 40
subjectivity, 6, 153; constitution and, 161–64; decreation and, 161–64; Dickinson and, 163–64; endogenous attention and, 161; exogenous attention and, 161–62; Whitman and, 163
subject of poetic attention, 10–11, 281n11
suspense, 238–39, 256, 269; Hölderlin and, 161, 171, 173–75, 178; Mallarmé and, 161
Svendsen, Lars, 247–48
swerves, in Retallack, 232–34
symbolism, imagination and, 134
Szondi, Peter, 109, 114, 298nn26–27, 299n41

tanka, *Urban Tumbleweed* and, 56, 71–74
Tape for the Turn of the Year (Ammons), 225–26
taste, 16
Taylor, Edward, 2

temporal inflection, 6, 153, 159; of anxiety, 160; *Un Coup de dés* and, 188; Hölderlin and, 171–72, 177–78, 180; hypotaxis and, 160–61; of nostalgia, 160; parataxis and, 160; of resignation, 192–93; of Rimbaud, 202; suspense as, 161, 171, 173–75, 178, 269; of vigilance, 160, 168–69; of C. Wright, 207

temporal suspension, boredom and, 238–39, 256

Tender Buttons (Stein), 35

testimony, 98, 107, 121

things, 11; in Bachmann, 100; in F. Ponge, 58–59; in W. Stevens, 48–49, 61, 65; in still lifes, 69–71, 291n29; thingliness (of language and body), 217; thing theory and, 16, 283n28; word and/as things (materiality of language), 95, 97, 255; in C. Wright, 195, 205–8

throw of the dice will never abolish chance, A. *See Coup de dés jamais n'abolira le hasard, Un*

"Tintern Abbey" (Wordsworth): Bloom on, 137; future experience in, 138; imagination in, 126, 132, 136–38; recollection in, 137; as revelation, 136

"To Boredom" (Simic), 242

Tocqueville, Alexis de, 248

"Todesfuge" (Celan), 108

Tomlinson, Charles, 93

tools, indirect objects as, 157

"Tradition and the Individual Talent" (Eliot), 266

transhistoricity, 7; boredom and, 238, 243; elegy and, 102; idleness and, 6, 235; recollection and, 108, 297n24. *See also* historical inflection of poetic attention

transitive attention, 5, 25; current discourse focus on, 152; direct perception and, 26–28; double transitivity and, 14, 26–28; imaginative focalization and, 27–28; mental representation and, 26–28. *See also* apprehension; contemplation; desire; intentionality (transitive); interest; recollection; selectivity; spatiotemporal remove

trauma, 99–108

truth, Nietzsche on, 285n4

Twelfth Night (Shakespeare), 82, 293n8

Urban Tumbleweed (Mullen): contemplation in, 56, 71–74; Epstein on, 73; *flaneur* in, 73; privilege in, 56, 71–74

utopia, 247–48

Vattimo, Gianni, 194, 308n8

Vaughn, James, 302n11

Vendler, Helen: O'Hara and, 293n17; Sonnet 18 and, 86–87; C. Wright and, 210

verisimilitude, imagination and, 134

Verwindung, resignation and, 194–95, 308n8

"Very rainy light, an eclogue" (O'Hara), 220–223

vigilance, 6, 164–65; alertness and, 167, 176, 181, 305n2; Blanchot on, 168–69, 172–73; desire and, 169–70; grace and, 170; meditative practice and, 167; nonrevelatory, 168, 170, 181–90; practice and, 167–68; revelatory, 167–68, 170–80, 209; Rimbaud and, 199; suspense and, 161, 171, 173–75, 178, 269; temporal inflection of, 160, 168–69; Weil on, 168–70; will and, 169 walking: Ammons and, 224–31, 314*n*28; *Urban Tumbleweed* and, 56, 71–74

Waste Land, The (Eliot), 38; boredom in, 243, 256–61; desire in, 259–60; "Engführung" and, 108, 113; love absent from, 88

Weil, Simone, 55; boredom and, 321*n*59; decreation and, 169; desire and, 169–70; friendship and, 314*n*16; grace and, 170; interest and, 79; Meltzer on, 169, 288*n*1; prayer and, 168–70, 193, 210; vigilance and, 168–70; C. Wright and, 205, 210

Whitman, Walt: scope in, 158; selectivity and, 36–37; "Song of Myself," 37; subjectivity in, 163

"Wie wenn am Feiertage . . ." ("As on a Holiday . . .") (Hölderlin), 170–74

will, vigilance and, 169

Williams, William Carlos, 11, 56

Williamson, Sonny Boy, 245

"Wind in the Streets" (Gunn), 249–51

"Winkel von Hahrdt, Der" (Hölderlin), 173

Winters, Yvor, 248

Wittgenstein, Ludwig, 299*n*39

Wolff, Christian, 303*n*23

wonder, 315*n*30

Wordsworth, William: Eliot on, 266; imagination and, 129–30, 132, 302*n*11; *Lyrical Ballads* and, 129–30, 136; *The Prelude*, 132, 302*n*18; "The Ruined Cottage," 132; "Tintern Abbey," 126, 132, 136–38

Wright, Charles, 312*n*73; "Autumn Begins in Martins Ferry, Ohio," 1–3; blanks in, 207; death in, 208–10; divinity in, 208–11; dropped lines in, 207, 311*n*57; God and, 205, 208, 210–11, 312*n*64; grace in, 210; meditative practice in, 196, 204–11, 311*n*46; prayer and, 312*n*64; repetition in, 206; resignation in, 196, 204–11; selectivity and, 36; "Sitting Outside at the End of Autumn," 206; temporal inflection of, 207; Vendler on, 210; Weil and, 205, 210

Wright, James, 1–3

written poems, as object of attention, 11

Yeats, William Butler, 114

yoga, 201, 316*n*47

Žižek, Slavoj, 295*n*2

Printed in the USA
CPSIA information can be obtained
at www.ICGtesting.com
JSHW021423010424
60356JS00004B/82